[英 汉 对 照]

西方学术经典文库

原始社会结构与功能

STRUCTURE AND FUNCTION
IN PRIMITIVE SOCIETY

[英] A.R.拉德克利夫-布朗 著

丁国勇 译

(一)

九 州 出 版 社
JIUZHOUPRESS

图书在版编目(CIP)数据

原始社会结构与功能/(英)布朗著;
丁国勇译. —北京:九州出版社,2006.12
(西方学术经典文库)
ISBN 7-80195-582-X

Ⅰ.原… Ⅱ.①布…②丁… Ⅲ.原始社会—社会人类学—文集—汉、英 Ⅳ.C912.4-53

中国版本图书馆 CIP 数据核字(2006)第 141689 号

原始社会结构与功能

作　　者	[英]A.R.拉德克利夫-布朗　著　　丁国勇　译
责任编辑	郑闯琦　　特约编辑　孙淑慧
出版发行	九州出版社
地　　址	北京市西城区阜外大街甲 35 号(100037)
发行电话	(010)68992190/2/3/5/6
网　　址	www.jiuzhoupress.com
电子信箱	jiuzhou@jiuzhoupress.com
印　　刷	三河东方印刷厂
开　　本	630×970mm　1/16
印　　张	33.25
字　　数	356 千字
版　　次	2007 年 1 月第 1 版
印　　次	2007 年 1 月第 1 次印刷
书　　号	ISBN　7-80195-582-X/C·102
定　　价	68.00 元(全二册)

出版说明

在西方学术思想的发展流变中，出现过很多影响深远的经典著作，这些著作穿越时空，为人们长久研读，有的甚至影响了整个人类文明的发展进程。这套《西方学术经典文库》(英汉对照本)，精选了其中最有代表性的一些名著，计划达到一百部，将陆续分批出版直至全部完成。

《西方学术经典文库》由多位专家学者指导分类选目，内容涵盖哲学、文学、宗教学、政治学、经济学、社会学、人类学、心理学、法学、历史学等类，注重权威性、学术性和影响性，收录了不同国家、不同时代、不同流派的诸多名著。

《西方学术经典文库》中译本译自英文原著或其他文种的英文译本，以英汉对照的形式出版，读者可以参照原文对作品有更加客观的理解，更好地把握西方学术思想的精髓。

为加以区别，原文中的英文注释，注释号用①、②……形式表示；中文译者注释则以〔1〕、〔2〕……形式表示。至于英译本中出现的原文页码和特殊索引等问题，中文译者在"译者后记"中将予以解释、说明。另外，在英文原著中，有一些表示着重意义的斜体或大写等字体，考虑到读者可以在对照英文阅读中看到，因此在中译文中，没有照样标出，还望读者理解。

九州出版社

Structure And Function In Primitive Society
By *A. R. Radcliffe-Brown*

本书根据 The Free Press 1968 年版本译出

CONTENTS

目　录

INTRODUCTION

The papers reprinted here are occasional papers in the fullest sense of the term; each of them was written for a particular occasion. They do, however, have some measure of unity as being written from a particular theoretical point of view.

What is meant by a theory is a scheme of interpretation which is applied, or is thought to be applicable, to the understanding of phenomena of a certain class. A theory consists of a set of analytical concepts, which should be clearly defined in their reference to concrete reality, and which should be logically connected. I propose, therefore, by way of introduction to these miscellaneous papers, to give definitions of certain concepts of which I make use for purposes of analysis of social phenomena. It must be remembered that there is very little agreement amongst anthropologists in the concepts and terms they use, so that this Introduction and the papers that follow are to be taken as an exposition of one particular theory, not of a commonly accepted theory.

History And Theory

The difference between the historical study of social institutions and the theoretical study can be easily seen by comparing economic history and theoretical economics, or by comparing the history of law with theoretical jurisprudence. In anthropology, however, there has been and still is a great deal of confusion which is maintained by discussions in which terms such as 'history' and 'science' or 'theory' are used by disputants in very different meanings. These confusions

导 论

这些重新出版的论文都是我在不同时期,根据特定的不同场合而写的。由于它们之间内在理论观点的统一性,所以可以把这些文章作为一个整体来看待。理论就是指人们可以用它,或认为可以用它来理解某种现象的表述。它包括一整套的分析概念,这套分析概念既要有现实意义,同时又要有内在的逻辑关联性。因此,通过给这些文章写导论的方式,我会给一些概念加以定义,应用这些概念分析社会现象。需要记住的是,在人类学家使用概念和术语时,他们几乎很少达成共识,因此,此篇导论以及后面的文章所给出的解释仅仅是对某种理论的解释,还不能看做是一种被普遍接受的理论解释。

历史和理论

社会制度史研究和社会理论研究之间有明显的区别,这一点可以通过比较经济史和理论经济学,或比较法律史和理论法学而得出。然而,人类学领域却始终没有弄清楚这种区别的真正含义。这种混乱的存在,主要是由于在学术交流中,人们对他们使用的基本术语,如“历史”、“科学”或“理论”的含义没有达成一

could be to a considerable extent avoided by using the recognised terms of logic and methodology and distinguishing between *idiographic* and *nomothetic* enquiries.

In an idiographic enquiry the purpose is to establish as acceptable certain particular or factual propositions or statements. A nomothetic enquiry, on the contrary, has for its purpose to arrive at acceptable general propositions. We define the nature of an enquiry by the kind of conclusions that are aimed at.

History, as usually understood, is the study of records and monuments for the purpose of providing knowledge about conditions and events of the past, including those investigations that are concerned with the quite recent past. It is clear that history consists primarily of idiographic enquiries. In the last century there was a dispute, the famous *Methodenstreit*, as to whether historians should admit theoretical considerations in their work or deal in generalisations. A great many historians have taken the view that nomothetic enquiries should not be included in historical studies, which should be confined to telling us what happened and how it happened. Theoretical or nomothetic enquiries should be left to sociology. But there are some writers who think that a historian may, or even should, include theoretical interpretations in his account of the past. Controversy on this subject, and on the relation between history and sociology, still continues after sixty years. Certainly there are writings by historians which are to be valued not solely as idiographic accounts of the facts of the past but as containing theoretical (nomothetic) interpretations of those facts. The tradition in French historical studies of Fustel de Coulanges and his followers, such as Gustave Glotz, illustrates this kind of combination. Some modern writers refer to it as sociological history or historical sociology.

In anthropology, meaning by that the study of what are called the primitive or backward peoples, the term ethnography applies to what

致。但是,在大家一致接受的逻辑和方法论术语的基础上,通过区分个案研究和法则研究,可以有效地避免这种混乱情况。

个案研究和法则研究的目的是有区别的,前者是希望建立相对于具体和实际情况的可被接受的理论,而后者着眼于范围更广的一般理论。我们的研究究竟属于哪种性质,要看我们希望从中得出什么样的结论。

历史学在一般人眼里就是通过对文献和遗物的研究,得到对于发生在过去的事情的判断和描述,这里面也包括对最近才发生的事情的调查研究。显然,可以认为历史学主要是以个案研究为基础的。而发生在20世纪的著名的"方法论之争"的核心问题就是,是否应该把理论思考引入历史学家的工作之中,他们是否应该总结出历史的基本规律。许多历史学家们认为历史研究的主要作用是记录过去发生的事件,以及这些事件是如何发生的。所以,通则研究不应当包含在其中,而应把它们归入社会学研究领域。但是,也有一些学者认为,历史学家在描述过去的事件时可以,甚至是应该进行理论性阐释。对这一问题的争论以及对历史学与社会学之间关系的争论,60年后的今天仍在继续着。当然,有一些历史学家们的著作在这两方面的结合上做得很好,例如以菲斯泰尔·德·库朗热及其追随者古斯塔夫·格洛茨为代表的法国历史研究传统。他们的著作不仅仅是在对历史事件的个案描述上得到了重视,而且在对这些事件做出理论(通则)解释方面也得到了重视。因此,这种结合也被一些现代的学者们称为社会历史学或历史社会学。

人类学的研究对象是所谓的原始民族或落后民族,在研究中

is specifically a mode of idiographic enquiry, the aim of which is to give acceptable accounts of such peoples and their social life. Ethnography differs from history in that the ethnographer derives his knowledge, or some major part of it, from direct observation of or contact with the people about whom he writes, and not, like the historian, from written records. Prehistoric archaeology, which is another branch of anthropology, is clearly an idiographic study, aimed at giving us factual knowledge about the prehistoric past.

The theoretical study of social institutions in general is usually referred to as sociology, but as this name can be loosely used for many different kinds of writings about society we can speak more specifically of theoretical or comparative sociology. When Frazer gave his Inaugural Lecture as the first Professor of Social Anthropology in 1908 he defined social anthropology as that branch of sociology that deals with primitive societies.

Certain confusions amongst anthropologists result from the failure to distinguish between *historical explanation of institutions* and *theoretical understanding*. If we ask why it is that a certain institution exists in a particular society the appropriate answer is a historical statement as to its origin. To explain why the United States has a political constitution with a President, two Houses of Congress, a Cabinet, a Supreme Court, we refer to the history of North America. This is historical explanation in the proper sense of the term. The existence of an institution is explained by reference to a complex sequence of events forming a causal chain of which it is a result.

The acceptability of a historical explanation depends on the fullness and reliability of the historical record. In the primitive societies that are studied by social anthropology there are no historical records. We have no knowledge of the development of social institutions among the Australian aborigines for example. Anthropologists, thinking of their study as a kind of historical study, fall back on conjecture and imagination, and invent 'pseudo-historical' or 'pseudo-causal' explanations. We have had, for example, innumerable and sometimes

通常采用的个案研究的特定模式是民族志,它清楚地记录了所研究的民族及其社会生活。与历史学家不同的是,民族志学者是通过直接观察和亲身体验的方式获得他们对于研究对象的全部或大部分的知识,而历史学家是从文献记录中获得相关知识。史前考古学是人类学的另一个分支,它明显也是属于个案研究,为我们提供了史前的知识。

社会学一般是指对总体社会制度的理论研究,有时它的范畴还可以扩展到包括许多与社会有关的不同种类的著作,因此,我们最好把这种理论研究更加具体地称为理论社会学或比较社会学。弗雷泽可以说是第一个社会人类学教授,在 1908 年发表就职演说时,他对社会人类学做了如下定义:社会人类学是社会学的一个分支,它的研究对象是原始社会。

存在于人类学家中的确定的混乱,主要来源于不能够区分理论的认识和对于制度的历史的解释。回答诸如为什么某社会存在其特定的制度时,适当的方法就是从对这个制度起源的历史陈述中寻找答案。要解释为什么美国的政治构造是由一个总统、两个议院、一个内阁和一个最高法院构成,就需要我们对北美历史进行考察。因此对历史解释的恰当的理解就是,它是通过一系列复杂事件所形成的因果关系解释某一制度的存在,并把它作为这个因果关系的要素之一。

历史记载的完整性及可靠性对历史解释是否能被大家接受具有决定性的作用。可是,社会人类学家所研究的原始社会并无历史记载。例如,我们对澳大利亚土著的社会制度发展过程就没有任何了解。如果要把他们的研究归于历史研究的范畴,人类学家们只能在推测和猜想的基础上,对研究臆测出一些“伪历史”和“伪

conflicting pseudo-historical accounts of the origin and development of the totemic institutions of the Australian aborigines. In the papers of this volume mention is made of certain pseudo-historical speculations. The view taken here is that such speculations are not merely useless but are worse than useless. This does not in any way imply the rejection of historical explanation but quite the contrary.

Comparative sociology, of which social anthropology is a branch, is here conceived as a theoretical or nomothetic study of which the aim is to provide acceptable generalisations. The theoretical understanding of a particular institution is its interpretation in the light of such generalisations.

Social Process

A first question that must be asked if we are to formulate a systematic theory of comparative sociology is: What is the concrete, observable, phenomenal reality with which the theory is to be concerned? Some anthropologists would say that the reality consists of 'societies' conceived as being in some sense or other discrete real entities. Others, however, describe the reality that has to be studied as consisting of 'cultures', each of which is again conceived as some kind of discrete entity. Still others seem to think of the subject as concerned with both kinds of entities, 'societies' and 'cultures', so that the relation of these then presents a problem.

My own view is that the concrete reality with which the social anthropologist is concerned in observation, description, comparison and classification, is not any sort of entity but a process, the process of social life. The unit of investigation is the social life of some particular region of the earth during a certain period of time. The process

因果”解释。例如，这种现象曾经出现在对澳大利亚土著图腾制度的起源和发展研究中，各种解释多种多样，有时它们之间甚至是相互冲突的。在这本书中，我也在一些文章中谈论到一些伪历史猜测，在我看来，这种猜测不但毫无用处，而且甚至起到反面的作用。但这并不是说对历史解释持拒绝的态度，恰恰相反，我们应该接受它。

我们这里所说的社会人类学包含在比较社会学之中，而比较社会学以理论研究或通则研究为其研究方法，就是为了能够得出可接受的，并且能够用来解释特定制度的一般理论。

社会过程

如果我们要形成一个系统的比较社会学理论，首先要回答下述问题：这个理论最关心的具体的、可以观察到的明显事实是什么？一些人类学家会说，组成这个事实的要素是不同的“社会”，而在某种意义上，这些社会的本质实际上又可以被看作是一种存在，或是其他个别的客观实体。然而，还有一些人类学家认为，组成这种事实的要素其实是“文化”，他们也把每一种文化看作是某种独立的、抽象的实体。此外，还有一些人似乎认为，这个事实涵盖了“社会”和“文化”两种实体，因而，我们还要研究这两者之间的关系问题。

在我看来，社会人类学家们对之考察、描述、对比及分类的具体事实其实并不是任何实体，而是一种过程，一种社会生活的过程。社会生活作为我们调查研究的对象，总是存在于某个特定阶段和某一地区。过程本身是由人类的各种行为及其之间的交往

itself consists of an immense multitude of actions and interactions of human beings, acting as individuals or in combinations or groups. Amidst the diversity of the particular events there are discoverable regularities, so that it is possible to give statements or descriptions of certain general features of the social life of a selected region. A statement of such significant general features of the process of social life constitutes a description of what may be called a *form of social life*. My conception of social anthropology is as the comparative theoretical study of forms of social life amongst primitive peoples.

A form of social life amongst a certain collection of human beings may remain approximately the same over a certain period. But over a sufficient length of time the form of social life itself undergoes change or modification. Therefore, while we can regard the events of social life as constituting a process, there is over and above this the process of change in the form of social life. In a synchronic description we give an account of a form of social life as it exists at a certain time, abstracting as far as possible from changes that may be taking place in its features. A diachronic account, on the other hand, is an account of such changes over a period. In comparative sociology we have to deal theoretically with the continuity of, and with changes in, forms of social life.

Culture

Anthropologists use the word 'culture' in a number of different senses. It seems to me that some of them use it as equivalent to what I call a form of social life. In its ordinary use in English 'culture', which is much the same idea as cultivation, refers to a process, and we can define it as the process by which a person acquires, from contact with other persons or from such things as books or works of art, knowledge, skill, ideas, beliefs, tastes, sentiments. In a particular society we can discover certain processes of *cultural tradition*, using the word tradition in its literal meaning of handing on or handing

构成,而这种行为的表现方式或是通过个人,或是通过集体显现出来。由于我们可以发现某种所谓的规律性的东西存在于不同种类的具体事件中,所以,基于此我们就可能把某一特定地区的社会生活的某种普遍特征描述出来。而这种对社会生活过程的一个普遍特征的描述过程,也就构成了对我们所说的社会生活形式的描述。我认为,社会人类学实际上是一种比较理论研究,它的研究对象是不同原始民族的社会生活方式。

一定群体的人们的社会生活方式在一定时期内会具有一定的稳定性,社会生活方式本身的发展与变迁需要经历一个相当长的时期。因此,我们所说的社会生活的过程不仅仅包括社会生活中的各种事件,而且,还包括社会生活方式的演变过程。通过共时性描述,我们刻画了存在于某一特定时期的社会生活方式,并尽可能地排除掉那些对其特征施加影响的变化。相反,历时性描述却主要用来反映一段时间以来发生的社会生活方式的变化。在比较社会学中,我们需要对社会生活方式的延续和变化给以理论上的说明。

文化

人类学家基于许多不同的含义使用“文化”一词。而且,我似乎觉得其中一些人类学家把文化的意义等同于社会生活方式。“文化”一词在英文中的普通用法与“教养”一词极为相似,它是指一个过程,含义就是指一个人通过与其他人接触或从书籍、艺术作品这类东西中获得知识、技巧、思想、信仰、品味及情感。在所研究的特定社会中,我们可以发现某种文化传统的过程,这里传

down. The understanding and use of a language is passed on by a process of cultural tradition in this sense. An Englishman learns by such a process to understand and use the English language, but in some sections of the society he may also learn Latin, or Greek, or French, or Welsh. In complex modern societies there are a great number of separate cultural traditions. By one a person may learn to be a doctor or surgeon, by another he may learn to be an engineer or an architect. In the simplest forms of social life the number of separate cultural traditions may be reduced to two, one for men and the other for women.

If we treat the social reality that we are investigating as being not an entity but a process, then culture and cultural tradition are names for certain recognisable aspects of that process, but not, of course, the whole process. The terms are convenient ways of referring to certain aspects of human social life. It is by reason of the existence of culture and cultural traditions that human social life differs very markedly from the social life of other animal species. The transmission of learnt ways of thinking, feeling and acting constitutes the cultural process, which is a specific feature of human social life. It is, of course, part of that process of interaction amongst persons which is here defined as the social process thought of as the social reality. Continuity and change in the forms of social life being the subjects of investigation of comparative sociology, the continuity of cultural traditions and changes in those traditions are amongst the things that have to be taken into account.

Social System

It was Montesquieu who, in the middle of the eighteenth century, laid the foundations of comparative sociology, and in doing so formulated and used a conception that has been and can be referred to by the use of the term *social system*. His theory, which constituted

统的字面意思是传承。从这个意义上说,正是通过对文化传统过程的传承,才使得我们对语言的理解及使用得以持续。一位英国人在这个过程中,可以学会掌握并使用英语,不过在社会的其他领域里,他也可以学会拉丁语、希腊语、法语或威尔士语。许多独立文化传统存在于复杂的现代社会中,例如,在某种传统之下,某人可能成为医生或外科医生,而另一种传统却可能将他塑造为一名工程师或建筑师。在最简单的社会生活形式中,可能只需要把这许多不同种类的文化传统分为两类,一类专为男人而设,相应地女人就需要遵循另外一类。

如果我们把正在研究的社会事实看做是一个过程而不是实体的话,那么我们就只能把文化及文化传统看做是这一过程中可知部分的名称而已,而并不能认为文化和文化传统代表整个过程。采用这些术语的原因只是在于,使我们在研究人类社会生活的某些方面时论述起来方便罢了。而人类社会生活与其他动物种类的社会生活之间,只是由于文化及文化传统的作用,才会显得区别是如此之大。这里所说的文化过程由诸如思考、情感和行为习惯方式的传递组成,它们构成了人类社会生活的独有特征。当然,这只是人与人之间作为社会事实的互动过程的一部分。由于比较社会学研究的对象包括社会生活形式的延续及改变,所以,它也要必须考虑文化传统的延续及这些传统的变化。

社会体系

在 18 世纪中叶,正是孟德斯鸠为比较社会学奠定了基础,与此同时,他还形成并使用了一个可以表述为“社会体系”的概念。

what Comte later called 'the first law of social statics', was that in a particular form of social life there are relations of interconnection and interdependence, or what Comte called relations of solidarity, amongst the various features. The idea of a natural or phenomenal system is that of a set of relations amongst events, just as a logical system, such as the geometry of Euclid, is a set of relations amongst propositions, or an ethical system a set of relations amongst ethical judgments. When one speaks of the 'banking system' of Great Britain this refers to the fact that there is a considerable number of actions, interactions and transactions, such for example as payments by means of a signed cheque drawn on a bank, which are so connected that they constitute in their totality a process of which we can make an analytical description which will show how they are interconnected and thus form a system. We are dealing, of course, with a process, a complex part of the total social process of social life in Great Britain.

In these essays I have referred to 'kinship systems'. The idea is that in a given society we can isolate conceptually, if not in reality, a certain set of actions and interactions amongst persons which are determined by the relationships by kinship or marriage, and that in a particular society these are interconnected in such a way that we can give a general analytical description of them as constituting a system. The theoretical significance of this idea of systems is that our first step in an attempt to understand a regular feature of a form of social life, such as the use of cheques, or the custom by which a man has to avoid social contact with his wife's mother, is to discover its place in the system of which it is part.

The theory of Montesquieu, however, is what we may call a theory of a total social system, according to which all the features of social life are united into a coherent whole. As a student of jurisprudence

在此之后，孔德以孟德斯鸠的理论为“社会静力学第一法则”的基本内容。按照这个法则，在某一特定社会生活形式中，存在一种相互关联、相互依赖的关系，孔德将这种关系称为“团结关系”。像在逻辑体系中那样，把自然，或可感知的体系这一概念描述为各种事件中的一系列关系的体现。例如，欧几里德几何学就是许多命题中的一系列关系，类似的例子还有，伦理体系就是各种道德判断之间的一系列关系。当我们说英国的“金融体系”时，实际是在指这个概念所代表的这样一件事实：大量的个人行动、人们之间的互动及交易（如签署支票从银行取款）被紧密联系在一起，从而在整体上构成一个可以进行描述分析的过程。通过这种过程会向我们展示它们是怎样相互联系，怎样形成一个体系的。当然，我们正在讨论的只是一种过程，它只是英国社会生活中整体社会过程一个复杂部分而已。

在本书的一些文章中，我曾提到过“亲属制度”的概念。此概念的意思是指在某一个特定社会中，我们即使不是在事实上，也可以在概念上将人们中那些由亲属关系或婚姻关系所决定的一系列行为和相互作用区隔出来；还指在一个特定社会中，这些行为和相互作用联系得如此紧密，以至于我们可以将其作为一个体系来做总的分析和描述。它的理论意义在于，在我们试图要理解社会生活中的特殊形式时，如使用支票，或回避与岳母有社会接触这样的习俗，我们首先要做的是揭示这些体系中的具体形式在整个体系中的位置。

然而，孟德斯鸠的理论却可以被看做是对整个社会体系进行描述的理论。社会生活中的所有特征在这种理论看来，都是相互

Montesquieu was primarily concerned with laws, and he sought to show that the laws of a society are connected with the political constitution, the economic life, the religion, the climate, the size of the population, the manners and customs, and what he called the general spirit (*esprit général*)—what later writers have called the 'ethos' of the society. A theoretical law, such as this 'fundamental law of social statics', is not the same thing as an empirical law, but is a guide to investigation. It gives us reason to think that we can advance our understanding of human societies if we investigate systematically the interconnections amongst features of social life.

Statics And Dynamics

Comte pointed out that in sociology, as in other kinds of science, there are two sets of problems, which he called problems of statics and problems of dynamics. In statics we attempt to discover and define conditions of existence or of co-existence; in dynamics we try to discover conditions of change. The conditions of existence of molecules or of organisms are matters of statics, and similarly the conditions of existence of societies, social systems, or forms of social life are matters for social statics. Whereas the problems of social dynamics deal with the conditions of change of forms of social life.

The basis of science is systematic classification. It is the first task of social statics to make some attempt to compare forms of social life in order to arrive at classifications. But forms of social life cannot be classified into species and genera in the way we classify forms of organic life; the classification has to be not specific but typological, and this is a more complicated kind of investigation. It can only be reached by means of the establishing of typologies for features of

关联从而结成一个整体的。作为一名法理学家,孟德斯鸠主要关注的是法律,他试图向人们展示一个社会的法律是与组成社会的其他要素结合在一起的。这些要素包括:政治制度、经济生活、宗教、气候、人口规模、生活方式、习俗以及被他称作总体精神而被后来一些学者们称为社会"精神"的要素。虽然像"社会静力学基本法则"这样的理论法则与经验法则不同,但理论法则仍旧可以指导调查研究。如果我们对社会生活特征之间的相互联系进行系统的调查研究,那么我们就有理由认为我们可以提高对人类社会的理解。

静力学和动力学

孔德指出,社会学也像其他科学领域一样,也存在静力学和动力学这两类问题。静力学研究的是,如何对特定社会现实或各个社会中共同的因素进行揭示和规定;而动力学主要是研究如何揭示变化的状态。分子和机体的存在环境是静力学问题,相应地,社会制度或社会生活方式的存在环境就是社会静力学要研究的问题。然而,社会生活方式变化的状态则是社会动力学研究的对象。

科学是建立在系统分类的基础上的。社会静力学就是要承担对不同的社会生活方式进行比较并加以分类的重要任务。但是,我们不能够把对有机生命按"种"和"属"进行分类的方法用于社会生活方式分类中;而且对于社会生活方式的这种划分既不能太细,但又要有代表性,因此这是一种更为复杂的调查研究。这种分类需要建立在一定的基础之上,这个前提就是首先要建立有关

social life or the complexes of features that are given in partial social systems. Not only is the task complex but it has been neglected in view of the idea that the method of anthropology should be a historical method.

But though the typological studies are one important part of social statics, there is another task, that of formulating generalisations about the conditions of existence of social systems, or of forms of social life. The so-called first law of social statics is a generalisation affirming that for any form of social life to persist or continue the various features must exhibit some kind and measure of coherence or consistence, but this only defines the problem of social statics, which is to investigate the nature of this coherence.

The study of social dynamics is concerned with establishing generalisations about how social systems change. It is a corollary of the hypothesis of the systematic connection of features of social life that changes in some features are likely to produce changes in other features.

Social Evolution

The theory of social evolution was formulated by Herbert Spencer as part of his formulation of the general theory of evolution. According to that theory the development of life on the earth constitutes a single process to which Spencer applied the term 'evolution'. The theory of organic and super-organic (social) evolution can be reduced to two essential propositions: (1) That both in the development of forms of organic life and in the development of forms of human social life there has been a process of diversification by which many different forms of organic life or of social life have been developed out of a very much smaller number of original forms. (2) That there has been a general trend of development by which more complex forms of structure and organisation (organic or social) have arisen from simpler forms. The acceptance of the theory of evolution only requires the acceptance of

社会生活特征的类型学或部分社会体制中的特征群的类型学的方法。这项工作不但很复杂，而且还因为人类学方法被看成一种历史学方法而一直受到忽略。

但是，社会静力学中除了类型学研究这个重要部分之外，还需要做另外一项工作，即对社会制度或社会生活方式的存在环境进行概括总结。前面所谓的静力学第一法则就是一种概括总结，它强调，任何一种社会生活方式内在的某种程度的连贯性或一致性，是其想要继续存在或使其各种特征延续下去的保证。但这只是规定了对这种连贯性本质的研究属于社会静力学研究的问题而已。

社会动力学研究主要关注的是，如何对社会体系的变化进行概括总结。它是一种假设的推论，认为在相互联系的各种社会生活的特征中，某些特征的变化很可能会导致另一些特征的变化。

社会进化

社会进化理论是赫伯特·斯宾赛提出的总体进化理论的一部分。根据这种理论，地球上生命的发展构成了斯宾赛所称的“进化”过程。有机体或超机体（社会）进化理论，可以归结为两个命题：(1)机体生命形式和社会生活方式的发展是多种多样的，在这个多样化的过程中初始数量很少的原始形式会逐步发展成数量众多的机体生命形式和社会生活方式。(2)有一种普遍的发展趋势，即更为复杂的结构形式和组织形式（机体的或社会的）是从较简单的形式中发展而来。要接受这个进化理论只需承认上述

these propositions as giving us a scheme of interpretation to apply to the study of organic and social life. But it must be remembered that some anthropologists reject the hypothesis of evolution. We can give provisional acceptance to Spencer's fundamental theory, while rejecting the various pseudo-historical speculations which he added to it, and that acceptance gives us certain concepts which may be useful as analytical tools.

Adaptation

This is a key concept of the theory of evolution. It is, or can be, applied both to the study of the forms of organic life and to the forms of social life amongst human beings. A living organism exists and continues in existence only if it is both internally and externally adapted. The internal adaptation depends on the adjustment of the various organs and their activities, so that the various physiological processes constitute a continuing functioning system by which the life of the organism is maintained. The external adaptation is that of the organism to the environment within which it lives. The distinction of external and internal adaptation is merely a way of distinguishing two aspects of the *adaptational system* which is the same for organisms of a single species.

When we come to the social life of animals another feature of adaptation makes its appearance. The existence of a colony of bees depends on a combination of the activities of the individual worker bees in the collection of honey and pollen, the manufacture of wax, the building of the cells, the tending of eggs and larvae and the feeding of the latter, the protection of the store of honey from robbers, the ventilation of the hive by fanning with their wings, the maintenance of temperature in the winter by clustering together. Spencer uses the term 'co-operation' to refer to this feature of social life. Social life and social adaptation therefore involve the adjustment of the behaviour of individual organisms to the requirements of the process by which the social life continues.

When we examine a form of social life amongst human beings as an adaptational system it is useful to distinguish three aspects of the

命题即可,因为我们可以依靠这些命题本身提供的解决办法来研究生命机体和社会生活。但是我们需要知道的是,这种进化的假设并不被一些人类学家接受。我们可以暂时接受斯宾塞的基础理论,但要摈弃他所附加的一些伪历史推测,我们可以从他的理论中了解到一些概念,它们可以作为有用的分析工具。

适应

进化理论一个非常重要的概念就是适应。此概念被用来、或可以被用来研究各种有机生命的形式和各种人类社会生活方式。一个生命机体要想得以生存或继续存在的基础,就是它必须做到内外适应。内部适应依赖于其各种器官及其活动的调节,以便各种生理过程可以成为一个能够维系机体生命的持续运转的体系。外部适应,是指机体如何来适应其生存的环境。区分内部适应和外部适应仅仅是区别适应体系两个方面的一种方法,该适应体系对于同一种类的机体来说是一样的。

当我们在考察动物的社会生活时,另一种适应特征就会出现。一群蜜蜂要想生存,就必须依赖各种活动的相互配合。这些活动包括:每只工蜂采集蜂蜜和花粉、生产蜂蜡、建造蜂房、照顾蜂卵和幼蜂、养育幼蜂、保护蜂蜜防止被盗、通过扇动翅翼给蜂房通风、冬天簇聚在一起保持适当的温度等。斯宾塞对这些社会生活特征使用了“合作”一词描述它们。因此,社会生活和社会适应需要对个体机能的行为进行调整来满足社会生活这一过程的延续。

当我们把人类的社会生活形式作为适应的体系来考察时,如

total system. There is the way in which the social life is adjusted to the physical environment, and we can, if we wish, speak of this as the ecological adaptation. Secondly, there are the institutional arrangements by which an orderly social life is maintained, so that what Spencer calls co-operation is provided for and conflict is restrained or regulated. This we might call, if we wished, the institutional aspect of social adaptation. Thirdly, there is the social process by which an individual acquires habits and mental characteristics that fit him for a place in the social life and enable him to participate in its activities. This, if we wish, could be called cultural adaptation, in accordance with the earlier definition of cultural tradition as process. What must be emphasised is that these modes of adaptation are only different aspects from which the total adaptational system can be looked at for convenience of analysis and comparison.

The theory of social evolution therefore makes it a part of our scheme of interpretation of social systems to examine any given system as an adaptational system. The stability of the system, and therefore its continuance over a certain period, depends on the effectiveness of the adaptation.

Social Structure

The theory of evolution is one of a trend of development by which more complex types of structure come into existence by derivation from less complex ones. An address on Social Structure is included in this volume, but it was delivered in war time and was printed in abbreviated form, so that it is not as clear as it might be. When we use the term structure we are referring to some sort of ordered arrangement of parts or components. A musical composition has a structure, and so does a sentence. A building has a structure, so does a molecule or an animal. The components or units of social structure are *persons*, and a person is a human being considered not as an organism but as occupying

果按三个方面来划分这个整体体系,会为我们的分析带来很多益处。首先,社会生活会为了适应自然环境而进行调整,这种调整的方式,如果我们愿意的话可以称之为生态适应。其次,存在一种维系有序社会生活的制度安排,因此斯宾塞所说的合作、限制或调和冲突才能实现,对这种方式如果我们愿意的话,可以称其为制度适应层面。第三,存在一种社会过程,通过此过程,人们可以获得适应其社会生活的习惯和智力特征,并能够使其参与到社会活动中,如果我们愿意的话可以称其为文化适应。这种定义方式与前文中把文化传统看做一种过程的定义是类似的。我们必须强调的是,我们只是为了在考察适应体系时便于进行分析和比较才分析这些层面,这些适应模式只是整体适应体系的三个不同方面而已。

因此,社会进化理论作为社会体制的阐释方案的一部分,是把某一特定体系作为适应体系来考察。体系的稳定性,及其在一定时期范围内的延续取决于适应的有效性。

社会结构

进化理论是关于发展趋势的理论,根据此理论,更为复杂的结构类型是由简单的结构类型发展而来的。我的一篇有关社会结构的讲演也包含在本书中,但由于战争年代的缘故,因此这篇文章是以简略的形式印出来的,在表述上显得并不充分。当我们在使用结构这个术语时,我们其实是在指事物的组成部分或成分之间的有规律的联系。东西有结构,句子也是这样。建筑物有结构,分子和动物也同样有结构。人是社会结构的组成成分或单

position in a social structure.

One of the fundamental theoretical problems of sociology is that of the nature of social continuity. Continuity in forms of social life depends on structural continuity, that is, some sort of continuity in the arrangements of persons in relation to one another. At the present day there is an arrangement of persons into nations, and the fact that for seventy years I have belonged to the English nation, although I have lived much of my life in other countries, is a fact of social structure. A nation, a tribe, a clan, a body such as the French Academy, or such as the Roman Church, can continue in existence as an arrangement of persons though the personnel, the units of which each is composed, changes from time to time. There is continuity of the structure, just as a human body, of which the components are molecules, preserves a continuity of structure though the actual molecules, of which the body consists, are continually changing. In the political structure of the United States there must always be a President; at one time it is Herbert Hoover, at another time Franklin Roosevelt, but the structure as an arrangement remains continuous.

The social relationships, of which the continuing network constitute social structure, are not haphazard conjunctions of individuals, but are determined by the social process, and any relationship is one in which the conduct of persons in their interactions with each other is controlled by norms, rules or patterns. So that in any relationship within a social structure a person knows that he is expected to behave according to these norms and is justified in expecting that other persons should do the same. The established norms of conduct of a particular form of social life it is usual to refer to as *institutions*. An institution is an established norm of conduct recognised as such by a distinguishable social group or class of which therefore it is an institution. The institutions refer to a distinguishable type or class of social relationships and interactions. Thus in

位,人并不是因为他是一个有机体才被称为人,而是因为他在社会结构中占据一定位置。

在社会学研究中,一个最根本的理论性问题是社会延续的本质。社会结构的内容包括人们之间关系的安排,它的延续性是社会生活方式得以延续的依赖条件。目前,这种社会结构内容是按人们所处的国家来对他们进行不同的划分。这种社会结构问题以我为例的话就是,尽管我生命中许多时间都在其他国家度过,但我 70 年来却一直属于英国。一个国家、一个部落、一个氏族或一个团体如法兰西学院或罗马教会等等,都会被看做是一种社会结构中的人事安排而得以延续,尽管在组成这些社会生活方式的人员或构成单位会时不时发生改变。这种对社会结构延续性的分析就像我们分析人体一样,作为人体来说其结构性是一直延续的,但组成人体的分子却是在一刻不停地发展变化的。还有,美国总统是一种政治安排,必须有总统持续地存在于美国的政治结构中,随着时间的变化,总统在某一期是赫伯特·胡佛,而在另一期却是富兰克林·罗斯福,但是这个结构作为一种安排却一直在延续。

社会关系中不断延续的网络构成了社会结构,这些社会关系的决定因素并不在于偶然存在于人们之间的联合,而是在于社会过程。人们之间发生关系的行为过程会受到不同的规范、规则或范式的制约,而这种行为过程包含于任何一种关系之中。因此,每个人都有理由相信,在社会结构的任何一种关系中,关系的双方都知道一方在期望对方按规范行事的同时,对方也有理由希望他按规章做事。制度通常是指那些已建立起来的某种社会生活方式的行为模式,这种行为模式是明确的,并且得到可以区分的社会群体或阶层承认。制度还可以是指一种可区分的社会关系

a given locally defined society we find that there are accepted rules for the way a man is expected to behave towards his wife and children. The relation of institutions to social structure is therefore twofold. On the one side there is the social structure, such as the family in this instance, for the constituent relationships of which the institutions provide the norms; on the other there is the group, the local society in this instance, in which the norm is established by the general recognition of it as defining proper behaviour. Institutions, if that term is used to refer to the ordering by society of the interactions of persons in social relationships, have this double connection with structure, with a group or class of which it can be said to be an institution, and with those relationships within the structural system to which the norms apply. In a social system there may be institutions which set up norms of behaviour for a king, for judges in the fulfilment of the duties of their office, for policemen, for fathers of families, and so on, and also norms of behaviour relating to persons who come into casual contact within the social life.

A brief mention may be made of the term *organisation.* The concept is clearly closely related to the concept of social structure, but it is desirable not to treat the two terms as synonymous. A convenient use, which does not depart from common usage in English, is to define social structure as an arrangement of persons in institutionally controlled or defined relationships, such as the relationship of king and subject, or that of husband and wife, and to use organisation as referring to an arrangement of activities. The organisation of a factory is the arrangement of the various activities of manager, foremen, workmen within the total activity of the factory. The structure of a family household of parents, children and servants is institutionally controlled. The activities of the various members of the persons of the household will probably be subject to some regular arrangement, and the organisation of the life of the household in this sense may be different in different families in the same society. The structure of a modern army consists, in the first place, of an arrangement into groups— regiments, divisions, army corps, etc., and in the second place an arrangement into ranks—generals, colonels, majors, corporals, etc. The organisation of the army consists of the arrangement of the

及社会互动的类型或类别。因而,我们通过对一个特定的社会的观察可以发现,在一位男子对待其妻子和孩子的行为方面,存在着被人们普遍接受的规则。因此,制度与社会结构之间存在着双重的关系:一方面,制度在像家庭这样的社会结构中,是作为其构成关系的规范存在的;另一方面,还存在像社区社会这样的群体,由于大家把规范公认为一种适当的行为,从而把它建立起来。如果认为制度这一术语的含义是社会为处于社会关系中的人们之间的互动提供一种秩序的话,那么制度与结构之间也存在双重的关系:首先是制度与采用它的那些群体或阶级相关联;其次是制度与结构体系内部那些适于规范的关系相联。例如,在一种社会体系中,国王、履行职责的法官、警察、家庭中的父亲等等都会有相应的制度来为他们确定相应的行为规范,同时对于那些在社会生活中偶尔会发生接触的人们也会存在相应的行为规范。

我要简单阐述一下组织这个术语。虽然在概念上组织与社会结构是紧密联系的,但这两个术语还是不能被看做是同义词。一个与英语的普通用法相似、并且更简便的用法是:把社会结构定义成一种人事安排,而且是受制度控制或受到确定的关系制约的,例如国王同臣民的关系,或丈夫同妻子的关系;而把组织当做是对某种活动的安排,例如在一个工厂中,整个工厂范围内对经理、工头、工人的各种活动安排就构成了这个工厂的组织。尽管制度可以控制包含父母、孩子、用人等成员的家庭住户结构,但是却可能存在某种常规性的安排来制约这些成员的各种活动。因此,从这个意义上说,同一社会中不同住户可能有不同的生活组织。现代军队的结构,首先包括团、师、军等群体设置安排,其次则是将军、上校、少校、下士等军衔设置安排。而军队的组织包括

activities of its personnel whether in time of peace or in time of war. Within an organisation each person may be said to have a *role*. Thus we may say that when we are dealing with a structural system we are concerned with a system of social *positions*, while in an organisation we deal with a system of *roles*.

Social Function

The term function has a very great number of different meanings in different contexts. In mathematics the word, as introduced by Euler in the eighteenth century, refers to an expression or symbol which can be written on paper, such as 'log. *x*', and has no relation whatever to the same word as used in such a science as physiology. In physiology the concept of function is of fundamental importance as enabling us to deal with the continuing relation of structure and process in organic life. A complex organism, such as a human body, has a structure as an arrangement of organs and tissues and fluids. Even an organism that consists of a single cell has a structure as an arrangement of molecules. An organism also has a life, and by this we refer to a process. The concept of organic function is one that is used to refer to the connection between the structure of an organism and the life process of that organism. The processes that go on within a human body while it is living are dependent on the organic structure. It is the function of the heart to pump blood through the body. The organic structure, as a living structure, depends for its continued existence on the processes that make up the total life processes. If the heart ceases to perform its function the life process comes to an end and the structure as a living structure also comes to an end. Thus process is dependent on structure and continuity of structure is dependent on process.

In reference to social systems and their theoretical understanding one way of using the concept of function is the same as its scientific use in physiology. It can be used to refer to the interconnection between the social structure and the process of social life. It is this use

其人员的各种活动(无论是和平时期还是战争时期的活动)安排。每个人都可以说在组织内拥有一定的角色,所以,我们可以说,当我们研究结构体系时,我们所关注的是社会位置体系,然而当我们研究组织时,我们所强调的是角色体系。

社会功能

"功能"这一术语,在不同的语境下有不同的含义。例如在数学领域中,就像18世纪奥依勒提出的那样,功能就是指像"log. x"这样的用于书面的表达或符号。因此无论怎样,都不能把这种用法与生理学中使用的功能概念建立关系。然而功能的概念在生理学领域中却是非常重要的,对机体生命的结构和过程的延续性的研究就需要它的帮助。结构存在于任何一个复杂的机体中,比如说人体,就是由器官、细胞组织、体液等的排列构成的。有时结构甚至还存在于由单细胞构成的生物之中,也就是它的分子的排列。同时,机体也有生命,因此我们将其看做一个过程。机体结构与机体生命过程之间的关系就构成了我们这里所说的机体功能的概念。机体的结构决定了当人体活着的时候其生命过程在人体内的运行,例如心脏就担负着向人体各个部分输送血液的功能。但机体结构作为一个有生命的结构,它的存在又要依赖于形成整个生命过程的其他各个过程。如果心脏不能够执行其功能,不仅生命过程将会结束,一个有生命的结构也会终结。因此,过程取决于结构,而结构的延续又依赖于过程。

功能概念的用法如果从社会体系及其理论认识方面来说,与在生理学中的科学用法是相似的,可以用来代表社会结构和社会

of the word function that seems to me to make it a useful term in comparative sociology. The three concepts of process, structure and function are thus components of a single theory as a scheme of interpretation of human social systems. The three concepts are logically interconnected, since 'function' is used to refer to the relations of process and structure. The theory is one that we can apply to the study both of continuity in forms of social life and also to processes of change in those forms.

If we consider such a feature of social life as the punishment of crime, or in other words the application, by some organised procedure, of penal sanctions for certain kinds of behaviour, and ask what is its social function, we have a fundamental problem of comparative sociology towards which a first contribution was made by Durkheim in his *Division du Travail Social*. A very wide general problem is posed when we ask what is the social function of religion. As it has been pointed out in one of the papers in this volume, the study of this problem requires the consideration of a large number of more limited problems, such as that of the social function of ancestor worship in those societies in which it is found. But in these more limited investigations, if the theory here outlined is accepted, the procedure has to be the examination of the connection between the structural features of the social life and the corresponding social process as both involved in a continuing system.

The first paper in this collection may serve to illustrate these theoretical ideas. It deals with an institution by which a sister's son is allowed privileged familiarity in his conduct towards his mother's brother. The custom is known in tribes of North America such as the Winnebago and others, in peoples of Oceania, such as the inhabitants of Fiji and Tonga, and in some tribes of Africa. My own observations on this institution were made in Tonga and Fiji, but as the paper was addressed to a South African audience it seemed preferable to refer to a single South African example, since a wider comparative discussion would have called for a much longer essay. The usual way of dealing with this institution, both in Oceania and in Africa, was to offer a

生活之间的相互联系。对我来说,在比较社会学中我认为功能的这种用法会让它成为一个有用的术语。因此,过程、结构和功能这三个概念就包含在对人类社会体系阐释的方案之中。这三个概念在逻辑上的相互关联,原因就在于"功能"一词描述过程和结构之间的关系。我们可以将这一理论用来研究社会生活方式的延续,也可以研究这些方式的变化过程。

比较社会学的根本问题是,考察社会生活特征的社会功能。因此,如果我们认为社会生活的特征包括惩罚犯罪,换句话说就是按照某种有组织的程序来对某种行为做出惩罚性制裁的话,假如追问它的社会功能是什么,那么我们就抓住了这个根本问题。杜尔干在《社会劳动分工》中,首次对它进行了研究。当我们问及什么是宗教的社会功能时,我们实际是提出了一个非常广泛而又普遍的问题。正如本书中一篇文章中指出的那样,研究此类问题需要对大量具体的问题进行考察,比如对许多地方发现的祖先崇拜在其社会中的功能这样具体问题的考察。然而,如果把本文中归纳的理论应用在这些较为具体的调查中,我们就必须考察社会生活的结构特征和与之相应的社会过程之间的关系,因为两者都在体系的延续过程中相互交织。

本书的第一篇文章会阐释这些理论观点。它谈到了一种外甥可以在舅父面前有放肆行为的制度。据我们了解,这种习俗在北美存在于温内巴戈或其他部落中,在大洋洲存在于诸如斐济和汤加等地区的民族部落中,还存在于非洲的一些部落中。我当时是在斐济和汤加对该制度进行考察的,因为需要很长的篇幅才能对此问题进行更广泛的讨论,况且文章是讲给南非的听众,所以引用南非的例子看起来是比较合适的。在讨论大

pseudo-historical explanation to the effect that it was a survival in a patrilineal society from a former condition of mother-right.

The alternative method of dealing with the institution is to look for a theoretical understanding of it as a part of a kinship system of a certain type, within which it has a discoverable function. We do not yet have a systematic general typology of kinship systems, for the construction of such is a laborious undertaking. I have indicated some partial and provisional results of such an attempt to determine types in a recent publication in the form of an Introduction to a book on African Systems of Kinship and Marriage. Amongst the great diversity of kinship systems we can, I think, recognise a type of what we may call father-right, and another of mother-right. In both these types the kinship structure is based on lineages with maximum emphasis on lineage relationships. In mother-right the lineage is matrilineal, a child belonging to the lineage of the mother. Practically all the jural relations of a man are those with his matrilineal lineage and its members, and therefore he is largely dependent on his mother' s brothers, who exercise authority and control over him and to whom he looks for protection and for inheritance of property. In a system offather-right, on the other hand, a man is largely dependent on his patrilineal lineage and therefore on his father and father' s brothers, who exercise authority and control over him, while it is to them that he has to look for protection and for inheritance. Father-right is represented by the sysyem of *patria potestas* of ancient Rome, and there are systems that approximate more or less closely to the type to be found in Africa and elsewhere. We may regard the BaThonga as so approximating. Mother-right is represented by the systems of the Nayar of Malabar and the Menangkubau Malays, and again there are systems elsewhere that approximate to the type.

The point of the paper on the mother' s brother may be said to be to contrast with the explanation by pseudo-history the interpretation of the institution to which it refers as having a function in a kinship system with a certain type of structure. If I were to rewrite the paper after thirty years I should certainly modify and expand it. But it has been

洋洲和非洲的这种制度时,目前普通的做法就是提供一个伪历史解释,即认为它是一种前母权环境在父系社会中的残余。

研究这种制度的另一种方法,是通过把该制度作为一种亲属制度的一部分来寻找其理论认识,并且可以在这种亲属制度中发现某种功能。我们还没有建立一种有关亲属制度的系统的总体类型学,因为这是一项极为耗费精力的工作。在最近出版的名为《非洲的亲属制度和婚姻制度》一书的导言中,我曾经表明了有关确定亲属关系类型的部分和暂时的结果。我认为,在种类繁多的亲属关系制度类型中,我们可以采纳那种我们称之为父权型和母权型分类的亲属制度,它们都是以极端重视世系关系的世系群为基础的。在母权型中,世系群是母权制,孩子属于母方世系群。事实上,一位男子的一切权利义务关系都与其母系世系群及其成员有关。因此,该男子大多数情况都要依赖其舅父,后者拥有着对这位男子掌控的权威,同时,他从舅父那里得到庇护和财产。相反,在父权型中,父系世袭群是一位男子主要依赖的对象,主要是父亲及父亲的兄弟,他从属于他们的权威和掌控,同时可以从他们那里得到保护和财产。父权制的典型代表是古代罗马父权制,与此或多或少相似的一些制度在非洲和其他一些地方也可以找到,例如,巴聪加人的制度。马拉巴尔的纳亚尔人和米南卡保罗来人的制度是母权制的代表,同时,与之相似的其他制度在其他地区也可以发现。

在有关舅父的那篇文章中,我提出的观点可以说是与伪历史的解释相对立的一种观点。亲属制度在社会结构中具有什么样的功能是它研究的主要内容。如果这篇文章放到30年后让我重

suggested to me that the paper may have a certain minor historical interest in relation to the development of thought in anthropology and it is therefore reprinted almost as it was written with only minor alterations.

Any interest this volume may have will probably be as an exposition of a theory, in the sense in which the word theory is here used as a scheme of interpretation thought to be applicable to the understanding of a class of phenomena. The theory can be stated by means of the three fundamental and connected concepts of 'process', 'structure' and 'function'. It is derived from such earlier writers as Montesquieu, Comte, Spencer, Durkheim and thus belongs to a cultural tradition of two hundred years. This introduction contains a reformulation in which certain terms are used differently from the way they were used in the early papers here reprinted. For example, in the earliest papers written twenty or more years ago the word 'culture' is used in the accepted meaning of that time as a general term for the way of life, including the way of thought, of a particular locally defined social group.

写，我想修改和扩充就必不可少。但是这篇文章提醒了我，也许它还具有一些人类学思想发展的历史韵味，因此，我只做了一点小小的修正，几乎按原样重印了它。

本书的所有趣味也许就是对这种理论的阐释。理论一词在这里是指一种解释方法，用来对某种现象进行认识。通过使用“过程”、“结构”、“功能”这三个最基本的、相互关联的概念，可以对这个理论进行详细论述。由于该理论来源于孟德斯鸠、孔德、斯宾塞、杜尔干等早期的学者，因此，它具有二百年的文化传统。在这篇导论中包含有对一些术语用法的改进，可能与过去所写的但收集于此书中文章中的用法不同。例如，在写于二三十年前的一篇很早的文章中，“文化”一词是作为一个概括性的术语被人们所接受的，其含义是指某一特定地区、特定社会群体的一种包括思维方式在内的生活方式。

CHAPTER I

The Mother's Brother In South Africa[①]

Amongst primitive peoples in many parts of the world a good deal of importance is attached to the relationship of mother's brother and sister's son. In some instances, the sister's son has certain special rights over the property of his mother's brother. At one time it was usual to regard these customs as being connected with matriarchal institutions, and it was held that their presence in a patrilineal people could be regarded as evidence that that people had at some time in the past been matrilineal. This view is still held by a few anthropologists and has been adopted by Mr. Junod in his book on the BaThonga people of Portuguese East Africa. Referring to the customs relating to the behaviour of the mother's brother and the sister's son to one another, he says: 'Now, having enquired with special care into this most curious feature of the Thonga system, I come to the conclusion that the only possible explanation is that, in former and very remote times, our tribe has passed through the matriarchal stage.' (Junod, *The Life of a South African Tribe*, 1913, *Vol. I*, *p.* 253.)

It is with this theory that I wish to deal in this paper; but I do not propose to repeat or add to the objections that have been raised against it by various critics in recent years. Purely negative criticism

---

① A paper read before the South African Association for the Advancement of Science, 9 July 1924, and printed *in South African Journal of Science*, *Vol. XXI*, *pp.* 542-55.

第一章　南非的母舅[①]

世界许多地方的原始人群中，舅父与外甥的关系被格外重视。在一些例证中，外甥对于其舅父的财产拥有某种特殊的权利。曾经有一段时间，这些习俗被认为是与母系氏族体制有关，而且如果该习俗出现于某一父系氏族群中，就证明该族群曾在过去某一时段经历过母系氏族阶段。一些人类学家至今仍旧持有这种观点，朱诺德先生在他的有关葡属东非的巴聪加人的书中也曾采用了这种观点。在谈到舅父与外甥相互关系的习俗时，朱诺德先生说："在特别关注巴聪加人制度这种令人好奇的特征后，我的结论是：对此特征唯一可能的解释就是，在从前很久远的时代，我们的部落曾经历过母系氏族阶段。"（朱诺德：《一个南非部落的生活》，1913 年，卷 1，第 253 页。）

此章我所讨论的正是这一理论。对此理论，近年来很多评论家提出了不少反对意见，在此，我并不想进行重复或补充。单纯的反对无助于推动一门科学的进展。如果认为一种假设不合理，去除它的唯一方法就是找到一个更令人满

① 本文曾作为论文在 1924 年 7 月 9 日的南北科学与进步协会的会议上宣读，后被收入《南非科学杂志》卷 21，第 542～545 页。

does not advance a science. The only satisfactory way of getting rid of an unsatisfactory hypothesis is to find a better one. I propose, therefore, to put before you an alternative hypothesis, and if I am successful, not in proving my hypothesis, but in showing that it does give a possible explanation of the facts, I shall at least have refuted the view of Mr. Junod that the explanation he accepts is the 'only possible' one.

For many African tribes we have almost no information about customs of this kind. Not that the customs do not exist, or are not important to the natives themselves, but because the systematic and scientific study of the natives of this country has as yet hardly begun. I shall, therefore, have to refer chiefly to the customs of the BaThonga as recorded by Mr. Junod. These are to be found in the first volume of the work quoted above (pp. 225 *et seq.*, and pp. 253 *et seq.*). Some of the more important of them may be summarised as follows:

1. The uterine nephew all through his career is the object of special care on the part of his uncle.
2. When the nephew is sick the mother's brother sacrifices on his behalf.
3. The nephew is permitted to take many liberties with his mother's brother; for example, he may go to his uncle's home and eat up the food that has been prepared for the latter's meal.
4. The nephew claims some of the property of his mother's brother when the latter dies, and may sometimes claim one of the widows.
5. When the mother's brother offers a sacrifice to his ancestors the sister's son steals and consumes the portion of meat or beer offered to the gods.

It must not be supposed that these customs are peculiar to the BaThonga. There is evidence that similar customs may be found amongst other African tribes, and we know of the existence of similar customs amongst other peoples in various parts of the world. In South Africa itself customs of this kind have been found by Mrs. Hoernle amongst the Nama Hottentots. The sister's son may behave with great freedom towards his mother's brother, and may take any particularly fine beast from his herd of cattle, or any particularly fine object that he may possess. On the contrary, the mother's brother may take from

意的假设。所以，即使我没能成功地证明我将要提出的假设，但只要我能对所论述的那些事实提供一个可能的解释，我就至少把朱诺德先生的那种“唯一可能的”观点驳倒了。

我们至今还没有在一些非洲部落中发现这方面的资料。我想，并不是因为这种习俗对于这里的土著人来说不重要，而是我们对于这个国家的土著人几乎还没有开始进行系统、科学的研究。因此，我只能主要依照朱诺德先生关于巴聪加人习俗的记载作为参考。你也可以在我刚才引述的朱诺德先生著作的第一卷中找到这些记载（第225页以下及253页以下），以下是一些重要观点的概述：

1. 舅父承担着对同母异父外甥的一生进行特别照顾的义务。

2. 如果外甥生病，舅父应该代替外甥献祭。

3. 外甥可以对舅父有放肆行为。例如，外甥可以到舅父家把为舅父准备的饭菜吃光。

4. 如果舅父去世，外甥对其舅父的部分财产有索取的权利，甚至可以拥有其舅父的一个寡妇。

5. 当舅父祭祀祖先时，容许外甥偷走并吃掉献给神的一部分酒肉。

大家不要认为这种习俗只存在于巴聪加人中，有证据表明，与之类似的习俗不仅被发现于其他非洲部落中，而且也存在于世界其他地区的民族中。对南非而言，豪恩莱夫人就在纳马霍屯督人中发现了这种习俗。在这些部落中，外甥在其舅父面前的行为极其自由，可以随意从其舅父的畜群中带走最好的牲畜，或拿走最好的物品。而与之相对，舅父只

his nephew's herd any beast that is deformed or decrepit, and may take any old and worn-out object he may possess.

What is particularly interesting to me is that in the part of Polynesia that I know best, that is, in the Friendly Islands (Tonga) and in Fiji, we find customs that show a very close resemblance to those of the BaThonga. There, also, the sister's son is permitted to take many liberties with his mother's brother, and to take any of his uncle's possessions that he may desire. And there also we find the custom that, when the uncle makes a sacrifice, the sister's son takes away the portion offered to the gods, and may eat it. I shall, therefore, make occasional references to the Tongan customs in the course of this paper.

These three peoples, the BaThonga, the Nama, and the Tongans, have patrilineal or patriarchal institutions; that is, the children belong to the social group of the father, not to that of the mother; and property is inherited in the male line, passing normally from a father to his son. The view that I am opposing is that the customs relating to the moth er's brother can only be explained by supposing that, at some past time, these peoples had matrilineal institutions, such as are found today amongst other primitive peoples, with whom the children belong to the social group of the mother, and property is inherited in the female line, passing from a man to his brother and to his sister's sons.

It is a mistake to suppose that we can understand the institutions of society by studying them in isolation without regard to other institutions with which they coexist and with which they may be correlated, and I wish to call attention to a correlation that seems to exist between customs relating to the mother's brother and customs relating to the father's sister. So far as present information goes, where we find the mother's brother important we also find that the father's sister is equally important, though in a different way. The custom of allowing the sister's son to take liberties with his mother's brother seems to be generally accompanied with an obligation of particular respect and obedience to the father's sister. Mr. Junod says little about the father's sister amongst the BaThonga. Speaking of a man's behaviour to this relative (his *rarana*) he says simply: 'He shows her great respect. However, she is not in any way a mother (*mamana*)' (op. cit., p. 223). About the Nama Hottentots we have better information, and

能得到外甥的畜群中那些老弱病残的牲畜，或其破旧的物品。

最令我感兴趣的是，在我所了解最多的波利尼亚的友爱岛（汤加）和斐济中，我们发现了与巴聪加人习俗极为相似的习俗。在他们的部落中，外甥也被允许去任意取笑舅父，只要他愿意就可以随意取走舅父的财产。同时，我们发现，当舅父祭祀时，外甥也可拿走献给神的一部分祭品，并把它吃掉。因此，我会在本文的论述过程中偶尔参考汤加人的习俗。

巴聪加人，纳马人和汤加人这三个民族中都存在父系或父权制度，也就是说，子女从属于父亲的生活圈子，而不属于母亲的；在氏族中男子继承财产，通常是由父亲传给儿子。我所反对的观点是，与舅父相关的习俗只能用以下假设来解释：即在过去某一段时期，这些民族曾是母系社会，子女从属于母亲的生活圈子，氏族中由女子继承财产，由一男子传给其兄弟，再传给外甥。

必须排除一种错误的观点，即可以忽视那些与之共存的或与之相联系的其他制度，而仅仅以孤立的研究就认为能理解这些社会制度。我想要强调一种关联，这种关联似乎存在于与舅父有关的习俗和与姑母有关的习俗之中。就目前的资料显示，我们发现，姑母在舅父具有重要性的地方以不同的作用和方式似乎也体现出了同样的重要性。外甥可以随意取笑舅舅，但对姑母却表现出特别的尊敬与服从，这两种习俗通常是相伴相生的。对巴聪加人中有关姑母的习俗，朱诺德先生几乎没有怎么论述。当谈到一名男子对这一亲属（他的拉拉娜）的行为时，朱诺德先生只是简单地说道："他对拉拉娜表示出极大的尊重。然而，无论从哪方面讲，拉拉娜都不是一位母亲（妈妈娜）。"（见前书第223

there the father's sister is the object of the very greatest respect on the part of her brother's child. In Tonga this custom is very clearly defined. A man's father's sister is the one relative above all others whom he must respect and obey. If she selects a wife for him he must marry her without even venturing to demur or to voice any objection; and so throughout his life. His father's sister is sacred to him; her word is his law; and one of the greatest offences of which he could be guilty would be to show himself lacking in respect to her.

Now this correlation (which is not confined, of course, to the three instances I have mentioned, but seems, as I have said, to be general) must be taken into account in any explanation of the customs relating to the mother's brother, for the correlated customs are, if I am right, not independent institutions, but part of one system; and no explanation of one part of the system is satisfactory unless it fits in with an analysis of the system as a whole.

In most primitive societies the social relations of individuals are very largely regulated on the basis of kinship. This is brought about by the formation of fixed and more or less definite patterns of behaviour for each of the recognised kinds of relationship. There is a special pattern of behaviour, for example, for a son towards his father, and another for a younger brother towards his elder brother. The particular patterns vary from one society to another; but there are certain fundamental principles or tendencies which appear in all societies, or in all those of a certain type. It is these general tendencies that it is the special task of social anthropology to discover and explain.

Once we start tracing out relationship to any considerable distance the number of different kinds of relatives that it is logically possible to distinguish is very large. This difficulty is avoided in primitive society by a system of classification, by which relatives of what might logically be held to be of different kinds are classified into a limited number of kinds. The principle of classification that is most commonly adopted in primitive society may be stated as that of the equivalence of brothers. In other words if I stand in a particular relation to one

页)我们对纳马霍屯督人的情况了解得更多一些,在这个部落中,侄子女给予姑母以极大尊重是他们的义务。在汤加人中,也可以明显地观察到这个习俗,即姑母必须得到尊敬和服从,并且高于其他的亲属。如果姑母为一个侄子选择妻子,他必须毫无拖延和毫无疑义地娶她,而且一生都如此。姑母对他来说是神圣的,她的话就是法律,他所犯的最大的错误就是对她不敬。

因此,在解释任何有关舅父习俗时,必须考虑到这种关联性。我曾说过,这种关联性是普遍存在的,并不仅仅限于我们所提到的三个民族。我认为,这些相关联的习俗之间并不是独立的制度,而是某种体系的一部分;如果我的看法是对的,那么单独地分析这个体系的一个组成部分,而不将这种分析与对整个体系的分析协调一致起来,是得不到满意结果的。

原始社会的部族中,亲属制度是个人社会关系调节的基础。那些固定了的、并且是或多或少为每一种公认的亲属关系确定了的行为模式,促成了这种现象的形成。例如,儿子对待其父亲、弟弟对待其哥哥之间都存在某种特殊的行为模式。不同的社会里有各自独特的行为模式,与此同时,某些根本的原则和趋势却存在于所有的社会之中。发现并阐释这些总的趋势是人类学家特有的任务。

如果我们开始在大范围内讨论亲属关系,那么我们所关注的数目将是庞大的,因为逻辑上可能加以区分的不同亲属种类的数目是很庞大的。如果我们按照某种分类体系的方式来研究原始社会,就可以避免这种困难。根据这种分类体系,可以把在逻辑上被认为是不同种类的亲属分成有限的几类。在大多数对原始社会研究中所采用的一般分类原则,可以说是“兄弟的同等原

man I regard myself as standing in the same general kind of relation to his brother; and similarly with a woman and her sister. In this way the father's brother comes to be regarded as a sort of father, and his sons are, therefore, relatives of the same kind as brothers. Similarly, the mother's sister is regarded as another mother, and her children are therefore brothers and sisters. The system is the one to be found amongst the Bantu tribes of South Africa, and amongst the Nama Hottentots, and also in the Friendly Islands. By means of this principle primitive societies are able to arrive at definite patterns of behaviour towards uncles and aunts and cousins of certain kinds. A man's behaviour towards his father's brother must be of the same general kind as his behaviour towards his own father and he must behave to his mother's sister according to the same pattern as towards his mother. The children of his father's brother or of the mother's sister must be treated in very much the same way as brothers and sisters.

This principle, however, does not give us immediately any pattern for either the mother's brother or the father's sister. It would be possible, of course, to treat the former as being like a father and the latter as similar to a mother, and this course does seem to have been adopted in a few societies. A tendency in this direction is found in some parts of Africa and in some parts of Polynesia. But it is characteristic of societies in which the classificatory system of kinship is either not fully developed or has been partly effaced.

Where the classificatory system of kinship reaches a high degree of development or elaboration another tendency makes its appearance: the tendency to develop patterns for the mother's brother and the father's sister by regarding the former as a sort of male mother and the latter as a sort of female father. This tendency sometimes makes its appearance in language. Thus, in South Africa the common term for the mother's brother is *malume* or *umalume*, which is a compound formed from the stem for 'mother'—*ma*—and a suffix meaning 'male'. Amongst the BaThonga the father' 's sister is called *rarana*, a term which Mr. Junod explains

则”。换言之,我与某男子之间的某种独特关系,同样适用于我与他的兄弟之间的关系,即我认为同他的兄弟之间也存在大致相同的关系。相应地,我与一个女子和她的姐妹之间,也适用于这种原则。在这种方式下,视父亲的兄弟为与父亲同类的人,视他的儿子们为自己兄弟一类的亲属;同样,母亲的姐妹被看做是另一个母亲,而她的孩子则被看做是自己的兄弟姐妹。在南非的班图部落、纳马霍屯督部落以及友爱群岛上,都可以发现这种体系存在的痕迹。原始社会中个人对其叔伯舅父、姑母姨妈和堂兄弟姐妹的行为方式,是从属于这种分类原则的,在此范畴内才能得出明确的行为模式。在此原则下,一个人必须像对待父亲一样对待叔伯父,像对待母亲一样对待其姨母,像对待自己的亲兄弟姐妹一样对待其堂表兄弟姐妹。

但是,这一原则并没有直接为我们提供对待舅父和或对待姑母的任一行为模式。当然,把舅父等同于叔伯父,像对待父亲一样对待他;对姑母就像姨母一样,把她们也像母亲一样对待,这种方式是可能的。而且,这种做法似乎的确被一些社会所采用。例如,在非洲和波利尼西亚的一些地方可以发现这种现象。但这种做法只是那些亲属分类制没有完全发展或已经隐没的社会里的特点。

还存在可以把舅父看成是一种男性母亲,而将姑母看成是一种女性父亲的这样一种对待舅父和姑母的模式,这种趋势曾出现在亲属分类体系达到一个较高的发展程度或细化的地方。而且,有的语言中也能看见端倪。在南非,舅父通常被称作 *malume* 或 *umalume*。这是一个复合词,词根“*ma*”来自母亲,每个词的后缀表示“男性”。姑母在巴聪加人中被称作 *rarana*,朱诺德

as meaning 'female father'. In some South African languages there is no special term for the father's sister; thus in Xosa, she is denoted by a descriptive term *udade bo bawo*, literally 'father's sister'. In Zulu she may be referred to by a similar descriptive term or she may be spoken of simply as *ubaba*, 'father', just like the father's brothers. In the Friendly Islands the mother's brother may be denoted by a special term *tuasina*, or he may be called *fa' e tangata*, literally 'male mother'. This similarity between South Africa and Polynesia cannot, I think, be regarded as accidental; yet there is no possible connection between the Polynesian languages and the Bantu languages, and I find it very difficult to conceive that the two regions have adopted the custom of calling the mother's brother by a term meaning 'male mother' either from one another or from one common source.

Now let us see if we can deduce what ought to be the patterns of behaviour towards the mother's brother and the father's sister in a patrilineal society on the basis of the principle or tendency which I have suggested is present. To do this we must first know the patterns for the father and the mother respectively, and I think that it will, perhaps, be more reassuring if I go for the definition of these to Mr. Junod's work, as his observations will certainly not have been influenced by the hypothesis that I am trying to prove.

The relationship of father, he says, 'implies respect and even fear. The father, though he does not take much trouble with his children, is, however, their instructor, the one who scolds and punishes. So do also the father's brothers' (op. cit., p. 222). Of a man's own mother he says: 'She is his true *mamana*, and this relation is very deep and tender, combining respect with love. Love, however, generally exceeds respect (op. cit., p. 224). Of the mother's relation to her children we read that 'She is generally weak with them and is often accused by the father of spoiling them.'

There is some danger in condensed formulæ, but I think we shall not be far wrong in saying that in a strongly patriarchal society, such as we find in South Africa, the father is the one who must be

先生将其解释为"女性父亲"。而在一些南非语言中,却没有特殊的术语来称呼姑母。在科萨语中,用 *udade bo bawo* 来表示姑母,这是一个描述性的语言,其字面意思是"父亲的姐妹";在祖鲁语中,也用描述性的术语来表示"她",或干脆将其等同于父亲的兄弟们,也称她为父亲。在友爱岛中,舅父用一个特殊的术语 *tuasina* 来表示,或被称为 *fa'e tangata*,字面意思也是"男性母亲",像在南非一样。我认为,存在于南非和波利尼西亚之间的这种相似性并不仅仅是一种巧合;然而,波利尼西亚语与班图诸语言中不可能存在联系,这两个地区也不可能同时采纳了来自于同一地区的把舅父称作"男性母亲"的习俗,也不可能相互采纳。

现在让我们看看,父系社会中对待舅父和姑母应具有的行为模式能否在我所提出的原则或趋势的基础上推导出来。在推导之前,首先必须了解当时的人们如何来对待自己的父亲和母亲。我想,如果也可以从朱诺德先生的作品中寻求如何解释这些模式的话,可能会更加可靠些,因为在我要证实的假设之前,他的观察肯定不会受到这些假设的干扰。

他说:"与父亲的关系隐含着尊敬甚至是恐惧。尽管父亲并没有为孩子做过多少事,但是,他却是孩子们的指导者,是批评和惩罚他们的人。父亲的兄弟们也是如此。"(见前书,第 222 页。)关于母亲,他说:"她是真正的 *mamana*,这种关系非常深切、温和,并包含着尊重与爱意,尽管爱往往超过了尊敬。"(见前书,第 224 页。)当我们读到母亲与自己的孩子之间的关系时,他写道:"她通常对孩子心软,丈夫经常会由于她溺爱孩子而责怪她。"

过于简单的假设总是包含了一些危险的元素。但是我认为,在一个如我们在南非发现的那种牢固的父权制社会里,以下观点

respected and obeyed, and the mother is the one from whom may be expected tenderness and indulgence. I could show you, if it were necessary, that the same thing is true of the family life of the Friendly Islanders.

If, now, we apply the principle that I have suggested is at work in these peoples it will follow that the father's sister is one who must be obeyed and treated with respect, while from the mother's brother indulgence and care may be looked for. But the matter is complicated by another factor. If we consider the relation of a nephew to his uncle and aunt, the question of sex comes in. In primitive societies there is a marked difference in the behaviour of a man towards other men and that towards women. Risking once more a formula, we may say that any considerable degree of familiarity is generally only permitted in such a society as the BaThonga between persons of the same sex. A man must treat his female relatives with greater respect than his male relatives. Consequently the nephew must treat his father's sister with even greater respect than he does his own father. (In just the same way, owing to the principle of respect for age or seniority, a man must treat his father's elder brother with more respect than his own father.) Inversely, a man may treat his mother's brother, who is of his own sex, with a degree of familiarity that would not be possible with any woman, even his own mother. The influence of sex on the behaviour of kindred is best seen in the relations of brother and sister. In the Friendly Islands and amongst the Nama a man must pay great respect to his sister, particularly his eldest sister, and may never indulge in any familiarities with her. The same thing is true, I believe, of the South African Bantu. In many primitive societies the father's sister and the elder sisters are the objects of the same general kind of behaviour, and in some of these the two kinds of relatives are classified together and denoted by the same name.

We have deduced from our assumed principle a certain pattern of behaviour for the father's sister and for the mother's brother.

应该不会离事实太远:对于父亲来说,孩子必须尊重他、听从他;而对于母亲来说,她是孩子们希望可以得到温柔与溺爱的人。必要的话,我还可以列举出这种现象在友爱岛的家庭中存在的事实。

现在,如果按我所提出的理论来考察上述民族中对舅父和姑母的行为模式,那么一个人如何对待其舅父和姑母将会遵循以下原则:必须听从并尊敬姑母,同时可以从舅父处得到溺爱和关怀。但是,我们仍然要考虑会使情况变得更加复杂的另一些因素。性别问题就是在我们考虑一个外甥同他的舅父和姑母之间的关系时有可能使情况复杂化的因素。在原始社会中,一名男子与男人之间的行为模式和他与女人之间的行为模式存在明显的区别。如果再一次进行简单化的假设,我们可以说,这种同性之间的亲昵关系,只存在于像巴聪加人这样的社会中。对一位男子来说,其女性亲属必须获得比其男性亲属更大的尊敬。因而,侄子对姑母的尊敬必须胜过他对待自己的父亲。(同理,由于尊敬年长者或高辈分者的原则,一名男子必须给予他们比给予父亲更多的敬意。)相反,一名男子对待其舅父所体现的亲昵程度,是不可以表现在他与女性亲属,甚至在与他母亲的关系中的。性别对亲属行为的影响,在兄弟姐妹中也可以得到最好的体现。在友爱岛和纳马人中,一名男子必须给予其姐妹,尤其是年长的姐姐以极大的尊敬,并且永远不得与她有任何过分亲昵的行为。我认为,同样的情况在南非班图人中也存在。在许多原始社会部落中,姑母和姐姐是同一种行为模式的对象,甚至这两类亲戚被归为一类,并用同一称呼来表示。

我们已经从假设的原则中推出对于姑母和舅父的特定行为

Now these patterns are exactly what we find amongst the BaThonga, amongst the Hottentots, and in the Friendly Islands. The father's sister is above all relatives the one to be respected and obeyed. The mother's brother is the one relative above all from whom we may expect indulgence, with whom we may be familiar and take liberties. Here, then, is an alternative 'possible explanation' of the customs relating to the mother's brother, and it has this advantage over Mr. Junod's theory that it also explains the correlated customs relating to the father's sister. This brings us, however, not to the end but to the beginning of our enquiry. It is easy enough to invent hypotheses. The important and difficult work begins when we set out to verify them. It will be impossible for me, in the short time available, to make any attempt to verify the hypothesis I have put before you. All I can do is to point out certain lines of study which will, I believe, provide that verification.

The first and most obvious thing to do is to study in detail the behaviour of the sister's son and the mother's brother to one another in matriarchal societies. Unfortunately, there is practically no information on this subject relating to Africa, and very little for any other part of the world. Moreover, there are certain false ideas connected with this distinction of societies into matriarchal and patriarchal that it is necessary to remove before we attempt to go further.

In all societies, primitive or advanced, kinship is necessarily bilateral. The individual is related to certain persons through his father and to others through his mother, and the kinship system of the society lays down what shall be the character of his dealings with his paternal relatives and his maternal relatives respectively. But society tends to divide into segments (local groups, lineages, clans, etc.), and when the hereditary principle is accepted, as it most frequently is, as the means of determining the membership of a segment, then it is necessary to choose between maternal or paternal descent. When a society is divided into groups with a rule that the children belong to the group of the father we have patrilineal descent, while if the children

模式。而这些行为模式恰恰与我们在巴聪加人、霍屯督人和友爱岛人那里所发现的行为模式一样。姑母是所有亲属中得到尊重和服从级别最高的人。而舅父则是人们最希望可以与他放纵并与他亲热的亲属,而且从他那里拿走财物。因此,对于有关舅父的习俗还有另外一个“可能的解释”。它相对于朱诺德先生理论的优势在于,这种解释同时阐述了有关姑母的一些相关习俗。然而,这仅仅是我们考察工作的开始而并非结尾。创立一种假设是很简单的事,但是,要证实这些假设却是个很重要也很困难的过程。要证明我所提出的假设,对我来说不是一个在短时间内可以完成的工作,我所能做的只是指出几种研究线索。我相信,这些线索会为证实假设提供证据。

在开始正式研究之前,深入研究母系社会中甥舅之间的相互行为显然是我们要做的第一件事。不幸的是,不仅我们在非洲根本找不到有关这方面的资料,而且在世界其他地方也只能找到很少的相关资料。另外,我们在开始进一步工作以前,还需要纠正一些有关母系社会和父系社会之区别的错误观点。

在所有的社会中,无论原始的还是先进的,亲属关系肯定都具有双边性。一个人与外界其他人的联系,既可以通过父亲一边,也可以通过母亲一边来进行。但是此人如何对待其父系亲属和其母系亲属却是有区别的,该社会的亲属制度规定了此种区别的特点。社会通常被划分为不同的部分(本地群、世系群、氏族等),为了确定一个部分的成员,我们通常依照世袭原则来判断。如果仍沿用这个方法,就有必要对母系继承和父亲继承加以选择。区分父系继承制和母系继承制,主要看该社会所依据的规则。如果该社会按孩子属于父方团体的规则来划分不同的团体,

always belong to the group of the mother the descent is matrilineal.

There is, unfortunately, a great deal of looseness in the use of the terms matriarchal and patriarchal, and for that reason many anthropologists refuse to use them. If we are to use them at all, we must first give exact definitions. A society may be called patriarchal when descent is patrilineal (i. e. the children belong to the group of the father), marriage is patrilocal (i. e. the wife removes to the local group of the husband), inheritance (of property) and succession (to rank) are in the male line, and the family is patripotestal (i. e. the authority over the members of the family is in the hands of the father or his relatives). On the other hand, a society can be called matriarchal when descent, inheritance and succession are in the female line, marriage is matrilocal (the husband removing to the home of his wife), and when the authority over the children is wielded by the mother's relatives.

If this definition of these opposing terms is accepted, it is at once obvious that a great number of primitive societies are neither matriarchal nor patriarchal, though some may incline more to the one side, and others more to the other. Thus, if we examine the tribes of Eastern Australia, which are sometimes spoken of as matriarchal, we find that marriage is patrilocal, so that membership of the local group is inherited in the male line, the authority over the children is chiefly in the hands of the father and his brothers, property (what there is of it) is mostly inherited in the male line, while, as rank is not recognised, there is no question of succession. The only matrilineal institution is the descent of the totemic group, which is through the mother, so that these tribes, so far from being matriarchal, incline rather to the patriarchal side. Kinship amongst them is thoroughly bilateral, but for most purposes kinship through the father is of more importance than kinship through the mother. There is some evidence, for example, that the obligation to avenge a death falls upon the relatives in the male line rather than upon those in the female line.

We find an interesting instance of this bilateralism, if it may be so called, in South Africa, in the OvaHerero tribe. The facts are not quite certain, but it would seem that this tribe is subdivided into two

我们称之为父系继承制；如果孩子们总是属于母亲团体时，就是母系继承制。

很不幸，关于“母权的”和“父权的”两个术语在用法上并没有很明确的定义，因此，许多人类学家拒绝使用这两个词。只有先给出准确定义，才能够使用它们。这样我们定义父权社会，指一个社会具有父系继承制（子女属于父方的团体），婚姻从夫居（即结婚后妻子移居至夫家），男子继承财产和承袭地位，家族以父亲为家长（即父亲及其亲属有权管理家族）。相对地，母权社会是指一个社会按照母系继承财产和承袭地位，婚姻从妻居（即丈夫婚后移居至妻家），孩子由妻方管教等。

如果大家可以接受这一对相互对立的术语的定义，那么我们立刻可以看出，在大部分原始社会部族中既不是母权制，也不是父权制，尽管有些倾向于母权制，另一些倾向于父权制。于是，当我们对那些有时被认为具有母权制的东澳大利亚部落进行考察时，我们会发现其婚姻是从夫居的，因而，当地团体的成员资格是按男子传承，并且父亲及其兄弟对孩子有主要的管教权利，有什么财产的话，主要由男子继承。同时，由于不存在认可的头衔，也就不存在承袭问题。那么仅存的母系体制是图腾集团的继承，并依母亲进行传递。因此，与其说这些部落具有母权制倾向，不如说具有父权制倾向。存在于这些部落中的亲属关系是具有双边性的。但是从实现目的的角度来看，父亲的亲属关系要比母亲的亲属关系更加重要。例如，有证据表明，为死者复仇的义务就落在男方亲属而非女方亲属身上。

在南非的奥瓦赫雷鲁人中，我们还可以找到这种双边主义的有趣例证。尽管事实并不是很确定，但是，这一部

sets of segments crossing one another. For one set (the *omaanda*) descent is matrilineal, while for the other (*otuzo*) it is patrilineal. A child belongs to the *eanda* of its mother and inherits cattle from its mother's brothers, but belongs to the *oruzo* of its father and inherits his ancestral spirits. Authority over the children would seem to be in the hands of the father and his brothers and sisters.

It is now clear, I hope, that the distinction between matriarchal and patriarchal societies is not an absolute but a relative one. Even in the most strongly patriarchal society some social importance is attached to kinship through the mother; and similarly in the most strongly matriarchal society the father and his kindred are always of some importance in the life of the individual.

In Africa we have in the south-east a group of tribes that incline strongly to patriarchy, so much so, in fact, that we may perhaps justifiably speak of them as patriarchal. Descent of the social group, inheritance of property, succession to chieftainship, are all in the male line; marriage is patrilocal, and authority in the family is strongly patripotestal. In the north of Africa, in Kenya and the surrounding countries, there is another group of strongly patriarchal peoples, some of them Bantu-speaking, while others are Nilotic or Hamitic. Between these two patriarchal regions there is a band of peoples stretching apparently right across Africa from east to west, on the level of Nyasaland and Northern Rhodesia, in which the tendency is towards matriarchal institutions. Descent of the social group, inheritance of property, and succession to the kingship or chieftainship are in the female line. In some of the tribes marriage seems to be matrilocal, at any rate temporarily if not permanently, i. e. a man on marriage has to go and live with his wife's people.

It is about these people and their customs that we urgently need information if we are to understand such matters as the subject of this paper. Of one tribe of this region we have a fairly full description in the work of Smith and Dale.[①] Unfortunately, on the very points with

① *The Ila-speaking People of Northern Rhodesia*, 1920

落似乎的确被划分为两个相互交叉的部分。一部分(奥玛安达)是母系传承,另一部分(奥图佐)是父系传承。孩子是母亲的 *eanda*,并且可以继承到舅父的牲畜,但他却是父亲的 *oruzo*,并从父亲那里继承其祖先精神。父亲及其兄弟姐妹有管教子女的权利。

我认为,现在应该可以清楚了,母权制社会和父权制社会的区别并不是绝对的,而是相对的。甚至是在最稳固的父系社会中,母系亲属也受到了一定的社会重视;同样,在最稳固的母系社会中,父亲及其亲属在个人生活中也受到某种程度的重视。

我们发现,在非洲东南部存在一些具有强烈父权制倾向的部落,这些部落的倾向如此之强,以至于我们无可非议地称其为父权制部落。这些部落都是依据父系来进行社会团体的传承、财产的继承、酋长的继任;婚姻为从夫居制,家庭是严重的父权家长制。我们还发现,一群具有明显父权制特征的部落存在于北非的肯尼亚及其周边的一些国家,其中一些部落操的是班图语,还有一些操的是尼罗特语和含米特语。在这两种父权制地区之间,有一条明显贯穿非洲东西的民族分布带,即具有母权制倾向的尼亚萨兰和北罗德西亚地区。社会团体财产、国王或酋长职位的继承都依照母系,其中一些部落的婚姻看起来即使不是永久性的,也是暂时性的从妻居制,即结婚的男子必须移居到妻子的家中。

想要理解像本文主题这样的问题,我们迫切需要关于这些民族及其习俗方面的资料。有关这一地区中某个部落的情况,我们可以在史密斯和达勒的著作中找到充分的描述。[①]

① 《居住在北罗得西亚的伊拉语部落》,1920 年。

which I am now dealing the information is scanty and certainly very incomplete. There are, however, two points I wish to bring out. The first concerns the behaviour of the mother's brother to his sister's son. We are told that 'the mother's brother is a personage of vast importance; having the power even of life and death over his nephews and nieces, which no other relations, not even the parents, have; he is to be held in honour even above the father. This is *avunculi potestas*, which among the BaIla is greater than *patria potestas*. In speaking of the mother's brother, it is customary to use an honorific title given to people who are respected very highly' (op. cit., Vol. I, p. 230). This kind of relation between the mother's brother and the sister's son is obviously what we might expect in a strongly matriarchal society. But how then, on Mr. Junod's theory, can we explain the change which must have taken place from this sort of relation to that which now exists among the BaThonga?

This brings me to another point which it will not be possible to discuss in detail but which has an important bearing on the argument. We have been considering the relation of the sister's son to his mother's brother; but if we are to reach a really final explanation, we must study also the behaviour of a man to his other relatives on the mother's side, and to his mother's group as a whole. Now in the Friendly Islands the peculiar relation between a sister's son and a mother's brother exists also between a daughter's son and his mother's father. The daughter's son must be honoured by his grandfather. He is 'a chief' to him. He may take his grandfather's property, and he may take away the offering that his grandfather makes to the gods at a kava ceremony. The mother's father and the mother's brother are the objects of very similar behaviour patterns, of which the outstanding feature is the indulgence on the one side and the liberty permitted on the other. Now there is evidence of the same thing amongst the BaThonga, but again we lack the full information that we need. Mr. Junod writes that a grandfather 'is more lenient to his grandson by his daughter than his grandson by his son' (op cit. p. 227). In this connection the custom of calling the mother's brother *kokwana* (grandfather) is significant.

Now here is something that it seems impossible to explain on Mr.

当然,很不幸,对于我所要讨论的问题,资料仍然贫乏而且很不完整。不过,我仍旧要提出两点。第一点是舅父如何对待其外甥。我们听说,“舅父是相当重要的人士,掌控着外甥和外甥女的生死大权,这种权力是其他亲属,甚至是父母都不拥有的;他享有的荣誉甚至高过父亲。”这就是舅权,在拜拉人中,它高于父权。谈到舅父,通常把这一荣誉性的称呼给予那些受到高度尊敬的人(见前书,卷1,第230页)。在一个坚固的母权制社会中出现这种舅甥关系是显而易见的。但是,仅根据朱诺德先生的理论,我们是不可能解释巴聪加人中这种关系从过去到现在的变化的。

这就不得不让我提出第二个论点。这一论点没有必要详谈,但是它却对争论有重要意义。如果我们想要对我们一直在讨论的外甥与舅父之间的关系给出一个真正的最终解释,我们就必须对外甥对待其母方的其他亲属的行为乃至对待整个母系集团的行为加以研究。目前,在友爱岛上,在外孙与外祖父之间同样存在着外甥与舅父之间的那种独特关系。外孙必须得到外祖父的尊敬,外孙就像是他的“酋长”一样,他可以取走外祖父的财产,包括外祖父在“卡瓦”仪式上献给神的祭品。作为行为模式的对象,外祖父与舅父之间有非常多的相似之处,这种行为模式的显著特征是一方放任另一方,而被放任的一方则放纵自己。尽管仍缺乏更充分的材料,但在巴聪加人中存在此种情况得到现有证据的支持。朱诺德先生写到:“外祖父对外孙比孙子仁慈得多。”(见前书,等227页。)在这方面,称舅父为*kokwana*(外祖父)的习俗就具有深刻的含义了。

这里有一些似乎是朱诺德先生的理论所无法解释的情况。

Junod' theory. In a strongly matriarchal society the mother's father does not belong to the same group as his grandchild and is not a person from whom property can be inherited or who can exercise authority. Any explanation of the liberties permitted towards the mother's brother cannot be satisfactory unless it also explains the similar liberties towards the mother's father which are found in Polynesia, and apparently to some extent in South Africa. This Mr. Junod's theory clearly does not do, and cannot do.

But on the hypothesis that I have put forward the matter is fairly simple. In primitive society there is a strongly marked tendency to merge the individual in the group to which he or she belongs. The result of this in relation to kinship is a tendency to extend to all the members of a group a certain type of behaviour which has its origin in a relationship to one particular member of the group. Thus the tendency in the BaThonga tribe would seem to be to extend to all the members of the mother's group (family or lineage) a certain pattern of behaviour which is derived from the special pattern that appears in the behaviour of a son towards his mother. Since it is from his mother that he expects care and indulgence he looks for the same sort of treatment from the people of his mother's group, i. e. from all his maternal kin. On the other hand it is to his paternal kin that he owes obedience and respect. The patterns that thus arise in relation to the father and the mother are generalised and extended to the kindred on the one side and on the other. If I had time I think I could show you quite conclusively that this is really the principle that governs the relations between an individual and his mother's kindred in the patriarchal tribes of South Africa. I must leave the demonstration, however, to another occasion. I can do no more now than illustrate my statement.

The custom, often miscalled bride-purchase and generally known in South Africa as *lobola*, is, as Mr. Junod has well shown, a payment made in compensation to a girl's family for her loss when she is taken away in marriage. Now, since in the patriarchal tribes of South Africa a woman belongs to her father's people, the compensation has to be paid to them. But you will find that in many of the tribes a certain portion of the 'marriage payment' is handed over to the mother's brother of the girl for whom it is paid. Thus, amongst the BaPedi, out of the *lenyalo* cattle one head (called *hloho*) is handed to the mother's

因为在一个牢固的母权制社会里,外祖父与外孙并不属于同一团体,外孙不可以从外祖父那继承到财产,同时,外祖父对外孙没有管教权。所以用任何有关外甥对舅父享有特权的解释来说明这种情况都不能让人满意,除非它能解释发生在波利尼西亚及非洲南部对外祖父的那种类似的特权现象。朱诺德先生的理论没有对这一现象进行解释,而且也不能解释。

但是根据我所提出的假设,对这种现象进行解释就会变得很容易。在原始社会中,个人会有一种被埋没在他或她所属的团体中的倾向,而且这种倾向具有一种强烈的、明显的趋势。这种结果与亲属关系有关,原因是那种最初同团体中某一个具体成员有关的行为模式扩展到了该团体的所有成员的倾向。对母亲的行为模式可以扩展到母亲所属团体(家族或世系群)的其他成员,这可能就是巴聪加部落具有那种倾向的起源。正是因为期盼从母亲那里得到关心和溺爱,所以也期盼能够从母方其他亲属那里得到同样的待遇。另一方面,其父系亲属也要得到尊敬和服从。因此,在各自的家族中,就可以确定对待母亲和父亲的行为模式并将之扩展开来。如果时间允许的话,我能够确定地证实这是南非父系部落中统治个人同其母方亲属之间关系的原则。然而,在此我仅表明我的观点,证明留到以后再做。

如朱诺德先生曾经详细说明过的当娶走新娘时对她的家族支付补偿的一种习俗,常被误称为“购买新娘”,这种习俗通常称为“罗保拉”。在南非的父权制部落中,补偿是交给他们的,因为女人属于父方成员。但是,在许多这样的父权制部落中,女孩的舅父也会得到一部分“婚姻补偿”。在巴佩迪人中,女孩的舅父会从“莱恩亚罗”中得到一只头畜。在巴索托

brother of the girl. Amongst the BaSotho a portion of the cattle received for a girl on her marriage may sometimes be taken by her mother's brother, this being known as *ditsoa*. Now the natives state that the *ditsoa* cattle received by the mother's brother are really held by him on behalf of his sister's children. If one of his sister's sons or daughters is ill he may be required to offer a sacrifice to his ancestral spirits, and he then takes a beast from the *ditsoa* herd. Also, when the sister's son wishes to obtain a wife, he may go to his mother's brother to help him to find the necessary cattle and his uncle may give him some of the *ditsoa* cattle received at the marriage of his sister, or may even give him cattle from his own herd, trusting to being repaid from the *ditsoa* cattle to be received in the future from the marriage of a niece. I believe that the Native Appeal Court has decided that the payment of *ditsoa* to the mother's brother is a voluntary matter and cannot be regarded as a legal obligation, and with that judgment I am in agreement. I quote this custom because it illustrates the sort of interest that the mother's brother is expected to take in his sister's son, in helping him and looking after his welfare. It brings us back to the question as to why the mother's brother may be asked to offer sacrifices when his nephew is sick.

In south-east Africa ancestor worship is patrilineal, i. e. a man worships and takes part in sacrifices to the spirits of his deceased relatives in the male line. Mr. Junod's statements about the BaThonga are not entirely clear. In one place he says that each family has two sets of gods, those on the father's side and those on the mother's; they are equal in dignity and both can be invoked (op. cit., II, p. 349, and I, p. 256, note). But in another place it is stated that if an offering has to be made to the gods of the mother's family this must be through the maternal relatives, the *malume* (op. cit., II, p. 367). Other passages confirm this and show us that ancestral spirits can only be directly approached in any ritual by their descendants in the male line.

The natives of the Transkei are very definite in their statements to me that a person's maternal gods, the patrilineal ancestors of his mother, will never inflict supernatural punishment upon him by making him sick. (I am not quite so sure about the Sotho tribes, but I

人中,女孩的舅父可能会带走她结婚时所收到的一部分牲畜,这称作“迪特索亚”。据当地人说舅父得到的迪特索亚只是代为外甥和外甥女保管。如果他们其中一个生了病,需要祭祀祖先的灵魂时,就会从迪特索亚中拿出一只牲畜来献祭。同样,当外甥想娶妻时,他也可以向舅父寻求帮助,并获得其所需的牲畜。这些牲畜可能来自其姐妹的婚姻中舅父收到的迪特索亚,也可能来自舅父自己的牲畜,当他确信可以从另一个外甥女的婚姻中得到偿还的话。对舅父迪特索亚的支付应当是自愿的行为,而并非是一种法律责任。对这个判断,我完全同意。我引用这一习俗的原因,是因为它解释了那种希望舅父帮助、关心外甥,并照看其财产的权利。这又把我们引导到另一个问题:为什么当外甥生病时,舅父被要求为其祭祀?

在非洲东南部,祖先崇拜是按照父系的世系,即一男子依据父系崇拜慰籍去世亲属的灵魂并参与祭祀。朱诺德先生有关巴聪加人这方面情况的叙述并不十分清楚。他曾在书中写道:“每个家族的神都由一组父方的神与一组母方的神组成,两组神都具有同样高的尊贵地位,并且都可以乞灵。”(见前引书,第二卷349页和第一卷256页的注释。)而在书中另一处,他说道:“如果必须对母方家族的神进行祭祀,则必须通过母方亲属 *malume* 来完成。”(见上书,第二卷367页。)但朱诺德先生的陈述又强调:只有在由父系子孙举行的仪式上,才能同祖先的灵魂直接接触。

特兰斯凯的土著人对他们的祖先崇拜方式曾向我非常明确地说明:某人母亲的父系祖先作为母方神灵,永远不会通过使他得病的方式来让他遭受超自然的惩罚。(我对索托部落的情况并不确定,但我认为,他们也许具有同样的观

think that they probably have similar views.) On the other hand a married woman can receive protection from the ancestral spirits of her patrilineal lineage, and so can her young children as long as they are attached to her. For children are only fully incorporated in their father's lineage when they reach adolescence. So in the Transkei a woman, when she marries, should be given a cow, the *ubulunga* cow, by her father, from the herd of her lineage, which she can take to her new home. Since she may not drink the milk from her husband's herd during the early period of her married life she can be provided with milk from this beast that comes from her lineage. This cow constitutes a link between herself and her lineage, its cattle, and its gods, for cattle are the material link between the living members of the lineage and the ancestral spirits. So if she is sick she can make for herself a necklace of hairs from the tail of this cow and so put herself under the protection of her lineage gods. Moreover, if one of her infant children is sick, she can make a similar necklace which is thought to give protection to the child. When her son is grown up he should receive an *ubulunga* bull from his father's herd, and thereafter it is from the tail of this beast that he will make a protective amulet; similarly the daughter, when she marries, is detached from her mother, and may receive an *ubulunga* cow from her father.

But though, according to the statements made to me, the maternal ancestors will not punish their descendant with sickness, they can be appealed to for help. When, therefore, a child is sick the parents may go to the mother's brother of the child, or to the mother's father if he is still living, and ask that a sacrifice shall be offered, and an appeal for help made to the child's maternal ancestors. This, at any rate, is stated as a practice in the Sotho tribes, and one of the purposes of the *ditsoa* cattle that go from the marriage payment to the mother's brother of the bride is said to be to make provision for such sacrifices if they should be needed.

This brings us to the final extension of the principle that I have suggested as the basis of the customs relating to the mother's brother. The pattern of behaviour towards the mother, which is developed in the family by reason of the nature of the family group and its social life, is extended with suitable modifications to the mother's sister and to the mother's brother, then to the group of maternal kindred as a whole, and finally to the maternal gods, the ancestors of the mother's group. In the same way the pattern of behaviour towards the father is extended to the father's brothers and sisters, and to the whole of the

点。)另一方面,一个已婚的女人及其孩子(只要这些孩子从属于她),都可以得到她父系祖先灵魂的保护。只有当孩子进入青春期时,才会完全融入父系的世系群中。因此,在特兰斯凯地区,一个女孩的父亲会从自己氏族的畜群中挑选出一头被称作“阿卜仑加”的牛,在其结婚时跟随她一起到夫家去。也许她在结婚初期不可以喝她丈夫牲畜的奶,所以她只能喝她从家里带来的那头牛的牛奶。这头奶牛在她和她的家族、家族的牲畜、神灵以及祖先的灵魂之间建立了一种联系,是人与神之间联系的载体。因此,在她和她未成年的孩子得病时,为祈求家族神灵的庇护,她可以用这头牛的尾毛为自己和孩子做个项链。但当她的儿子长大后,他会从父亲的畜群中得到一头阿卜仑加公牛,此后,他可以用这头牛的尾毛做一件护身物;女孩也是如此,结婚就意味着与母亲脱离,而从她父亲那里得到一头阿卜仑加奶牛。

但是根据别人对我的陈述,后辈们不但不会受到母方祖先降病的惩罚,而且还可以向他们乞求帮助。因此,父母会在孩子生病时到孩子的舅父,或外祖父那里(如果外祖父在世的话)寻求帮助,请求他们为孩子做祭祀,并祈求母方祖先的帮助。不管怎么说,这都是索托部落的一种习俗。据说事先要为这种祭祀做准备,这也就是新娘结婚时支付给舅父的迪特索亚牲畜的目的之一。

现在我们可以来讨论有关舅父的基本习俗原则的最终扩展了。通过适当的修正和补充,由家庭团体和社会生活本身发展而成的对待母亲的行为模式可以被扩展到对姨母、舅父,进而对整个母系集团,最终到母方神灵和母方祖先。以同样的原则对待父亲的行为模式,也能被扩展到父亲的兄弟姐妹及整个父系集团,

father' s group (or rather to all the older members of it, the principle of age making important modifications necessary), and finally to the paternal gods.

The father and his relatives must be obeyed and respected (even worshipped, in the original sense of the word), and so therefore also must be the paternal ancestors. The father punishes his children, and so may the ancestors on the father' s side. On the other hand, the mother is tender and indulgent to her child, and her relatives are expected to be the same, and so also the maternal spirits.

A very important principle, which I have tried to demonstrate elsewhere (*The Andaman Islanders*, Chapter V), is that the social values current in a primitive society are maintained by being expressed in ceremonial or ritual customs. The set of values that we here meet with in the relations of an individual to his kindred on the two sides must, therefore, also have their proper ritual expression. The subject is too vast to deal with at all adequately here, but I wish to discuss one point. Amongst the BaThonga, and also in Western Polynesia (Fiji and Tonga), the sister' s son (or in Tonga also the daughter' s son) intervenes in the sacrificial ritual. Mr. Junod describes a ceremony of crushing down the hut of a dead man in which the *batukulu* (sister' s children) play an important part. They kill and distribute the sacrificial victims and when the officiating priest makes his prayer to the spirit of the dead man it is the sister' s sons who, after a time, interrupt or 'cut' the prayer and bring it to an end. They then, among the BaThonga clans, seize the portions of the sacrifice that have been dedicated to the spirit of the dead man and run away with them, 'stealing' them (op. cit., I, p. 162).

I would suggest that the meaning of this is that it gives a ritual expression to the special relation that exists between the sister' s son and the mother' s brother. When the uncle is alive the nephews have the right to go to his village and take his food. Now that he is dead they

甚至延伸到祖辈(年龄原则起着重要的修正性作用),最终延伸到父方神灵。

父亲及其亲属必须得到服从和尊重(该词的原本意义为崇拜),因此,父方祖先也必须得到如此对待。父亲可以惩罚他的子女们,而父系祖先也同样承担这样的角色和权利。另一方面,母亲对子女充满着关心和溺爱,因此,母方亲属和孩子的母方神灵也被孩子们这样期待着。

我在《安达曼群岛岛民》第五章,曾尝试着说明一个重要原则:在某一个原始社会中,如何表达礼仪习俗是维持通行的社会价值的关键所在。因此,我们在这里所谈到的这个特定原始社会结构中,肯定存在某种恰当的礼仪形式来描述这个社会中个人与其双方亲属关系的价值。由于这个话题涉及的范围太广,我不能在这里对该话题进行充分地描述,但我希望谈谈其中的一点。在巴聪加人和西波利尼西亚(斐济和汤加人)中,外甥(在汤加人中还包括外孙)会干涉献祭仪式,成为其中的一名参与者。*batukulu*(外甥)在朱诺德先生描述的这个礼仪中起着重要的作用,他是作为推倒死者草房的人。他们宰杀并献出祭品,待主祭祭司为死者的灵魂做完祈祷,外甥就会通过干扰或打断祈祷的方式使仪式结束。在巴聪加人部落中,外甥们还会夺取献给死者灵魂的一部分祭品,而且不受死者灵魂的约束,即“偷走”这些祭品(见上引书,第一卷,第162页)。

我认为,这种礼仪表达了那种甥舅之间的特殊关系。在舅父生前,外甥有权到舅父的村子去并拿走他的食物。现在,舅父去

come and do this again, as part of the funeral ritual, and as it were for the last time, i. e. they come and steal portions of meat and beer that are put aside as the portion of the deceased man.

The same sort of explanation will be found to hold, I think, of the part played in sacrificial and other ritual by the sister's son both amongst the Bantu of South Africa and also in Tonga and Fiji. As a man fears his father, so he fears and reverences his paternal ancestors, but he has no fear of his mother's brother, and so may act irreverently to his maternal ancestors; he is, indeed, required by custom so to act on certain occasions, thus giving ritual expression to the special social relations between a man and his maternal relatives in accordance with the general function of ritual, as I understand it.

It will, perhaps, be of help if I give you a final brief statement of the hypothesis I am advancing, with the assumptions involved in it and some of its important implications.

1. The characteristic of most of these societies that we call primitive is that the conduct of individuals to one another is very largely regulated on the basis of kinship, this being brought about by the formation of fixed patterns of behaviour for each recognised kind of kinship relation.
2. This is sometimes associated with a segmentary organisation of society, i. e. a condition in which the whole society is divided into a number of segments (lineages, clans).
3. While kinship is always and necessarily bilateral, or cognatic, the segmentary organisation requires the adoption of the unilineal principle, and a choice has to be made between patrilineal and matrilineal institutions.
4. In patrilineal societies of a certain type, the special pattern of behaviour between a sister's son and the mother's brother is derived from the pattern of behaviour between the child and the mother, which is itself the product of the social life within the family in the narrow sense.
5. This same kind of behaviour tends to be extended to all the maternal relatives, i. e. to the whole family or group to which

世了，作为葬礼的一部分，外甥还会有同样的行为（这是最后一次）偷走献给已故之人的一部分酒肉。

我认为，这种用礼仪表达甥舅之间特殊关系的解释，同样适用于南非班图人、汤加人和斐济人的祭祀或其他礼仪中外甥所起的作用。男子对其父亲的畏惧与驯服，也使他同样害怕或敬畏其父系祖先。但是，他并不害怕其舅父，从而，对其母系祖先也无需有敬畏的行为。而且，在特定场合，他的行为也符合习俗的要求。根据我的理解，这样用特定仪式来表达一个人与母系亲属之间的那种特殊关系，与仪式的功能大体是相一致的。

我觉得，把我所提出的假设及假设内所包含的一些设想以及一些重要含义作个简要的概括，是有益的。

1. 大多数我们称之为原始社会的特点是：个人之间的相互行为主要基于亲属关系的调节，这种调节通过各种认定的亲属关系而形成的一种固定的行为模式得到实现。

2. 这种情况经常与社会的拆合组织，即整个社会被拆分成几个部分（世系群、氏族）的一种状态，相互联系。

3. 尽管亲属关系总是，并且必然是双边的，或是血脉传承的，但拆合组织却只能遵循单边世系原则，因此，必须在父系制度和母系制度中进行选择。

4. 在某种父系社会中，母子间的行为模式是甥舅之间的特殊行为模式的基础，狭义上说，母子行为模式本身产生于家庭内部的社会生活。

5. 所有母方亲属都有被这种行为模式涉及的倾向，包括舅父所

the mother's brother belongs. ①

6. In societies with patrilineal ancestor worship (such as the Ba-Thonga and the Friendly Islanders) the same type of behaviour may also be extended to the gods of the mother's family.
7. The special kind of behaviour to the maternal relatives (living and dead) or to the maternal group and its gods and sacra, is expressed in definite ritual customs, the function of ritual here, as elsewhere, being to fix and make permanent certain types of behaviour, with the obligations and sentiments involved therein.

In conclusion, may I point out that I have selected the subject of my contribution to this meeting because it is one not only of theoretical but also of practical interest. For instance, there is the question as to whether the Native Appeal Court was really right in its judgment that the payment of the *ditsoa* cattle to the mother's brother of a bride is not a legal but only a moral obligation. So far as I have been able to form an opinion, I should say that the judgment was right.

The whole subject of the payments at marriage (*lobola*) is one of considerable practical importance at the present time to missionaries and magistrates, and to the natives themselves. Now the study of the exact position in which a person stands to his maternal relatives is one without which it is impossible to arrive at a completely accurate understanding of the customs of *lobola*. One of the chief functions of *lobola* is to fix the social position of the children of a marriage. If the

---

① This extension from the mother's brother to the other maternal relatives is shown in the BaThonga tribe in the kinship terminology. The term *malume*, primarily applied to the mother's brother, is extended to the sons of those men, who are also *malume*. If my mother's brothers are dead it is their sons who will have to sacrifice on my behalf to my maternal ancestors. In the northern part of the tribe the term *malume* has gone out of use, and the mother's father, the mother's brother, and the sons of the mother's brother are all called *kokwana* (grandfather). However absurd it may seem to us to call a mother's brother's son, who may be actually younger than the speaker, by a word meaning 'grandfather', the argument of this paper will enable us to see some meaning in it. The person who must sacrifice on my behalf to my maternal ancestors is first my mother's father, then, if he is dead, my mother's brother, and after the decease of the latter, his son, who may be younger than I am. There is a similarity of function for these three relationships, a single general pattern of behaviour for me towards them all and this is again similar in general to that for grandfathers. The nomenclature is, therefore, appropriate.

属的整个家庭或团体。[①]

6. 在那些父系祖先崇拜的社会中(如巴聪加人和友爱岛人),母系家族的神灵也适用于同样的行为模式。

7. 对待母系亲属(无论是活着的还是已故的)、母系团体、母系家族的神灵和神物的特殊行为模式,在固定的礼仪习俗中都有所表达。这里所提到的仪式的功能,与世界上其他地方一样,都是用来确定或形成某种包含义务和情感在内的行为模式。

总之,我想说明的是,我为此会议选择的这一论文题目既具有理论意义,又具有实践意义。例如,在讨论关于土著上诉法庭,认为新娘支付给舅父迪特索亚牲畜不是法律义务而是道德义务的判决是否正确时,依我的观点,这个判决是正确的。

对于现在的传教士、地方官员以及土著人本身来说,关于婚姻聘金("罗保拉")的所有话题,具有相当重要的实践意义。目前,要完全准确地了解"罗保拉"的习俗,就必须对一个人在其母系亲属中所处的确切地位进行研究。孩子在婚姻中的社会地位由"罗保拉"来确定,这是"罗保拉"的主要功能之一。在

---

① 通过舅父扩展到母方其他的亲属,这种现象在巴聪加人的亲属称谓中有所显示。最初对将舅父称为 *malume*,随后这一称谓也用于舅父的儿子们,即他们也是 *malume*。如果我的舅父故去了,那么,他的儿子们必须为我向我的母方祖先做献祭。在该部落的北方地区,他们不再使用 *malume* 这一术语,而是统称外祖父、舅父和舅父的儿子们为 *kokwana*(祖父)。尽管舅父的儿子实际上可能比自己还小,在我们看来用一个意为"外祖父"的词来称呼他是荒谬的,但本文的论点将使我们看到其中的含义。那位必须为了我向我的母方祖先献祭的人,首先是我的外祖父;在他死后,就由我的舅父代替;假如舅父也去世了,就应该轮到他的儿子,尽管他实际上可能比我还年轻。这三种亲属关系具有类似功能,对他们的行为模式可以采用一种概念化的方式,即适用于外祖父的称谓也适用于他们。因此,上述称谓是合适的。

proper payment is made by a family, then the children of the woman who comes to them in exchange for the cattle belong to that family, and its gods are their gods. The natives consider that the strongest of all social bonds is that between a child and its mother, and therefore by the extension that inevitably takes place there is a very strong bond between the child and its mother's family. The function of the lobola payment is not to destroy but to modify this bond, and to place the children definitely in the father's family and group for all matters concerning not only the social but also the religious life of the tribe. If no lobola is paid the child inevitably belongs to the mother's family, though its position is then irregular. But the woman for whom the *lobola* is paid does not become a member of the husband's family; their gods are not her gods; and that is the final test. I have said enough, I hope, to show that the proper understanding of customs relating to the mother's brother is a necessary preliminary to any final theory of *lobola*.

一个家族支付了适当的聘金之后,那么这个用牲畜交换来的女人所生的孩子就从属于这个家族,此家族的神灵也便是他们的神灵。土著人认为,存在于母子之间的关系是所有社会关系中最稳固的关系,此种关系又延伸至孩子与母方家族的所有亲属中。支付“罗保拉”并不是要破坏这种关系,而是要对这种关系进行修正,以确定孩子在部落社会和宗教生活的所有方面处于父系家族和团体中的何种位置。如果结婚时没有支付“罗保拉”,那么孩子必然只属于母方家庭,尽管这种关系很不正规。但是,对于那些支付“罗保拉”,但并没有成为丈夫家庭成员的女人来说,丈夫家族的神灵不属于她的神灵,这是最终的结论。我已经说得够多了,我希望,我已经充分地说明,正确理解有关舅父的习俗是最终理解“罗保拉”的必要前提。

CHAPTER Ⅱ

Patrilineal And Matrilineal Succession[①]

If we are to understand aright the laws and customs of nonEuropean peoples we must be careful not to interpret them in terms of our own legal conceptions, which, simple and obvious as some of them may seem to us, are the product of a long and complex historical development and are special to our own culture. If, for instance, we attempt to apply to the customs of the simpler peoples our own precise distinctions between the law relating to persons and the law relating to things we shall produce nothing but confusion in the result.

With us one of the most important aspects of succession is the transmission of property by inheritance. Yet in some of the simplest societies this is a matter of almost no significance at all. In an Australian tribe, for example, a man possesses a few weapons, tools, utensils and personal ornaments, things of little value or permanence. On his death some of them may be destroyed, others may be distributed among his relatives and friends. But their disposal is of so little importance, unless in relation to ritual, that it is often difficult to find any rules of customary procedure. But even in such simple societies, where inheritance of private property may be said not to exist or to be of minimal importance, there are problems of succession in the widest sense of the term.

---

① Reprinted from *The Iowa Law Review*, Vol. XX, No. 2, January 1935.

第二章　父系继承和母系继承[①]

欧洲之外的民族其法律与习俗,是长期而复杂的历史发展产物,它对于我们自身的文化来说具有独特的内涵。虽然在我们看来,其他民族的某些法律及习俗很简单,但是想要正确地理解它们,我们须注意不要以自己民族的法律认知来做阐释。如果我们将我们对人和对物的明确法律区分应用于较简单的民族习俗中,那么,所得到的后果只能使我们自己混乱不堪。

对我们来说,通过继嗣进行财产转交是继承关系最重要的方面。然而,这种事情在一些最简单的社会中是根本没有意义的。例如,在一个澳大利亚部落中,一位男子拥有一些武器、工具、器皿、个人饰品,还有一些不值钱的和不耐用的物品。在他去世时,他的这些财产可能被销毁一部分,也会分发给他的亲属和朋友们。但是,除非这种处理与礼仪有关,否则,是没有多大意义的,在此很难找到任何原则来规范这些习惯程序。然而,尽管在那些简单的社会里,如那些基本没有私有财产继承或其意义不大的社会,从"继承"一词的最广泛意义上说,也存在着继承的问题。

① 根据《衣阿华法律评论》重印,第20卷,第2期,1935年2月。

The term ‘succession’ will here be taken as referring to the transmission of rights in general. A right exists in, and is definable in terms of, recognised social usage. A right may be that of an individual or a collection of individuals. It may be defined as a measure of control that a person, or a collection of persons, has over the acts of some person or persons, said to be thereby made liable to the performance of a duty. Rights may be classified as of three main kinds:

(*a*) Rights over a person imposing some duty or duties upon that person. This is the *jus in personam* of Roman law. A father may exercise such rights over his son, or a nation over its citizens.

(*b*) Rights over a person ‘as against the world’, i. e. imposing duties on all other persons in respect of that particular person. This is the *jus in rem* of Roman law in relation to persons.

(*c*) Rights over a thing, i. e. some object other than a person, as against the world, imposing duties on other persons in relation to that thing.

The rights classified under (*b*) and (*c*) are fundamentally of the same kind, distinguished only as they relate to persons or to things, and are of a different kind from those classified under (*a*).

We may consider a few examples from such a simple society as an Australian tribe. A man has certain rights over his wife. Some of them are rights *in personam* whereby he may require from her the performance of certain duties. Others are rights *in rem*. If anyone should kill the wife he commits an injury against the husband. If anyone should have sexual intercourse with the wife without the consent of the husband he commits an injury against the latter. In some tribes a man may lend his wife to another; this is an exercise by the husband both of his rights *in personam* and of his rights *in rem*.

In a great number of Australian tribes the custom of the levirate holds sway, By this, when a man dies all his rights over his wife (and over his immature children) are transferred to his younger brother, or failing such, to an agnatic cousin. This is a simple instance

“继承”一词的含义在这里一般定义为权利的转交。权利来自于公认的社会习惯。由这种公认的社会习惯规范其含义，其中，权利可分为个人的权利和集体的权利。它可以被定义为个人或集体对其他人或集体行为的控制标准，从而也包含了责任的履行。权利的三个主要种类是：

1. 对某人拥有的权利，即让某人承担责任的权利。也就是罗马法中的对人权。父亲对儿子，国家对公民都拥有这种权利。

2. 就整个世界而言，某人拥有的权利，即让其他所有人都对此人承诺义务的权利，这就是罗马法中就人而言的对物权。

3. 对物的权利，即对整个世界而言，对物而不是对人的权利，让其他人对此物承诺义务的权利。

第二类和第三类的权利仅在于对人和对物的有所不同，其余的内容基本相同，并且，两者都与第一类权利在种类上有所区别。

让我们看一些例子：例如，像在澳大利亚某部落那样简单的社会中，一位男子对其妻子有某种权利。权利包含有对人权，要求妻子对丈夫履行一定的义务；另外也包含有对物权。如果有人杀害了某人的妻子，那么此人对她的丈夫犯了伤害罪。如果有人在丈夫不知情的情况下与其妻子通奸，那么，他对后者也犯了伤害罪。在某些部落中，男人可将妻子借给别人，这表示他在同时行使对人权和对物权。

在许多澳大利亚部落中，叔娶嫂制的习俗占统治地位。这一习俗规定，当一男子死去，他对于其妻（和对于其未成年的孩子）的所有权利被移交至他的弟弟；若没有亲弟弟，则移交给他的叔

of fraternal succession. What is transferred is certain rights *in personam* and *in rem* over certain persons (the wife and children) and with these rights there go, of course, certain obligations or duties.

Let us next consider, in such a tribe as the Kariera of Western Australia, the nature of the group that I shall call a 'horde'. This is a body of persons who jointly possess, occupy and exploit a certain defined area of country. The rights of the horde over its territory can be briefly indicated by saying that no person who is not a member of the horde has the right to any animal, vegetable or mineral product from the territory except by invitation or consent of members of the horde. Acts of trespass against this exclusive right of a horde to its territory seem to have been very rare in the social life of the aborigines but it appears to have been generally held that anyone committing such a trespass could justifiably be killed. ① This exclusive use of its territory by a horde is modified by obligations of hospitality whereby, when there is an abundance of some kind of food at a certain time, members of friendly neighbouring hordes are invited to come in and share it. The son of any woman born in the horde and married elsewhere is always entitled to visit his mother's horde and hunt in its territory.

It is convenient to speak of such a group as the Kariera horde as a 'corporation' having an 'estate'. This is an extension of the terms 'corporation' and 'estate' as they are commonly used in law, but I think this extension is justifiable, and hope that at any rate it will be admitted for the purposes of the present exposition. By an estate is here meant a collection of rights (whether over persons or things) with the implied duties, the unity of which is constituted either by the fact that they are the rights of a single person and can be transmitted, as a whole, or in division, to some other person or persons, or that they are the rights of a defined group (the corporation) which maintains a

① We have records from a part of South Australia of occasional deliberate acts of trespass with armed force, a body of men invading a territory in which red ochre was found for the purpose of obtaining a supply. This was actually an act of war and as the invaders took care to come in force the horde whose rights were thus invaded had no effective remedy.

伯弟弟。这是兄弟继承的一个简单例证。所移交的是对某些人（妻子和孩子）的一定的对人和对物的权利，与这些权利同时转交的还有某些义务和责任。

接下来，让我们看一下来自西澳大利亚卡列拉这样的部落的情况，我称其性质为“队群”。队群是一群人，他们共同拥有、占领，并开发一块领土。队群对自己的领土的权利可以简述如下：任何不属于队群成员的人都无权动用当地的动物、植物或矿产品，除非接受到队群成员的邀请或同意。侵害队群对于领地的那种独有权利，这样的行为在土著人的社会生活中似乎非常少见。但是人们认为，任何犯有这种侵犯行为的人，都无可争议地会被处死。[①] 由于队群的热情好客，这种对领土的独占使用现象会有所减轻。当某一时期本部落的某种食物充裕时，友好邻家队群的成员就会被邀请来一起分享这种食物。队群中任何一位妇女所生的男孩在别处结婚，也同样有权拜访母亲的队群并在此领域进行狩猎。

我们把像卡列拉队群这样的团体说成是拥有“财产”的“法人”比较适当。这里延伸了常用于法律中的“法人”和“财产”两个术语所涵盖的范围。但我认为这种延伸是无可非议的，并且我希望，为着目前解说的效果，无论如何它将得到认可。这里，财产是指隐含着义务的权利（无论是对人还是对物）的集合。这些权利的集合要么是个人所具有的权利，能够全部或部分地转交给某人或某些人，要么是

① 在南澳部分地区曾经有偶发蓄意武装侵犯的记载，在一群男子侵入的领地内发现了他们为取得供给而设的赤赫石。这实际上是一种战争行为，表示侵略者有预谋地大举入侵，而权利受侵的队群对这种行为则没有有效的对付办法。

continuity of possession. A personal estate thus corresponds to that *universitas juris* which is what, in Roman law, was transmitted by inheritance.[①]. . .

The corporate estate of a Kariera horde includes in the first place its rights over its territory.

The continuity of the horde is maintained by the continuity of possession of the territory, which remains constant, not subject to division or increase, for the Australian aborigines have no conception of the possibility of territorial conquest by armed force. The relation of a horde to its territory does not correspond exactly to what we regard as 'ownership' in modern law. It has some of the qualities of corporate ownership, but also partakes of the nature of the relation of a modern state to its territory, which we may speak of as the exercise of 'dominion'. Rights of ownership over land and rights of dominion have seemingly both had their origin by development and differentiation from such a simple relation as that exemplified in the Australian horde.

The estate of a horde includes not only its rights over a territory, but also its rights, *in personam* and *in rem*, over its members. The adult male members of the horde owe certain duties to it so that it has rights *in personam* over them. It also has rights *in rem*, for if one of them is killed, by violence or by sorcery, the horde as a whole conceives itself to have been injured and takes steps to obtain satisfaction. Women and children are not members of the horde in the same sense as adult males. If a man's wife is 'stolen' it is he as an individual who seeks satisfaction though he will have the backing of the other members of the horde. But indirectly she also belongs to the horde so that when her husband dies she should by custom pass into the possession of some other member of the horde and not to some person outside.

---

① *Hereditas est successio in universum jus quod defunctus habuit*: an inheritance is a succession to the entire legal position of a deceased man.

某个团体(法人)的权利,它保持着这种占有的延续性。因此,个人财产就与罗马法律中的全部动产和不动产基本等同,它通过继承来转交。① ……

对领土的所有权在卡列拉队群的法人财产中具有首要的地位,这种所有权的继承维系着队群的连续性。对于澳大利亚土著人来说,这种所有权是永恒的,不能轻易地被分割或扩大,因为他们未曾想到过靠武力来征服领土。队群与其领土的关系和我们现代法律中认为的“所有权”在内涵上还不完全一致。在它的含义里不但具有法人所有权的特点,而且还具有现代国家与其领土关系的特点,我们可以把此关系称为“行使领土”权。看起来,土地所有权和领土主权都是从像澳大利亚队群这样的简单关系中发展和衍生出来的。

除了领土的所有权,队群的财产还包括对其成员所拥有的对人和对物的权利。队群中的成人男子对队群承担某种责任,因此,队群拥有其对人权。队群同时还具有对物权,队群作为一个整体,都会把对队群成员的伤害看做是对队群的伤害,如果队群中某一成员被杀害,无论是死于暴力还是巫术,整个队群都会采取报复行动。队群中的女人和孩子作为队群的成员与成年男性具有不同的意义。如果某男子的妻子被“盗”,那么,只有此男子独自去寻求补偿,尽管他拥有队群其他成员的支持。但是,她同时也间接属于队群,因为当她丈夫去世后,按照习俗,她将被移交至队群的其他成员,并成为那位成员的财产,而不属于队群外某个人的财产。

---

① 这种继承指的是对死者全部法律地位的承袭。

Since the Kariera horde is exogamous every female child passes by marriage out of the possession of her parents and out of the possession of the horde into the possession of her husband in another horde. By Australian custom this transfer of possession, i. e. of rights, *in personam* and *in rem*, over a person, should normally involve compensation or indemnification, which, in many tribes, is provided by the man who receives a wife giving his sister in exchange to be the wife of his brother-in-law. Male children may be said to pass out of the possession of the parents and into direct possession of the horde at initiation. This is, in some tribes, symbolically expressed in the initiation ritual.

The Kariera horde affords an example of perpetual corporate succession. It will be obvious, I think, that it contains the germs of the state and of sovereignty as we know them in more complex developments. Thus, as the terms have been used above, the United States of America is a ' corporation ' having as its constituent ' estate ' possession of, or dominion over, a certain territory (subject, unlike that of an Australian horde, to increase by conquest or purchase) and certain specific rights, *in personam* and *in rem*, over the persons of its citizens.

The continuity of a corporation such as the Australian horde is dependent on the continuity of its estate. In the first place there is continuity of possession of the territory. Secondly, there is a continuity which transcends the space of a human life by the fact that as the group loses some members by death it acquires new members by the birth of children and the initiation of boys into the status of men.

If now we turn from considering the horde as a whole to consider the individual male members we find here also a process of customary transmission of rights. Children ' belong ', we may say, primarily to the father, i. e. it is he who exercises over them rights in personam and in rem. As the father in turn belongs to the horde this horde has some rights over his children. When a girl reaches puberty the rights over her are transferred (perhaps not in entirety but in great part) from her father and his horde to her husband. When the boy reaches

因为卡列拉队群实行外婚制，所以，每一个女孩结婚后将不再是属于父母和队群的财产，而是属于生活在另一队群的她丈夫的财产。根据澳大利亚习俗，这种财产的转移，即关于某人的对人权和对物权的转移，通常是和补偿或赔偿联系在一起的。在许多部落中，这种赔偿是由娶妻子的那个男人通过把自己的姐妹嫁给他妻子的兄弟为妻的方式而进行。男孩在进行成年仪式时被认为是从为父母所有转移为队群直接所有，在某些部落中，这就是成年仪式所表达的象征性含义。

卡列拉队群在永久法人继承方面为我们提供了一个例证。我认为，很显然，它包含了那种在更加复杂的发展阶段中才存在的国家和主权的萌芽。因此，按照我们前面所使用的术语来说，美利坚合众国就是一个“法人”，它对所拥有的“财产”，即对特定领域（与澳大利亚队群的领域不同，此领域可以通过侵略或购买来扩张）拥有某些特定权利，就对其公民拥有对人和对物权。

保留澳大利亚队群法人的延续是依靠对其财产的延续来维持的。这种延续包括：首先，是对领土所有权的延续；其次，是一种超过个人生命时限的延续。在第二类延续中，由于成员的死去，群体需要另一些新的成员来补充，这些新成员由新出生的孩子和行成人礼仪获得男子地位的男孩构成。

现在，我们转换视角，把对队群整体关注转移到对队群中的个别男子成员的关注上，这时我们也会发现这种权利转移的习惯的过程。可以这样说，孩子最初是属于父亲的财产，即父亲对孩子有对人权和对物权。而父亲又是属于队群的财产，所以这一队群对他的孩子也有所有权。当一个女孩进入青春期，父亲和队群对她的权利就要转交给她的丈夫（也许不是全部转交，但也是大部分

puberty he is transferred from his position of dependence on his father to that of an adult member of the horde. Now a member of the horde has certain rights over other members and over the territory of the horde. These rights are part of his personal estate or status. Thus there is a process of ' patrilineal succession ' whereby the sons of male members of the horde become in their turn members, thus acquiring rights and having a share in the estate.

We are thus brought, after necessary and it is hoped not too tedious preliminary considerations, to the problem with which this paper is to deal, that of the nature and function of the unilineal transmission of rights. In the patrilineal succession of the Australian horde the most considerable part of the body of rights of a male person, his status, his personal estate as a sharer or co-parcener in the estate of a horde, are derived by him through his father to the exclusion of his mother and are transmitted in turn to his sons to the exclusion of his daughters. It is important, however, to recognise that in this instance, and, so far as we know, in all instances of patrilineal succession, some rights are also transmitted through the mother. Thus in the Kariera tribe a man has certain quite important rights over his mother's horde, over its individual members, and over its territory.

In matrilineal succession the greater part of the body of rights of an individual, over things, over persons, or as a member of a corporation, are derived by him through his mother and cannot be transmitted to his children but devolve upon his sister's children.

As an example of a very thorough system of matrilineal succession we may consider the *taravad* of the Nayar caste of Malabar. A *taravad* is an incorporated matrilineal lineage. It includes all living descendants in the female line of an original ancestress. It has therefore both male and female members, all of whom are children of female members of the group. It is constituted as a corporation (a joint-family in the terminology of Indian lawyers) by the possession of an estate which includes in the first instance possession of a house or houses and land, and in the second place rights over the persons of its members. The control of the estate is in the hands of a

转交)。当一男孩进入青春期时,他从原来依附于其父亲这种地位转变成队群中的一个成年成员的地位。此时,作为队群中的一名成员,他对其他成员及队群都拥有某些权利。这些权利在部分上构成了他的个人财产或地位。因此,这是一个“父系继承”过程,即队群中男性成员的儿子成为这个队群的新成员,从而可以得到以上权利,并分享队群的财产。

经过一些必要而且希望不是太冗长的初步思考后,该提出本文要讨论的问题了,即权利单系继承的本质和功能。在澳大利亚队群的父系继承中,一位成年男子的绝大部分权利,如他的地位,他作为队群财产的分享者和共同继承人所拥有的个人财产,都是由其父亲传递而并非他母亲传递给他的。然后他又将这些权利传递给他的儿子而非女儿。然而,根据目前为止我们所了解的,要认识到:在这一例证中,或所有父系继承的例证中,母亲也会转交某些权利。就像在卡列拉部落里,一名男子对其母亲的队群中的个体成员和领地,也有一定的、并且是非常重要的权利。

在母系继承制中,母亲也传递给个人对物、对其他人或作为法人团体中的成员所拥有的绝大部分权利。但是此人却不能把这些权利传递给他的儿子们,而是移交给他的外甥们。

作为一个完整的母系继承制度的例证,马拉巴尔地区纳亚尔种姓的“塔拉瓦德”是一个结构紧密的母系世系群。这一世系群由女始祖的所有活着的后代组成,所以它不但有男性成员,也有女性成员,他们都是这一群体内女性成员的子女。作为一个法人团体(印度的律师称之为联合家庭)它也拥有对相应财产的所有权。这种财产的所有权首先包括对房屋或土地的占有,其次是对其成员人身权的占有。在一个团体

'manager' who is normally the oldest male member of the group. In order that the group may retain complete and exclusive possession of the children born to its female members the Nayars have established a system which denies all legal rights to a male parent. A Nayar girl is 'married' while still very young to a suitable bridegroom by the Hindu religious ceremony of the tying of a jewel. (It is probable that in former times the 'bridegroom' ceremoniously deflowered the virgin 'bride'.) On the third day the newly-wedded pair are divorced by the Hindu ceremony of dividing a piece of cloth. Thereafter the divorced bridegroom has no rights over the person, the estate or the children of his bride. At a later period the girl takes a lover. In former times, amongst some of the Nayar, if not generally, a woman was permitted by custom to have two or more lovers at the same time. As the lover is not married to the woman he also has no legal claims over her person or estate or over any children that may be born of the union.

The Nayar system is the most thoroughgoing example of perpetual matrilineal succession. The lineage group maintains its continuity and its unity by not admitting any outside person to any share in its estate. It retains possession of its own women and claims exclusive rights over the children born to them.

The status① of an individual at a given moment of time may be defined as the totality of all his rights and duties as recognised in the social usages (laws and customs) of the society to which he belongs. The rights constituting a status, and similarly the duties, are of many different kinds, some relating to 'the world at large', to the society as a whole, others relating to some definite social group of which the individual is a member (e. g. a man's rights over and duties towards his own clan), or to some group of which he is not a member but to which

---

① It is well always to remember that *status*, *estate*, *state*, and the French état are all different forms of one and the same word, the late Latin *estatus*.

中,最年长的人拥有对财产的管理权利。纳亚尔人通过建立一种否定父亲所有合法权利的制度,使团体能够对其女性成员所生的孩子有全部的并且是独一无二的占有权。纳亚尔女孩在很小的时候就通过一种系珠宝的印度宗教仪式,“嫁给”一位与她相配的新郎。而在结婚后第三天(在这以前,“新郎”已仪式性地破了“新娘”的贞洁),通过另一种印度教仪式,即将一块布分割开来,新婚夫妇便离了婚。此后,离了婚的新郎对新娘及其财产或孩子没有任何权利。那个女孩子可能在过了一段时间之后,又找到了她的爱人。以前在纳亚尔部落中,这种现象虽然不是很普遍,不过习俗允许一个女人同时可以有两个甚至是更多的爱人。只要这个爱人不娶这个女人为妻,他就没有对这个女人及他们可能生育的孩子的任何法律权利。

纳亚尔部落的制度是永久母系继承的一个最完整的例证。它的世系群的统一和延续是通过不允许外人分享任何财产得以维系的。不仅部落中女性的所有权归世系群所有,它还对部落中女性所生的孩子拥有独占权。

个人在某一时刻的身份①也许可以说是他所属的社会中,受社会习惯(法律和习俗)承认的权利和责任的总和构成。与各种责任一样,构成地位的权利也具有不同的种类:有些与整个世界或作为整体的社会有关;而另一些则联系着他所在的特定的社会群体(如一男子对本氏族的权利和义务),还有的体现着他与那些虽然他并不是群体成员之一,但却与之有特殊关系的一些群体之

① 应该知道的是,地位、财产、领土及法语的身份,都是晚期拉丁语中的“estatus”这个词的各种不同形式。

he stands in a special relation (e. g. a man's relation to his mother's clan in a patrilineal clan system, or to his father's clan in a matrilineal system), and yet others concern his special relations as an individual with other individuals.

Everywhere in human society the status of an individual is very largely determined by birth as the child of a particular father and particular mother. Behind the question of succession, therefore, lies the question of what elements of status, i. e. what rights and duties, are transmitted to the child by the father on the one hand and by the mother on the other. Every society has to establish its system of rules in this matter and there is an immense diversity of systems to be found in surviving and historic communities. The almost universal rule is that an individual derives some elements of his status from or through his father, and others from or through his mother.

It has to be remembered that in all societies there is a general difference between the status of a man and that of a woman, and in some societies these differences are very marked and very important. Thus when a son 'succeeds' his father he may attain a status very similar to that of his father, but a daughter cannot do so to the same extent. The reverse holds true in the instance of a mother and her daughter on the one hand and her son on the other. Thus in African kingdoms where succession is matrilineal a king is succeeded by his younger brother and then by his sister's son. The heir therefore acquires, through his mother, important elements of the status of his mother's brother. The king's sister, who holds a very important position, is, of course, succeeded by her daughter.

One solution of the problem of the determination of status would be to let the sons derive from the father and daughters from the mother. This principle is only known to be adopted in a few tribes, about which we know very little, in East Africa and in New Britain. As a working arrangement it has weighty objections which cannot be gone into here.

间的关系(如在父系制度中,男子与其母系氏族的关系,或在母系制度中此人与父系氏族的关系);另外还有就是,他与其他个体之间的这种特殊关系只是作为个人之间所发生的特殊联系。

一个人的出身状况决定他的地位,这无论在人类社会的任何地方都适用。因此在继承问题的背后,还隐含的存在着地位的要素的问题。这个问题包括:父亲传给子女的是哪些权利和责任?而母亲传给的又是哪些权利和责任?每个社会在这方面都需要建立自己的规则体系。这种制度的种类极为繁多,在幸存下来的和历史上的群体中都有充分的体现。不过,普遍性的规则却是,从父亲处或通过父亲获得构成某人地位的一些要素,而从母亲处或通过母亲获得另一些要素。

我们应该记住,男子和女子的地位在所有社会中都有着广泛的区别,并且在一些社会中,这种区别非常明显,也很重要。因此,当儿子"超越"其父亲时,他可以获得与其父亲相似的地位,但是,女儿却不能这样。但也可以看到相反的情况存在于以母亲和女儿为一方,而儿子为另一方的例证中。例如在非洲各王国中,由于他们是依照母系传承的,所以由弟弟或是外甥来继承王位。因此,在舅父的地位中,通过母亲来确定的继承人构成了其重要因素。具有非常重要位置的国王的姐妹们,当然要由她们的女儿来接替。

儿子们从父亲那里获得地位,女儿们从母亲那里获得地位,这种方式是确定他们的地位的方法之一。据了解,这一原则只被东非和新不列颠的一些部落所采用,而我们还不是很了解这些部落的情况。作为一项进行中的整理工作,它还存在极大的反对呼声,因此,在这里不能进行讨论。

It is possible to have a system in which a child, by birth, acquires the same rights, of the same kind and to an equal degree, over the persons to whom he is related through his father and those to whom he is related through his mother. An instance of this is that where a person has an equal expectation of testamentary or intestate succession to the estate of the brothers and sisters of his father and those of his mother. A further instance is provided by the customs relating to *wergild* amongst the Teutonic peoples. By birth a man acquired rights over a number of persons who constituted his *sib*.① This included all his relatives through his father and through his mother, counting either through males or through females, within a certain range. This range varied in different Teutonic communities and perhaps in the same community at different times. Amongst some of the Anglo-Saxons it extended as far as fifth cousins. If a man were killed all the members of his sib could claim a share in the indemnity (*wergild*) paid by the killer, proportionate to the degree of the relationship. Inversely, if a man killed another all members of his sib were under obligation to contribute to the blood-money he had to pay, each contributing in the same proportion as he would receive if the man himself had been killed. The members of a man's sib had specific rights *in rem* in relation to him and specific duties *in personam* towards him.

The solution adopted by the great majority of human societies of the problem relating to the determination of status has been one by which a child derives certain rights and duties through the father and others of a different kind through the mother. Where the rights and duties derived through the father preponderate in social importance over those derived through the mother we have what

① Professor Lowie and some American writers use the term 'sib' as equivalent to what is here, in accordance with European usage, called a 'clan'. It seems desirable to retain the word 'sib' for the bilateral group of kindred to which it was originally applied.

可能存在这样的制度，孩子一出生就分别通过父亲和母亲获得了来自父方亲属和母方亲属享有的同等权利。根据这种制度，一个人对其父亲和母亲的兄弟姐妹的财产同样有希望获得遗嘱继承和非遗嘱继承，这是一个例证。此制度的另一例证，是日尔曼民族中与偿命金有关的习俗。男子从一出生就拥有对构成本氏族[①]某些成员的权利。那些成员既包括他父方的所有亲属，又包括他母方的所有亲属。在一定范围内，他们既依男方计算，又依女方计算。在不同的日尔曼社会，这一范围会有所不同，或许同一社会中在不同的时期也会有所不同。在一些盎格鲁－撒克逊部落中，此范围甚至延伸至第五代旁系亲属。如果一位男子被杀死，那么他氏族的所有成员根据与死者关系的远近程度，可以要求一份赔偿金。相反，如果是此人杀了另外的人，那么他氏族中所有成员同样也有责任为他献出他所必须支付的赔偿金。正反两种情况中得到或支付的赔偿金的数目是相同的，即每位成员所支付的赔偿金与在此男子被杀时所获得的赔偿金数目相同。一位男子在氏族中，所有的成员对他都拥有特定的对物权和对人权的责任。

关于地位确定的问题，在大部分地区的人类社会中是采用如下的解决方法，即让孩子从父亲那里获得一定的权利和责任，也从母亲那里获得另一些权利和责任。如果前者大于后者，即通过父亲所获得的权利和责任在社会中的重要性比通过母亲所获

---

① 此处罗维教授和其他美国学者使用的“sib”这个术语和按照欧洲人习惯所称的“clan”(氏族)，意义相当。看来，保留最初使用“sib”指代这种亲属团体是合适的。

it is usual to call a patrilineal system. Inversely a matrilineal system is one in which the rights and duties derived through the mother preponderate over those derived through the father.

There are, however, some societies in which there is a fairly even balance between the elements of status derived through the father and those through the mother. An example is provided by the Ova-Herero of south-west Africa. Through his mother a child derives membership in an *eanda*, a matrilineal clan; through his father he becomes a member of an *oruzo*, a patrilineal clan. There is thus a double system of clans crossing one another. As both kinds of clans are exogamous a man cannot belong to the *eanda* of his father or to the *oruzo* of his mother. Through his mother and as a member of her *eanda* he has certain rights over, and duties towards, that group and particularly his mother's brothers and his sister's children. Secular property is inherited only within the *eanda* so that a man inherits such property from his mother's brother and transmits it to his sister's son. On the other hand through his father and as a member of his *oruzo* he has rights and duties of other kinds in relation to that group. Certain sacred cattle may only be inherited within the *oruzo* and are therefore transmitted from father to son.

There are to be found in Africa and in Oceania other instances of systems in which patrilineal and matrilineal succession are combined and more or less balanced against one another. In a considerable part of Africa this is rationalised by a conception that every human being is compounded of two principles, one, called the 'blood' in Ashanti, derived from the mother, the other, the 'spirit', derived from the father.

Probably the most important factor in determining the nature of succession in the simpler societies is the need of defining rights *in rem* over persons. When a child is born there is the question, 'To whom

得的权利和责任大时,我们通常称之为父系制度。相反,当后者大于前者,即当通过母亲所获得的权利和责任的社会重要性比通过父亲处获得的权利和责任重要时,就是母系制度。

然而,在一些社会中,两者程度几乎一样,即从父亲那里获得的地位要素与从母亲那里获得的身份要素几乎完全平衡。西南非洲的奥瓦赫雷鲁人为我们提供了一个例证。孩子既通过母亲成为母系氏族"衣安达"的其中一员;又通过父亲成为父系氏族"奥鲁佐"的一员。因此,我们称之为双重氏族体系,并且系统内部相互交叉。因为两种氏族都采用外婚制度,所以此男子既不能属于母亲的"衣安达",又不能属于父亲的"奥鲁佐"。一方面通过与其母亲的关系和他作为衣安达成员的资格,他对母亲的团体,尤其是他舅父和他的外甥、外甥女拥有特定的权利和责任。由于世俗财产只在衣安达内部继承,因此,这位男子有权从其舅父那里继承财产,并把此财产再传递给他的外甥。另一方面,此男子,通过父亲及他作为奥鲁佐成员的关系,他对父方团体具有与以上不同的权利和责任。某种神牛只可在奥鲁佐内部继承,并且是父子相传。

在非洲和大洋洲地区,能够发现其他一些制度存在的例证,在这些制度中,父系继承和母系继承结合在一起,并且它们确定地位的重要性方面基本上是相互平衡的关系。在非洲的绝大部分地区,这种制度被那种每个人都是由两种原则构成的概念而理性化了。一种原则来自于母亲,阿散蒂人称之为"血液";而被称为"灵魂"的原则则来自于父亲。

也许,在更为简单的社会中,确定继承性质最重要的一个因素,是需要给人的对物权下定义。当一个孩子出生时,随之而

does the child belong?' It may, of course, be regarded as belonging jointly to the two parents. Both have an interest in it, both have rights *in personam* and *in rem* in relation to it. But there are other persons who have rights, *in personam* and *in rem* over the father (his parents, and brothers and sisters) and others who similarly have rights over the mother. In any society in which kinship is of fundamental importance in the total social structure, as it is in the majority of non-European societies, it is essential for social stability and continuity that the rights of different individuals over a given individual should be defined in such a way as to avoid as far as possible conflicts of rights. We have seen how the ancient Teutonic system gives similar, and in some instances equal, rights *in rem* to the father's kin and to the mother's kin of a given individual so that if he is killed all members of his sib (i. e. his kindred on both sides) are entitled to compensation. Let us now consider examples of the solution of this problem in matrilineal and patrilineal systems.

For a matrilineal system we may return to the Nayar as affording an extreme, and therefore crucial instance. In that system the *taravad*, or joint-family, maintains intact and absolute its rights *in rem* over all its members. Marriage normally gives the husband certain rights *in rem* over his wife and over the children. The Nayars may be said either to have eliminated marriage or to have eliminated this aspect of marriage. It is true that the union of a Nayar woman and her *sambandham* lover is often a life-long union of great affection and that the lover has a great attachment to the children. But legally he has no rights over his 'wife', if we call her such, or over the children. In turn the group has no rights *in rem* over him for these remain with his own *taravad*. The *taravad* as a corporation retains undivided and undisputed possession of its own estate.

来的问题就是:“这个孩子属于谁?”当然,这孩子也许被认为由双方父母共同拥有,双方父母对他都有利害关系,都具有与他有关的对人权和对物权。但是,还有一些人拥有对此父亲(他的父母和兄弟姐妹)的对人权和对物权,对此母亲也有同样的情况。在任何一种亲属关系在整个社会结构都具有重要意义的社会里,正如大多数欧洲以外的社会那样,以一种尽可能避免权利冲突的方式来规定不同个人对某个人的权利,这对保持社会稳定及其延续就具有非常重要的作用。我们已经看到在古日尔曼体系中,一个特定个体的父方亲属和母方亲属是如何拥有对其同样的对物权,它在某些情形下甚至是平等的。正因如此,一旦一个人被杀害,此人氏族中所有成员(即他双方的亲属)都有权得到赔偿。下面,让我们思考一下这一问题在母系制度和父系制度中是如何得到解决的例证。

对于母系制度,我们回想到纳亚尔种姓。这个例子是个极端,对于研究母系制度具有非常重要的意义。在纳亚尔制度中,所有成员的对物权都归“塔拉瓦德”或联合家庭所有,这个权利被要求是完整而绝对的。一般来说,婚姻赋予了丈夫某种对于其妻子及孩子的对物权。但纳亚尔人可以说已消除这种婚姻,或消除了这方面的婚姻。事实上,一位纳亚尔女子与她的“赛姆班海姆”情人结合,一般是终生相爱的,并且她的爱人也深爱着他们的孩子。但是从法律方面讲,他对“妻子”(如果我们可以这样称呼她的话)或孩子并不拥有任何权利。同样,“妻子”所属的“塔拉瓦德”对他也不拥有对物权,因为这些权利属于他自己的“塔拉瓦德”。作为一个法人团体,“塔拉瓦德”对属于它的财产的权利具有不可分割性和不可争议性。

As an instance of a definitely patrilineal solution of the problem of the distribution of rights *in rem* we may take the Zulu-Kaffir tribes of South Africa. In these tribes marriage requires the payment of an indemnity in the form of a number of cattle, called the *Ikazi*, the act of transfer of these being known as *uku-lobola*. An unmarried girl belongs to her father, or to her guardian (father's brother or brother) if her father be dead, and to her agnatic kindred. They have over her certain rights *in personam* and *in rem*. An offence committed against her, as rape, seduction, maiming or homicide, is an injury to her kin and they have the right to be indemnified. A father may bring before the chief an action for compensation for an offence committed against his daughter. By the act of marriage the father and the agnatic kindred surrender a great part of these rights over the daughter to her husband and to his agnatic kindred. The payment of cattle is an indemnification for this surrender of rights. For these people the great value of a woman is as the mother of children. (For this reason there is no more unhappy, unwanted person among them than a barren woman.) The act of *lobola* is therefore primarily a procedure whereby those paying the cattle acquire undivided and indisputable rights over all children born to the woman. This is readily demonstrated by an analysis that would be out of place here. The natives state the principle in two ways: 'Cattle beget children'; 'The children are where the cattle are not.' In case of divorce either the wife and her children return to her father and any cattle paid are returned, or if (as is usual) the husband retains the children he must abandon claim to the cattle he has paid or to some portion thereof. On the death of a wife who has borne children (a barren wife may be repudiated and the repayment of the cattle or the substitution of a sister may be claimed) if all the cattle have been paid, the children remain with the father and the mother's kin have no rights *in rem* over them. The system here outlined is a simple legal

南非的祖鲁-卡菲尔部落可以作为一个例证,解释如何按照明确的父方世系来解决对物权的分配问题。在这些部落中,婚姻必须以支付一些数量的牛作为补偿。他们称这些牛为“艾卡孜”,把这种交换行为称为“尤扣罗保拉”。一个未婚少女从属于父亲(如果父亲去世,则从属于她的监护人,即叔父或兄弟)及其父亲亲属。他们对她有对人权和对物权。他们把对此女子所做的任何侵犯,如强奸、引诱、伤害或杀害都看成是对自己的伤害,他们有权要求赔偿;父亲可以在酋长面前对女儿受到侵犯之事索赔。在女儿进行婚姻礼仪时,对女儿的大部分权利就由父亲及其父方亲属转交给其丈夫及其丈夫的父方亲属。夫方支付的牛群就是作为对其父亲及夫方亲属这种权利转交的一种补偿。对于这些部落来说,女人能够成为孩子的母亲就是她最大的价值所在。一个没有生育能力的女人是最不幸,也是最不受人欢迎的。因此,“罗保拉”行为主要是一种程序,即通过支付牛群,一方获得了对此妇女所生的孩子的不可分割和无可非议的权利。通过分析很容易证明这一观点,但我不想在这里讨论。土著人用两种方式形象地描述这一原则:“牛群带来孩子”,“有孩子的地方没有牛”。夫妻双方一旦离婚,如果妻子带着孩子回到她父亲那里,那么父亲必须退回所有当时收到的牛群;如果(通常如此)丈夫想保留孩子,他就必须全部或部分放弃对原来支付的牛群的索取权。如果生过孩子的妻子去世了(不生育的妻子可能会被抛弃,并且要求归还牲畜,或要求以她的姐妹来代替),并且夫家已经为其支付了牛群,那么,她所生育的孩子就跟随孩子的父亲,孩子的对物权也不再由母方亲属拥有。以上所描述的制度是一个简单

procedure for giving the father and his agnatic kindred indisputable and undivided rights *in rem* over his children.

Thus the system of patrilineal or matrilineal succession centres largely around the system of marriage. In an extreme matrilineal society a man has no rights in rem over his children, though he does usually have certain rights *in personam*. The rights remain with the mother and her relatives. The result is to emphasise and maintain a close bond between brother and sister at the expense of the bond between husband and wife. Consequently the rights of the husband over his wife are limited. In an extreme patrilineal society we have exactly the opposite. Rights *in rem* over the children are exclusively exercised by the father and his relatives. The bond between husband and wife is strengthened at the expense of the bond between brother and sister. The rights of the husband over his wife are considerable; she is *in manu*, under *his potestas*.

Extreme patrilineal systems are comparatively rare, and extreme matrilineal systems perhaps even rarer. Generally there is some modification by which, while the kindred on the one side have a preponderant right, some rights are recognised on the other side also. Thus in the Cherokee tribe of North American Indians, while a man belonged to his mother's clan, so that if he were killed they and they alone would demand satisfaction, yet he stood in a very special relation to his father and to his father's clan.

Little has been said so far about the inheritance of property. This is because in the simpler societies the transmission of property is generally dependent upon the transmission of status. Thus amongst the Nayar the important property (land, houses, etc.) is the undivided or joint possession of a corporation constituted by a matrilineal lineage. Amongst the Zulu-Kaffir tribes the sons succeed to a share of the father's estate to the exclusion of daughters and their descendants. In general, though there are a few exceptions, it may be said that the transmission of property follows the same line as does the transmission of status.

With regard to the institutions of patrilineal and matrilineal succession the question is frequently asked as to what is their origin. The term 'origin' is ambiguous. In one sense we may talk of the

的法律程序，它赋予了父亲及其父系亲属不可争议和不可分割的对孩子们的对物权。

因此，父系继承或母系继承主要围绕着婚姻制度。在一个极端的母系社会中，男子对他的孩子没有对物权。这种权利由母亲及其亲属来控制，其结果是以牺牲夫妻之间的关系来加强和保持兄弟姐妹之间的亲密关系。在极端的父系社会中，情况恰恰相反。对孩子的对物权完全由父亲及父方亲属独自占有。夫妻之间关系的加强是以牺牲兄弟姐妹之间的关系为代价的。丈夫对妻子的权利非常大，她完全在他的控制之下。

极端的父系制度是比较罕见的，而极端的母系制度更加少见。总的来说，双方都存在着一定的调和成分，当一方的亲属的权利具有某种优势时，另一方亲属的某些权利也会得到认可。比如，在北美印第安人的切罗基部落中，由于一男子属于母亲的氏族，所以，母方氏族就其被杀害便有权单独要求赔偿，不过他与父亲和父亲的氏族之间，仍保持着一种特殊的关系。

直到目前，有关财产继承的话题几乎没有怎么谈到，这是因为在更为简单的社会中，财产的继承一般是依赖于地位的继承。因而，在纳亚尔人中，那些重要的财产（土地、房屋等）要么不可分割，要么就由母系氏族构成的法人共同拥有。在祖鲁-卡菲尔部落中，父亲的财产仅由儿子们共同继承，而不包括女儿们及女儿的后代。总的来说，尽管有些例外，财产的转移可以说成是依据地位的转移路线而完成的。

当谈到父系继承制度和母系继承制度时，关于两种继承制度的起源问题经常会被问到。“起源”一词有些含糊，在一定意义

'historical origin'. The historical origin of the Nayar system, or that of the Zulu-Kaffirs, or of any other system, is a series of unique events extending often over a long period of gradual growth. The determination of the origin in this sense of any social system is the task of a historian. For the simpler peoples these histories are unknown and are the subject only of pure speculation, to my mind largely unprofitable. But the term 'origin' may be used in another sense, and very frequently it is used ambiguously with a confusion of the two meanings.

Any social system, to survive, must conform to certain conditions. If we can define adequately one of these universal conditions, i. e. one to which all human societies must conform, we have a sociological law. Thereupon if it can be shown that a particular institution in a particular society is the means by which that society conforms to the law, i. e. to the necessary condition, we may speak of this as the 'sociological origin' of the institution. Thus an institution may be said to have its general raison d'être (sociological origin) and its particular *raison d'être* (historical origin). The first is for the sociologist or social anthropologist to discover by the comparative method. The second is for the historian to discover by examination of records or for the ethnologist, in the absence of records, to speculate about.

One such law, or necessary condition of continued existence, is that of a certain degree of functional consistency amongst the constituent parts of the social system. Functional consistency is not the same thing as logical consistency; the latter is one special form of the former. Functional inconsistency exists whenever two aspects of the social system produce a conflict which can only be resolved by some change in the system itself. It is always a question of the functioning, i. e. the working of the system as a whole. Consistency is a relative matter. No social system ever attains to a perfect consistency, and it is for this reason that every system is constantly undergoing change.

上,我们可以讨论它的“历史起源”。作为一系列的独特事件,纳亚尔制度、祖鲁－卡菲尔人的制度或其他社会的制度,其历史起源是在一个较长时期中缓慢发展的。从某种意义上说,应该由历史学家来承担寻找任何一个社会制度起源的工作。对于那些更为简单的民族,尚有历史的未知,有的只是对历史纯粹的猜测。我认为,这种猜测没有多大意义。但是我们可以从另一个角度来看“起源”一词,而且使用时这两种含义经常是模糊地被混淆在一起。

任何一种社会制度必须遵从一定的条件才可以生存。如果我们能够为其中一个普遍性的条件下定义,即人类社会所必须遵从的条件,那么就产生了一种社会学的法规。某种制度的“社会起源”就是指这样的一些条件或的法规,即某种制度与必要的条件相一致——如果我们可以证明的话。那么可以这样说,每种制度都有它的一般存在理由(社会起源),也包括它的特殊存在理由(历史起源)。前者需要社会学家和社会人类学家通过对比的方法来发现,后者则需要历史学家通过考察文献记录来发现,或民族学家在缺少文献的情况下推测出来。

要维持一种存在的延续性,一般的原则或必要的条件是构成社会制度的各个组成部分须具备一定程度的功能连贯性。功能连贯性与逻辑连贯性是有区别的,逻辑连贯性是功能连贯性的一种特殊形式。当社会制度的两方面产生一种冲突,而这种冲突只能通过对制度本身进行调整才能解决时,便会产生功能的不连贯性。这是个功能问题,即整个制度的运行问题。连贯性是相对的,没有一种社会体制曾经达到了完美的连贯性。之所以如此,

Any insufficiency in this respect in a social system tends to induce change, sometimes, though by no means always, through the conscious recognition of the insufficiency by members of the society and the conscious seeking of a remedy. To this law of the necessity of a certain degree of functional consistency we may add a second, which is a special instance of the first. Any human social life requires the establishment of a social structure consisting of a network of relations between individuals and groups of individuals. These relations all involve certain rights and duties which need to be defined in such a way that conflicts of rights can be resolved without destroying the structure. It is this need that is met by the establishment of systems of justice and legal institutions.

Every system of rights necessarily involves the existence of common, joint or divided rights over the same person or thing. The father and the mother of a child both have rights *in personam* over their child. In an orderly family it is necessary that there should be no unresolved or unresolvable conflict between these rights. The same thing is true throughout a society as a whole in all the various relations into which persons are brought. When two persons A and B have rights over something Z or rights *in rem* over some person Z, there are three ways of adjusting these rights so as to avoid unresolvable conflicts. One is the mode of *rights in common*; A and B have similar and equal rights over Z and these are such that the rights of A will not conflict with those of B. An instance is to be found in the native tribes of South Africa in which, as the native saying is, 'grass and water are common'. Any member of a tribe has the right to graze his cattle or water them, or take water for his own use, in any part of the territory over which the tribe (represented by its chief) exercises dominion. A second is the mode of *joint rights* in which A and B (or any number of persons) exercise jointly certain rights over Z. The establishment of such joint rights immediately establishes what is here called a corporation. An infringement of the rights normally calls for a joint action on the part of the

是因为每一种制度都在不断地进行改变。社会制度中任何机能的失效都会带来变化。社会成员有时(尽管并非总是)会有意识地认识到这种不足,并且会主动寻求补救方法。在必须保持一定的功能连贯性这个法则的基础上,我们可以再加上第二个法则,作为前一个法则的特殊例证。任何方式的人类社会生活都建立在一定的社会结构上,这种社会结构是由各种个人之间或团体之间的关系网构成的。这些关系包括一定的权利和责任。规范这些权利和责任的原则在于:既不能破坏社会结构的完整,又可以解决各种权利之间的冲突。正是为了满足这种需求,司法机构和法律制度便得以建立。

每一套权利体系必然包含对同一人,或同一物所具有的共同权利、联合权利和不同权利。父母对他们的孩子都具有对人权。未解决或不能解决的权利冲突必然不会在一个有秩序的家庭里存在;总体上看,在人们被带入其间的所有各种关系中,这种相同的情况是真切地贯穿于一个社会的。如果A、B二者对某物Z都具有权利或对某人Z都有对物权,那么,可以有三种方法来调节他们的这些权利以避免那些不可解决的冲突。第一种方法是同等权利模式:A、B两人对某人Z具有相似并且是平等的权利而A与B的权利并不发生冲突。南非土著部落为我们提供了这种权利模式的实例。正如土著人所说:"草和水是公共所有的。"部落中的任何一位成员都有权在本部落行使主权的每一块领土上放养自己的牲畜,并为自己汲水。第二种方法是共同权利模式:在这种模式中,A、B两人(或其他成员)共同行使对Z的一定权利。像法人团体就是以这种共同权利为基础建立的。法人团体会采取一致行动来对

corporation, which may, of course, be carried out by its official representatives. A South African tribe has joint possession of its territory, the possession (the estate) being vested in the chief. An infringement of these rights may be adjusted by the chief or may lead to the action of war, in which, under the chief, the whole tribe seeks to maintain its rights. The third mode is that of *rights in division*. Here A has certain definite rights over Z and B has certain other definite rights; the respective rights may be defined either by custom or by a specific contract, or agreement. An example is the relation of owner and tenant of a leased land or building.

So far as rights over persons go the exercise of rights in common is necessarily very limited. In an unfamiliar region one may ask direction from any person one meets and expect to receive whatever information that person can give. In English law the king's officers can demand from any passer-by 'in the king'sname' assistance in the arrest of a malefactor. ①Rights over persons *in personam* are usually exercised either jointly or in division.

Rights over persons *in rem* can obviously never be exercised in common. We have seen, from the example of the Teutonic customs relating to *wergild*, that they can be held in division. But such a thing is rare and for the reason that it requires a complicated definition of the respective shares of various kindred in their interest in their kinsmen. One has only to glance at some of the early laws of Norway and Sweden relating to the division of the *wergild* between agnatic and cognatic kin of different degrees to realise with what difficulties such a system is confronted in its working.

It results from this that rights *in rem* over a person must as a general rule either be exclusively personal, i. e. confined to a single individual (a condition to which the rights of an owner over a slave

① The latter instance, however, might be interpreted as the exercise of a joint right, since the king is the representative of the nation which, as a corporation, has joint rights over the persons of its citizens.

抗对这种权利的侵犯，当然，一致行动也许会由法人团体的法定代表去执行。一个南非的部落对于领地里的共同占有权(财产)可能就会授予其酋长来施行。由酋长来调和任何对这种权利的侵犯，或者在其领导下，整个部落通过进行战争来维护这种权利。第三种是分别权利模式：即成员 A 和成员 B 都对成员 Z 具有一定的权利，而二者的权利内容有所不同；这种各自的权利是根据习俗或通过特定的合同或协议来规定的。例如在土地和房屋出租方面，地主和佃户之间的关系就是这种关系。

以共同权利模式行使的对人权必然会受到诸多的限制。某人在一个陌生的地区可以向他所遇到的人问路，并且希望能从对方那里得到信息。英国法律中规定，国王的官员在拘捕罪犯时有权以“国王的名义”要求任何过路人给予帮助。① 通常情况下，对人的对人权可以共同行使，也可以分别行使。

很明显，对人的对物权不可能被共同行使。从日尔曼民族中关于赔偿金的习俗例证我们就可以看出，这些权利是被分别行使的。但这种情况极为少见，因为它需要精确地考察那些处于利益关系中的男性亲属各自享有的份额，这是一项极其复杂的工作。挪威和瑞典关于如何在父方和母方不同级别的亲属之间分配偿命金的早期法律，就充分体现了这种复杂性。想要体会这种体制在运行时所面临的怎样的困难，只需看看这些法律就是了。

原因在于，作为一种普通规律，对人的对物权必须是在归个体所

---

① 然而，这后一个例子或许应该看做是联合权利的行使，既然国王是这个国家的代表，那么作为一个法人团体，国家对其公民就具有联合权利。

may approximate in some instances) or must be joint. The rights of a Roman father over his children were nearly exclusive but even these, at certain periods of history certainly, were subject to the rights, exercised jointly, of the *gens* or of the state; even the *potestas* of a *pater familias* was not absolute. Thus we may say that any society that recognises rights in rem over persons (and all known societies do so to some extent) will normally, and with only the rarest exceptions, make some provision for the joint exercise of such rights. This implies the existence of corporations of some kind, since a corporation is here defined as a collection of persons who jointly exercise some right or rights.

A corporation can only form itself on the basis of a common interest. In the simplest societies the easiest, perhaps almost the only, ways in which common interests can be created are on the basis of locality, i. e. residence in the same local community or neighbourhood, or kinship. Corporations therefore tend to be established either on the one basis or the other or on both combined (the Kariera horde is an example of the latter) or else a double system of local groups and kinship groups is formed.

We must here appeal to another sociological law, the necessity not merely for stability, definiteness and consistency in the social structure, but also for continuity. To provide continuity of social structure is essentially a function of corporations. Thus a modern nation has its continuity as a corporation exercising joint rights over its territory and over the persons of its citizens.

We can imagine as a possibility an incorporated local community which was completely endogamous and which would therefore not have to face the issue of choosing between matrilineal and patrilineal succession, since any child born in the community would have both its parents there. But the moment there are intermarriages between two corporate local groups the question of linealsuccession does arise. In such a situation it is possible that no customary rule may be established, each instance being adjusted by agreement

有(近似于主人对奴隶的权利)的同时,也是共同所有的。在罗马人中,尽管父亲对其孩子的权利是接近于排他的,但在历史的某一阶段,这些权利曾被共同行使,要么属于氏族,要么属于国家,甚至族长的权利也不是绝对的。因此,我们敢说,在任何承认对人的对物权的社会(以及那些在某种程度承认这种权利的社会)中,几乎都毫无例外地要对如何共同行使这些权利做出一些规定。因为,法人团体在此被定义为共同行使某一权利或某些权利的一群人,所以这就意味着在上述的社会中会有某种法人团体的存在。

一个法人团体只能基于其成员的共同利益而形成。在最简单的社会里,法人团体建立起共同利益最容易或是唯一的方法就是以地域性,即以相同的地域籍贯,或居住在同一地区,或拥有共同的亲属关系为共同体基础。因此,法人团体既可能建立在一种关系的基础上,也可能建立在另一种关系的亲属上,或者可以以这两种关系的合并为基础(卡列拉游牧部落属于这种关系的例证),或者形成一种具有地域团体和亲属团体的双重制度。

我们有必要在这里求助于另一种社会学法则,这不仅是保持社会结构的稳定、有序和连贯的需要,也是为了社会延续的需要,而维持社会结构的连续性是法人团体的基本功能。因此,作为法人团体,一个现代国家行使对其领土和公民的共同权利时是有连续性的。

我们可以想象这样一种可能性,即在一个联系紧密的地域社区中,由于该社区完全采用内婚制度,出生于该社区的任何一个孩子的父母都在社区内,所以无需面对选择母系继承还是父系继承问题。但是,当两个当地的法人团体通婚时,就会出现世系继

of the persons most nearly concerned. It seems that this was the case of the hordes or local groups of the Andaman Islanders. The result is to produce a loose and indefinite structure. If any definite rule does arise it must usually take the form of one either of matrilineal or of patrilineal succession.

If any society establishes a system of corporations on the basis of kinship—clans, joint-families, incorporated lineages—it must necessarily adopt a system of unilineal reckoning of succession. It would, of course, be theoretically possible to establish some sort of rule whereby, when the parents belong to different groups, in certain definite circumstances the children belong to the father's group and in others to the mother's. This would produce complicated conditions, and in general any complicated definition of rights is likely to be functionally inefficient as compared with a simpler one.

Thus the existence of unilineal (patrilineal or matrilineal) succession in the great majority of human societies can be traced to its sociological 'cause' or 'origin' in certain fundamental social necessities. Chief amongst them, I have suggested, is the need of defining, with sufficient precision to avoid unresolvable conflicts, the rights *in rem* over persons. The need of precise definition of rights *in personam* and of rights over things would seem to be secondary but still important factors.

There are many facts which might be adduced to support this hypothesis. I will mention only one kind. In societies organised on the basis of clans one of the most important activities of the clan is to exact vengeance or indemnification when a clansman is killed. The list of known instances of this would fill many pages. The clan as a corporation has rights in rem over all its clansmen. If one is killed the clan is injured and it has the right, and its members are under an obligation, to proceed to some action towards receiving satisfaction, either through vengeance or by receiving an indemnity.

Thus the cause of the decay of the clan (the *genos* or *gens*) in ancient Greece and Rome was the transfer of its rights *in rem* (and necessarily therefore of some of its rights *in personam*) to the city or state, the nature of these rights being inevitably considerably

承的问题。在这种状况下,可能不会建立习俗规则,每一件诉讼都是由第一当事人之间的协议来协调解决的。这似乎与队群或安达曼岛的当地团体的情况相同。这会产生一种松散且不稳定的社会结构。如果一旦任何一种稳定的规则产生了,那么该社区所采用的规则必定会是母系继承制或父系继承制。

一旦某一社会根据亲属关系——氏族、联合家庭、联合的世系群——建立一种法人体系,那么该社会的继嗣制度肯定是采取单系继承的。当然,当父母双方不属于同一群体时,从理论上说,会出现在某些情况下孩子属于父方团体,而在另一些情况下,孩子属于母方团体的可能性。但是由此将会产生复杂的情况,并且一般来说,与一个关于权利的简单定义相比,任何复杂的定义从功能上说都不是很有效。

因此,存在于大多数人类社会中的单系继承制度(父系或母系)可以在某种最基本的社会需求中追溯其社会学"起因"或"起源"。我曾经说过,其中最主要的需求是:为了避免那些无法解决的冲突,就需要对人的对物权加以精确的规定。尽管对于对人权和针对于物的对物权的精确定义似乎是第二位的,但却是重要的因素。

我只选用可以支持这一假设的许多事实中的一种来阐述。在以氏族为基础而组织起的社会中,作为氏族中最重要的活动之一,当氏族某一成员被杀害时,整个氏族会进行报复或要求赔偿。有关这一点可以列出很多已知例证。作为一个法人团体,氏族对其所有成员都有对物权。如果杀害氏族中某一成员,就会被视为是对整个氏族的侵犯,从而这个氏族有权利,其成员也有义务,采取行动进行报复或要求赔偿。

因此,在古希腊和古罗马,氏族(*genos* 或 *gens*)衰落的起因在于它把对物权(必然也有些对人权)转交给城市或城邦国家,而这些

modified in the process of transference. But the decay of the *gens* in Rome still left the patriarchal family as a corporation (as Maine long ago pointed out) the basis of which, however, was not merely the exercise of rights *in rems* by the *pater familias* over his children, but also the exercise of joint rights over property and the maintenance of a religious cult of ancestorworship.

The sociological laws, i. e. the necessary conditions of existence of a society, that have here been suggested as underlying the customs of unilineal (patrilineal or matrilineal) succession are:

1. The need for a formulation of rights over persons and things sufficiently precise in their general recognition as to avoid as far as possible unresolved conflicts.
2. The need for continuity of the social structure as a system of relations between persons, such relations being definable in terms of rights and duties.

By American ethnologists who object to the method of explanation adopted in the preceding argument it is said that any sociological laws that can be formulated must necessarily be truisms. The laws formulated above, if they be true, as I believe, even if not adequately expressed, may be truisms. But even so they would seem to need to be brought to the attention of at least some ethnologists. A recent writer on the subject of matrilineal and patrilineal succession① makes the following statements: 'Unilateral institutions are in themselves anomalous and artificial. Matrilineal ones are doubly so.' 'Unilateral institutions, wherever found, represent deviations from the expectable, abnormalities in the social structure.' 'Unilateral reckoning contradicts the duality of parenthood and results in an unnatural stressing of one side of the family to the exclusion of the other.' On the basis of these assertions he seems to conclude that unilineal determination of status must have had a single origin in some one aberrant people and

---

① Ronald L. Olson, 'Clan and Moiety in North America', *University of California Publications*, Vol. 33, pp. 409, 411.

权利的本质却在这种转换过程中被大大改变了。但是,在罗马,氏族的衰落仍旧保留了父权制度家庭作为法人团体的习俗(正如梅因很久前所指出的那样)。然而,这种父权家庭的法人团体的基础并不仅仅只是族长对孩子所行使的对物权,而且还有其行使对财产的共同权利及维持对祖先的宗教崇拜。

这里建议的支持单系继承(父系继承或母系继承)习俗的社会学法则,即社会存在的必要条件如下所示:

1. 需要在大众认知中确立一种明确的对人权和对物权的公式,从而尽可能避免不可解决的冲突。

2. 根据一定的权利和责任构建的社会结构规定了人们之间的关系体系,这种社会结构需要得到延续。

反对在上述讨论中采用这种解释方法的美国民族学家们认为,任何可以公式化的社会学法则都必然是自明之理。正如我所认为的那样,如果以上被公式化的法则是正确的,即使没有充分的表述,也可能是自明之理。但尽管如此,至少也需要让一些民族学家对那些法则有所关注。最近,一位学者在其文章中对母系继承和父系继承[①]这一主题做了以下陈述:“单系制度自身是无规则的、人为的。母系制度则更是如此。”“无论在哪里发现的单系制度都肯定会与所期待的有偏差,并且代表着社会结构中的反常态。”“单系计算与父母身份的二元性相冲突,导致不自然地重视家庭的一方而排斥另一方。”基于以上断言,他似乎做出了以下

① 奥尔森:《北美的氏族和半偶族》,《加利福尼亚大学出版物》第 33 卷,第 409、411 页。

to have spread from them, by a process of 'diffusion', to vast numbers of peoples in Europe, Asia, Africa, Australia, Oceania and America.

(One wonders, of course, why so many societies of so many different types should have accepted and retained such 'anomalous', 'abnormal' and 'unnatural' institutions.)

I hope that the argument of this paper has shown, on the contrary, that unilineal institutions in some form, are almost, if not entirely, a necessity in any ordered social system. What is therefore unusual or rare (we need not say abnormal or anomalous and still less unnatural) is the discovery of a people such as the Teutonic peoples of Europe (apparently alone amongst IndoEuropean speaking peoples) maintaining for some period, until the coming of feudalism and Roman law, a system in which there is considerable, if not quite complete, avoidance of the unilineal principle, in which a person derives similar and equal rights through the father and through the mother. ①

It might well be expected that such a paper as this would deal with the question of what general factors determine the selection by some people of the matrilineal and by others of the patrilineal principle in determining status or succession. My opinion is that our knowledge and understanding are not sufficient to permit us to deal with this problem in any satisfactory manner.

① There are systems of bilateral kinship with succession through both males and females in some parts of Indonesia, e. g. in the Ifugao of the Philippine Islands. The discussion of these would be complex and require space that is not available.

结论:地位的单系确定必然有唯一的起源,源自于一个反常的民族,此民族通过某种"传播"的过程将其扩展到欧洲、亚洲、非洲、澳洲大陆、大洋洲和美洲等许多民族中。

(当然,人们会问为什么这种"不规则"、"反常"及"不自然"的制度会被如此多不同类型的社会接受并保留。)

相反,我希望我在本文的讨论已经证明了,即使在某些时候可能不是必须的,但某种形式的单系制度,是任何有秩序的社会制度中必要的基础。因此,说某个发现是不寻常、少见的(而不必像上面所说的不规则、反常、及不自然)仅仅是指:像欧洲日尔曼这样的民族(显然,即使在印欧语诸民族中也是独特的)在封建制度和罗马法出现以前,曾经维持着一种明显区别于单系原则的制度,尽管这种区别并不是完全的。在这种制度中,通过父亲和母亲都可以获得相似的和平等的权利。①

大家可能期待像本文这样的文章能解决这样的问题:即在确定地位和继承问题时,某个民族决定采用母系原则一般是基于哪些因素,又是哪些因素使其他的民族决定采用父系原则。我认为,想以令人满意的方式来解决这一问题,目前我们的知识和理解水平还达不到。

---

① 在印度尼西亚的某些部落,依然存在着父系与母系的双血亲继承制度,比如在菲律宾群岛的伊富高人。关于这些问题的讨论十分复杂,限于篇幅,无法展开。

CHAPTER Ⅲ

The Study Of Kinship Systems①

For seventy-five years the subject of kinship has occupied a special and important position in social anthropology. I propose in this address to consider the methods that have been and are being used in that branch of our studies and the kinds of results that we may reasonably expect to arrive at by those methods. I shall consider and compare two methods which I shall speak of as that of conjectural history and that of structural or sociological analysis.

One of these methods was first applied to some social institutions by French and British (mostly Scots) writers of the eighteenth century. It was of this method that Dugald Stewart wrote in 1795: 'To this species of philosophical investigation, which has no appropriated name in our language, I shall take the liberty of giving the title of *Theoretical* or *Conjectural History*; an expression which coincides pretty nearly in its meaning with that of *Natural History*, as employed by Mr. Hume (see his *Natural History of Religion*), and with what some French writers have called *Histoire Raisonnée*.' I shall accept Dugald

① Presidential Address to the Royal Anthropological Institute, 1941. Reprinted from the *Journal of the Royal Anthropological Institute*.

第三章　亲属制度研究[①]

75 年来,对亲属关系问题的研究在社会人类学中一直占有特殊且重要的位置。在这次演讲中,我会谈到在这一研究领域中一直或正在使用的一些方法,以及根据这些方法可能得出的结论。在此我将讨论两种方法并对之进行比较,我将它们称为历史推测的方法和结构分析或社会学分析方法。

18 世纪法国和英国(主要是苏格兰)的学者将其中一个方法首次运用到社会制度研究中。斯图尔特于 1795 年就这一方法写道:"对于这一具有哲理性的调查研究,由于在我们的语言中没有恰当的名称,我将冒昧地给其命名为'理论上或推测的历史';这种表达方式在意义上与休谟先生在'自然历史'(参见他的《宗教自然史》)中所使用的相一致。同时也与一些法国学者所

① 1941 年为皇家人类学会作的会长演说,重印自《皇家人类学会杂志》。

Stewart's suggestion and shall use the name 'conjectural history'.

The method of conjectural history is used in a number of different ways. One is to attempt to base on general considerations, on what Dugald Stewart calls 'known principles of human nature', conjectures as to first beginnings—of political society (Hobbes), of language (Adam Smith), of religion (Tylor), of the family (Westermarck), and so on. Sometimes an attempt is made to deal with the whole course of development of human society, as in the works of Morgan, Father Schmidt and Elliot Smith. Sometimes we are offered a conjectural history of the development of a particular institution, as in Robertson Smith's treatment of sacrifice. The special form of the method with which we shall be concerned in what follows is the attempt to explain a particular feature of one or more social systems by a hypothesis as to how it came into existence.

An early example of the method of conjectural history applied to kinship is to be found in the essay on *Primitive Marriage* published by John F. M'Lennan in 1865. You will remember the two principal theses put forward in that book: the origin of the custom of exogamy from marriage by capture, and the proposition that 'the most ancient system in which the idea of blood relationship was embodied was a system of kinship through females only'. Six years later there appeared *The Systems of Consanguinity and Affinity* of Lewis Morgan, a monument of scholarly, patient research in the collection of data, to be followed in 1877 by his *Ancient Society*, in which he offered a conjectural outline history of the whole course of social development. These works of M'Lennan and Morgan were followed by a considerable mass of literature, which has continued to be produced down to the present day, in which the method of conjectural history has been applied in different forms to various features of kinship organisation.

说的‘推理历史’相一致。”我将接受斯图尔特的建议,采用“推测历史”的说法。

历史推测方法有不同的使用方式。这种方式以总体思考为基础,来推测不同社会方式的起源,如对政治社会(霍布斯)、语言(亚当·斯密)、宗教(泰勒)、家庭(韦斯特马克)等起源的推测,就是在斯图尔特所说的“人类本质的已知原则”的基础上进行的。有时,在摩尔根、施密特神父和艾略特·史密斯等人的作品中能够看到他们尝试应用这种方法对人类社会的整个发展过程进行分析。有时,它也应用于对某一制度的发展进行历史推测,比如罗伯逊·史密斯关于祭祀的阐述。下面将要研究的方法的特殊形式是,通过假设一种或多种社会制度的起源来解释它的某种特征。

用推测历史的方法研究亲属制度的一个早期例证可以在约翰·麦克伦南1865年发表的《原始婚姻》一书中找到。此书提出了两个主要观点:一、异族通婚习俗起源于劫掠婚;二、“具有血缘观念的最古老的制度只能是母系制度”。6年后路易斯·摩尔根发表了名为《血亲和姻亲制度》一书,此书被认为是在资料收集方面潜心研究的里程碑式的著作。此后,他在于1877年发表的《古代社会》一书中,提出一部描述社会发展整个过程的推测史纲。随着麦克伦南和摩尔根著作的发表,相继又有许多著作问世,直至今日,学者们在这些著作中一直采用不同的历史推测方法来研究亲属组织的不同特征。

As I think you know, I regard the pursuit of this method as one of the chief obstacles to the development of a scientific theory of human society. But my position has often been misunderstood. My objection to conjectural history is not that it is historical, but that it is conjectural. History shows us how certain events or changes in the past have led to certain other events or conditions, and thus reveals human life in a particular region of the world as a chain of connected happenings. But it can do this only when there is direct evidence for both the preceding and succeeding events or conditions and also some actual evidence of their interconnection. In conjectural history we have direct knowledge about a state of affairs existing at a certain time and place, without any adequate knowledge of the preceding conditions and events, about which we are therefore reduced to making conjectures. To establish any probability for such conjectures we should need to have a knowledge of laws of social development which we certainly do not possess and to which I do not think we shall ever attain.

My own study of kinship began in 1904 under Rivers, when I was his first and at that time his only student in social anthropology, having for three years previously studied psychology under him. I owe a great deal to that contact with Rivers, and more rather than less because from the outset it appeared that we disagreed on the subject of method. For Rivers followed the method of conjectural history, at first under the influence of Morgan, and later in the form of what he called ethnological analysis, as exemplified in his *History of Melanesian Society* (1914*a*). But in his field work Rivers had discovered and revealed to others the importance of the investigation of the behaviour of relatives to one another as a means of understanding a system of kinship. In what follows I shall be criticising one side of Rivers' work, but the position I now hold is the one I held in my friendly discussions with him during a period of ten years, ending in an agreement to go on disagreeing. My esteem for Rivers as man, as teacher, and as scientist, is in no way diminished by the fact that I find myself obliged to

我认为,对这种方法的盲目使用是人类社会科学理论发展的主要障碍。但是,我的观点却经常被人误解。对于这种推测历史的方法,我反对的并非是其历史的一面,而是推测的一面。某些事件或变化会受到发生在过去的事件或某种变化的影响,通过对这种变化影响的阐释,历史向我们揭示了世界上某一地区的人类生活就像是相互联系在一起的一系列连锁事件。要做到这一点,关键是必须要有以前和随后所发生事件或条件的直接依据,以及这些事件和条件相互关系的真实证据。在推测历史的方法中,我们只对发生于某一时间和某一地点的事件的状态有直接地了解,但却没有充分了解这以前的事件和条件。因而,我们只能推测其历史。为了使推测成为可能,我们应当了解社会发展的规律,但我们目前还远没有具备这种知识,而且我认为我们永远不会拥有这种知识。

我在里弗斯的指导下于 1904 年开始研究亲属关系。我是他第一个也是那时他唯一的学习社会人类学的学生。在此之前,我曾跟随他学习了 3 年心理学。我很感激与里弗斯相处的那段日子,主要是因为从一开始我俩就在方法问题上存在分歧。里弗斯最初在摩尔根的影响下采用推测历史的方法,后来,他又运用了他叫做民族学分析法的方法,而且具体体现在他的《美拉尼西亚社会史》(1914a)一书中。里弗斯通过实地考察,发现并向人们揭示了运用对亲属之间相互行为的研究方法理解亲属制度的重要意义。以下的评论我只是针对里弗斯著作的一个方面,我和他最初达成了一致的观点,但随后又发生了分歧,现在我仍然坚持在与他十年友好讨论中一直持有的观点。我反对并批评他采用推测历史方法,但这并不妨碍我把里弗斯当做朋友、老师和科学家来尊重。

criticise adversely his use of the method of conjectural history.

At the outset it is necessary to give a definition. I shall use the term 'kinship system' as short for a system of kinship and marriage or kinship and affinity. It is a pity that there is no inclusive term in English for all relationships which result from the existence of the family and marriage. It would be very tiresome to speak all the time of a system of kinship and affinity. I hope, therefore, that my use of the term will be accepted. It need not lead to ambiguity.

The unit of structure from which a kinship system is built up is the group which I call an 'elementary family', consisting of a man and his wife and their child or children, whether they are living together or not. A childless married couple does not constitute a family in this sense. Children may be acquired, and thus made members of an elementary family, by adoption as well as by birth. We must also recognise the existence of compound families. In a polygynous family there is only one husband with two or more wives and their respective children. Another form of compound family is produced in monogamous societies by a second marriage, giving rise to what we call step-relationships and such relationships as that of half-brothers. Compound families can be regarded as formed of elementary families with a common member.

The existence of the elementary family creates three special kinds of social relationship, that between parent and child, that between children of the same parents (siblings), and that between husband and wife as parents of the same child or children. A person is born or adopted into a family in which he or she is son or daughter and brother or sister. When a man marries and has children he now belongs to a second elementary family, in which he is husband and father. This interlocking of elementary families creates a network of what I shall call, for lack of any better term, genealogical relations, spreading out indefinitely.

首先,有必要对要讨论的问题下个定义。我将使用“亲属制度”一词作为亲属和婚姻制度或亲属和姻亲制度的简称。很遗憾,在英语中还找不到一个词可以概括由家庭和婚姻引起的各种关系。但是一直用“亲属和姻亲制度”这个名称,让人觉得十分乏味。因此,我希望大家接受我使用“亲属制度”来代替它。这个词应该不会让大家感到模棱两可。

我把构成亲属制度的结构单位称为“基本家庭”,包括一对夫妇及其子女(无论他们是否住在一起)。所以一对夫妻如果还没有孩子的话,按这种定义来说就不算是组成了一个家庭。通过生育和收养,可以使孩子成为基本家庭的成员。同时我们还必须认识到,也存在复合家庭的形式。例如一夫多妻就是复合家庭的一种形式,它由一个丈夫和两个或两个以上的妻子及她们各自的孩子组成。一夫一妻制社会中也可能产生复合家庭的另一种形式:由于第二次婚姻,出现了所谓的继父母关系,以及同父异母(或同母异父)的兄弟关系。复合家庭可以看做是围绕一个共同成员所组成的许多基本家庭的总合。

在基本家庭中以及它们之间,存在着三种社会关系,即父母与孩子之间、同父母子女之间以及这些孩子的父母之间的关系。如果一个孩子因为出生或被收养,他或她就成了这个基本家庭的儿子或女儿、兄弟或姐妹。当一个男人结婚生子之后,他就属于另一个基本家庭的成员,在这个基本家庭中,他是丈夫或父亲。这种由基本家庭之间相互联结形成的网络,在没有更合适的称呼的情况下,可以暂且称为“谱系关系”。这种谱系关系可以无限延续。

The three relationships that exist within the elementary family constitute what I call the first order. Relationships of the second order are those which depend on the connection of two elementary families through a common member, and are such as father's father, mother's brother, wife's sister, and so on. In the third order are such as father's brother's son and mother's brother's wife. Thus we can trace, if we have genealogical information, relationships of the fourth, fifth or *n*th order. In any given society a certain number of these relationships are recognised for social purposes, i. e. they have attached to them certain rights and duties, or certain distinctive modes of behaviour. It is the relations that are recognised in this way that constitute what I am calling a kinship system, or, in full, a system of kinship and affinity.

A most important character of a kinship system is its range. In a narrow range system, such as the English system of the present day, only a limited number of relatives are recognised as such in any way that entails any special behaviour or any specific rights and duties. In ancient times in England the range was wider, since a fifth cousin had a claim to a share of the *wergild* when a man was killed. In systems of very wide range, such as are found in some non-European societies, a man may recognise many hundreds of relatives, towards each of whom his behaviour is qualified by the existence of the relationship.

It must be noted also that in some societies persons are regarded as being connected by relationships of the same kind although no actual genealogical tie is known. Thus the members of a clan are regarded as being kinsmen, although for some of them it may not be possible to show their descent from a common ancestor. It is this that distinguishes what will here be called a clan from a lineage.

Thus a kinship system, as I am using the term, or a system of kinship and affinity if you prefer so to call it, is in the first place a system of dyadic relations between person and person in a community, the behaviour of any two persons in any of these relations being regulated

我把存在于基本家庭中的这三种关系称作第一顺序。第二顺序是两个基本家庭的联合,这种联结方式都围绕着一个共同成员,如祖父、舅舅、姨母等。第三顺序是堂兄弟或舅母。因此,第四、第五或任何一级顺序的亲属关系都可以在谱系资料中追溯出来。在任何特定的社会里,一定数量的亲属关系背后总是存在一定的社会目的,即这些关系是与一定的权利和责任或一定的行为模式联系在一起的。我所说的亲属制度就是由这种方式建立的关系构成,它的完整说法就是亲属和姻亲制度。

亲属制度的范围是区别不同亲属制度类型的一个最重要的特征。在一个较为狭窄的亲属制度中,如现代英国亲属制度,只有数目有限的亲属被承认有特别的行为或特定的权利和责任。而在古代的英格兰,亲属制度的范围较宽,因此当一个男子被杀害后,就连处于第五顺序的堂表兄弟也有分享偿命金的权利。在那些范围最宽的社会中,如欧洲以外的一些社会,一名男子可以辩认出他的数百位亲戚,依据亲属关系的存在规范他与他们中每一位的行为。

同时必须要注意,在一些社会中,人们是靠类似于谱系纽带的关系联系起来的,尽管事实上这种纽带并不存在。因此,同一氏族的成员往往都被看成是亲属,尽管他们可能并不来自于同一祖先,而且想证实他们拥有同一血统也几乎是不可能的。而正是这种血统的差异形成了氏族与世系群的区别。

因此,如果大家愿意,可以把我说的亲属制度叫做亲属及姻亲制度。这种制度首先表现为一个群体中人与人之间的一种二元关系体系,在这个体系中,由社会习惯按照一定的方式调节处

in some way, and to a greater or less extent, by social usage.

A kinship system also includes the existence of definite social groups. The first of these is the domestic family, which is a group of persons who at a particular time are living together in one dwelling, or collection of dwellings, with some sort of economic arrangement that we may call joint housekeeping. There are many varieties of the domestic family, varying in their form, their size, and the manner of their common life. A domestic family may consist of a single elementary family, or it may be a group including a hundred or more persons, such as the *zadruga* of the Southern Slavs or the *taravad* of the Nayar. Important in some societies is what may be called a local cluster of domestic families. In many kinship systems unilinear groups of kindred—lineage groups, clans and moieties—play an important part.

By a kinship system, then, I mean a network of social relations of the kind just defined, which thus constitutes part of that total network of social relations that I call social structure. The rights and duties of relatives to one another and the social usages that they observe in their social contacts, since it is by these that the relations are described, are part of the system. I regard ancestor worship, where it exists, as in a real sense part of the kinship system, constituted as it is by the relations of living persons to their deceased kindred, and affecting as it does the relations of living persons to one another. The terms used in a society in addressing or referring to relatives are a part of the system, and so are the ideas that the people themselves have about kinship.

You will perceive that by using the word 'system' I have made an assumption, an important and far-reaching assumption; for that word implies that whatever it is applied to is a complex unity, an organised whole. My explicit hypothesis is that between the various features of a particular kinship system there is a complex relation of interdependence. The formulation of this working hypothesis leads immediately

于这些关系中任意两者之间的行为。

亲属制度意味着存在确定的社会群体。而社会群体中首要的便是共食家庭。共食家庭是指一个群体,其中的人们在特定时期内生活在同一住所或同一住所群中,并且存在可以称为共同家政的经济安排。共食家庭有不同的种类,它们因形式、规模及共同生活方式而异。一个共食家庭的基本结构既可以是一个基本家庭,也可以是一个包括一百多人或更多人组成的群体,如南斯拉夫人所说的“扎德鲁加”群体或纳亚尔人所说的“塔拉瓦德”群体。所谓地区性共食家庭群在一些社会中占有很重要的位置,而单系亲属群体如世系群、氏族和半偶族,在许多亲属制度中也起着很重要的作用。

我认为,上述定义的那种社会关系网络就是我所说的亲属制度,不同的这种网络组成了总体社会关系网络,我们把它称为社会结构。亲属制度包含很多内容,首先在亲属制度中包括那些构建这种制度的根据,由亲属之间相互权利和责任以及他们在社会交往中应该遵守的社会习惯构成。我把目前的祖先崇拜习俗也包括在所谓真正意义的亲属制度中。祖先崇拜构建在活人与死者之间的关系之上,并对存在于活着的人们之间的相互关系施加影响。这种制度还包括一个社会里人们的亲属称谓,因此人们如何认定自己亲属的概念就包括在亲属制度之中。

我已经做了一个重要并且具有深远影响的假设,通过使用“体系”一词,大家可能已经意识到了这一点。关于“体系”一词,无论怎样使用它,都隐含着存在一个复杂的联合体,一个有组织的整体。我的具体假设是:在特定亲属制度的各种特征之间,存在一种复杂的相互依赖的关系。这一具有可操作性假设的形式

to the method of sociological analysis, by which we seek to discover the nature of kinship systems as systems, if they be really such. For this purpose we need to make a systematic comparison of a sufficient number of sufficiently diverse systems. We must compare them, not in reference to single, superficial, and therefore immediately observable characters, but as wholes, as systems, and in reference, therefore, to general characters which are only discovered in the process of comparison. Our purpose is to arrive at valid abstractions or general ideas in terms of which the phenomena can be described and classified.

I propose to illustrate the two methods, that of conjectural history and that of system analysis, by means of a particular example, and for this purpose I select a peculiar feature of the kinship terminology of a number of scattered tribes. When Morgan made his study of the terminology of kinship in North American tribes, he noted certain peculiarities in the terms for cousins. In the Choctaw tribe he found that a man calls his father's sister's son by the same term of relationship that he applies to his own father and his father's brother. We may say that the father's sister's son is thus treated in the terminology as though he were a younger brother of the father. Reciprocally a man calls his mother's brother's son by the term for 'son'. Consistently with this he applies one term of relationship to his father's sister and her daughter, and speaks of his mother's brother's daughter as a 'daughter'. In the Omaha tribe, on the other hand, Morgan found that a man calls his mother's brother's son 'uncle', i. e. mother's brother, and calls his mother's brother's daughter 'mother', so that reciprocally he speaks of his father's sister's son by the term that he uses for his sister's son, and a woman uses a single term for her own son, her sister's son and her father's sister's son. Figs. 1 and 2 will help to make these terminologies clear.

会直接引导出一种社会学分析方法。通过这种分析方法我们可以发现作为体系的亲属制度(如果亲属制度真的是一种体系的话)的本质。为达到这一目的,我们要对大量不同的制度进行系统对比。在制度对比过程中,我们不应当参照那些单一的、表面的,因而可以立刻观察到的特征,而应该把它们作为一个总体或系统比较,并把那些只有在比较过程中才能发现的普遍特征作为参照。我们的目的就是要通过现象得出概念,即通过那些可以进行描述和分类的现象来总结出有效的抽象或总体概念。

以下,我举例说明历史推测和系统分析这两种方法。为此,我挑选一些分散部落中的独特亲属称谓作为例子。当摩尔根在研究北美部落亲属称谓时,他发现了表亲称谓的某些特点。他发现,在乔克托部落中,一名男子对父亲姐妹的儿子的称谓与他对父亲以及父亲的兄弟的称谓相同。因此,我们可以说,他在称谓上将父亲姐妹的儿子与父亲的弟弟似乎同样对待。相反地,一位男子把母亲兄弟的儿子称为"儿子"。同理,一位男子也会使用同一称谓来称呼父亲的姐妹和她们的女儿,并且称呼母亲兄弟的女儿为"女儿"。然而,在奥马哈部落中,摩尔根发现一位男子将其母亲兄弟的儿子称为"舅父",即和母亲的兄弟的称谓相同,而将母亲兄弟的女儿称呼为"母亲"。相应地,他也用同一称谓来称呼他姐妹的儿子和他父亲姐妹的儿子。而且一位女子在称呼自己的儿子、她姐妹的儿子以及她父亲姐妹的儿子时,也可使用同一称谓。图 1 及图 2 将帮助我们对这些称谓有一个清楚的认识。

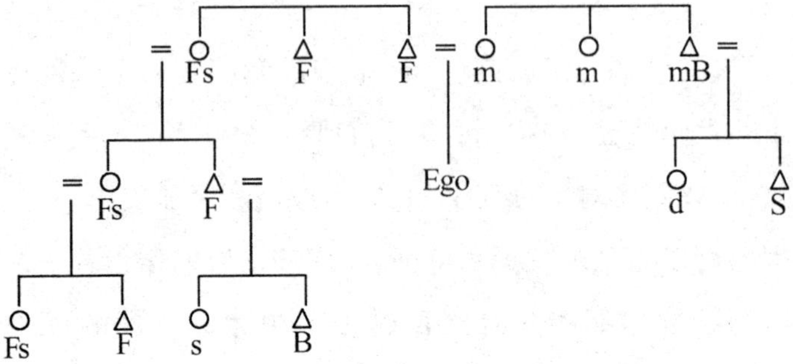

FIG. 1—CHOCTAW

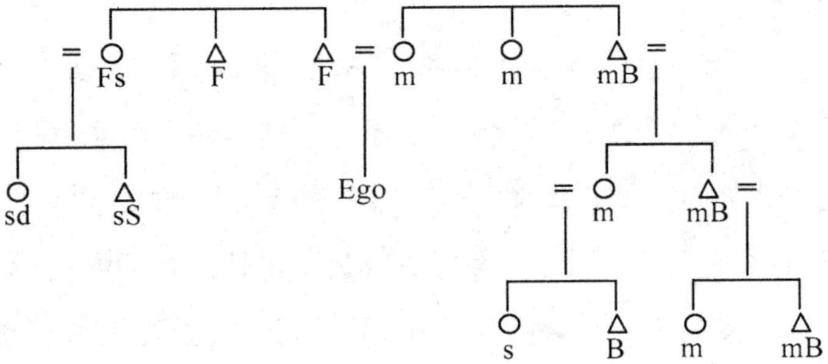

FIG. 2—OMAHA

F = Father	m = mother
B = Brother	d = daughter
S = Son	s = sister

Terminologies similar to the Omaha are found in a number of regions: (1) in the Siouan tribes related to the Omaha, such as the Osage, Winnebago, etc.; (2) in certain Algonquian tribes, of which we may take the Fox Indians as an example; (3) in an area of California which includes the Miwok; (4) in some tribes of East Africa, both Bantu and non-Bantu, including the Nandi and the Ba-Thonga; (5) amongst the Lhota Nagas of Assam; and (6) in some New

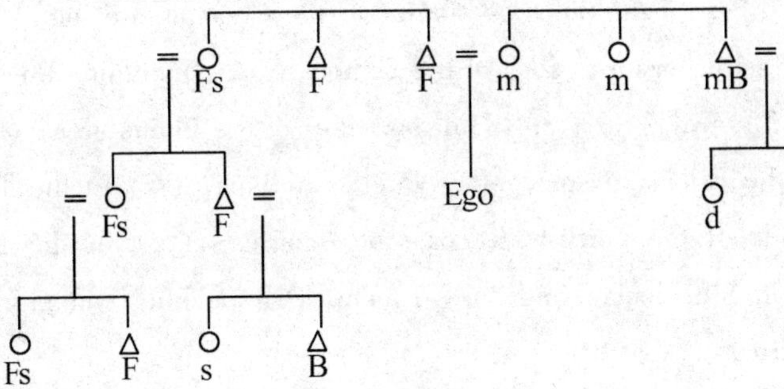

图 1　乔克托称谓

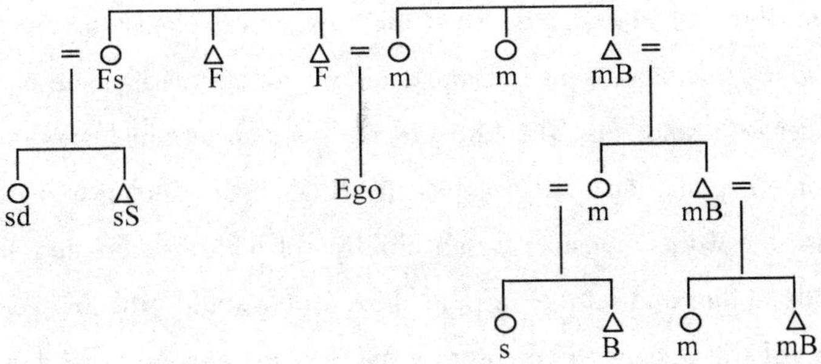

图 2　奥马哈称谓

F = 父亲　　m = 母亲

B = 兄弟　　d = 女儿

S = 儿子　　s = 姐妹

与奥马哈部落的称谓有相似情况的地区有：(1)与奥马哈部落有联系的苏人部落，如奥萨格人、温内巴格人等等；(2)一些阿尔衮琴部落，如福克斯印第安人；(3)包括米沃克人在内的部分加利福尼亚地区；(4)东非的一些部落，如全部的班图语族和非班图语族，包括南迪人和巴聪加人；(5)生活在阿萨姆

Guinea tribes. Terminologies similar to the Choctaw are found: (1) in other south-eastern tribes of the United States, including the Cherokee; (2) in the Crow and Hidatsa tribes of the Plains area; (3) amongst the Hopi and some other Pueblo Indians; (4) in the Tlingit and Haida of the north-west coast of America; (5) in the Banks Islands in Melanesia; and (6) in one Twi-speaking community of West Africa.

There are some who would regard this kind of terminology as 'contrary to common sense', but that means no more than that it is not in accordance with our modern European ideas of kinship and its terminology. It ought to be easy for any anthropologist to recognise that what is common sense in one society may be the opposite of common sense in another. The Choctaw and Omaha terminologies do call for some explanation; but so does the English terminology, in which we use the word 'cousin' for all children of both brothers and sisters of both mother and father—a procedure which would probably seem to some non-Europeans to be contrary not only to common sense but also to morals. What I wish to attempt, therefore, is to show you that the Choctaw and Omaha terminologies are just as reasonable and fitting in the social systems in which they occur as our own terminology is in our own social system.

I would point out that the Choctaw system and the Omaha system exhibit a single structural principle applied in different ways, in what we may perhaps call opposite directions. We shall therefore consider them together, as varieties of a single species.

Attempts have been made to explain these terminologies by the method of conjectural history. The first was that of Kohler in 1897, in his essay 'Zur Urgeschichte der Ehe'. Kohler set out to defend Morgan's theory of group-marriage, and used the Choctaw and Omaha

地区的沃塔那加人;(6)部分新几内亚部落。与乔克托人的称谓有相似情况的地区有:(1)包含切罗基人在内的部分生活在美国东南部的部落;(2)在平原地区的克劳部落和希达察部落;(3)霍皮人和其他普埃布洛印第安人;(4)美洲西北海岸的特林吉特人和海达人;(5)美拉尼西亚的班克斯岛地区;(6)说特维语的西非的一个社区。

这种亲属称谓看似“有悖常理的”,但它只不过是与现代欧洲人的亲属观念及其称谓不一致而已。对于任何一位人类学家来说,经常会发现在某一社会中被正常接受的事在另一社会中却被认为是违反常理的。确实需要对乔克托人和奥马哈人与我们对亲属称谓的不同方式做些解释。但是,我认为同样也有必要解释一下英国人的称谓。在非洲某些部落,如果用一个词来表示父母双方的兄弟姐妹的所有子女,不但是与习惯不符,甚至是有违道德的,但在英语称谓中,我们使用“Cousin”一词代表了所有这些子女。对于我们的社会制度,我们所使用的称谓语是合适的;相应的,我希望证明给你们,对于乔克托人和奥马哈人的制度,他们关于亲属的称谓同样合理并且适合他们的制度。

我要指出,在乔克托亲属制度和奥马哈亲属制度之间,显示出了相对立的结构原则。因此,我们可以认为它们是同一种类的不同变体,两种制度可以结合到一起考察。

有很多人已经使用过历史推测方法试图去解释这些称谓。科勒在 1897 年的《史前婚姻》一文中,首先运用这一方法反驳摩尔根的群婚理论,当时他使用的论据就是乔克托人

systems for his argument. He explained the Choctaw terminology as the result of marriage with the mother's brother's wife, and the Omaha system as the result of a custom of marriage with the wife's brother's daughter. Kohler's essay was reviewed by Durkheim (1898) in what was an important, if brief, contribution to the theory of kinship. He rejected Kohler's hypotheses, and pointed out the connection of the Choctaw and Omaha systems with matrilineal and patrilineal descent respectively.

The subject was considered again by Rivers in reference to the Banks Islands, and, without bringing in, as Kohler had done, the question of group-marriage, he explained the Banks Islands terminology as resulting from a custom of marriage with the mother's brother's widow. Gifford (1916), having found the characteristic feature of the Omaha system in the Miwok of California, followed the lead of Kohler and Rivers, and explained it as the result of the custom of marriage with the wife's brother's daughter. About the same time, and independently, Mrs. Seligman (1917) offered the same explanation of the Omaha feature as it occurs in the Nandi and other tribes of Africa.

Let me summarise the argument with reference to the Omaha type. The hypothesis is that in certain societies, mostly having a definite patrilineal organisation, a custom was for some reason adopted of permitting a man to marry his wife's brother's daughter. Referring to Fig. 3, this means that D would be allowed to marry f. When such a marriage occurred, then for G and h, f, who is their mother's brother's daughter, would become their step-mother, and E, their mother's brother's son, would become the brother of their step-mother. The hypothesis then assumes that the kinship terminology was so modified as to anticipate this form of marriage wherever it might occur. G and h will call f, their mother's brother's daughter and therefore their possible future step-mother, 'mother', and her brother E they will call 'mother's brother'. Reciprocally f will call G 'son' and E

和奥马哈人的制度。在他看来，在乔克托人中由于存在可以与母亲兄弟的妻子结婚的习俗，所以产生了适应这一社会制度的称谓制度；而奥马哈人的称谓制度则来自人们可以与妻子兄弟的女儿结婚的习俗。杜尔干（1898）对科勒的文章给予了评论并认为它对亲属理论做了重要的贡献。但是杜尔干并不赞成科勒的假设，他认为乔克托与奥马哈制度分别与母系和父系继承有联系。

里弗斯也曾研究过这一问题，但他并没有像科勒那样涉及群婚的问题。在考察班克斯岛时，他认为正是由于习俗允许人们可以娶母亲兄弟的寡妻，才产生了班克斯岛上的亲属称谓制度。吉福德（1916）在加利福尼亚米沃克人中发现了奥马哈制度的特点后，运用科勒和里弗斯的研究方法，把这一特点归因于可以与妻弟的女儿结婚的习俗。大约在同一时期，赛丽格曼夫人（1917）也用同样的理论解释了在南迪及非洲其他部落中发现的奥马哈制度的特点。

对奥马哈亲属制度类型的论述可以概括如下。这些论述的假设前提是：在大多数具有明确父系组织结构的社会中，由于某些原因，习俗允许一位男子与其妻弟的女儿结婚。在图 3 中，表示 D 可以娶 f。一旦这种婚姻发生了，f 对于 G 和 h 来说将变成他们的继母，而原本她只是他们母亲兄弟的女儿。相应地，E 现在就是他们继母的兄弟，而他原来是他们母亲的兄弟的儿子。根据这个假设，亲属称谓是和婚姻形式联结在一起的，不管此种形式的婚姻在何地发生，都需要改变原有的亲属称谓来适应新的婚姻形式。对于 G 和 h 来说，现在 f（他们母亲兄弟的女儿、未来可能的继母）被称呼为“母亲”；同时，她的兄弟 E 被称为“母亲的兄弟”。

will call him 'sister's son'. There is an exactly parallel argument for the Choctaw system. A custom arises by which a man may occasionally marry the widow of his mother's brother. In the figure, G would marry b, the wife of his mother's brother A. Thus E and f would become his step-children. If this marriage is anticipated in the terminology, then E and f will call G 'father' and h 'father's sister'.

Let us note that in the Omaha tribe and in some others having a

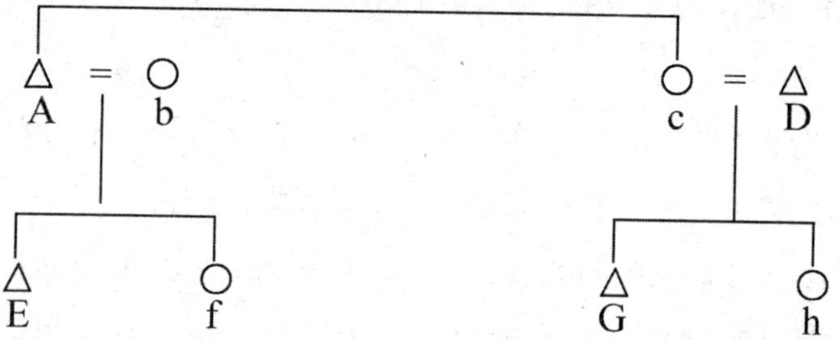

FIG. 3

Note—A and c are brother and sister

similar terminology it is regarded as permissible for a man to marry his wife's brother's daughter. Marriage with the mother's brother's widow does not seem to occur regularly with the Choctaw terminology, and does certainly occur without it, even in tribes with an Omaha terminology such as the BaThonga.

The basis of what we may call the Kohler hypothesis is the obvious fact that in each of the two varieties the terminology and the special form of marriage are consistent; the two things fit together in what may be called a logical way. This, I think, anyone can see by inspection of the data. But the hypothesis goes far beyond this. It supposes that there is some sort of causal connection such that the marriage custom can be said to have caused, produced, or resulted in, the special terminology. No evidence is adduced that this is actually the way in which things happened. The argument is entirely a priori. It is the essential weakness of conjectural history that its hypotheses

相应地,将称呼G为"儿子",而E将G称为"姐妹的儿子"。在乔克托制度中,这种方式以反向方式运用。按照习俗,一位男子有时可以与母亲兄弟的寡妻结婚。在图中,G可以与b结婚,而她原本是G母亲的兄弟A的妻子。因而,E和f就变成G的继子女。如果预计到这种婚姻发生的可能,那么称谓制度做出的适应性改变就是,E和f称呼G为"父亲",称呼h为"父亲的姐妹"。

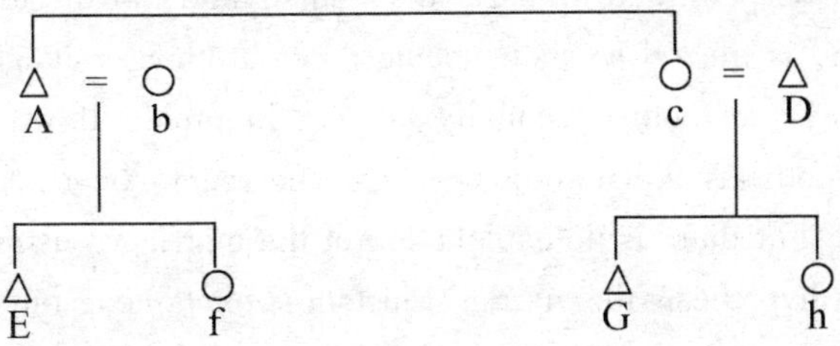

图3

(注:A和c是兄弟和姐妹)

此处我们应该注意,在奥马哈部落和一些具有相似称谓制度的部落中,一位男子可以娶妻子兄弟的女儿为妻。但在和母亲兄弟的寡妻结婚以后,称谓形式却与乔克托的称谓制度有所不同。在使用奥马哈称谓制度的部落如巴聪加人中,虽然出现过这种婚姻形式,但却没有使用过象乔克托部落这样的称谓制度。

所谓的科勒假设是基于这样一个明显的事实:在上述的两种称谓变异中,特有的婚姻形式决定了各自的称谓制度,两者的结合在逻辑上没有冲突。我认为,通过分析资料可以很容易得出这一结论。但,在假设中还蕴涵着更深层次的内容,即在婚姻与称谓制度之间存在某种因果关系,婚姻习俗是亲属称谓制度的起因,是它引起、产生或导致了特有的亲属称谓制度。但论点只是

cannot be verified. Thus this hypothesis cannot be considered as anything more than a speculation or conjecture as to how things might have happened.

Now it would be equally plausible to suggest that the special form of marriage is the result of the terminology. If, as in the terminology of the Omaha type, I treat my wife's brother's daughter as being the younger sister of my wife, and, by the custom of the sororate, it is considered proper for me to marry my wife's younger sister, then I might well be permitted to marry the woman who, in the terminological system, is treated as such, namely her brother's daughter. This hypothesis is, of course, equally lacking in proof. If we adopt the Kohler hypothesis the terminology is conceived to be in some sense explained, but there is no explanation of the marriage custom. By the alternative hypothesis the marriage custom is explained, but the terminology is not. I do not see how there can be any ground for a choice of one of these two hypotheses in preference to the other except purely personal predilection.

However, while we could conceive of the marriage custom as being the immediate result of the terminology in a society which already has sororal polygyny, the terminology cannot be the immediate result of the marriage custom without the concomitant action of some other undetermined factor. We have examples of societies in which a man sometimes marries the widow of his mother's brother, but only uses the terminology which this marriage makes appropriate after the marriage has taken place. Although we have no recorded instance of this procedure in marriage with the wife's brother's daughter it is at least conceivable that it might occur. What is lacking in the hypothesis we are examining is some reason why the whole terminology should be adjusted so as to fit a particular form of marriage which only occasionally occurs.

Let us now leave the hypothesis and examine the structural principles of those kinship systems in which this terminology occurs, whether in the Choctaw or the Omaha form. It is necessary, however,

先验的假设,没有事实能证明事情确实是这样的。历史推测法的本质弱点就在于此,不能够对其假设加以检验。因此,我们只能把这种假设看作是对发生的某些事情进行了某种推测而已。

现在,我们同样也可以认为特殊的婚姻形式是称谓制度的结果。如果像奥马哈类型称谓那样,把妻弟的女儿称为妻子的妹妹。那么,按照妻姐妹婚的习俗,我就可以娶妻子的妹妹为妻,从而理论上也可以娶在称谓上是我妻子的妹妹而事实上是我妻弟的女儿为妻。当然,此假设同样缺少论据。而科勒的假设却只能在某种程度上对这种称谓进行解释,仍然不能解释婚姻的习俗。但如果采用目前的假设,却又只能对婚姻习俗进行解释,而对称谓制度无能为力。我们选择一种假设而不是另一种假设的理由除了纯粹的个人偏好外,我想不出还有其他什么理由。

然而,我们可以想象,在一个已经有着妻姐妹婚习俗的社会中,此婚姻习俗是称谓制度的直接结果,但称谓制度却不可能是婚姻习俗的直接结果,除非附加上某些不确定因素的附带作用。在一些例子中我们可以看到,在一些社会中,一位男子有时可以娶母亲兄弟的寡妻为妻。但使其婚姻得体的称谓却是在这种婚姻发生后才使用的。尽管与自己妻弟的女儿结婚以后称谓会发生怎样变化的记载目前还没有,但至少我们可以想象这种情况是可能发生的。而我们此处要考察的假设中,缺少的是某种理由,去说明为什么整个称谓形式都要被调整,去适应一种仅仅是偶然发生的特殊婚姻形式。

现在,我们离开以上假设,单纯分析具有这种称谓形式的亲属制度的结构原则,无论这种结构原则是属于乔克托的亲属制度

to say something on the subject of kinship terminologies, about which there has been a great deal of controversy. Morgan's first interest in the subject was as an ethnologist, i. e. one seeking to discover the historical relations of the peoples of the earth. He thought that by collecting a sufficient sample of terminologies and comparing them he could reveal the historical relation of the American Indians (the Ganowanian peoples as he called them) to the peoples of Asia. In the course of his work, however, he decided that these terminologies could be used to infer the former existence of forms of social organisation. He supposed that the classificatory terminology which he found in North American tribes such as the Iroquois was inconsistent with the form of social organisation with which it is actually found, and therefore could not have arisen in a society so organised, but must be a 'survival' from some different kind of social system.

This was, of course, pure assumption, but it is the kind of assumption that the method of conjectural history encourages us to make, often unconsciously or implicitly. Morgan was thus led to a hypothesis that is one of the most fantastic in a subject that is full of fantastic hypotheses. The truth is that he had quite failed to understand the nature and function of the classificatory terminology. There is nothing that so effectively prevents the perception and understanding of things as they are as hypotheses of conjectural history, or the desire to invent such hypotheses.

One of Morgan's early critics, Starcke (1889), was, I believe, the first to maintain the position which has always been my own. He held that in general a kinship nomenclature is 'the faithful reflection of the juridical relations which arise between the nearest kinsfolk in each tribe'. He condemned as unsound the attempt to use such nomenclatures to make historical reconstructions of past societies. It would be interesting to consider why it is that Starcke has had so few followers and Morgan so many, but that I cannot here undertake.

In 1909 Kroeber published in our *Journal* a paper on 'Classi-ficatory

还是属于奥马哈社会的亲属制度。不过在此之前,仍然有必要讨论一下存在很大争议的关于亲属称谓的话题。对这一问题,摩尔根曾产生过极大的兴趣,并首次以民族学家的视角对其进行过研究,试图揭示地球上各民族之间的历史关系。按照他的观点,在收集足够的有关称谓的资料基础上,对其进行比较研究,就可以揭示美洲印弟安人(他称之为加诺万尼亚人)与亚洲民族间的历史关系。然而,在研究的过程中,他认为以前的社会组织存在形式也可以靠这些称谓来推断。因为他在研究中发现,在北美部落的易洛魁人中,分类称谓与社会组织结构形式不一致,因此,此种称谓形式不可能在这样的社会中产生,而只能是另一种不同种类的社会制度"幸存"下来的东西。

当然,这纯粹是一种假设,但它正是在历史推测法引导下做出的。而这种引导通常是无意识的或源于方法本身的。摩尔根就是受这种方法的引导得出一个在充满各种奇幻假设的学科中最具幻想的假设。事实上,他没有很确切地理解分类称谓的本质和功能。在我看来,在阻碍人们对事物的认识和理解方面,没有什么能比历史推测假设或发明此类假设的渴望更有效。

我认为,摩尔根早期的一位批评者之一,斯达克(1889)是第一位与我持有相同观点的人。他认为,试图依靠历史推测方法,用这种称谓方式来重建往日社会历史的做法是极不可靠的。在他看来,亲属称谓本质上是"每个部落内近亲之间法律关系的可靠反应"。但为什么斯达克只拥有较少的追随者,而摩尔根却赢得众多的追随者呢?我在这个场合不能对这个值得探讨的有趣问题加以评论。

克罗伯于1909年在我们的《刊物》上发表了《分类亲属制

Systems of Relationship'. To the contentions of that paper Rivers made a reply in his lectures on *Kinship and Social Organisation* (1914*b*), and Kroeber answered the criticisms of Rivers in his *California Kinship Systems* (1917).

I discussed Kroeber's paper with Rivers when it appeared and found myself in the position of disagreeing with both sides of the controversy. Kroeber wrote: 'Nothing is more precarious than the common method of deducing the recent existence of social or marital institutions from a designation of relationship.' This is a restatement of Starcke's contention of 1889, and with it I was, and still am, in complete agreement, thereby disagreeing with Rivers. Kroeber also wrote: 'It has been an unfortunate characteristic of the anthropology of recent years to seek in a great measure specific causes for specific events connection between which can be established only through evidence that is subjectively selected. On wider knowledge and freedom from motive it is becoming increasingly apparent that causal explanations of detached anthropological phenomena can be but rarely found in other detached phenomena.' With this statement I am in agreement.

But both Kroeber and Rivers seemed to agree that causal explanations are necessary for the constitution of what Kroeber calls 'true science'. For Rivers anthropology is a true science because, or to the extent that, it can show causal connections; for Kroeber it is not a true science. Here I disagree with both Kroeber and Rivers, holding that a pure theoretical science (whether physical, biological or social) is not concerned with causal relations in this sense. The concept of cause and effect belongs properly to applied science, to practical life and its arts and techniques and to history.

This brings us to the crux of the Rivers-Kroeber debate. Rivers held that the characteristics of a kinship nomenclature are determined by social or sociological factors, that particular features of terminology

度》一文。针对这篇文章中提出的观点，里弗斯在《亲属关系和社会组织》(1914b)的讲座中给予了评论。而对于里弗斯的评论，克罗伯又在《加利福尼亚的亲属制度》(1917)一书中做了回答。

当克罗伯的文章发表之后，通过与里弗斯就此文章进行的探讨，我发觉我与争论双方的观点都不一致。克罗伯写道："没有比习惯上通过亲属称谓来推断现存的社会制度或婚姻制度的方法更不妥当的了。"在此他重申了斯达克1889年的观点，这个观点不管在过去还是现在我都持完全同意的态度，从而也就意味着我不赞同里弗斯的观点。克罗伯又写道："在人类学中近年来出现了一个令人遗憾的特点，即极力寻找特殊事件之间的关联，而支撑这些关系的证据却都是主观遴选的。只要有更全面的知识，而且摈弃主观的左右，就可以明显地看出，在互相孤立的人类学现象间建立因果联系十分困难。"我同意这个观点。

但是，克罗伯所说的"真正科学"要建立在因果解释之上，对于这个观点克罗伯和里弗斯似乎都同意。但二人的分歧在于，里弗斯认为人类学是真正的科学，因为在某种意义上，人类学展示了因果关系；而对于克罗伯来说，它并不是一门真正的科学。这里我不同意克罗伯和里弗斯的观点，我认为一门纯粹的理论科学(无论是自然的、生物的还是社会的)并不是构建于因果关系之上的。因果概念应属于应用科学、现实生活、艺术、技术和历史学范畴。

里弗斯与克罗伯之争的关键之处在于，里弗斯认为亲属关系与特定社会是有一定因果联系的，社会或社会学方面的因素决定

result from particular features of social organisation. Against this Kroeber held that the features of a system of terminology 'are determined primarily by language' and 'reflect psychology not sociology'. 'Terms of relationship', he wrote, 'are determined primarily by linguistic factors and are only occasionally, and then indirectly, affected by social circumstances.' But in his later paper Kroeber explains that what he calls psychological factors 'are social or cultural phenomena as thoroughly and completely as institutions, beliefs or industries are social phenomena'. His thesis is therefore concerned with a distinction between two kinds of social phenomena. One of these he calls institutional, defined as 'practices connected with marriage, descent, personal relations, and the like'. These are what he called in his first paper 'social factors'. The other kind he speaks of as the 'psyche' of a culture, 'that is, the ways of thinking and feeling characteristic of the culture'. These constitute what he calls the psychological factors.

Thus Kroeber's thesis, on its positive side, is that similarities and differences of kinship nomenclature are to be interpreted or understood by reference to similarities and differences in the general 'manner of thought'. On its negative side, and it is with this that we are concerned, Kroeber's thesis is that there is no regular close connection between similarities and differences of kinship nomenclature and similarities and differences of 'institutions', i. e. practices connected with marriage, descent and personal relations. He admits, in 1917, the existence of 'undoubted correspondence of terminology and social practice in certain parts of Australia and Oceania', but denies that such are to be found in California. It may be pointed out that in Australia and Oceania they have been deliberately looked for, in California they have not. It may well be that in the remnants of Californian tribes it is now too late to look for them.

In opposition to Kroeber, and in a certain sense in agreement with Rivers, I hold that all over the world there are important correspondences between kinship nomenclature and social practices. Such

了亲属称谓的特征。并且,这些称谓的具体特征是由特定的社会组织结构导致的。而克罗伯却认为,某一称谓制度的特征“主要是由语言来决定的”,并且“反映的是心理学,却不是社会学”。他写道:“亲属称谓主要由语言因素决定,社会情况只是给予它偶然的、间接的影响。”但在克罗伯后来的文章中,他把他所说的心理因素解释为“完全的社会或文化现象,就像制度、信仰或生活完全是社会现象一样”。在他的文章中,论述了两种社会现象的区别。一种社会现象是制度性的,即关于婚姻、传承、个人关系等关系的实践。他在第一篇文章中称其为“社会因素”。另一种社会现象是他所说的文化“精神”,“即思维方式和文化的情感特征”。这些构成了他所说的心理因素。

我认为,克罗伯观点中可取的部分是,他认为“思维方式”之间的差异是理解和诠释亲属称谓差异的出发点。而其不可取的部分是(这也正是我们关注的),他认为亲属称谓的异同与“制度”的异同之间,并不存在有规律的密切联系,即那些与婚姻传承和个人关系相关联的行为之间的差别不会造成亲属称谓的差异。虽然克罗伯于1917年承认,在澳大利亚和大洋洲的一些地区中,称谓和社会习俗之间存在着毋庸置疑的一致性,但他同时又认为在加利福尼亚并不存在这种情况。也许需要指出,为了寻找这种一致性而特意在澳洲和大洋洲做的考察并没有在加利福尼亚也这样做。但是现在想再到加利福尼亚部落的后裔中去做这种考察可能已经太晚了。

我的观点与克罗伯相反,某种意义上近似于里弗斯的观点。我认为亲属称谓与社会习俗之间存在的这种一致性,在全世界各个地方都有据可查。但是这种一致性存在的证据必须通过实地

correspondences are not to be simply assumed; they must be demonstrated by field work and comparative analysis. But their absence may not be assumed either; and Kroeber's arguments from their alleged absence in California remain, I think, entirely unconvincing.

For Kroeber the kinship nomenclature of a people represents their general manner of thought as it is applied to kinship. But the institutions of a people also represent their general manner of thought about kinship and marriage. Are we to suppose that in Californian tribes the way of thinking about kinship as it appears on the one hand in the terminology and on the other hand in social customs are not merely different but are not connected? This seems to be in effect what Kroeber is proposing.

Kroeber pointed out in 1917 that his original paper represented 'a genuine attempt to understand kinship systems as kinship systems'. But by 'kinship system' Kroeber means only a system of nomenclature. Moreover, Kroeber is an ethnologist, not a social anthropologist. His chief, if not his sole, interest in the subject is in the possibility of discovering and defining the historical relations of peoples by comparison of their systems of nomenclature.

My own conception is that the nomenclature of kinship is an intrinsic part of a kinship system, just as it is also, of course, an intrinsic part of a language. The relations between the nomenclature and the rest of the system are relations within an ordered whole. My concern, both in field work in various parts of the world and in comparative studies, has been to discover the nature of these relations.

In the actual study of a kinship system the nomenclature is of the utmost importance. It affords the best possible approach to the investigation and analysis of the kinship system as a whole. This, of course, it could not do if there were no real relations of interdependence between the terminology and the rest of the system. That there are such

考察和对比分析才能得到,不能仅仅通过简单的假设来想象。但是,我们同样也不可以仅仅依靠假设而不是实地考察和对比分析得出两者之间不存在这种一致性的结论。所以,我认为克罗伯由于加利福尼亚的部落中缺乏这种一致性便得出整体上两者之间不存在有规律联系的结论根本不能让人信服。

克罗伯认为,就像思维方式是亲属关系的反映一样,一个民族的亲属称谓也是这个民族大致思维方式的反映。但是,一个民族的制度同样也反映了本族人民关于亲属和婚姻的总体思维模式。在此,我们难道是在说加利福尼亚部落中那种既体现在称谓中,同时又体现在社会习俗中的亲属关系的思维方式之间不仅不同,而且根本无关吗?克罗伯的观点似乎的确如此。

克罗伯于 1917 年提出,他最初的一篇文章代表了“把亲属制度作为亲属制度来理解的一次真正尝试”。对克罗伯来说,“亲属制度”只是称谓制度的意思。另外,克罗伯只是一位民族学家,并不是社会人类学家。对于这个课题,他主要(如果不是唯一)的兴趣是尽可能通过比较研究各民族的称谓体制,发现和阐释这些民族之间的历史关系。

我认为,正如亲属称谓理所当然是语言的一个内在组成部分一样,它也是亲属制度的一个内在组成部分。称谓与制度中其他部分共同构成了一个有序的整体,它们之间的关系体现了有序整体内部的关系。通过在世界各地进行的实地调查和比较研究,我希望能够得出关于这些关系本质的一些结论。

在真正研究亲属制度中,称谓是极其重要的,因为称谓形式为我们提供了调查和分析作为整体的亲属制度一个最可行的方法。当然,如果在称谓和制度其他部分之间不存在相互依赖的关

relations I can affirm from my own field work in more than one region. It will be borne out, I believe, by any anthropologist who has made a thorough field study of a kinship system. ①

I have dealt with the controversy between Kroeber and Rivers because, as both the controversialists point out, the real issue is not simply one concerning kinship terms, but is a very important question of the general method of anthropological studies. It seemed to me that I could best make clear my own position by showing you how it differs from that of Rivers on the one side and that of Kroeber on the other.

Kinship systems are made and re-made by man, in the same sense that languages are made and re-made, which does not mean that they are normally constructed or changed by a process of deliberation and under control of conscious purpose. A language has to work, i. e. it has to provide a more or less adequate instrument for communication, and in order that it may work it has to conform to certain general necessary conditions. A morphological comparison of languages shows us the different ways in which these conditions have been complied with by using different morphological principles such as inflection, agglutination, word order, internal modification or the use of tone or stress. A kinship system also has to work if it is to exist or persist. It has to provide an orderly and workable system of social relations defined by social usage. A comparison of different systems shows us how workable kinship systems have been created by utilising certain structural principles and certain mechanisms.

---

① My position has been misunderstood and consequently misrepresented by Dr. Opler (1937b) in his paper on 'Apache Data concerning the Relation of Kinship Terminology to Social Classification'; but the first two paragraphs of another of Dr. Opler's papers (1937a) on 'Chiricahua Apache Social Organisation', state what was at that time his, and is also my, point of view.

系,那么这一点是不可能做到的。从我在许多地区所做的实地考察中可以证明,这种关系是存在的。我相信,任何对亲属制度做出详尽研究的社会人类学家都可以得出这一结论。①

我对克罗伯－里弗斯之间争论进行讨论的原因,正如这两位争论者所指出的那样,是由于他们之间争论的真正所在不仅仅和亲属称谓问题有关,而且更重要的是还关系到如何进行人类学研究的一般方法问题。对我来说,我将通过指出我与里弗斯和克罗伯观点的不同之处,清晰地表明我自已的立场。

亲属制度与语言一样,是通过人们构建、再构建形成的。但这并不是说这种构建、再构建过程是经过人们深思熟虑或是有意识控制的。一种语言必须能被人们使用,也就是说,它必须为人们的沟通提供足够的工具。为了能被使用,一种语言必须与某种普遍的、必要的条件相一致。通过语言的形态学方面的比较,我们能够获得语言在遵循这些条件时采取的不同方式。方式的不同主要表现为形态学规则的不同,例如屈折变化规则、黏着规则、语序变化规则、内部变形或声调与重音的运用规则等。同理,一种亲属制度必须能够被人们使用才能够存在或保持下去。作为一种社会关系制度,它必须符合特定的社会习俗规定,同时也必须是有序、可行的。通过不同制度的对比可以表明利用一定的结构原则和一定的机制是如何创造出有效的亲属制度来的。

① 奥普勒博士原来误解了我的观点,以致他在《关于亲属称谓与社会分类的关系的阿帕切材料》(1937b)一文中做了误述;然而,他在另一篇《奇里卡华阿帕切人的社会组织》(1937a)的论文的开头两段提出的观点和我的观点相同。

One common feature of kinship systems is the recognition of certain categories or kinds into which the various relatives of a single person can be grouped. The actual social relation between a person and his relative, as defined by rights and duties or socially approved attitudes and modes of behaviour, is then to a greater or less extent fixed by the category to which the relative belongs. The nomenclature of kinship is commonly used as a means of establishing and recognising these categories. A single term may be used to refer to a category of relatives and different categories will be distinguished by different terms.

Let us consider a simple example from our own system. We do what is rather unusual in the general run of kinship systems: we regard the father's brother and the mother's brother as relatives of the same kind of category. We apply a single term originally denoting the mother's brother (from the Latin *avunculus*) to both of them. The legal relationship in English law, except for entailed estates and titles of nobility, is the same for a nephew and either of his uncles; for example, the nephew has the same rights of inheritance in case of intestacy over the estate of either. In what may be called the socially standardised behaviour of England it is not possible to note any regular distinction made between the maternal and the paternal uncle. Reciprocally the relation of a man to his different kinds of nephews is in general the same. By extension, no significant difference is made between the son of one's mother's brother and the son of one's father's brother.

In Montenegro, on the contrary, to take another European system, the father's brothers constitute one category and the mother's brothers another. These relatives are distinguished by different terms, and so are their respective wives, and the social relations in which a man stands to his two kinds of uncles show marked differences.

There is nothing 'natural' about the English attitude towards uncles. Indeed many peoples in many parts of the world would regard this failure to distinguish between relatives on the father's side and those on the mother's side as u nnatural and even improper. But the terminology is consistent with our whole kinship system.

不同亲属制度的一个共同特征是可以规范一个人由各种亲属组成的不同亲属范畴或种类。一个人与其亲属的社会关系实际地表现形式遵循权利、责任或社会允许的态度和行为模式的规定,并且在一定程度上由亲属所属的范畴或种类确定。可以通过亲属称谓方式建立和识别这些范畴,一个特定称谓用来对应亲属中一个特定范畴,这样不同的范畴就由不同的称谓区分。

下面我们考察一个我们自己制度中的简单例子。相对于一般的亲属制度,我们的亲属制度有鲜明的特点:父亲的兄弟和母亲的兄弟是同一类别的亲属,我们使用同一称谓母亲的兄弟(源于拉丁语 *avunculus*)来指代两者。在英国法律中,除了承袭等级和贵族头衔以外,一个人和舅、叔的法律关系是相同的。例如,在没有遗嘱的情况下,一个人对舅、叔有相同的遗产继承权。在所谓英格兰标准化的社会行为中,看不到对母方舅舅和父方叔叔有任何有规律的区分。相应地,一位男子与外甥和侄子的关系也并无差别。同理,在母亲兄弟的儿子与父亲兄弟的儿子之间也是等同的,不会存在显著的区别。

相反,还存在一种欧洲亲属制度,例如在黑山,人们认为父亲的兄弟和母亲的兄弟是不同的亲属范畴。为了区分这两类范畴,对他们采用不同的称谓,相应地他们妻子的称谓也不相同,而且一个人与叔叔和舅舅的社会关系也存在明显的区别。

事实上,对于大多数民族来说,英国人对叔叔和舅舅的态度在他们看来是不"自然"的。的确,世界上许多地方的民族都认为应该区分父方亲属和母方亲属,这种不加区分的现象是不自然甚至是不规范的。但是,(我们)这种不加区分的称谓形式正是与我

The kinship systems with which we shall be concerned here all have certain forms of what Morgan called the 'classificatory' terminology. What Morgan meant by this term is quite clear from his writings, but his definition is often ignored, perhaps because people do not bother to read him. A nomenclature is classificatory when it uses terms which primarily apply to lineal relatives, such as 'father', to refer also to collateral relatives. Thus by Morgan's definition the English word 'uncle' is not a classificatory term, but the very opposite, since it is used only for collateral relatives. Kroeber (1909) criticises Morgan and rejects his conception of classificatory terminologies, and then proceeds to make use of the same distinction by taking as one of the important features of terminologies the extent to which they separate or distinguish lineal from collateral relatives. It seems to be merely the word 'classificatory' that Kroeber does not like. Doubtless it is not the ideal word; but it has long been in use and no better one has been suggested, though others have been put forward.

I do not propose to deal with all systems in which the classificatory principle is applied in the terminology, but only with a certain widespread type. In these systems the distinction between lineal and collateral relatives is clearly recognised and is of great importance in social life, but it is in certain respects subordinated to another structural principle, which can be spoken of as the principle of the solidarity of the sibling group. A group of siblings is constituted by the sons and daughters of a man and his wife in monogamous societies, or of a man and his wives where there is polygyny, or of a woman and her husbands in polyandrous communities. The bond uniting brothers and sisters together into a social group is everywhere regarded as important, but it is more emphasised in some societies than in others. The solidarity of the sibling group is shown in the first instance in the social relations between its members.

From this principle there is derived a further principle which I

们的整个亲属制度相一致的形式。

我们这里要关注的亲属制度都具有摩尔根所说的“类分式”称谓的某种形式。也许是因为人们不想费力去阅读他的文章，从而经常忽视摩尔根在其著作中对这一术语含义所做的清楚概述。摩尔根认为所谓类分式称谓制度就是指主要用来称呼像“父亲”这样的直系亲属的称谓同时也可用来称呼旁系亲属。根据摩尔根的定义，英语词 uncle 只用于称呼旁系亲属，所以它就不属于类分式称谓。尽管克罗伯(1909)对摩尔根的这种关系进行了评论，并反对他提出的类分称谓概念，然而实际上后来他也开始使用同样的区分方式，即认为亲属称谓的重要特点就在于如何准确区分直系和旁系亲属。克罗伯似乎只是不大喜欢“类分式”这个词而已。毫无疑问，即使这种说法已经使用很长时间，但类分式并不是一个理想的说法，不过至今还没有提出比它更恰当的其他说法。

我不准备对所有使用这个制度的称谓概而论之，将只讨论广为流传的类型。这些制度明确给出了直系和旁系亲属的区别，这种区别在社会生活中起着非常重要的作用。但是，就某些方面来说，它又从属于所谓的同胞群体团结原则。同胞群体的构成在不同的社会制度中有不同的内容，在单偶制社会中是指一个男人及其妻子所生的子女；在一夫多妻制社会中包括一位男子与其众多妻子的子女；而在一妻多夫制社会中包括一个女人和其众多丈夫所生的子女。连结兄弟姐妹成为一个整体的纽带在任何地方都会得到重视，在某些社会中，这种重视程度甚至更高。而同胞群团结也成为社会成员之间社会关系最早的表现形式。

我把从这一原则中推出的另一个原则称之为氏族群团的

shall speak of as that of the unity of the sibling group. This refers not to the internal unity of the group as exhibited in the behaviour of members to one another, but to its unity in relation to a person outside it and connected with it by a specific relation to one of its members.

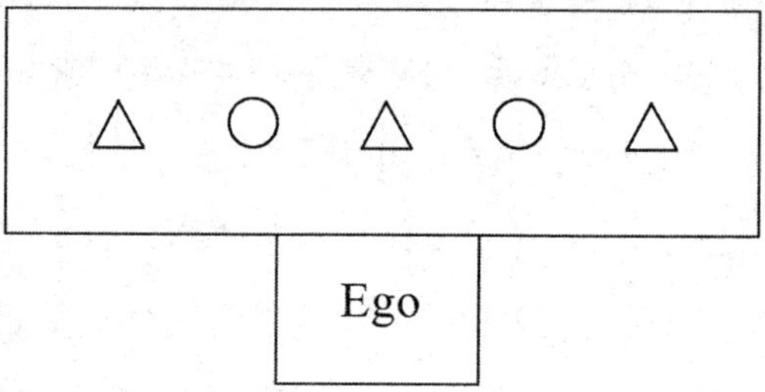

Fig. 4

A diagram may help the discussion. Fig. 4 represents a sibling group of three brothers and two sisters, to which Ego is related by the fact that he is the son of one of the three men. In the kinship systems with which I am now dealing, Ego regards himself as standing in the same general kind of relation to all the members of the group. For him it constitutes a unity. His relation to the brothers and sisters of his father is conceived as being of the same general kind as his relation to his father. Within the group, however, there are two principles of differentiation, sex and seniority, which have to be taken into account. In systems in which seniority is not emphasised a man treats his father's brothers, both older and younger, as being like his father. He refers to them or addresses them by the same term of kinship that he applies to his own father, and in certain important respects his behaviour towards them is similar to his behaviour towards his own father. What defines this behaviour is, of course, different in different systems. Where seniority is strongly emphasised, a man may distinguish between the senior brother and the junior brother either in behaviour alone or both in behaviour and terminology, but there still remains a common element in the pattern of behaviour towards all 'fathers'.

统一。这一次生原则是指那种与群体外部人相关的统一,外部人通过与群体内部某一成员的特殊关系而与群体发生关系。

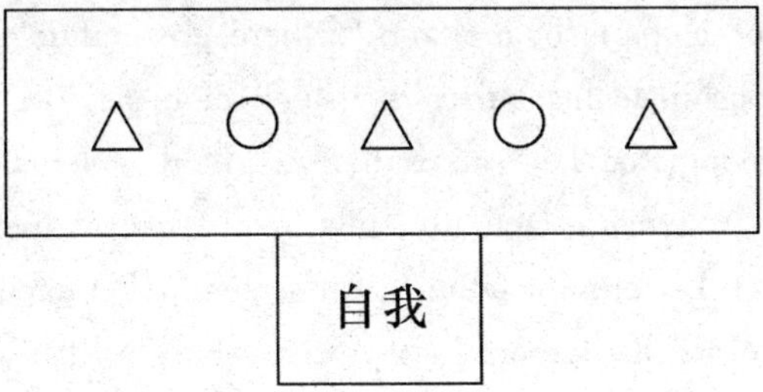

图4

我们的讨论在图表的帮助下会更清晰。图表4代表的同胞群包含三个兄弟和两个姐妹。作为这三位男子中某一位的儿子,自我与这个同胞群发生了关联。就我们现在讨论的亲属制度而言,自我认为自己与这个群体所有成员存在大致相同的关系,这些关系构建了一个统一体。他与其父亲的兄弟姐妹的关系大致等同与他与其父亲的关系。然而,在这个群体内部也存在性别和辈分原则,它们同样应该得到重视。是否强调辈分对人们在社会中的行为会有一定影响,不过在对所有"父辈"的行为方式上,仍旧会存在一个共同的行为模式。在忽视辈分的社会制度中,一位男子无论是对待父亲的哥哥还是弟弟,都会与对待父亲一样,使用称呼父亲的称谓来称呼他们,并在某些重要的方面,对待他们的行为与对待父亲的行为也很相似。当然,这些行为在不同制度中会有不同的表现。在那些辈分得到重视的社会中,父亲的哥哥或弟弟可能会得到区分,要么在行为上有所区别,要么就在行为和称谓上都有区别。

The difference of sex is more important than the difference of seniority, and in this matter there is considerable variation in the systems we are considering. But in quite a considerable number of systems, in different parts of the world, there are certain features of a man's relationship to his father's sister which can be correctly described by saying that he regards her as a sort of female father. In some of these systems he actually calls her 'female father', or some modification of the term for father. If it seems to you impossible that a man should regard his father's sister as a relative of the same kind as his own father, this is because you are thinking, not about social relationships as defined by modes of behaviour, with which we are here concerned, but about the physiological relationship, which is irrelevant.

The same kind of thing happens with the sibling group of the mother. The mother's sisters are treated as relatives of the same kind as the mother, both in terminology and in certain principles of behaviour or attitude. In a number of systems the mother's brother is also treated as a relative of the same kind as the mother. He may be called 'male mother', as in Bantu tribes of Africa and in Tonga in the Pacific. If the principle of seniority is stressed, the mother's brothers may be distinguished according as they are older or younger than the mother.

Those of you who have never had any direct contact with systems of this kind may find it difficult to comprehend how a father's sister can be regarded as a female father or a mother's brother as a male mother. This is due to the difficulty of dissociating the terms 'father' and 'mother' from the connotations they have in our own social system. It is absolutely essential to do this if the kinship systems of other societies are ever to be understood. Perhaps it will help somewhat if I refer to another terminology which seems to us peculiar. Most of the systems with which I am now dealing have a word for 'child', or words for 'son' and 'daughter', which a man applies to his own children

和辈分相比性别的差别更加重要，我们研究的各种制度在这方面有极大的差异。在世界不同地区的众多制度中，一位男子与其父亲姐妹的关系的某种特征如果用一句话正确描述就是，此男子把她们看成女性父亲。事实上，在某些这类亲属制度中，她们确实被称为“女性父亲”，或是对父亲这个词略做些变动。如果一位男子把其父亲的姐妹看做是与其父亲相同的亲属，这种现象对你来说似乎是不可想象的，那是因为你只是从我们并没有关注的生理学关系角度考察这个问题，而没有从社会关系的角度看待它。而这里，我们关注的正是，由行为模式规定的社会关系。

相应地，这种情况也会出现在母亲同胞群中。母亲的姊妹会被看做和母亲一样，这种相似性不仅表现在称谓上，而且也表现在一定的行为原则或态度方面。甚至在许多制度中，母亲的兄弟也被看成是与母亲同类的亲属，在非洲的班图部落和大洋洲的汤加，他甚至被称呼为“男性母亲”。如果这里再加上辈分原则，母亲的兄弟们将会根据他们年龄大于或是小于母亲加以区分。

如果从来没有和这类制度有过直接接触，那么人们也许很难理解父亲的姐妹是如何被认为是女性父亲，或是把母亲的兄弟看做是男性母亲这一问题。这是因为我们拘泥于在我们自己的社会制度中如何定义“父亲”和“母亲”这些称谓，而没有摆脱出来，把它们放到所要考察的社会中去理解。但是，这种摆脱对于理解其他社会的亲属制度来说是绝对必要的。或许，我再提出另一个对我们来说很特别的称谓会有帮助。我现在讨论的大部分制度，对“孩子”的称谓都用一个词来表示，或者用一些词来称呼“儿子”或“女儿”。不管是一个男子称呼自己的孩子和他兄弟的孩子，还是一个女子称呼自己的孩子和她姐妹的孩子，都可以使用它们。但

and his brother's children, and a woman applies to her own children and her sister's children. But in some Australian tribes there are two different words for 'child'. One is used by a man for his own child (or his brother's child) and by a woman for her brother's child; the other is used by a woman for her own or her sister's child, and by a man for his sister's child. I think you will see that this is another way of expressing in the terminology the unity that links brother and sister in relation to the child of either of them. I am called by one term by my father and his brothers and sisters; and by another term by my mother and her sisters and brothers.

The same principle, that of the unity of the sibling group, is applied to other sibling groups. Thus the father's father's brother is regarded as belonging to the same category as the father's father, with the result that his son is a somewhat more distant relative of the same kind as the father and his brothers. By means of such extension of the basic principle, a very large number of collateral relatives of different degrees of distance can be brought under a limited number of categories. A man may have many, even hundreds, of relatives whom he thus classifies as 'fathers', 'brothers', 'mother's brothers' and so on. But there are different ways in which this extension of the basic classificatory principle can be applied, so that there result systems of different types. What is common to them all is that they make some use of this structural principle which I have briefly illustrated.

What I am trying to show you is that the classificatory terminology is a method of providing a wide-range kinship organisation, by making use of the unity of the sibling group in order to establish a few categories of relationship under which a very large number of near and distant relatives can be included. For all the relatives who are denoted by one term, there is normally some element of attitude or behaviour that is regarded as appropriate to them and not to others. But within a category there may be and always are important distinctions. There is, first, the very important distinction between one's own father and his brother. There are distinctions within the category between nearer and more distant relatives. There is sometimes an im portant distinction between relatives of a certain category who belong to other clans.

是,在澳洲一些部落中,称呼"孩子"却需要两个词,其中一个是用于男人称呼自己的孩子(或自己兄弟的孩子),以及用于女人称呼自己兄弟的孩子;另一个用于女人称呼自己的或其姐妹的孩子,以及用于男人称呼自己姐妹的孩子。上述表述就是所谓在称谓中的表达统一性的另一种方式,这种统一性通过顾及各自的子女从而把兄弟和姐妹联系起来。父亲及其兄弟姐妹们对我的称呼是一致的;而母亲及其兄弟姐妹们则用另一种称谓来称呼我。

这种同胞群一致原则同样也可以扩展到其他同胞群中。因而,祖父的兄弟和祖父同属一类范畴。因此可以推出,祖父兄弟的儿子与父亲及父亲的兄弟同属一类亲属,只是关系稍微有点远。大量的、但疏远程度不同的旁系亲属就可以在这个基本原则及其扩展形式之下,被归结到数个有限范畴内。按这种方式一位男子可以把他拥有的可能达上百位的亲属分为"父亲"、"兄弟"、"母亲的兄弟"等等不同范畴。但是,由于存在很多种这类基本原则的扩展方式,所以不同的扩展方式也就对应了不同类型的制度。它们的共同之处就是,都多少运用了我简述的结构原则。

我试图要向你们表明,作为一种建立大范围亲属组织结构的方法,类分式称谓通过采用同胞群一致原则建立的范畴,可以将大量的远近亲属包括进来。对于那些被一种称谓指代的所有亲属们来说,他们之间通常总会存在一些共同的、不能适用于别人的态度或行为要素。但是,一些重要的区分总是会存在的,即使是在同一范畴之内。至少,一个人的父亲和他父亲的兄弟之间就存在着很重要的区分。区分也可以产生在同一范畴的近亲和远亲之间;也可以产生在某一亲属范畴中那些属于其他氏族的亲属之

There are other distinctions that are made in different particular systems. Thus the categories represented by the terminology never give us anything more than the skeleton of the real ordering of relatives in the social life. But in every system that I have been able to study they do give us this skeleton.

If this thesis is true, if this is what the classificatory terminology actually is in the tribes in which it exists, it is obvious that Morgan's whole theory is entirely ungrounded. The classificatory system, as thus interpreted, depends upon the recognition of the strong social ties that unite brothers and sisters of the same elementary family, and the utilisation of this tie to build up a complex orderly arrangement of social relations amongst kin. It could not come into existence except in a society based on the elementary family. Nowhere in the world are the ties between a man and his own children or between children of one father stronger than in Australian tribes, which, as you know, present an extreme example of the classificatory terminology.

The internal solidarity of the sibling group, and its unity in relation to persons connected with it, appear in a great number of different forms in different societies. I cannot make any attempt to deal with these, but for the sake of the later argument I will point out that it is in the light of this structural principle that we must interpret the customs of sororal polygyny (marriage with two or more sisters), the sororate (marriage with the deceased wife's sister), adelphic polyandry (marriage of a woman with two or more brothers, by far the commonest form of polyandry), and the levirate (marriage with the brother's widow). Sapir, using the method of conjectural history, has suggested that the classificatory terminology may be the result of the customs of the levirate and sororate. That the two things are connected is, I think, clear, but for the supposed causal connection there is no evidence whatever. Their real connection is that they are different ways of applying or using the principle of the unity of the sibling group, and they may therefore exist together or separately.

间。另外不同的制度也还会对应其他种不同的区分。因此,由称谓所代表的范畴只能告诉我们社会生活中的实际亲属关系框架内的事。而我能研究的每一个制度的确都给我提供了这种框架。

如果上述论题成立的话,这种类分式称谓在各个部落中存在的情况果真如此,那么,很明显,摩尔根的整套理论就是没有根据的。根据上述这种解释,类分式称谓制度不仅取决于对那种联结同一基本家庭中的兄弟姐妹的强有力的社会纽带的认可,而且取决于如何利用这种纽带在亲属中建立一种复杂有序的社会关系。因此可以看出,这种类分式称谓只可能产生于以基本家庭为基础的社会中。对于父子关系和同父同胞关系来说,没有比在澳大利亚部落中发现的这种关系更牢固的了。正如你们了解的那样,澳大利亚部落在类分式称谓方面为我们提供了一个极端例证。

对应于不同的社会制度,同胞群的内部团结原则以及将个人联结起来的统一性会有不同的表现形式。在此我不能对其加以讨论,但为了以后的论述,我要指出,解释以下这些婚姻习俗,根据的正是这一结构原则。这些婚姻包括:姊妹共夫婚(两个或两个以上姊妹嫁给一个男子)、妻姊妹婚(与已故妻子的姊妹结婚)、兄弟共妻的一妻多夫婚(一个女子与两个或两个以上的兄弟结婚,这是一妻多夫制的最普遍形式)、夫兄弟婚(与兄弟的寡妻结婚)。萨皮尔利用历史推测的方法,得出是夫兄弟婚和妻姐妹婚习俗导致了类分式称谓产生的结论。我想,对这种因果关系的假设没有任何根据,虽然两者之间显然是有关联的。它们之间的真正关联是:它们是使用或体现同胞群一致原则的不同方式,因而,既可以共同存在,也可以分开存在。

An organisation into clans or moieties is also based on the principle of the solidarity and unity of the sibling group in combination with other principles. Tylor suggested a connection between exogamous clans and the classificatory terminology. Rivers put this in terms of conjectural history, and argued that the classificatory terminology must have had its origin in the organisation of society into exogamous moieties.

II

It is necessary, for our analysis, to consider briefly another aspect of the structure of kinship systems, namely the division into generations. The distinction of generation has its basis in the elementary family, in the relation of parents and children. A certain generalising tendency is discoverable in many kinship systems in the behaviour of relatives of different generations. Thus we find very frequently that a person is expected to adopt an attitude of more or less marked respect towards all his relatives of the first ascending generation. There are restraints on behaviour which maintain a certain distance or prevent too close an intimacy. There is, in fact, a generalised relation of ascendancy and subordination between the two generations. This is usually accompanied by a relation of friendly equality between a person and his relatives of the second ascending generation. The nomenclature for grandparents and grandchildren is of significance in this connection. In some classificatory systems, such as those of Australian tribes, the grandparents on the father's side are distinguished, in terminology and in behaviour, from those on the mother's side. But in many classificatory systems the generalising tendency results in all relatives of the generation being classed together as 'grandfathers' and 'grandmothers'.

We may note in passing that in classificatory terminologies of what Morgan called the Malayan type and Rivers the Hawaiian type, this generalising process is applied to other generations, so that all relatives of the parents' generation may be called 'father' and 'mother' and all those of one's own generation may be called 'brother' and 'sister'.

同胞群的团结和一致原则也是氏族或半偶族组织发展和演变的基础,当然也存在其他的原则基础。泰勒指出,某种关联存在于外婚制氏族和类分式称谓之间,里弗斯根据历史推测的方法,认为类分式称谓必定起源于社会组织向外婚制半偶族社会发展的过程中。

Ⅱ

辈分划分作为亲属制度结构的另一方面,为了我们的分析目的,有必要进行简要的考察。辈分划分源于基本家庭中父母与孩子之间的关系。不同辈分亲属之间的某种一般性行为模式存在于许多亲属制度中。因而,我们经常可以发现一个人会对其父辈的所有亲属采取或多或少的尊敬态度。为保持一定的距离或防止过于亲密,对他们之间的行为也会有一定的限制。事实上,在父与子两代人之间存在一种一般化的主导与从属关系。但与这种主导与从属关系伴随的是此人与其祖辈亲属之间的友好平等关系。在这种关系中,祖孙两辈之间的称谓就会具有极其重要的含义。例如在某些澳大利亚部落中,根据其部落的类分式称谓制度,对待父方的祖父母与母方的祖父母在称谓及行为方面都是有区别的。但是,更一般化的趋势存在于大多数的类分式称谓制度中,即把那一辈的所有亲属不加区分的称为“祖父”或“祖母”。

这里顺便提一下,这种一般化的称谓形式也可以被应用到其他的辈分中,这种情况出现在摩尔根说的马来型和里弗斯说的夏威夷型的分类称谓中,因此在那里,所有父辈亲属可以被称呼为“父亲”和“母亲”,而所有与自己同辈的亲属被称呼为“兄弟”和“姐妹”。

There are many kinship systems in various parts of the world that exhibit a structural principle which I shall speak of as the combination of alternate generations. This means that relatives of the grandfather's generation are thought of as combined with those of one's own generation over against the relatives of the parents' generation. The extreme development of this principle is to be seen in Australian tribes. I shall refer to this later.

While some systems emphasise the distinction of generations in their terminology or in their social structure, there are also systems in which relatives of two or more generations are included in a single category. So far as I have been able to make a comparative study, the various instances of this seem to fall into four classes.

In one class of instances the term of relationship does not carry a connotation referring to any particular generation and is used to mark off a sort of marginal region between non-relatives and those close relatives towards whom specific duties and over whom specific rights are recognised. The application of the term generally only implies that since the other person is recognised as a relative he or she must be treated with a certain general attitude of friendliness and not as a stranger. A good example is provided by the terms *ol-le-sotwa* and *en-e-sotwa* in Masai. I would include the English word 'cousin' in this class.

A second class of instances includes those in which there is conflict or inconsistency between the required attitude towards a particular relative and the required general attitude towards the generation to which he belongs. Thus in some tribes in South-East Africa there is conflict between the general rule that relatives of the first ascending generation are to be treated with marked respect and the custom of privileged disrespect towards the mother's brother. This is resolved by placing the mother's brother in the second ascending generation and calling him 'grandfather'. An opposite example is found in the Masai. A man is on terms of familiarity with all his relatives of the second descending generation, who are his 'grandchildren'. But it is felt that the relation between a man and the wife of his son's son should be one not of familiarity but of marked reserve. The inconsistency

世界不同地区的许多亲属制度都表现出一种结构原则，我将其称呼为“隔代联合体的结构原则”。意思是说，一个人的祖辈一代的亲属可以跨过其父辈一代人而与此人的同辈亲属联结到一起。在澳大利亚部落中可以看到这一原则的充分展现。我将在下面再对此进行讨论。

某些亲属制度特别看重辈分在称谓和它们的社会结构方面的区别，但仍有一些亲属制度不加区分地把两代或两代以上的亲属包含在一个范畴内。通过我能做的对比性研究，我将它们分为四种类型。

第一种，亲属称谓并不具有特指某一辈分的含义。而只是作为一种标志用来区分非亲属和那些给予特定责任和权利的近亲。运用亲属称谓称呼某人一般暗含着：既然对方被看做是一位亲属，那么对待他或她就不能像对待陌生人那样，态度应该是友好的。在马赛人称谓中的 *ol-le-sotwa* 和 *en-e-sotwa* 为我们提供一个很好的例证。我认为英语中“cousin”一词也属于这一种类型。

第二种，是指态度上的区别。因为在对待某一特定亲属和他同辈人时，使用的行为方式应该有所区别，对待他们二者所持有的态度存在冲突或不一致。比如，在东南非洲的一些部落中，就存在对父辈亲属要给予明显尊重的一般原则和对母亲的兄弟可以不尊重习俗之间的冲突。通过把母亲的兄弟的地位放到祖父辈一代亲属中并称呼为“祖父”，可以使这一冲突得到解决。但在马赛人中却存在与此相反的例证。一位男子与其孙辈的所有亲属有亲昵关系，这些亲属是他的“孙子”。但是一般认为他与其“孙子”的妻子不可以有亲昵关系，要有明显的节制。这种不一致

is resolved by a sort of legal fiction by which she is moved out of her generation and is called 'son's wife'.

A third class of instances are those resulting from the structural principle, already mentioned, whereby alternate generations are combined. Thus the father's father may be called 'older brother' and treated as such, and the son's son may be called 'younger brother'. Or a man and his son's son may be both included in a single category of relationship. There are many illustrations of this in Australian tribes and some elsewhere. An example from the Hopi will be given later.

The fourth class of instances includes the systems of Choctaw and Omaha type and also certain others, and in these the distinction between generations is set aside in favour of another principle, that of the unity of the lineage group.

Since the word lineage is often loosely used, I must explain what I mean by it. A patrilineal or agnatic lineage consists of a man and all his descendants through males for a determinate number of generations. Thus a minimal lineage includes three generations, and we can have lineages of four, five or n generations. A matrilineal lineage consists of a woman and all her descendants through females for a determinate number of generations. A lineage group consists of all the members of a lineage who are alive at a particular time. A clan, as I shall use the term here, is a group which, though not actually or demonstrably (by genealogies) a lineage, is regarded as being in some ways similar to a lineage. It normally consists of a number of actual lineages. Lineages, both patrilineal and matrilineal, exist implicitly in any kinship system, but it is only in some systems that the solidarity of the lineage group is animportant feature in the social structure.

Where lineage groups are important we can speak of the solidarity of the group, which shows itself in the first instance in the internal relations between the members. By the principle of the unity of the lineage group I mean that for a person who does not belong to the lineage but is connected with it through some important bond of kinship or

性通过一种习惯做法，即把她从她那一代人脱离出来，并称为“儿媳”的方式解决，虽然她实际上并不是“儿媳”。

第三种，是由这种结构原则（上面已提到过）引起的，把隔代亲属联为一体的现象。因而，也许会称父亲的父亲为“大哥”，并相应地对待他；同理，儿子的儿子也许会被叫作“小弟”。或者，一位男子与其孙子辈亲属会被归为同一个关系范畴。这方面的例证有很多，例如在澳大利亚一些部落中和世界上其他地方都可以发现。在下面，我会就这种情况向你们谈论一下霍皮人的例子。

第四种，包括乔克托型、奥马哈型和其他一些类型的亲属制度。它们采用的是世系群一致原则，而不考虑辈分之间的区分。

由于“世系群”一词的用法通常很不严谨，因此，我必须解释一下我使用该词的意思。一个父系或男系世系群是由一位男子及其所有的依男性计算的若干代子孙组成。最小的世系群至少要包括三代人，当然，我们的世系群可以由四代人、五代人或若干代人构成。母系氏族群是由一位女子及其所有的依女性计算的若干代后代组成。不论依父方世系还是母方世系计算，世系中所有在世的成员都会被包括在某一特定时期世系群中。正如我在此文中的用法，氏族尽管实际上不是或不能根据家谱证明是一个世系群，但在某些方面与世系群相似。氏族通常是由好几个事实上的世系群构成。所有的亲属制度中都会有这些世系群（包括父系的和母系的）的存在，但世系群的团结只在某些制度中才会成为社会结构的重要特征。

讨论群体团结只有在那些世系群起重要作用的社会中才有意义。这种团结，首先表现在其成员的内部关系中。我认为，世系群一致原则是指，由于某种重要的亲属关系或婚姻的纽带，使

by marriage, its members constitute a single category, with a distinction within the category between males and females, and possibly other distinctions also. When this principle is applied in the terminology a person connected with a lineage from outside applies to its members, of one sex, through at least three generations, the same term of relationship. In its extreme development, as applied to the clan, a person connected with a clan in a certain way applies a single term of relationship to all members of the clan. An example will be given later.

The Omaha type of terminology may be illustrated by the system of the Fox Indians, which has been carefully studied by Dr. Sol Tax (1937). The features of the system that are relevant to the argument are illustrated in the accompanying diagrams (Figs. 5-9).①

---

① In these diagrams △ represents a male person and ○ a female. The sign = connects a man and his wife and the lines descending from it indicate their children. The letters (capitals for males and lower case for females) stand for the kinship terms of a classificatory system, in which the same term is applied to a number of relatives. CF stands for the term used in referring to a grandfather, and similarly gm for grandmother; the others are F, father, m, mother, ms, mother's sister, fs, father's sister, MB, mother's brother, FL, father-in-law, ml, mother-in-law, B, brother, sis, sister, BL, brother-in-law, sl, sister-in-law, S, son, d, daughter, N, nephew (strictly speaking sister's son) n, niece (sister's daughter of a male) GC or gc, grandchild.

一个不属于某一世系群的人与该世系群联结到一起,而此人会将该世系群的成员看做构成了一个单独的范畴,在此范畴内,存在男女之间的区别或是其他的区别。当此原则被运用到称谓上,这个来自世系群外部并与此世系群有关联的人,对该世系群内至少三代以上的同性成员,会只使用一种亲属称谓。这一与世系群相关的原则发展到可被应用于氏族时,与某个氏族相关联的人会用一种关系称谓来称呼氏族中所有的成员。稍后,我会给出一个例证。

奥马哈型称谓可以通过福克斯印第安人的制度来解释。对此,索尔·泰克斯博士(1937)曾经做过仔细的研究。通过附图可以解释这个制度的一些特征(见图5-9)。[1]

① 在这些附图中,"△"代表男性"○"代表女性。"="表示夫妻关系,它向下的线条代表他们的子女。字母(大写的为男性,小写的为女性)代表类分制度的亲属称谓,同一称谓可以表示多个亲属。GF代表对祖父的称谓,gm代表对祖母的称谓;其他字母代表的称谓是:F为父亲,m为母亲,ms为母亲的姐妹,fs为父亲的姐妹,MB为母亲的兄弟,FL为岳父,ml为岳母,B为兄弟,sis为姐妹,BL为联姻兄弟,al为联姻姐妹,S为儿子,d为女儿,N为侄或外甥,严格地讲是指姐妹的儿子,即外甥,n为外甥女,GC或gc为孙儿孙女。

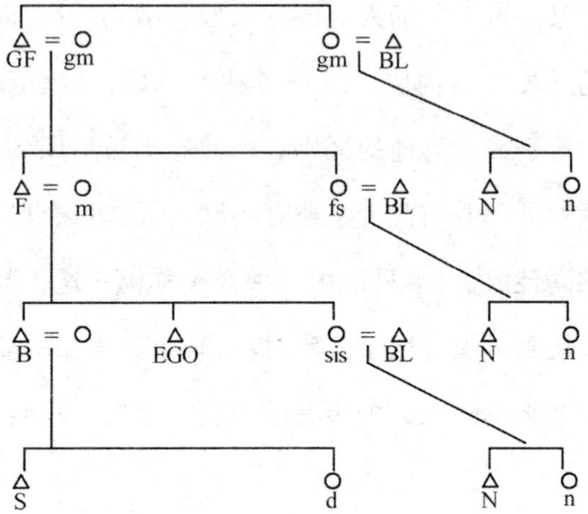

FIG. 5—Fox

Father's Lineage

In his own patrilineal lineage a man distinguishes his relatives according to generation as 'grandfather' (GF), 'father' (F), 'older or younger brother' (B), 'son' (S), 'grandmother' (gm), 'father's sister' (fs), 'sister' (sis), and 'daughter' (d). I would draw your attention to the fact that he applies a single term, 'brother-in-law' (BL), irrespective of generation, to the husbands of the women of the lineage through three generations (his own and the two ascending generations), and that he calls the children of all these women by the same terms, 'nephew' (N) and 'niece' (n). Thus the women of Ego's own lineage of these generations constitute a sort of group, and Ego regards himself as standing in the same relationship to the children and husbands of all of them, although these persons belong to a number of different lineages.

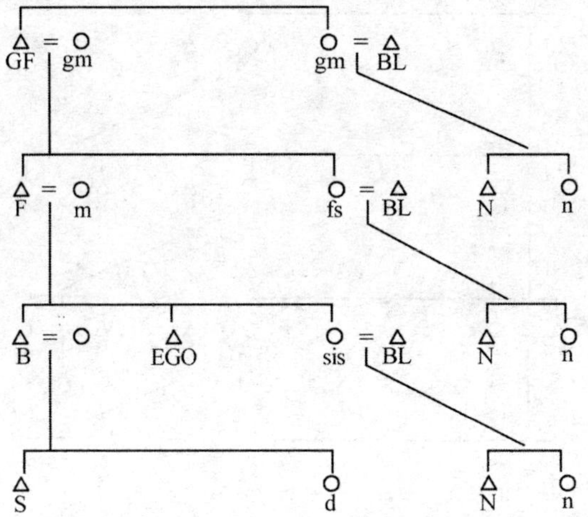

图 5　福克斯

（父亲的世系群）

在自己的父方世系群中(图 5),一个男子按照辈分划分他的亲属。这些辈分包括:"祖父"(GF)、"父亲"(F)、"兄弟"(B)、"儿子"(S)、"祖父"(gm)、"父亲的姐妹"(fs)、"姐妹"(sis)、"女儿"(d)。在此请注意以下事实:对世系群中三代(他这一代和上溯两代)所有女人的丈夫,不管辈分高低都用"联姻兄弟"(BL)称呼;对这些女人的子女都用"外甥"(N)和"外甥女"(n)称呼。自我世系群中的所有女人形成了一种群体;尽管这些女人的丈夫和孩子可能分属不同的世系群,但自我认为与他们的关系相同。

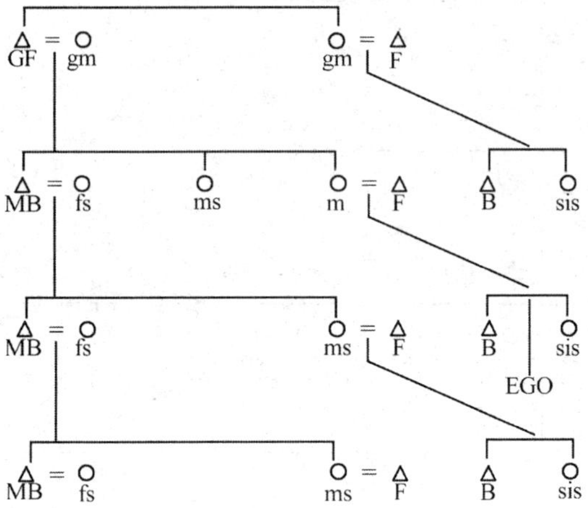

FIG. 6—Fox

Mother's Lineage

Turning to the mother's patrilineal lineage, it can be seen that a man calls his mother's father 'grandfather', but calls all the males of the lineage in the three succeeding generations 'mother's brother' (MB). Similarly he calls the women of these three generations, except his own mother, by a term translated as 'mother's sister' (ms). He applies the term 'father' (F) to the husbands of all the women of the lineage through four generations (including the husband of the mother's father's sister) and the children of all these women are his 'brothers' and 'sisters'. He is the son of one particular woman of a unified group, and the sons of the other women of the group are therefore his 'brothers'.

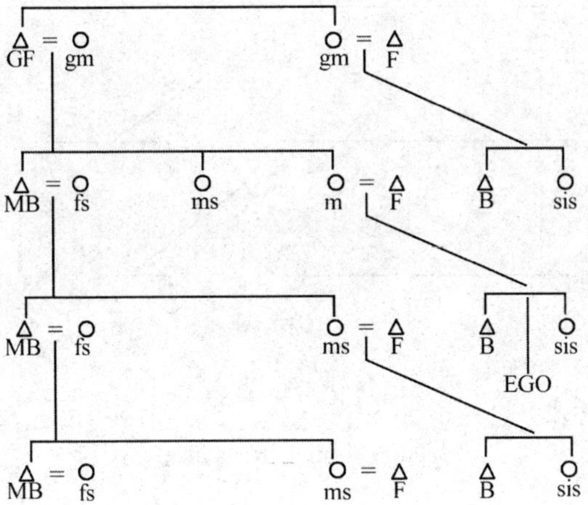

图六　福克斯

（母亲的世系群）

让我们转向母亲的父系世系群的话题，大家可以看到，一位男子将其母亲的父亲称为“祖父”，但他称呼该世系群以后三代的所有男性为“母亲的兄弟”（MB）。同样，他也称除母亲的以外的所有女人为“母亲的姐妹”（ms）。对他的世系群中四代所有女人（包括母亲的父亲的姐妹）的丈夫，他都使用“父亲”（F）这同一个称谓来称呼，并且，他将所有这些女人的孩子都称作“兄弟”和“姐妹”。因为他是一个统一群体内某个女人的儿子，所以此群体内其他女人所生的儿子就是他的“兄弟”。

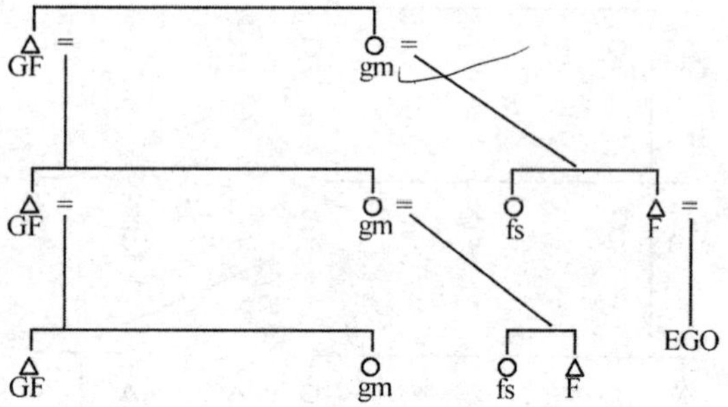

FIG. 7—Fox

Father's Mother's Lineage

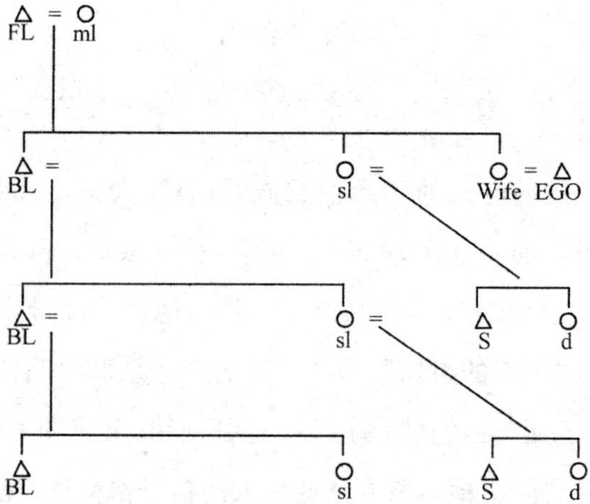

FIG. 8—Fox

Wife's Lineage

In his father's mother's lineage Ego calls all the men and women throughout three generations 'grandfather' and 'grandmother'. The children of these 'grandmothers' are all his 'fathers' and 'father's sisters', irrespective of generation. In his mother's mother's lineage he also calls all the males 'grandfather' and the females grandmother', but I have not thought it necessary to include a figure to show this.

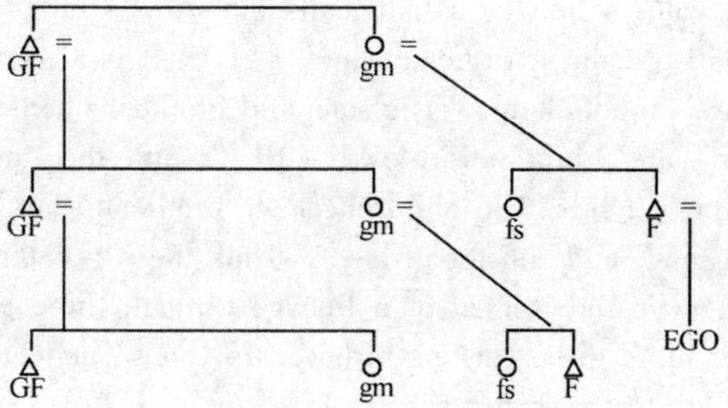

图 7　福克斯

（父亲的母亲的世系群）

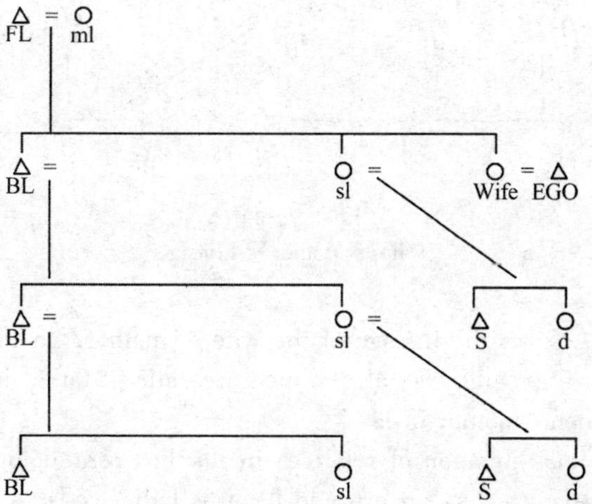

图 8　福克斯

（妻子的世系群）

在父亲的母亲世系群中，自我用“祖父”和“祖母”称谓来称呼三代人中所有的男人和女人。不论辈分高低，所有这些“祖母”的孩子们都称作他的“父亲”和“父亲的姐妹”。在他母亲的母亲的世系群中，他称呼所有的男性为“祖父”，所有的女姓为“祖母”，图示同前，所以没有必要再用图来说明。

In his wife's lineage a man calls his wife's father by a term which we will translate 'father-in-law' (FL). It is a modification of the word for 'grandfather'.[①] The sons and brother's sons of the 'fathers-in-law' are 'brothers-in-law' (BL), and the daughters are 'sisters-in-law' (sl). The children of a 'brother-in-law' are again 'brother-in-law' and 'sister-in-law'. Thus these two terms are applied to the men and women of a lineage through three generations. The children of all these 'sisters-in-law' are 'sons' and 'daughters'.

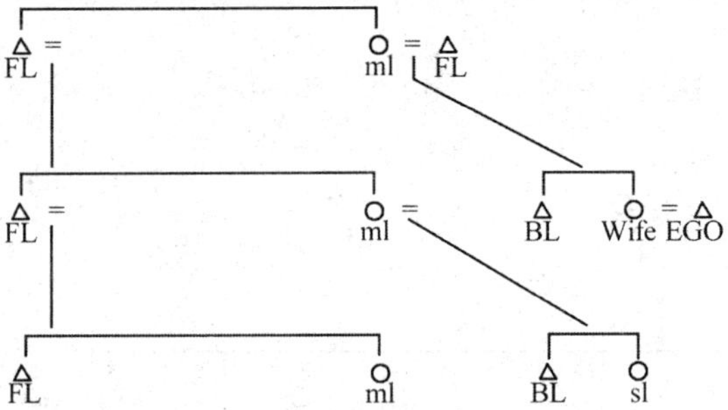

FIG. 9—Fox
Wife's Mother's Lineage

Fig. 9 shows the lineage of the wife's mother. In this lineage, through three generations, all the men are called 'father-in-law' and all the women 'mother-in-law'.

Is the classification of relatives in the Fox terminology simply a matter of language, as some would have us believe? Dr. Tax's observations (1937) enable us to affirm that it is not. He writes:

The kinship terminology is applied to all known relatives (even in some cases where the genealogical relationship is not traceable) so that the entire tribe is divided into a small number of types of relationship pairs. Each of these types carries with it a more or less distinct traditional pattern of behaviour. Generally speaking,

① The Fox terms for father-in-law and mother-in-law are modificatioms of the terns for grandfather and grandmother. In the Omaha tribe the terms for grandparents, without modification, are applied to the parents-in-law and to those who are called 'father-in-law' and 'mother-in-law' in the Fox tribe.

在他妻子的世系群中(图8),我们把他称呼妻子父亲的称谓翻译为"岳父"(FL),它是"祖父"一词的变体。① 称呼和自己同代的男子,即"岳父"及其兄弟的儿子为"联姻兄弟"(BL),而将同代的女子,即他们的女儿称作"联姻姐妹"(sl)。但是,下一代的子女,即"联姻兄弟"的子女又被称作"联姻兄弟"和"联姻姐妹"。就这样整个这个世系群中三代的男人和女人都可以用"联姻兄弟"和"联姻姐妹"这两个词来称呼。不过,所有这些"联姻姐妹"的子女都被称作"儿子"和"女儿"。

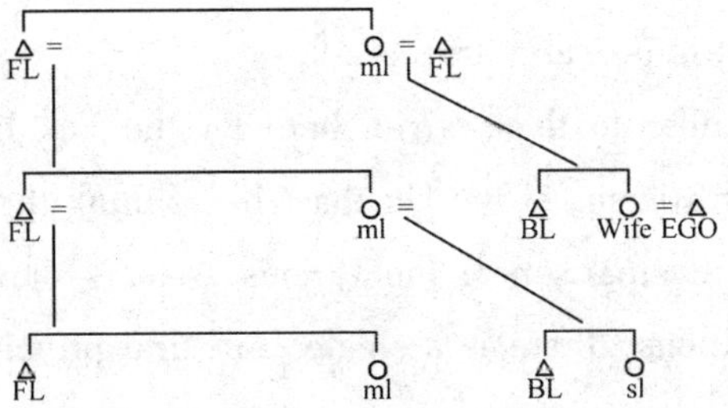

图9　福克斯

(妻子母亲的世系群)

图9展示给我们的是妻子母亲的世系群。在这个世系群中,对三代中所有的男性称呼为"岳父",而将所有女人称作"岳母"。

福克斯关于亲属分类的称谓是否单纯是个语言问题,正如一些人要我们相信的那样?泰克斯博士(1937)的考察向我们证实,并不仅仅是语言的问题。他写道:

由于亲属称谓应用的范围包括所有已知的有时甚至是关系

① 在福克斯的称谓中对岳父和岳母的称谓分别来自对祖父和祖母称谓的变体。在奥马哈部落中,称呼祖父母的称谓可以直接用来称呼岳父母,同时也用来称呼福克斯部落中那些称谓是"岳父"和"岳母"的人。

the behaviour of close relatives follows the pattern in its greatest intensity, that of father relatives in lesser degree; but there are numerous cases where, for some reason, a pair of close relative do not behave towards each other at all as they should'.

Dr. Tax goes on to define the patterns of behaviour for the various types of relationship. Thus the classification of relatives into categories, carried out by means of the nomenclature, or therein expressed, appears also in the regulation of social behaviour. There is good evidence that this is true of other systems of the Omaha type, and, contrary to Kroeber's thesis, we may justifiably accept the hypothesis that it is probably true of all.

Charts similar to those given here for the Fox Indians can be made for other systems of the Omaha type. I think that a careful examination and comparison of the various systems shows that, while there are variations, there is a single structural principle underlying both the terminology and the associated social structure. A lineage of there (or sometimes more) generations is regarded as a unity. A person is related to certain lineages at particular points: in the Fox tribe to the lineages of his mother, his father's mother, his mother's mother, his wife, and his wife's mother. In each instance he regards himself as related to the succeeding generations of the lineage in the same way as he is related to the generation with which he is actually connected. Thus all the men of his mother's lineage are his 'mother's brothers', those of his 'grand mother's lineage his 'grandfathers', and those of his wife's lineage are his 'brothers-in-law'.

This structural principle of the unity of the patrilineal lineage is not a hypothetical cause of the terminology. It is a principle that is directly discoverable by comparative analysis of systems of this type; or, in other words, it is an immediate abstraction from observed facts.

不能追溯的亲属,所以整个部落被划分为少数几类关系对儿。它们或多或少都具有自己独特的传统行为模式。一般的,近亲间的相互行为最接近这种模式,远亲则次之;但仍有许多种情况显示,由于某种原因,一对近亲并不按照他们应该遵循的模式对待对方。

泰克斯博士又继续定义了各种亲属关系之间的行为模式。不同的亲属范畴的划分是称谓划分的结果和体现,而且在社会行为的规范中也有所表现。在奥马哈型的其他制度中,有充足的证据可以说明此种情况。与克罗伯的论点相反,我们可以毋庸置疑地接受这一假设,认为在所有的制度中都有可能存在这种情况。

在这里制作了图表以说明福克斯印第安人的世系群,同样,也可以制作图表来说明奥马哈型的其他制度。我认为,通过制度间的对比研究,在对各种制度仔细研究和对比后可以发现,只要在他们之间出现差异,就可以肯定,在称谓和与之相联系的社会结构背后有一个结构原则在起作用。三代人(有时更多)的世系群被看做是一个整体。一个人可以通过不同方式和各种世系群相联系。在福克斯部落里,此人可以与母亲的世系群、父亲的母亲的世系群、母亲的母亲的世系群、妻子的世系群以及妻子的母亲的世系群相联系。他可以认为自己与世系中同代人的关系也可以扩展到与世系中其他各代人之间。因此,按称谓原则,他将母亲世系群中的所有男性看做“母亲的兄弟”,而他“祖母”世系群中的所有男性成了他的“祖父”,他妻子世系群的男性则成了他的“联姻兄弟”。

父系世系群的统一结构原则不是称谓制度的一个假设性原因,而是通过对这类制度的对比分析得出的结论性原则;也就是说,这种原则是对实际情况考察的理论抽象。

Let us now examine a society in which the principle of the unity of the lineage group is applied to matrilineal lineages. For this I select the system of the Hopi Indians, which has been analysed in a masterly manner by Dr. Fred Eggan (1933) in a Ph. D. thesis which has, unfortunately, not yet been published. 1① The most significant features of the system are illustrated in the accompanying figures.

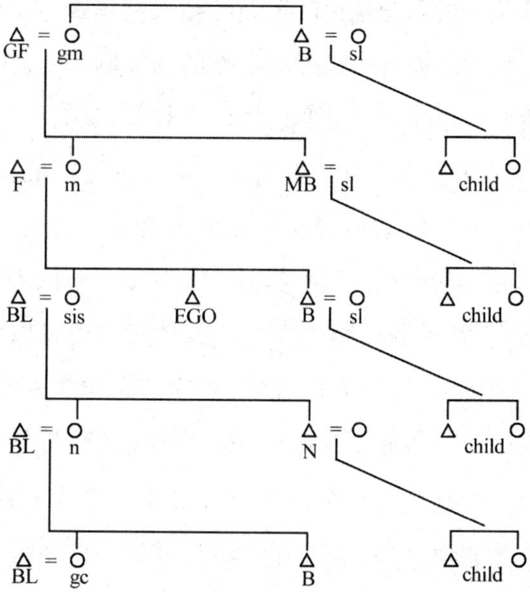

FIG. 10—HOPI

Mother's Lineage

A man's own lineage is, of course, that of his mother. He distinguishes the women of his lineage by generation as 'grandmother' (gm), 'mother' (m), 'sister' (sis), 'niece' (n), and 'grandchild' (gc). Amongst the men of his lineage he distinguishes his 'mother's brothers' (MB), 'brothers' (B) and 'nephews' (N).

① The thesis, in a revised form, has now been published. Eggan: *Social Organisation of the Western Pueblos*. The University of Chicago Press, 1950.

现在让我们研究将世系群一致原则应用到母系世系群社会的情况。为此,我选择了霍皮印第安人的制度。弗雷德·伊根博士(1933)在博士论文中曾详细地分析过这一制度,不过很遗憾,这篇论文没有发表。① 在图 10 中可以看出该制度的一些最重要的特征。

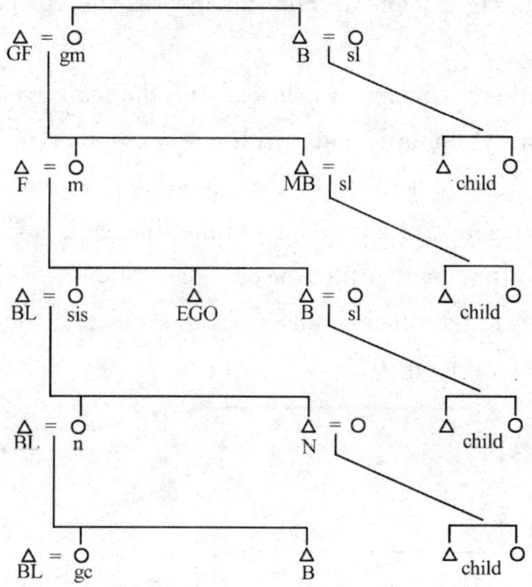

图 10　霍皮

(母亲的世系群)

当然,在图中可以看出,他母亲的世系群也就是这个男子自己的世系群。对这个世系群之内的妇女是通过划分不同辈分的方式加以区分的,他称呼她们为:"祖母"(gm)、"母亲"(m)、"姐妹"(sis)、"甥女"(n)以及"孙女"(gc)等。同样,他也用这种方式

---

① 这篇论文修改后已经发表。伊根:《西普埃波洛人的社会组织》,芝加哥大学出版社,1950 年版。

But he includes his mother's mother's brother and his sister's daughter's son in the same category as his brothers. The structural principle exhibited here is that already referred to as the combination of alternate generations. It should be noted that a man includes the children of all men of his own lineage, irrespective of generation, in the same category as his own children. Fig. 10 should be carefully compared with Fig. 5, for the Fox Indians, as the comparison is illuminating.

In his father's lineage a man calls all the male members through five generations 'father' and, with the exception of his father's mother (his 'grandmother'), he calls all the women 'father's sister'. The husband of any woman of the lineage is a 'grandfather', and the wife of any man of the lineage is a 'mother'. The children of his 'fathers' are 'brothers' and 'sisters'. Fig. 11 should be carefully compared with Fig. 6.

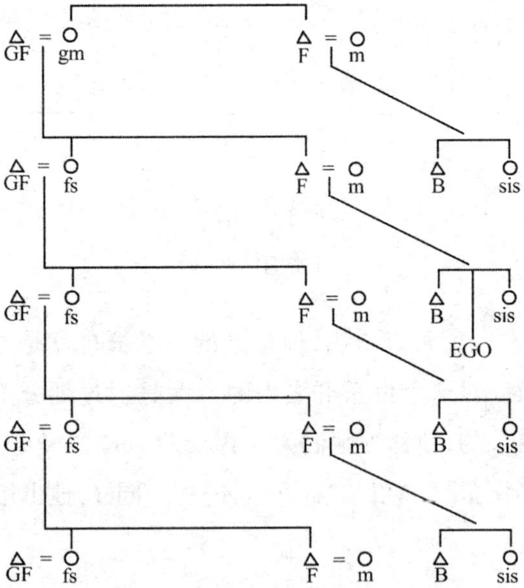

FIG. 11 —HOPI
Father's Lineage

区分这个世系群中的男人，称呼他们为“母亲的兄弟”(MB)、“兄弟”(B)、和“外甥”(N)。但是，我们在图中也发现，他的母亲的母亲的兄弟、他自己姐妹的女儿的儿子以及他的兄弟同归于一个范畴。在这里所表现出的结构原则是我们已经谈到过的隔代合并原则。此处还应该注意到，这个世系群中所有男人的孩子不论辈分，都被他划归为自己的孩子这类范畴中。为了更好地理解这一原则，可以把图10和描述福克斯印第安人的图5进行比较。

从图示可以看出，在他父亲的世系群中，这五代人中所有男子都被称为“父亲”，所有的女人为“父亲的姐妹”，但是他称呼他父亲的母亲为“祖母”。世系群中所有女人的丈夫都是他的“祖父”，所有男人的妻子都是他的“母亲”。于是，所有他称呼为“父亲”的人所生的孩子都是他的“兄弟”和“姐妹”。让我们把图11和图6进行仔细的比较是有益的。

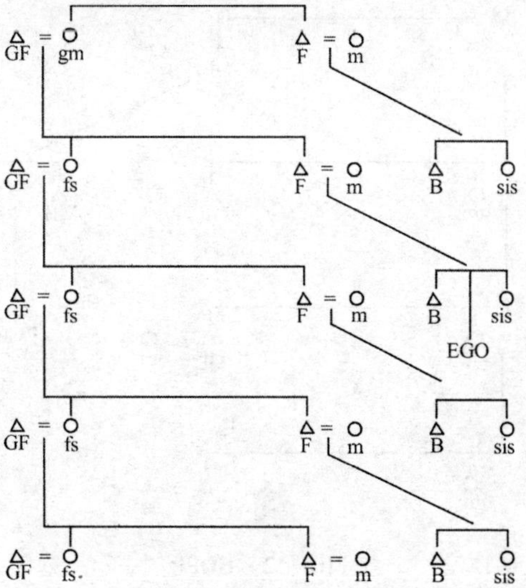

图11　霍皮

(父亲的世系群)

In his mother's father's lineage a man calls all the men and women through four generations 'grandfather' and 'grand mother'.

The Hopi do not regard a man as related to his father's father's lineage as a whole, and the principle is therefore not applied to it. He does call his own father's father 'grandfather'.

Dr. Eggan has shown that for the Hopi this classification of relatives into categories is not simply a matter of terminology or language, but is the basis of much of the regulation of social life.

What is, I think, clearly brought out by a comparison of the Fox and Hopi systems is their fundamental similarity. By the theories of conjectural history this similarity is the accidental result of different historical processes. By my theory it is the result of the systematic application of the same structural principle, in one instance to patrilineal and in the other to matrilineal lineages.

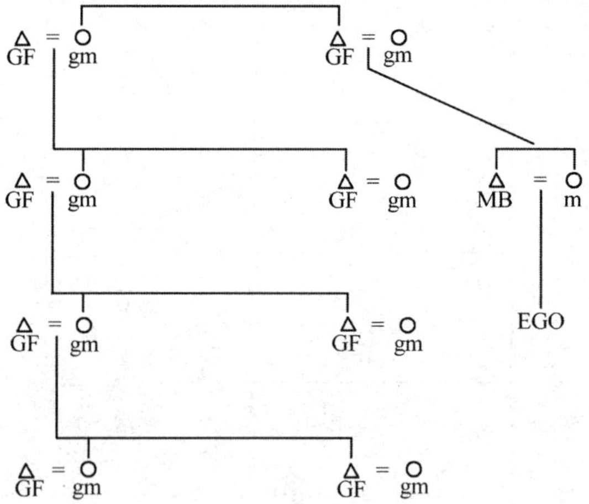

FIG. 12—HOPI

Mother's Father's Lineage

同样，我们也可以看出，图中所示的他母亲的父亲的世系群中，四代人中所有的男人和妇女分别被称为“祖父”和“祖母”。

在霍皮人看来，一个男子与其父亲的父亲的整个世系群并无关系。因此，此结构原则就不能运用到这个世系群中来。不过他也称呼他父亲的父亲为“祖父”。

伊根博士的研究表明，在霍皮人中，对于将亲属范畴分类的原因，实际上更多的是根据社会生活规范的需要，而不仅仅是称谓和语言的问题。

我认为，通过对福克斯和霍皮制度的比较，使我们清楚地发现它们根本上的相似性。但是按照历史推测理论的观点，仅仅是不同历史过程的一种巧合造成了这种相似性结果。然而根据我的理论，正是在父亲世系群和母亲世系群中分别应用了同一种结构原则才产生了这种相似性的结果。

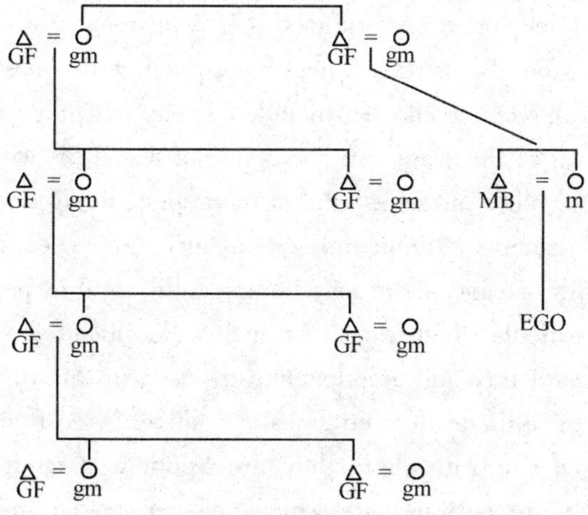

图 12　霍皮

（母亲的父亲的世系群）

I cannot, of course, discuss all the various systems of Choctaw and Omaha type. The variations that they show in certain features are very interesting and important. If you wish to test my theory you will examine them, or some of them, for yourselves, and the easiest way to analyse any system is to reduce it to a set of lineage charts similar to those given here for the Fox and the Hopi. For any system such a set of charts will reveal the exact way in which the general principle of the unity of the lineage is applied. The manner of application varies somewhat, but the principle appears in each system of the type.

You will doubtless already have noticed that in these systems there are an extraordinary number of relatives of all ages to whom a man applies the terms 'grandfather' and 'grandmother'. There is, I believe, a good reason for this, which should be briefly indicated. It is a general rule in societies having a classificatory terminology that for all the various relatives included under a single term there is some more or less definite pattern of behaviour which is regarded as normal or appropriate. But there are important differences in this matter. In certain instances the pattern can be defined by reference to specific rights and duties, or by specific modes of behaviour. For example, in the Kariera tribe of Australia a man must practice the most careful avoidance of all women who are included in the category of 'father's sister', of whom there are very many and of whom his wife's mother is one. But in other instances all that the application of a term implies is a certain general attitude rather than any more specific relation. Within such a category there may be a specific jural or personal relation to a particular individual. In many classificatory systems the terms for grandfather and grandmother are used in this way, as implying a general attitude of friendliness, relatively free from restraint, towards all persons to whom they are applied. Grandparents and grandchildren are persons with whom one can be on free and easy terms. This is connected with an extremely widespread, indeed almost universal, way of organising the relation of alternate generations to one another.

当然,我不能对乔克托型和奥马哈型中所有的制度都进行讨论,尽管它们在某些特征上显示出的多样性是非常有趣和重要的。如果想检验我的理论,就需要对这些多样性进行全面或部分的研究。把这些多样的制度简化为类似于用来分析福克斯人和霍皮人的一组世系群图表的方法,再分析起来可能就非常容易。对于任何一种制度,人们在特定世系群中应用统一普遍原则时采用的准确方式都会由这样一组图表显示出来。虽然相对于不同制度应用的方式略有不同,但上述原则在每种类型的制度中都存在。

毫无疑问,你们必定已经多次发现,在所有这些制度中,一位男子会使用"祖父"和"祖母"这两个称谓来称呼所有不同年龄层的亲属。我认为,这种现象必定有其原因。关于这一点,我要给予简单说明。在具有类分式称谓的社会中,存在一个普遍原则:某种规范的行为模式会体现在那些具有同一称谓所有亲属的相互行为之中。但这一模式的形式存在很大的差异。在一些情况下,这种模式是由特定的权利和责任或根据特定的行为方式确定的。例如,在澳大利亚的卡列拉部落中,一位男子必须小心翼翼地避免与那些属于"父亲的姐妹"范畴的女人接触。他妻子的母亲就是这众多女人中的一个。但在其他情况下,使用这种称谓只是意味某种大致态度而不是指任何具体关系。在某种特定称谓定义的范畴中,涵盖着与某人有关的特定法律或人身关系。在许多类分式称谓制度中,对祖父和祖母称谓的使用是为了对所有被称呼的人表现出一种普遍友好的态度,而不至于使人感到拘谨。对于某个男人来说,他和他祖辈和孙辈的人可以保持某种亲昵关系。这种现象与那种广泛分布,甚至非常普遍的、在隔代人之间建立关系的方法紧密联系。

In the Fox and Hopi systems all the members of the lineage of a grandparent are included in one category with the grand parents and the attitude that is appropriate towards a grandparent is extended to them. This does not imply any definite set of rights and duties, but only a certain general type of behaviour, of a kind that is regarded as appropriate towards relatives of the second ascending generation in a great many societies not belonging to the Choctaw and Omaha type.

I should have liked to discuss this further and to have dealt with those varieties of the Omaha type (such as the VaNdau) in which the mother's brother and the mother's brother's son are called 'grandfather'. But I have only time to draw your attention to a special variety of the Choctaw type which is of great interest in this connection. The Cherokee were divided into seven matrilineal clans. In the father's clan a man called all the men and women of his father's and all succeeding generations 'father' and 'father's sister', and this clan and all its individual members had to be treated with great respect. A man could not marry a woman of his father's clan, and of course he could not marry into his own clan. In the clan of his father's father and that of his mother's father a man calls all the women of all generations 'grandmother'. He thus treats, not the lineage, but the whole clan as a unity, although a clan must have numbered many hundreds of persons. With any woman whom he calls 'grandmother' a man is allowed to be on free and easy terms. It was regarded as particullary appropriate that a man should marry a 'grandmother', i. e. a woman of his mother's father's or father's father's clan.

Let us now return to a brief consideration of the special customs of marriage that have been proposed as causes of the Choctaw and Omaha terminologies respectively. Marriage with the wife's brother's daughter is theoretically possible and does perhaps actually, though only occasionally, occur in some of the tribes having a system of Omaha type.

在福克斯和霍皮制度中,祖父母世系群的所有成员与祖父母同属一个亲属范畴,同时,适用于对待祖父母的态度也被扩展到这个世系群的所有成员。这只是一种普遍的行为模式,而并不意味着与任何确定的权利和责任相关,在许多不属于乔克托型和奥马哈型的社会中它被认为是适合于对待上溯第二代亲属。

我本想对此问题做进一步讨论,并涉及到奥马哈类型的不同种类(例如万道人)。在那些不同的类型中,"祖父"称谓适用于母亲的兄弟和母亲的兄弟的儿子。但时间只能允许我对属于乔克托类型的一个特殊种类重点评论,因为它在这一问题上具有重要意义。这个特殊类型是切罗基人,他们整个分为七个母系氏族。在父亲的氏族中,对于父辈以及下溯各辈分的所有男人,一位男子把他们都称为"父亲";而将父辈以及下溯各辈分的所有女人称为"父亲的姐妹"。而且,对这个氏族及氏族中所有成员必须给予极大的尊重。一位男子不可以娶父亲氏族的女人为妻,当然,他也不可以娶自己氏族内部的女人。他对于所有他父亲的父亲的氏族和他母亲的父亲的氏族中的各代的女人的称呼是一致的,他称她们为"祖母"。因而,尽管一个氏族可能拥有几百人,他仍将其作为一个统一体对待,而不是仅将氏族中的特定世系群看做一个统一体。对于他称之为"祖母"的所有女人,他可以与她们有亲昵关系。在氏族中,最合适的婚姻就是一位男子娶一位"祖母",即与他母亲的父亲的氏族中的一个女人结婚。

现在,让我们简单回顾一下被认为分别导致了乔克托和奥马哈称谓的那些婚姻习俗。与妻子兄弟的女儿结婚在理论上是可能的,S 在某些具有奥马哈类型称谓的制度中,出现这种习俗尽管只是偶然的,但它确实是存在的。据说这种婚俗在以前的福克斯

Though there has been no marriage of this kind in the Fox tribe in recent times it is spoken of as a custom that formerly existed. We have seen that the marriage custom and the terminology fit consistently. The reason for this should now be easy to understand, for a little consideration will show that this particular marriage is an application of the principle of the unity of the lineage combined with the custom of the sororate or sororal polygyny. In the usual form of these customs we are concerned only with the principle of the unity of the sibling group. A man marries one woman of a particular sibling group and thereby establishes a particular relation to that group as a unity. The men are now permanently his brothers-in-law. Towards one of the women he stands in a marital relationship, and therefore towards the others he is conceived as standing in a similar relationship which may be called a quasi-marital relationship. For instance, they will regard his children as being their 'children'. Thus it is appropriate that when he takes a second wife, whether before or after the death of his first, he should marry his wife's sister.

I am quite aware that sororal polygyny can be attributed to the fact that co-wives who are sisters are less likely to quarrel seriously than two who are not so related, and that the sororate may similarly be justified by the fact that a stepmother is more likely to have proper affection for her stepchildren if they are the children of her own sister. These propositions do not conflict with my explanation but support it, for the principle of the unity of the sibling group as a structural principle is based on the solidarity of brothers and sisters within one family.

When we turn to systems of the Omaha type, we see that in place of the unity of the sibling group we now have a unity of the larger group, the lineage group of three generations. When a man marries one woman of this group he enters into a relation with the group as a unity, so that all the men are now his brothers-in-law, and he at the same time enters into what I have called a quasimarital relationship with all the women, including not only his wife's sisters but also his wife's brother's daughters, and in some systems his wife's father's sisters.

部落中曾经出现过，但在近代的福克斯部落中一直也没有发现这方面的痕迹。但显而易见，这种婚俗与称谓形式是一致的。出现这种形式的原因我们只要简单地考察一下就能很容易地看出来，这种特殊的婚姻是世系群一致原则与妻姐妹婚相结合的产物。在这些习俗的基本形式中，我们仅应用了同胞群一致原则。一位男子通过与某一同胞群中一位女人的婚姻，而与整个同胞群建立了一定关系。该同胞群中所有的男人就成为他的永久联姻兄弟。由于这种婚姻关系，使得他与此群体内其他女人之间也存在着这种相似的关系，可称之为亚婚姻关系。譬如，群体内其他女人会把此男子的孩子看做她们的“孩子”。不管他第一个妻子是否去世，如果他想娶第二个妻子，合适的做法就是娶第一位妻子的姐妹。

我明显地感觉到，姐妹共夫制其实是源于这样一个事实：两个妻子如果是两姊妹的话，她们之间的争吵可能会比没有这种关系的两个妻子少些。同时，以下情况也可能是妻姐妹婚存在的合理证明：如果继子女是继母自己姐妹的孩子，那么继母很有可能对孩子们有更多的爱。这些事实不仅与我的解释并不冲突，反而对我的解释是一种支持，因为同胞群一致原则作为一种结构原则，是以一个家庭内的兄弟姐妹的团结为基础的。

当我们阐述奥马哈类型的制度时，我们可以看到同胞群统一体被三代世系群统一体这个更大的群体统一体取代。通过与这种大群体内的一位女子结婚，一位男子可以与整个群体建立关系。从而，他与这个群体中所有男人都成为联姻兄弟，而与该群体中所有的女人之间处于我刚才所说的亚婚姻关系。这种女人的范围很广，他妻子的姐妹、妻子兄弟的女儿都包括在其中，在某

The group within which, by the principle of the sororate, he may take a second wife without entering into any new social bonds is thus extended to include his wife's brother's daughter; and the custom of marriage with this relative is simply the result of the application of the principle of the unity of the lineage in a system of patrilineal lineages. The special form of marriage and the special system of terminology, where they occur together, are directly connected by the fact that they are both applications of the one structural principle. There is no ground whatever for supposing that one is the historical cause of the other.

The matter is much more complex when we come to the custom of marriage with the mother's brother's widow. This form of marriage is found associated with terminology of the Choctaw type in the Banks Islands, in the tribes of North-West America and in the Twi-speaking Akim Abuakwa. But it is also found in many other places where that type of terminology does not exist. Nor is it correlated with matrilineal descent, for it is to be found in African societies that are markedly patrilineal in their institutions. There does not seem to be any theoretical explanation that will apply to all the known instances of this custom. There is no time on this occasion to discuss this subject by an analysis of instances.

I must briefly refer to another theory, which goes back to Durkheim's review (1898) of Kohler, and by which the Choctaw and Omaha terminologies are explained as being the direct result of emphasis on matrilineal and patrilineal descent respectively. We have, fortunately, a crucial instance to which we can refer in this connection, in the system of the Manus of the Admiralty Islands, of which we have an excellent analysis by Dr. Margaret Mead (1934). The most important feature of the Manus system is the existence of patrilineal clans (called by Dr. Mead 'gentes') and the major emphasis is on patrilineal descent. The solidarity of the patrilineal lineage is exhibited in many features of the system, but not in the terminology. However this emphasis on patrilineal descent is to a certain extent counterbalanced by the recognition of

些制度中，甚至妻子父亲的姐妹也在其中。根据妻姊妹婚原则，在一个群体内娶第二个妻子不会带来新的社会关系。这个群体的范围甚至可以扩展到妻子兄弟的女儿。可以认为由于世系群一致原则在父亲世系群制度中的运用，从而使这种婚姻习俗得以实现。作为同一种结构原则的产物，在这种特殊的婚姻形式和特殊的称谓制度共同出现的地方，它们紧密联系在一起。没有理由认为其中一个是另一个的历史原因。

谈到与母亲兄弟的寡妻结婚的习俗时，问题会变得更加复杂。有人认为这种婚姻形式与某些部落的乔克托型称谓有一定联系，如班克斯岛人、美洲西北部的一些部落和讲维特语的阿金阿布亚克马人。但也有发现说，在不存在乔克托型称谓的一些地方也有这种习俗。而且这种习俗在非洲社会中也被发现，从而证明它与母系继承无关，因为这些非洲社会明显是父系社会。似乎没有任何一种理论可以解释这一习俗所有已知的例征。但现在，我没有时间通过分析案例来讨论这一问题。

我必须简述一下另一种理论，它可以回溯到杜尔干(1898)对科勒的评论。这个理论认为，乔克托和奥马哈称谓是分别重视母系和父系继承制的结果。幸运的是，我们有一个很关键的例证可以说明这一点：玛格丽特·米德博士(1934)曾对阿默勒尔蒂群岛马努人的制度做过详尽、彻底的分析。不同于别的部族，在马努人制度中不仅存在父系氏族(米德博士称其为“gentes”)，并且特别强调父系继承。在该制度中，许多独特的地方都能体现出父方世系群的团结，但在称谓中却不能表现出这一点。然而，父系继承会同对母方世系的承认发生一定的冲突，对它重视的程度在某种程度上会因此受

matrilineal lineages, and this does appear in the terminology in features that make it similar to the Choctaw type. Thus a single term, *pinpapu*, is applied to the father's father's sister and to all her female descendants in the female line, and a single term, *patieye*, is applied to the father's sister and all her descendants in the female line. The unity of the matrilineal lineage is exhibited not only in the use of these terms, but also in the general social relation in which a person stands to the members of it, and is an important feature of the total complex kinship structure.

One of the strange ideas that has been, and I fear still is, current is that if a society recognises lineage at all it can only recognise either patrilineal or matrilineal lineage. I believe the origin of this absurd notion, and its persistence in the face of known facts, are the result of that early hypothesis of conjectural history that matrilineal descent is more primitive, i. e. historically earlier, than patrilineal descent. From the beginning of this century we have been acquainted with societies, such as the Herero, in which both matrilineal and patrilineal lineages are recognised; but these were dismissed as being 'transitional' forms. This is another example of the way in which attachment to the method and hypotheses of conjectural history prevents us from seeing things as they are. It was this, I think, that was responsible for Rivers' failing to discover that the Toda system recognises matrilineal lineage as well as patrilineal, and that the islands of the New Hebrides have a system of patrilineal groups in addition to their matrilineal moieties. Apart from the presuppositions of the method of conjectural history, there is no reason why a society should not build its kinship system on the basis of both patrilineal and matrilineal lineage, and we know that there are many societies that do exactly this.

In my criticism of the method of conjectural history I have insisted on the need for demonstration in anthropology. How then am I to demonstrate that my interpretation of the Choctaw-Omaha terminologies is the valid one? There are a number of possible arguments, but I have time for only one, which I hope may be considered sufficient.

到削弱。这种现象在称谓中确有体现，并与乔克托类型的特点相似。因而，“贫帕扑”代表父亲的父亲的姐妹和她的所有女性后代，而“帕泰也”代表父亲的姐妹以及她所有的女性后代。这个复杂亲属结构的一个重要特征就是母系世系群的统一性，它不仅仅体现在这些称谓的使用上，而且还表现在个人与本世系群其他成员建立的普遍的社会关系上。

过去一直流行、恐怕现在仍旧流行的一个奇怪观点是，父方世系和母方世系是矛盾的，二者只能保留其一，假如一个社会确实承认世系的话。我认为，历史推测的初期假设是造成这一怪论的根本原因，它完全没有参照目前已知的事实。此假设认为从历史上出现的时间来说，母系传承要比父系传承更早，因此母系传承更加古老。早在本世纪初，我们就已经知道存在像赫雷罗这样母系和父系世系群都得到承认的社会。但他们只是简单地被认为是一种“过渡”形式被忽视掉了。这完全是不能够认清事物的本质而只依靠历史推测方法和其假设的结果。我认为，正是这一点导致了里弗斯没有能够发现托达人的制度既承认母亲世系群又承认父亲世系群；也没有发现新赫布里底群岛除了拥有母系半偶族外，还存在父系群体。除非仅以历史推测方法为假设前提，否则无法解释一个社会为何不在父系和母系世系群的基础上建立其亲属制度。但是，目前事实已经表明，许多社会亲属制度的确是以此为基础的。

在我批判历史推测方法时，我坚持认为有必要从人类学的角度进行论证。那么，我该怎样论证才能支持我对乔克托—奥马哈称谓解释的正确性呢？可以从几方面来说明，但由于时间关系，我只能选其一，但我希望它能够充分说明问题。此论证取自世系

This is drawn from the existence—of terminologies in which the unity of lineage or clan is exhibited, but which do not belong to either the Choctaw or the Omaha type; and I will mention one example, that of the Yaralde tribe of South Australia.

The Yaralde are divided into local patrilineal totemic clans. A man belongs to his father's clan, and we will consider his relation to three other clans: those of his mother, his father's mother and his mother's mother. The Yaralde, like many other Australian tribes, such as the Aranda, have four terms for grandparents, each of which is applied to both men and women. The term *maiya* is applied to the father's father and his brothers and sisters and to all members of a man's own clan of the second ascending generation. A second term, *ŋaitja*, is applied to the mother's father and his brothers and sisters, i. e. to persons of the mother's clan of the appropriate generation. The third term, *mutsa*, is applied not only to the father's mother and her brothers and sisters, but to all persons belonging to the same clan, of all generations and of both sexes. The clan is spoken of collectively as a man's *mutsaurui*. Similarly the term *baka* is applied to the mother's mother and her brothers and sisters and to all members of her clan of all generations, the clan being spoken of as a man's *bakaurui*. The structural principle here is that for the outside related person the clan constitutes a unity within which distinctions of generation are obliterated. Compare this with the treatment of lineages or clans of grandparents in the Fox, Hopi and Cherokee systems.

群或氏族统一性中所体现出的称谓，但该称谓既不属于乔克托型，也不属于奥马哈型。我将提到一个有关南澳大利亚雅拉尔德部落的例子。

雅拉尔德人由一些地方性父系图腾氏族组成。在这里一位男子属于父亲的氏族，同时，我们再考察他与另外三个氏族的关系：即与他母亲的氏族的关系、与他父亲的母亲的氏族的关系和与他母亲的母亲的氏族的关系。雅拉尔德人在对祖父母的称谓上类似于澳大利亚的其他部落，例如阿兰达人，总共有四种之多，而且每一种称谓都是对男女通用的。下面具体列出雅拉尔德人的称谓及其对应的亲属范畴。父亲的父亲以及他的兄弟姐妹还有这个男子本氏族中上溯至第二代的所有成员用 *maiya* 来称呼；母亲的父亲以及他的兄弟姐妹用 *ŋaitja* 来称呼，它指代了母亲氏族中辈分合适的人；父亲的母亲以及她的兄弟姐妹和她氏族中各辈分的男女成员都可以用 *mutsa* 来称呼，从而这个氏族就可以叫做这个男人的 *mutsaurui*；同理，因为可以用 *baka* 称呼母亲的母亲以及她的兄弟姐妹还有她氏族中各辈分的成员，所以这个氏族也可以叫做这个男子的 *bakaurui*。结构原则在此的表现方式是：如果一个人不属于某个氏族，但与这个氏族有某种关系，那么这个氏族会以一个统一体的形式对待他，对于他来说这个统一体内不同人之间辈分的区别消失了。在对福克斯、霍皮和切罗基制度中祖父母世系群或祖父母氏族所做的研究中上述现象可以作为一个参照。

The Yaralde terminology for relatives in the mother's clan is shown in Fig. 13. It will be noted that the mother's brother's son and daughter are not called mother's brother (*wano*) and mother (*neηko*) as in Omaha systems. But the son's son and daughter of the mother's brother are called 'mother's brother' and 'mother'. If we wish to explain this by a special form of marriage it would have to be marriage with the wife's brother's son's daughter. I am not certain that such a marriage would be prohibited by the Yaralde system, but I am quite sure that it is not a custom so regular as to be regarded as an effective cause in producing the Yaralde terminology, and it would afford no explanation whatever for the terminological unification of the clans of the father's mother and the mother's mother. The structural principle in volved is obviously that of the merging of alternate generations, which is of such great importance in Australia, and which we have also seen in the Hopi system. A system very similar to the Yaralde is found in the Ungarinyin tribe of North-West Australia, but I will not do more than refer to it.

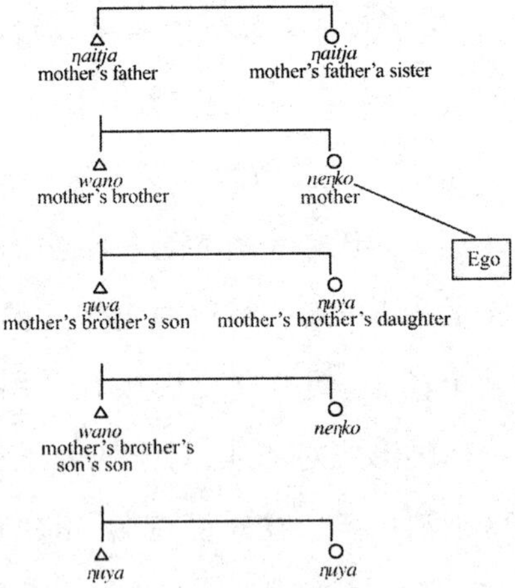

FIG. 13—YARALDE

Mother's lineage

ηaitja
neηko } η is $\bar{n}$g
ηuya

雅拉尔德人对母系氏族亲属使用的称谓可以参见图 13。应该注意的是,在这里和奥马哈人的不同之处在于,并不是将母亲的兄弟的儿子和女儿称呼为母亲的兄弟(*wano*)和母亲(*neηko*),而是将母亲的兄弟的儿子的子女称呼为"母亲的兄弟"和母亲。如果非要用一种特殊的婚姻形式来解释这个现象的话,那么只能用可以与妻子兄弟的儿子的女儿结婚这种婚姻形式来表述它了。我不确定雅拉尔德是否会禁止这种婚姻,但是,我可以非常确信地说:这种习俗并不是产生雅拉尔德称谓的原因,而且它也不能解释父亲的母亲的氏族和母亲的母亲的氏族在称谓上的一致性这种现象。明显地,这里所用的结构原则是隔代合并原则,它在澳大利亚各部落占有极为重要的位置。同时,这个原则在霍皮制度中也可以见到。此处我只会稍微提一下,在澳大利亚西北部的翁加里宁部落中可以发现和雅拉尔德制度非常相似的制度。

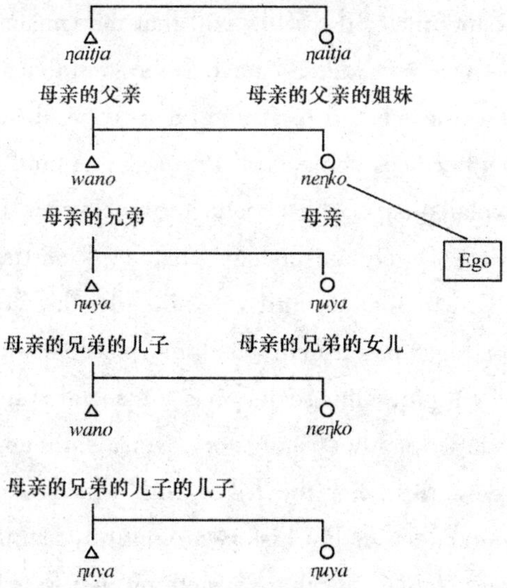

图 13　雅拉尔德

(母亲的世系群)

Earlier in this address I said that I would try to show you that the Omaha type of terminology is just as reasonable and fitting in those social systems in which it is found as our own terminology is in our system. I hope I have succeeded in doing this. On the basis of the elementary family and the genealogical relationships resulting therefrom, we English have constructed for ourselves a certain kinship system which meets the necessities of an ordered social life and is fairly self-consistent. The Fox or the Hopi have on the same basis constructed a relatively self-consistent system of a different type which provides for the needs of social cohesion in a different way and over a wider range. We understand the terminology in each instance as soon as we see it as part of an ordered system. The obvious connection of the Omaha terminology with the custom of marriage with the wife's brother's daughter is seen as a relation between two parts of a self-consistent working system, not as a relation of cause and effect.

If you ask the question, 'How is it that the Omaha (or any other of the tribes we have considered) have the system that they do?' then it is obvious that the method of structural analysis does not afford an answer. But neither does conjectural history. The proffered but purely hypothetical explanation of the Omaha terminology is that it resulted from the adoption of a certain unusual custom of marriage. This obviously gives us no explanation until we know why the Omaha and other tribes came to adopt this custom. The only possible way of answering the question why a particular society has the social system that it does have is by a detailed study of its history over a sufficient period, generally several centuries. For the tribes with which we are here concerned the materials for such a history are entirely lacking. This is, of course, very regrettable, but there is nothing that we can do about it. If you want to know how England comes to have its present system of constitutional monarchy and parliamentary government, you will go to the history books, which will give you the details of the growth of the

在演讲刚开始时，我就说过，我会向你们证明奥马哈型称谓对于它所在的那些制度来说，就像我们的称谓对于我们的制度一样，是合理并且适用的。我希望我已经做到了这一点。在基本家庭和由此产生的谱系关系基础上，我们英国人已经为自己构建了一种亲属制度，它满足了有序的社会生活和自身持续发展的需求。福克斯人和霍皮人的制度是不同的类型，但同样是在相同的基础上构建的并且能够满足其自身的持续发展。这种制度对社会内聚性需求的满足从不同方面和在更广阔的范围得到扩展。在任何一种情况下，如果我们能将称谓看做是有序制度的一个组成部分，我们就可以说掌握了这种称谓。很明显，在奥马哈称谓与可以娶妻子兄弟的女儿为妻的婚俗之间存在的那种联系可以看做是具有维系自我发展制度的两个部分之间的关系，但它们之间并无因果关系。

如果你要问："奥马哈部落（或我们所考察的任何其他部落）为什么拥有其现存的制度？"显然结构分析的方法不能为我们提供答案。但是，历史推测方法同样也不能给予回答。目前只能对其提出纯粹的假设性解释，即奥马哈的称谓制度是由采取特定的、不寻常的婚姻习俗引起的。很明显，只有我们知道为什么奥马哈和其他部落采用这一习俗之后，我们才可以得到对这个问题清楚的解释。为什么某一特定社会拥有其现有的社会制度？对这类问题唯一可能的解答办法，就是对这一社会的历史做长时间的（一般为几个世纪）详细的分析。但是，很令人遗憾的是，这些我们讨论的部落的相关历史资料非常缺乏，我们对此无能为力。如果你想要知道英格兰为什么形成了现存的君主立宪制度和议会政府，你可以参考历史文献，那里面记载着这些制度发展的具

system. If there were no records at all of this historical development, would the anthropologists think it worth while to spend their time in making conjectures as to what it might have been?

Even when there are historical records, they only enable us to discover how a particular system has grown out of a somewhat different particular system. Thus it would be possible to write a historical account of the changes of the kinship system of England during the past ten centuries. This would take us back to the Teutonic bilateral sib system, as exhibited in the institution of *wergild*. But we still should not know why the Teutonic peoples had this kind of system, while the Romans had a different system of agnatic lineages. The great value of history for a science of society is that it gives us materials for the study of how social systems change. In this respect conjectural history is absolutely worthless.

But if you ask, not how the English kinship system or the English political system came into existence, but how it works at the present time, that is a question that can be answered by research of the same kind as anthropological field-work, and historical considerations are relatively, if not absolutely, unimportant. Such knowledge of how social systems work is of great value for any understanding of human life. It often has been and still is neglected by anthropologists who consider it their principal task to write the history of peoples or institutions that have no history.

If you accept the analysis that I have given, but still wish to apply the method of conjectural history, what you have to conjecture is why all the tribes that have been enumerated elected to construct their kinship systems on the basis of the unity of the lineage.

What kind of results can we expect to obtain from the method of sociological analysis? Nothing, of course, that will be acceptable as significant by those who demand that any explanation of a social phenomenon must be a historical explanation, or by those who demand

体情况。但是如果根本没有对这些历史发展的记载,那么,花费时间去对过去发生的事进行猜测在人类学家们看来是不是值得呢?

即使有了历史记载,也只能够帮助我们懂得一个特定的制度是怎样从另一个不同的制度中演化过来的。不过这一点也足够帮助我们对英格兰过去十个世纪的亲属制度发展做一历史叙述。这又把我们带回到日耳曼人的双边氏族制度中,此制度在偿命金制度中已经体现出来。但我们仍旧不明白条顿人为什么拥有这种制度,而同时期的罗马人却拥有另一种不同的父系制度。历史为我们提供了研究社会制度变化的资料,这就是它作为一门科学对社会的巨大价值所在。在这一方面,历史推测方法是绝对没有价值的。

但是,如果你要问的是英国亲属制度或英国政治制度在现阶段如何运作的,而不是它如何产生的,那么这就是另一个问题了。类似于人类学家实地调查的研究方法可能会给出这个问题的答案。但在这种方法中,历史材料可能相对地不那么重要,即使这种程度不是绝对地。像社会制度是如何运作这样的知识,对于理解社会生活具有极大的价值。但是,无论是过去还是现在,这类知识都被那些认为他们的基本任务是写出各民族历史和那些无历史民族的制度的人类学家们所忽视。

如果你们尽管已经同意了我的分析,但仍对运用历史推测的方法念念不忘的话,那么你们应该推测的是:为什么世系群统一的原则是所有那些被列举的部落构建其亲属制度的共同基础。

我们期望从社会学分析方法中得到什么呢?当然,有些人认为任何对于社会现象的解释都是一种历史的解释,而有些人认为应该从

what is called psychological explanation, i. e. explanation in terms of the individual and his motives. I suggest that the results that we may reasonably expect are as follows:

1. It will enable us to make a systematic classification of kinship systems. Systematic classification is an essential in any scientific treatment of any class of phenomena, and such classification must be in terms of general properties.

2. It enables us to understand particular features of particular systems. It does this in two ways: (*a*) by revealing the particular feature as a part of an organised whole; (*b*) by showing that it is a special example of a recognisable class of phenomena. Thus I have tried to show that the Choctaw and Omaha terminologies belong to a class which also includes the Yaralde terminology, and that these are all special applications of the general principle of the solidarity and continuity of the lineage, which appears in many other forms in a great number of different societies.

3. It is the only method by which we can hope ultimately to arrive at valid generalisations about the nature of human society, i. e. about the universal characteristics of all societies, past, present, and future. It is, of course, such generalisations that are meant when we speak of sociological laws.

In the method of conjectural history single problems are usually considered in isolation. On the other hand, the method of structural analysis aims at a general theory, and a great many different facts and problems are, therefore, considered together and in relation to one another. It is obvious that in this address, inordinately long as it has been, I have only been able to touch on a few points in the general theory of kinship structure. I have dealt briefly with one or two other points in earlier publications. That particular part of the general theory which has occupied us today may be said to be the theory of the establishment of type relationships. I have mentioned the tendency present in many societies to set up a type relationship between a person and all his relatives of the parents' generation, and the even more marked tendency to establish a type relationship, usually one of free and easy behaviour, towards the relatives of the grandparents' generation. I have not tried to deal with this except incidentally.

心理学方面解释社会现象,即根据一个人的动机来解释。以下我认为我们可以得出的合理结果对于上述这些人来说,既没有意义,也无法接受。我认为这些有充分理由的结果是:

1. 社会学分析方法可以帮助我们对亲属制度做系统的分类。在科学研究中,系统分类是必要的,并且分类必须具有普遍意义。

2. 社会学分析方法揭示了各种制度的特征。方法有两种:(a)将该特征作为一个有组织整体的一部分;(b)证明这些特征是一种可认识现象中的一个独特例证。因而,根据世系群团结和延续这个总的原则特征,我曾经尝试去证明乔克托和奥马哈型称谓属于同一种类。雅拉尔德型称谓也应该包括在这个种类中,因为这些不同类型的称谓都是对这一原则特征的特殊应用。这一原则还在不同的社会中以其他的形式出现过。

3. 社会学分析方法是对人类社会本质,即对有关所有社会的过去、现在和将来的普遍特征做出有效总结的唯一方法。当然,此处的总结指在社会学法则意义上的那种总结。

人们在使用历史推测方法时,往往只独立地考察每一个问题。相反,运用结构分析方法,将大量不同的事实及问题联系起来研究,能得出一般性的结论。尽管这次演讲的时间较长,但我也只能提及亲属结构一般理论的几个要点问题。其他的一些观点,我曾在以前发表的文章中提到过。今天我们一直讨论的是一种关于建立类型关系的理论,对于以它作为一个特定组成部分而提炼出的一般理论应该已被大家接受。我曾提到过目前社会上流行的趋势是与父辈一代所有亲属之间建立一种类型关系,另一种更为明显的趋势是与祖父母辈间建立一种在行为上自在轻松的类型关系。对于这一问题我只是碰巧提到而已。我在这里主要探

The major part of the exposition has been concerned with two structural principles which are themselves examples of a more general structural principle or class of principles. By the principle of the unity of the sibling group a type relationship is set up between a given person and all the members of a sibling group to which he is related in a certain way. It is by reference to this principle, I hold, that we must interpret the classificatory terminology and such customs as the sororate and levirate. By the principle of the unity of the lineage group a type relationship is set up between a given person and all the members of a lineage group to which he is related in a certain way. It is by reference to this principle, I hold, that we must interpret the terminologies of the Fox, the Hopi and the Yaralde, and other similar systems in many scattered parts of the world.

If you will take the time to study two or three hundred kinship systems from all parts of the world you will be impressed, I think, by the great diversity that they exhibit. But you will also be impressed by the way in which some particular feature, such as an Omaha type of terminology, reappears in scattered and widely spread regions. To reduce this diversity to some sort of order is the task of analysis, and by its means we can, I believe, find, beneath the diversities, a limited number of general principles applied and combined in various ways. Lineage solidarity in one form or another is found in a majority of kinship systems. There is nothing at all surprising in the fact that terminologies of the Choctaw and Omaha type, in which it finds what may be called an extreme development, should be encountered in separated regions of America, Africa, Asia and Oceania, in many different families of languages, and in association with many different types of 'culture'.

Last year I explained in general terms how I conceive the study of social structure (Radcliffe-Brown, 1940b). In this address, by means of a particular example, I have tried to show you something of the nature of a certain method of investigation. But do not think that this method can be applied only to the study of kinship. It is applicable in one way or another to all social phenomena, for it is simply the method of abstractive generalisation by the comparison of instances, which is the characteristic method of the inductive sciences.

讨了两个结构原则，而它们只是某些更一般原则的特例而已或者可能是众多原则中的一种罢了。同胞群一致原则指出，和一同胞群之间发生某种联系的人会和这个同胞群的所有成员之间形成某种类型关系。我认为，这一原则正是用来诠释类分式称谓和像妻姐妹婚和夫兄弟婚这样的习俗的。同理，对于世系群一致原则来说，与某个世系群依某种关系联系在一起的人会与这个世系群中所有的成员建立一种类型关系。同样我也认为，必须根据这一原则，来诠释福克斯人、霍皮人和雅拉尔德人的称谓制度以及分布于世界各地的其他相似的制度。

我认为只要能花费时间对二三百种世界各地区的亲属制度进行研究，你们就会深切地感受到它们之间体现出的极大不同。但是，你也可能深切体会到某种如奥马哈称谓制度这样共性的特征竟会分布得如此广泛。要将这些差异梳理得有条理，就必须依靠分析的方法。我相信，通过此方法可以将一些以不同方式运用和结合起来的普遍原则从众多的差异中剥离出来。因此，世系群团结原则作为一种普遍原则会在大多数亲属制度中以不同的形式出现。正因如此我们才丝毫不奇怪为什么在乔克托人和奥马哈人中得到极端发展的所谓乔克托型和奥马哈型称谓在美洲、非洲、亚洲和大洋洲的不同地区、不同语系中都可以遇到，并能够与不同的类型文化相联系。

去年，我曾大致谈过我理解的社会结构研究到底是什么样子（拉德克利夫-布朗，1940b）。在此次讲演中，通过举例，我试图向你们表明关于调查方法的本质内容。它是一种独特的科学归纳方法，通过资料对比得出归纳结论，所以请不要认为它仅能用于研究亲属关系，它还可以应用于所有的社会现象研究中，当然是以不同方式出现的。

'Why all this fuss about method?' some of you may perhaps ask. We cannot reach agreement as to the validity or the value of results unless we first reach some agreement as to objectives and the proper methods of attaining them. In the other natural sciences there is such agreement; in social anthropology there is not. Where we disagree, it should be the first purpose of discussion to define as precisely as possible the ground of difference. I have put my case before you, without, I hope, any unfairness towards those with whom I disagree. It is for you to judge which of the two methods that I have compared is most likely to provide that kind of scientific understanding of the nature of human society which it is the accepted task of the social anthropologist to provide for the guidance of mankind.

REFERENCES

Durkheim, E.

(1898). 'Zur Urgeschichte der Ehe, Prof. J. Kohler', Analyses III, La Famille, *Année Sociologique*, Vol. I, pp. 306-319.

Eggan, F.

(1933). 'The Kinship System and Social Organisation of the Western Pueblos with Special Reference to the Hopi', *Ph. D. thesis*, University of Chicago.

Gifford, E. W.

(1916). 'Miwok Moieties', *Arch. and Ethn. Publ.*, *Univ. California*, Vol. XII, No. 4.

Gilbert, William H., Jr. (1937). 'Eastern Cherokee Social Organisation', in *Social Anthropology of North American Tribes* (ed. Fred Eggan). Chicago University Press, pp. 283-338.

Kohler, J. (1897). 'Zur Urgeschichte der Ehe', *Zeitschrift für Vergleichende Rechtswissenschaft* (Stuttgart), Bd. II.

你们其中一些人也许会问:“为什么总是在讨论方法论的问题呢?”原因在于,如果在使用的方法上无法统一,那么对于研究结果的正确性以及结果的价值也无法达成统一。这里所指的方法必须是客观准确的,能够带来适当的、有价值的成果。虽然其他的自然科学领域已就方法问题达成共识,但在社会人类学领域还没有做到这一点。当我们对问题的结论产生争论时,我们首先要做的是对它进行讨论,并尽可能准确地表明产生争论的原因。我已经把我的观点阐述清楚,并希望没有对我持反对态度的观点表现出任何的偏见。对于我比较的两种方法,科学的探究人类社会本质究竟应该靠哪个,需要你们来评判。社会人类学家的任务就是提供认识人类社会本质的指南。

参考书目:

杜尔干:

1898,《J.科勒教授和〈史前婚姻〉》

伊根:

1933,《从霍皮人的特例看西普埃布洛人的亲属制度和社会组织》

吉福德:

1916,《米沃克人的半偶族》

吉尔伯特,威廉:

1937,《东切罗基人的社会组织》

科勒:

1897,《史前婚姻》

克罗伯:

Kroeber, A. L. (1909). 'Classificatory Systems of Relationship', *fJ. R. Anthrop. Inst.*, Vol. XXXIX, pp. 77-84.

— (1917). 'California Kinship Systems', *Arch. and Ethn. Publ. Univ. California*, Vol. XII, No. 9.

Mead, Margaret (1934). 'Kinship in the Admiralty Islands', *Anthrop. Papers Amer. Mus. Nat. History*, Vol. XXXIV, Pt. II, pp. 181-358.

M'Lennan, John F. (1865). *Primitive Marriage.* Edinburgh: Adam & Charles Black.

Morgan, Lewis H. (1871). 'The Systems of Consanguinity and Affinity', *Smithsonian Institution Contributions to Knowledge*, Vol. XVII.

— (1877). *Ancient Society or Researches in the Lines of Human Progress from Savagery to Civilisation.* London: Macmillan; New York: Henry Holt.

Opler, M. E. (1937a). 'Chiricahua Apache Social Organisation', in *Social Anthropology of North American Tribes* (ed. Fred Eggan), Chicago University Press.

— (1937b). 'Apache Data Concerning the Relation of Kinship Terminology to Social Classification', *Amer. Anthrop.*, Vol. XXXIX, pp. 201-212.

Radcliffe-Brown, A. R. (1918). 'Notes on the Social Organisation of Australian Tribes', Pt. I, *f. R. Anthrop. Inst.*, Vol. XLVIII, pp. 222-253.

—(1924). 'The Mother's Brother in South Africa', *South African J. Science*, Vol. XXI.

— (1930-31). 'The Social Organisation of Australian Tribes', Pts. I-III, *Oceania*, Vol. I, pp. 34-63, 206-246, 322-341, 426-456.

— (1935). 'Patrilineal and Matrilineal Succession', *Iowa Law Review*, Vol. XX, No. 2.

— (1940a). 'On Joking Relationships', *Africa*, Vol. XIII, No. 3, pp. 195-210.

— (1940b). 'On Social Structure', *f. R. Anthrop. Inst.*, Vol. LXX, pp. 1-12.

Rivers, W. H. R. (1907). 'On the Origin of the Classificatory System of Relationship', in *Anthropological Essays Presented to Edward Burnett Tylor.* Oxford: Clarendon Press. (Reprinted in *Social Organisation.*

London: Kegan Paul, 1924, App. I, pp. 175-192.)

— (1914*a*). *History of Melanesian Society. Cambridge University Press.*

— (1914*b*). *Kinship and Social Organisation. London: London School of Economics.*

1909,《类分式亲属制度》

1917,《加利福尼亚的亲属制度》

玛格丽特·米德：

1934《阿德默勒尔拜岛上的亲属关系》

麦克伦南：

1865《原始婚姻》

摩尔根：

1871《血亲和姻亲制度》

1877《古代社会——人类从野蛮到文明发展线索探究》

奥普勒：

1937a《奇里卡华阿帕切人的社会组织》

1937b《关于亲属称谓与社会分类的关系的阿帕切材料》

拉德克利夫-布朗：

1918《关于澳大利亚部落社会组织的笔记》

1924.《南非的母舅》

1930~31《澳大利亚亚部落的社会组织》

1935《父系继承制和母系继承制》

1940a《论戏谑关系》

1940b《论社会结构》

里弗斯：

1907《论类别式亲属制度的起源》

1914a《美拉尼西亚社会史》

1914b《亲属关系和社会组织》

Seligman, Brenda Z.

(1917). '*The Relationship Systems of the Nandi Masai and Thonga*', *Man*, *Vol. XVII*, 46.

Starcke, C. N.

(1889). *The Primitive Family* (*The International Scientific Series*, *Vol. LXVI*). *London*: *Kegan Paul*.

Stewart, Dugald

(1795). *Introduction to Essays of Adam Smith*.

Tax, Sol

(1937). '*The Social Organisation of the Fox Indians*', *in Social Anthropology of North American Tribes* (*ed. Fred Eggan*). *Chicago University Press*, *pp*. 241-282.

塞丽格曼：

1917《南迪人、马赛人和聪加人的亲属制度》

斯达克：

1889《原始家庭》

斯图尔特：

1795《亚当·史密斯论文集》导论

索尔·泰克斯：

1937《福克斯印第安人的社会组织》

CHAPTER Ⅳ

On Joking Relationships[①]

The publication of Mr. F. J. Pedler's note[②] on what are called 'joking relationships', following on two other papers on the same subject by Professor Henri Labouret[③] and Mademoiselle Denise Paulme,[④] suggests that some general theoretical discussion of the nature of these relationships may be of interest to readers of *Africa*.[⑤]

What is meant by the term 'joking relationship' is a relation between two persons in which one is by custom permitted, and in some

---

① Reprinted from Africa, Vol. XIII, No. 3, 1940, pp. 195-210.

② 'Joking Relationships in East *Africa*', Africa, Vol. XIII, p. 170.

③ 'La Parentéà Plaisanteries en *Afrique* Occidentale', Africa, Vol. II, p. 244.

④ 'Parent Plaisanteries et Alliance par le Sang en Afrique Occidentale', Africa, Vol. XII, p. 433.

⑤ Professor Marcel Mauss has published a brief theoretical discussion of the *subject in the Annuaire de l' École Pratique des HautesÉtudes, Section des Sciences religieuses*, 1927-8. It is also dealt with by Dr. F. Eggan in *Social Anthropology of North American Tribes* 1937. *pp*,75-81.

第四章 论戏谑关系①

弗·季·佩德勒先生发表了一篇关于什么是“戏谑关系”的笔记,②在此之前,关于这一论题亨利·拉布雷③教授和马德穆瓦瑟勒·德尼瑟·波尔默教授④也发表了两篇文章,以上表明了《非洲》杂志的读者也许对戏谑关系本质的一般理论性讨论感兴趣。⑤

所谓“戏谑关系”是指两人之间的一种关系。其中一方在社会习俗允许下,并在特定场合要求下,可以嘲弄另一方或开另

① 重印自《非洲》,1940 年,卷 13,3 期,195~210 页。

② 《东非的戏谑关系》,《非洲》,卷 13,第 170 页。

③ 《西非的亲属关系》,《非洲》,卷 2,第 244 页。

④ 《西非的亲属关系和家族联盟》,《非洲》,卷 12,第 433 页。

⑤ 马塞尔·莫斯教授在《实践学派高级研究年刊,宗教科学分册》(1927~1928 年)对这一理论有过简要探讨。弗·伊根教授在《北美诸部落的社会人类学》,1937 年版第 75~81 页中也对此问题有过探讨。

instances required, to tease or make fun of the other, who in turn is required to take no offence. It is important to distinguish two main varieties. In one the relation is symmetrical; each of the two persons teases or makes fun of the other. In the other variety the relation is asymmetrical; A jokes at the expense of B and B accepts the teasing good humouredly but without retaliating; or A teases B as much as he pleases and B in return teases A only a little. There are many varieties in the form of this relationship in different societies. In some instances the joking or teasing is only verbal, in others it includes horse-play; in some the joking includes elements of obscenity, in others not.

Standardised social relationships of this kind are extremely widespread, not only in Africa but also in Asia, Oceania and North America. To arrive at a scientific understanding of the phenomenon it is necessary to make a wide comparative study. Some material for this now exists in anthropological literature, though by no means all that could be desired, since it is unfortunately still only rarely that such relationships are observed and described as exactly as they might be.

The joking relationship is a peculiar combination of friendliness and antagonism. The behaviour is such that in any other social context it would express and arouse hostility; but it is not meant seriously and must not be taken seriously. There is a pretence of hostility and a real friendliness. To put it in another way, the relationship is one of permitted disrespect. Thus any complete theory of it must be part of, or consistent with, a theory of the place of respect in social relations and in social life generally. But this is a very wide and very important sociological problem; for it is evident that the whole maintenance of a social order depends upon the appropriate kind and degree of respect being shown towards certain persons, things and ideas or symbols.

Examples of joking relationships between relatives by marriage are very commonly found in Africa and in other parts of the world.

一方的玩笑,而另一方并没有觉得这是一种侵犯。区分两种主要戏谑类型非常重要。在第一种类型中,戏谑是对称的;双方可以互相取笑及嘲弄。在第二种类型中,戏谑是不对称的。A 取笑 B,B 诙谐地接受这种取笑,但并不给予报复;或者 A 随意取笑 B,而 B 只能稍微地给予回敬。不同的社会会存在各种各样的戏谑关系形式。在某些地方只是口头上的取笑及嘲弄;而在另一些地方,这种取笑具有恶意性;还有些地方嘲弄具有淫秽性,而其他地方则没有。

像戏谑关系这种标准化的社会关系分布极其广泛,不仅仅存在于非洲,亚洲、大洋州及北美洲也都存在。为了能够对这种现象有个科学的理解及认识,做一个广泛的对比性研究是非常有必要的。一些关于这方面的材料可以在人类学文献中找到,但并非都能够被运用,因为,遗憾的是,很少有人能精确地观察并描述这种关系。

戏谑关系是友好和敌对这两种情绪的特殊结合。在任何其他社会背景下,戏谑这种行为都会表达并会引起敌意;但这并不是很严肃的敌意,而且被戏谑者也无需严肃地对待。戏谑行为其实是在敌对情绪伪装下表达真正的友谊。也就是说,戏谑关系是在允许不被尊重的情况下产生的。戏谑关系的任何一种完整理论都必须是关于尊敬在社会关系和总体社会生活中所起作用的理论的一部分,或与之相合。这是个范围非常广泛和重要的社会学问题;因为很明显,整个社会秩序的维护必须依靠对于社会特定的人、事、思想及符号表示适当的、得体的尊敬。

在非洲及世界其他地区,戏谑关系在亲属间非常常见。根据

Thus Mademoiselle Paulme[1] records that among the Dogon a man stands in a joking relationship to his wife's sisters and their daughters. Frequently the relationship holds between a man and both the brothers and sisters of his wife. But in some instances there is a distinction whereby a man is on joking terms with his wife's younger brothers and sisters but not with those who are older than she is.

This joking with the wife's brothers and sisters is usually associated with a custom requiring extreme respect, often partial or complete avoidance, between a son-in-law and his wife's parents.[2]

The kind of structural situation in which the associated customs of joking and avoidance are found may be described as follows. A marriage involves a readjustment of the social struc ture whereby the woman's relations with her family are greatly modified and she enters into a new and very close relation with her husband. The latter is at the same time brought into a special relation with his wife's family, to which, however, he is an outsider. For the sake of brevity, though at the risk of over-simplification, we will consider only the husband's relation to his wife's family. The relation can be described as involving both attachment and separation, both social conjunction and social disjunction, if I may use the terms. The man has his own definite position in the social structure, determined for him by his birth into a certain family, lineage or clan. The great body of his rights and duties and the interests and activities that he shares with others are the result of his position. Before the marriage his wife's family are outsiders for him as he is an outsider for them. This constitutes a social disjunction which is not destroyed by the marriage. The social conjunction results from the continuance, though in altered form, of the wife's relation to

---

① *Africa*, Vol. XII, p. 438.

② Those who are not familiar with these widespread customs will find descrip tions in Junod, *Life of a South African Tribe*, Neuchatel, Vol. I, pp. 229-37, and in *Social Anthropology of North American Tribes*, edited by F. Eggan, Chicago, 1937, PP. 55-7.

马德穆瓦瑟勒·波尔默[1]的记载,在多贡人中,一位男子与其妻子的姐妹及他们的女儿们保持着戏谑关系。一位男子经常会与其妻子的兄弟姐妹有着戏谑关系。但在一些地方,一位男子可以与其妻子的弟弟妹妹们开玩笑,却不能与其妻子的哥哥姐姐开玩笑。这种与妻子的兄弟姐妹的戏谑关系经常是与特定习俗联系的,这就要求女婿和岳父母之间相互极端尊重,两方要部分或完全回避。[2]

在与戏谑和回避相关的社会习俗的这种结构状态里,请看以下描述。婚姻会使社会结构发生重构,因为一位女子与其家庭的关系在发生极大改变的同时,她进入一个新的家庭并与丈夫有非常亲密的关系。同时,丈夫也与妻子的家庭形成了特殊的关系,然而,对于妻子的家庭来说,他仍旧是个外人。尽管冒着过于简单化的危险,但为了简洁明了地表达,我们在这里只关注丈夫与其妻子家庭的关系,它可以被描述为既包含附属又包含分离。如果可以这么说的话,我认为这种关系既包含社会关联又包含社会分离。男人在社会结构中有其特定的地位,是由他出生的家庭、世系群或氏族决定。他大部分的权利、责任及兴趣以及和其他人共享的社会活动都是社会地位带来的结果。在结婚之前他妻子的家庭对他来说是局外人,正如他对于他妻子的家庭是局外人一样。这就构成了社会的分离。婚姻并不能破坏这种分离。社会关联正来源于他妻子与其娘家关系的延续,尽管这种关系的形式

① 《非洲》,卷12,第438页。

② 不太熟悉这种普遍的习俗的人们可以参见,朱诺德:《一个南非部落的生活》,卷1,第229~237页,和弗·伊根编:《北美诸部落的社会人类学》,第55~57页。

her family, their continued interest in her and in her children. If the wife were really bought and paid for, as ignorant persons say that she is in Africa, there would be no place for any permanent close relation of a man with his wife's family. But though slaves can be bought, wives cannot.

Social disjunction implies divergence of interests and therefore the possibility of conflict and hostility, while conjunction requires the avoidance of strife. How can a relation which combines the two be given a stable, ordered form? There are two ways of doing this. One is to maintain between two persons so related an extreme mutual respect and a limitation of direct personal contact.

This is exhibited in the very formal relations that are, in so many societies, characteristic of the behaviour of a son-in law on the one side and his wife's father and mother on the other. In its most extreme form there is complete avoidance of any social contact between a man and his mother-in-law. This avoidance must not be mistaken for a sign of hostility. One does, of course, if one is wise, avoid having too much to do with one's enemies, but that is quite a different matter. I once asked an Australian native why he had to avoid his mother-in-law, and his reply was, 'Because she is my best friend in the world; she has given me my wife'. The mutual respect between son-in-law and parents-in-law is a mode of friendship. It prevents conflict that might arise through divergence of interest.

The alternative to this relation of extreme mutual respect and restraint is the joking relationship, one, that is, of mutual disrespect and licence. Any serious hostility is prevented by the playful antagonism of teasing, and this in its regular repetition is a constant expression or reminder of that social disjunction which is one of the essential components of the relation, while the social conjunction is maintained by the friendliness that takes no offence at insult.

The discrimination within the wife's family between those who have to be treated with extreme respect and those with whom it is a duty to be disrespectful is made on the basis of generation and sometimes of seniority within the generation. The usual respected relatives are those of the first ascending generation, the wife's mother and her sisters, the wife's father and his brothers, sometimes

已经改变,但娘家的亲戚仍旧关爱着她和她的子女。如果像一些无知人士所说的,妻子是非洲人,因此是买来的,那么丈夫则与其娘家没有任何持久的亲密关系。虽然奴隶可以买,但是妻子却不能。

社会分离意味着兴趣的分歧,并且可能会产生冲突和敌意情绪。然而,社会关联则需要回避冲突。怎样才能将一种既包含社会分离又包含社会关联的关系达到一个稳定、有序的形式呢?有两种方法能够做到。第一种方法是保持双方相互极度尊重的关系,并限制直接的个人接触。这在那些非常正式的关系中得以展现出来,即女婿和岳父母双方的行为在许多社会中表现出的特征。这种关系最极端的形式,就是女婿和岳母的社会关系的完全回避。

回避不应当误以为是敌对情绪的标志。当然如果一个人足够聪明,就不会与其敌人有太多的接触,但那却是另一回事。我曾经向一澳大利亚土著人询问过为什么他要尽量回避他的岳母,他的回答是:“因为在这个世界上,她是我最好的朋友;她使我拥有了妻子。”女婿与岳父母之间的相互尊重是一种友谊的模式。这种尊重避免了由于利益分歧而可能产生的冲突。

在这种极度相互尊重和抑制的关系外,还有另一种就是戏谑关系。戏谑关系是一种对方相互不尊重和允许相互放纵的关系。嘲弄带来的玩笑般的敌对阻止了对方产生任何严肃的敌对情绪。经常反复的戏谑常常表现或暗示社会分离是构成戏谑关系的主要因素,同时,对于戏谑所采取的无动于衷态度则维持了社会关联。

在妻子的亲属中,对哪些人应给予极度的尊重,哪些人不给予尊重是根据辈分加以区分的,有时也根据年代资历区分。通常受到尊重的那些亲属都是上一辈的人,如岳母及其姐妹、岳父及

the wife's mother's brother. The joking relatives are those of a person's own generation; but very frequently a distinction of seniority within the generation is made; a wife's older sister or brother may be respected while those younger will be teased.

In certain societies a man may be said to have relatives by marriage long before he marries and indeed as soon as he is born into the world. This is provided by the institution of the required or preferential marriage. We will, for the sake of brevity, consider only one kind of such organisations. In many societies it is regarded as preferable that a man should marry the daughter of his mother's brother; this is a form of the custom known as cross cousin marriage. Thus his female cousins of this kind, or all those women whom by the classificatory system he classifies as such, are potential wives for him, and their brothers are his potential brothers-in-law. Among the Ojibwa Indians of North America, the Chiga of Uganda, and in Fiji and New Caledonia, as well as elsewhere, this form of marriage is found and is accompanied by a joking relationship between a man and the sons and daughters of his mother's brother. To quote one instance of these, the following is recorded for the Ojibwa. 'When cross-cousins meet they must try to embarrass one another. They "joke" one another, making the most vulgar allegations, by their standards as well as ours. But being "kind" relations, no one can take offence. Cross-cousins who do not joke in this way are considered boorish, as not playing the social game.'①

The joking relationship here is of fundamentally the same kind as that already discussed. It is established before marriage and is continued, after marriage, with the brothers- and sisters-in-law.

In some parts of Africa there are joking relationships that have nothing to do with marriage. Mr. Pedler's note, mentioned above,

---

① Ruth Landes in Mead, *Co-operation and Competition among Primitive Peoples*, 1937, *p.* 103.

其兄弟们,有时也包括岳母的兄弟们。戏谑关系通常发生在同辈之间,但经常要考虑年纪的区别;有时需要尊重妻子的姐姐和哥哥,但可以戏谑其弟弟妹妹们。

在一些社会中,由于存在指定婚或优先婚习俗,一位男士可以说在结婚前很久,或是从他出生起,就有了姻亲。为了简明之便,我们在这里只谈这类习俗中的一种。在许多社会里,人们一般认为男人最好能娶舅父的女儿为妻,这种形式的习俗被称作"交表婚"。因此他的表姐妹,或者在这个划分体系中所有的女人都有可能成为他的妻子。而她们的兄弟们则有可能成为他的妻兄或妻弟。在北美奥吉布瓦印第安人和乌干达的奇加人中,还有在斐济和新喀里多尼亚,以及世界上其他地方,都可以发现这种联姻现象,并且伴有男子与舅父的孩子们之间的戏谑关系。奥吉布瓦人的一个例子,可以描述这种现象:"当交表亲们相见时,他们必须试图使对方困窘。他们彼此'戏谑'。他们所说的话,无论是从我们的标准,还是他们的标准来衡量,都是最粗俗的。但由于彼此间的亲密关系,没有人会发怒。那些不用这种方式开玩笑的表亲们被认为是粗鲁的人,因为他们不会玩这种社会游戏。"①

刚才谈到的这种姻亲间的戏谑关系与我们已讨论过的戏谑关系基本上是一样的。它早在结婚之前就已确立,并在婚后又在妻兄、妻弟、嫂子和弟媳之间继续延续。

而在非洲的一些地区,戏谑关系却与婚姻没有任何关系。例

---

① 鲁思·兰德斯,载米德《原始民族中的合作与竞争》,1937 年版,第 103 页。

refers to a joking relationship between two distinct tribes, the Sukuma and the Zaramu, and in the evidence it was stated that there was a similar relation between the Sukuma and the Zigua and between the Ngoni and the Bemba. The woman's evidence suggests that this custom of rough teasing exists in the Sukuma tribe between persons related by marriage, as it does in so many other African tribes. ①

While a joking relationship between two tribes is apparently rare, and certainly deserves, as Mr. Pedler suggests, to be carefully investigated, a similar relationship between clans has been observed in other parts of Africa. It is described by Professor Labouret and Mademoiselle Paulme in the articles previously mentioned, and amongst the Tallensi it has been studied by Dr. Fortes, who will deal with it in a forthcoming publication. ②

The two clans are not, in these instances, specially connected by intermarriage. The relation between them is an alliance involving real friendliness and mutual aid combined with an appearance of hostility.

The general structural situation in these instances seems to be as

---

① Incidentally it may be said that it was hardly satisfactory for the magistrate to establish a precedent whereby the man, who was observing what was a permitted and may even have been an obligatory custom, was declared guilty of common assault, even with extenuating circumstances. It seems quite possible that the man may have committed a breach of etiquette in teasing the woman in the presence of her mother's brother, for in many parts of the world it is regarded as improper for two persons in a joking relationship to tease one another (particularly if any obscenity is involved) in the presence of certain relatives of either of them. But the breach of etiquette would still not make it an assault. A little knowledge of anthropology would have enabled the magistrate, by putting the appropriate questions to the witnesses, to have obtained a fuller understanding of the case and all that was involved in it.

② Fortes, M., *The Dynamics of Clanship among the Tallensi*. Oxford University Press, 1945.

如两个不同部落,苏库马人和扎拉莫人之间的戏谑关系曾在佩德勒先生的笔记中被提及。另外现有资料也显示了苏库马人和齐瓜人之间,及恩戈尼人和本巴人之间存在相似的关系。正如那位妇女所说的,与非洲其他部落一样,在有姻亲关系的人之间可以相互戏谑的风俗在苏库马部落也存在。①

然而,两个部落之间存在戏谑关系的情况却极少出现。因此,正如佩德勒先生所说,这种情况值得仔细调查研究。在非洲其他地区的不同氏族间也存在一种与此相似的关系,部分学者已经研究了这种关系。例如这种关系曾在拉布雷和马德穆瓦瑟勒·波尔默两位教授的文章中描述过,而福茨博士曾研究过存在于塔兰西人中的这种关系,他在即将出版的一本书中将再次讨论这一问题。②

在那些例子中,两个氏族并不只是靠联姻联系在一起,而是由在敌对伪装下的真正友谊和相互帮助结成的联盟联系在一起的。

可以把这些例子中显示的一般结构状态大体描述如下:个人

---

① 顺便提一下,人们对那位法官并不满意,因为他开创了一个先例,判决那个男人犯了一般伤害罪,但实际上存在减罪的理由,因为这种习俗甚至可能是必须履行的。看来极有可能的是,因为当着那女人舅舅的面嘲笑她这一点败坏了礼俗。因为在世界上许多地区,两个有戏谑关系的人在有任何一方的某些亲戚在场的情况下互相取笑(特别是含有淫秽成分时),都被视为不道德的事。但伤风败俗并不是一种伤害。如果那位法官有一些人类学方面的知识,他就可以向证人提出适当问题,以对这一案件及与相关的一切事情全面考虑。

② 福茨:《塔伦西人氏族制度发展史》,牛津大学出版社,1945 年版。

follows. The individual is a member of a certain defined group, a clan, for example, within which his relations to others are defined by a complex set of rights and duties, referring to all the major aspects of social life, and supported by definite sanctions. There may be another group outside his own which is so linked with his as to be the field of extension of jural and moral relations of the same general kind. Thus, in East Africa, as we learn from Mr. Pedler's note, the Zigua and the Zaramu do not joke with one another because a yet closer bond exists between them since they are *ndugu* (brothers). But beyond the field within which social relations are thus defined there lie other groups with which, since they are outsiders to the individual's own group, the relation involves possible or actual hostility. In any fixed relations between the members of two such groups the separateness of the groups must be recognised. It is precisely this separateness which is not merely recognised but emphasised when a joking relationship is established. The show of hostility, the perpetual disrespect, is a continual expression of that social disjunction which is an essential part of the whole structural situation, but over which, without destroying or even weakening it, there is provided the social conjunction of friendliness and mutual aid.

The theory that is here put forward, therefore, is that both the joking relationship which constitutes an alliance between clans or tribes, and that between relatives by marriage, are modes of organising a definite and stable system of social behaviour in which conjunctive and disjunctive components, as I have called them, are maintained and combined.

To provide the full evidence for this theory by following out its implications and examining in detail its application to different instances would take a book rather than a short article. But some confirmation can perhaps be offered by a consideration of the way in which respect and disrespect appear in various kinship relations, even though nothing more can be attempted than a very brief indication of a few significant points.

属于某一特定的群体，例如一个氏族，他与群体内其他成员之间的行为模式依靠以下方式进行：由一套复杂的涵盖社会生活各个重要方面的权利和责任体系确定他们之间的关系，而由制裁维持其长期存在。这里还可能有其他群体存在，他们与本群体有紧密关系，这些群体都受到相同的法律和道德的约束。因此，正如佩德勒先生笔记记载的那样，在东非，由于群体之间的紧密联系，并把对方视为 ndugu（兄弟），所以在齐瓜人和扎拉莫人之间并不相互取笑。但是，在这种紧密联系的社会关系以外还有些其他群体，他们就像局外人一样，所以本群体与他们之间会涉及到可能的或真正的敌对关系。群体的分离性是这样的两个群体中成员之间存在的任何关系的基本特征。准确地说，建立戏谑关系就表明确立了这种群体间的分离性，而且会使其程度得到加强。社会分离作为整个结构状态的一部分必须不断地通过群体间的敌对情绪和永久的不尊重加以确立。尽管表示友好和互助的社会联合存在于社会分离之上，但是这种社会联合既不能消除也不能削弱社会分离。

因此，我的观点是：作为不同模式的基本组成部分，构成氏族及部落联盟的戏谑关系和姻亲间的戏谑关系都能建立起独特及稳定的社会行为体系。我谈到的构成社会联合及分离的元素在这个体系中得以维持并结合在一起。

彻底阐明我的观点、详细考察它在不同情况下的表现形式、充分论证它，要完成这个任务，需要写一本书，而不能仅仅靠一篇短文。但，我们或许可以通过考察如何在各种亲属关系中表达尊敬和不敬的方式，得到一些启示，尽管这里我只能非常简单地指出一些要点。

In studying a kinship system it is possible to distinguish the different relatives by reference to the kind and degree of respect that is paid to them. ① Although kinship systems vary very much in their details there are certain principles which are found to be very widespread.

One of them is that by which a person is required to show a marked respect to relatives belonging to the generation immediately preceding his own. In a majority of societies the father is a relative to whom marked respect must be shown. This is so even in many so-called matrilineal societies, i. e. those which are organised into matrilineal clans or lineages. One can very frequently observe a tendency to extend this attitude of respect to all relatives of the first ascending generation and, further, to persons who are not relatives. Thus in those tribes of East Africa that are organised into age-sets a man is required to show special respect to all men of his father's age set and to their wives.

The social function of this is obvious. The social tradition is handed down from one generation to the next. For the tradition to be maintained it must have authority behind it. The authority is therefore normally recognised as possessed by members of the preceding generation and it is they who exercise discipline. As a result of this the relation between persons of the two generations usually contains an element of inequality, the parents and those of their generation being in a position of superiority over the children who are subordinate to them. The unequal relation between a father and his son is maintained by requiring the latter to show respect to the former. The relation is asymmetrical.

When we turn to the relation of an individual to his grand parents and their brothers and sisters we find that in the majority of human societies relatives of the second ascending generation are treated with very much less respect than those of the first ascending generation, and instead of a marked inequality there is a tendency

---

① See, for example, the kinship systems described in Social *Anthropology of North American Tribes*, edited by Fred Eggan, University of Chicago Press, 1937; and Margaret Mead, 'Kinship in the Admiralty Islands', *Anthropological Papers of the American Museum of Natural History*, Vol. XXXIV, pp. 243-56.

在亲属关系体系中，不同亲属可以根据他们得到的尊重种类及程度划分。① 在不同的亲属体系迥然不同的背后，仍旧存在某些广为流传的一般性原则。例如，在亲属体系中，上一辈的亲属会得到下一代人明显的尊重。我们发现父亲在大多数社会体系中都会得到明显的尊重，这种现象甚至在许多所谓的按照母系氏族和母系世系群组成的母系社会里，也是存在的。而且人们常常可以观察到，对所有上一辈的亲属有时甚至是非亲属的人都表示出这种尊重的趋势。因此，如果东非的部落中存在年龄组织，那么父亲辈年龄组中的所有男人以及他们的妻子们就会得到下一代人特别的敬意。

对于社会来说，保持这种敬意的作用非常明显。为了社会传统的代代传承，必须有某种权威作为保证。而正是上一代人才被认为拥有这种权威，也正是他们在运用这种权威。由于这种原因，一般来说两代人之间地位是不平等的，子女必须对父母及其同辈的人表示尊重，而这种下一代对上一代的尊重使地位上的不平等和优越感得以维持。而且他们之间的这种关系是不对称的。

下面考察一个人和其祖父母辈亲属之间的关系。在大多数人类社会中，相对于父辈亲属来说，祖辈亲属获得的尊敬要明显少得多。一个人和祖辈之间基本是友好相待的平等关系，而不是那

① 可参阅诸如弗雷德·伊根编:《北美部落的社会人类学》中描述的亲属体系，芝加哥大学出版社，1937 年版；玛格丽特·米德《阿默勒尔蒂群岛的亲属制度》，《美国自然历史博物馆人类学论文》，第 34 卷，第 243 ~ 256 页。

to approximate to a friendly equality. Considerations of space forbid any full discussion of this feature of social structure, which is one of very great importance. There are many instances in which the grandparents and their grandchildren are grouped together in the social structure in opposition to their children and parents. An important clue to the under standing of the subject is the fact that in the flow of social life through time, in which men are born, become mature and die, the grandchildren replace their grandparents.

In many societies there is an actual joking relationship, usually of a relatively mild kind, between relatives of alternate genera tions. Grandchildren make fun of their grandparents and of those who are called grandfather and grandmother by the classificatory system of terminology, and these reply in kind.

Grandparents and grandchildren are united by kinship; they are separated by age and by the social difference that results from the fact that as the grandchildren are in process of entering into full participation in the social life of the community the grandparents are gradually retiring from it. Important duties towards his relatives in his own and even more in his parents' generation impose upon an individual many restraints; but with those of the second ascending generation, his grandparents and collateral relatives, there can be, and usually is, established a relationship of simple friendliness relatively free from restraint. In this instance also, it is suggested, the joking relationship is a method of ordering a relation which combines social conjunction and disjunction.

This thesis could, I believe, be strongly supported if not demonstrated by considering the details of these relationships. There is space for only one illustrative point. A very common form of joke in this connection is for the grandchild to pretend that he wishes to marry the grandfather's wife, or that he intends to do so when his grandfather dies, or to treat her as already being his wife. Alternatively the grandfather may pretend that the wife of his grandchild

种明显的不平等。

由于篇幅的限制，不可能详尽描述社会结构的这一重要特征。但在很多例证中都可以看出，在社会结构中，祖孙三代之间祖辈会与孙辈联合在一起，而与第二代的父辈对抗。这一现象的一个重要的线索就是随着社会生活在时间中的流动，人们从出生到长大到死亡，孙辈逐渐取代祖辈。

在很多社会里，确实存在一种相对温和的隔代人之间的戏谑关系。孙辈们可以嘲弄祖辈和那些根据类分式称谓体系被叫作祖父祖母的人，而祖辈们则给以亲切的回应。

祖辈与孙辈的联系纽带依靠血缘关系；同时他们又被年龄差别及社会差别分隔开来，这种社会差别就是当孙辈们一步步完全踏入群体的社会生活时，祖辈们则逐渐从这种生活中退出。在社会生活中，一个人和同辈、父辈及祖辈之间的行为方式是不同的。对于同辈乃至父辈的亲属们，他会因为担负有重要的责任而受到诸多限制；但与其祖辈们，即其祖父母和祖辈的表亲们，却通常能建立起一种相对单纯的友谊关系，并且也没有那么多的限制。上述例子说明，戏谑关系可以用来建立一种社会联合与社会分离相结合的关系。

我相信，这一观点即使不经过细节考虑来证明，也能够得到充分的支持。在这里我只用一个很普通的玩笑来对这一观点加以说明。祖孙两辈都可以互相开关于对方妻子的玩笑，孙子可以假装要娶祖母为妻，或当祖父去世再娶她，甚至也可能直接把祖母看作妻子。相应地，祖父对孙子也可以如此，他可以假装

is, or might be, his wife.① The point of the joke is the pretence at ignoring the difference of age between the grandparent and the grandchild.

In various parts of the world there are societies in which a sister's son teases and otherwise behaves disrespectfully towards his mother's brother. In these instances the joking relationship seems generally to be asymmetrical. For example the nephew may take his uncle's property but not vice versa; or, as amongst the Nama Hottentots, the nephew may take a fine beast from his uncle's herd and the uncle in return takes a wretched beast from that of the nephew.②

The kind of social structure in which this custom of privileged disrespect to the mother's brother occurs in its most marked forms, for example the Thonga of South-East Africa, Fiji and Tonga in the Pacific, and the Central Siouan tribes of North America, is characterised by emphasis on patrilineal lineage and a marked distinction between relatives through the father and relatives through the mother. In a former publication③ I offered an interpretation of this custom of privileged familiarity towards the mother's brother. Briefly it is as follows. For the continuance of a social system children require to be cared for and to be trained. Their care demands affectionate and unselfish devotion; their training requires that they shall be subjected to discipline. In the societies with which we are concerned there is something of a division of function between the parents and other relatives on the two sides.

---

① For examples see Labouret, *Les Tribus du Rameau Lobi*, 1931, p. 248, and Sarat Chandra Roy, *The Oraons of Chota Nagpur*, Ranchi, 1915, pp. 352-4.

② A. Winifred Hoernl, 'Social Organisation of the Nama Hottentot'; *American Anthropologist*, N. S., Vol. XXVII, 1925, pp. 1-24.

③ 'The Mother's Brother in South Africa', *South African Journal of Science*, Vol. XXI, 1924. See Chapter I.

要娶孙子的妻子,或者直接把她看做妻子。[1] 在这里,关键是双方都假装无视他们之间的年龄差别。

在世界各地都存在这样的社会,那里外甥戏谑的对象可以是舅舅,而且在这些戏谑关系形式中双方之间似乎都是不对等的。例如,外甥可以拿走舅舅的财产,但舅舅却不可以有同样的行为;或者,像纳马霍屯督人那样,外甥可以赶走舅舅畜群中最健康的牲畜,但舅舅只能从外甥那里取走病弱的牲畜。[2]

这种可对舅舅表示不敬的习俗在某些社会结构中表现得十分明显,在非洲东南部的聪加人、太平洋中的斐济人和汤加人以及北美的中央苏人部落中,都可以看到这种习俗形式。在这些社会结构中,他们都强调父系,在父系亲属和母系亲属间存在明显的差别。

以前我曾发表过一篇关于亲近舅父习俗的文章。[3] 对这种习俗简单说来就是:孩子们是社会体系得以维系的基础,他们必须得到很好的照顾和训练。对他们的照顾应该是充满爱意的和一种无私的奉献;而对他们的训练则是以培养他们遵守纪律为目的的。在我们谈到的社会中,对孩子的父母以及其父系亲属和母系亲属的职能都有所划分,从而在担负对孩子的照顾和训练方面也会承担

---

① 案例可参见拉布雷:《洛比人支族的部落》,1931 年,第 248 页和萨拉特·霍恩莱:《乔塔纳格普尔的奥昂人》,兰契,1915 年,第 352 ~ 354 页。

② 阿·威尼弗雷德·霍恩莱《纳马雷屯督人的社会组织》,《美国人类学家》,第 17 卷,1925 年,第 1 ~ 24 页。

③ 《南非的母舅》,见第 1 章。

The control and discipline are exercised chiefly by the father and his brothers and generally also by his sisters; these are relatives who must be respected and obeyed. It is the mother who is primarily responsible for the affectionate care; the mother and her brothers and sisters are therefore relatives who can be looked to for assistance and indulgence. The mother's brother is called 'male mother' in Tonga and in some South African tribes.

I believe that this interpretation of the special position of the mother's brother in these societies has been confirmed by further field work since I wrote the article referred to. But I was quite aware at the time it was written that the discussion and interpre tation needed to be supplemented so as to bring them into line with a general theory of the social functions of respect and disrespect.

The joking relationship with the mother's brother seems to fit well with the general theory of such relationships here outlined. A person's most important duties and rights attach him to his paternal relatives, living and dead. It is to his patrilineal lineage or clan that he belongs. For the members of his mother's lineage he is an outsider, though one in whom they have a very special and tender interest. Thus here again there is a relation in which there is both attachment, or conjunction, and separation, or disjunction, between the two persons concerned.

But let us remember that in this instance the relation is asymmetrical. ① The nephew is disrespectful and the uncle accepts the disrespect. There is inequality and the nephew is the superior. This is recognised by the natives themselves. Thus in Tonga it is said that the sister's son is a 'chief' (*eiki*) to his mother's brother, and Junod② quotes a Thonga native as saying 'The uterine nephew is a chief! He takes any liberty he likes with his maternal uncle'.

---

① There are some societies in which the relation between a mother's brother and a sister's son is approximately symmetrial, and therefore one of equality. This seems to be so in the Western Islands of Torres Straits, but we have no information as to any teasing or joking, though it is said that each of the two relatives may take the property of the other.

② *Life of a South African Tribe*, Vol. I, p. 255.

不同的任务。父亲及其兄弟(有时也包括父亲的姐妹),主要是对孩子进行管治,使他们遵守纪律,孩子必须听从并尊敬他们;而母亲主要负责照顾、关心孩子,孩子可以从母亲及其兄弟姐妹那里得到救助有时甚至是溺爱。比如在汤加人和南非的一些部落那里,舅舅就被称作“男性母亲”。

我相信,在我刚才提到的文章发表后,通过进一步的实地调查,我对这些社会中舅父的特殊地位阐述的正确性得到了进一步的证实。但在写那篇文章的时候,我就意识到这种讨论和解释的不完全性,为使之能与有关尊敬和不敬的社会功能的一般理论统一起来,有必要对其补充和完善。

和舅父间的戏谑关系似乎与这里略述的关于戏谑关系的一般理论极为符合。一个人是从属于父系的世系群或氏族的,这种社会结构中他所有的最重要的责任与权利决定了他不论是生前还是死后都要依附于父系亲属。但对于其母系亲属来说,他是个局外人,尽管母系亲属们对他有着极体贴的、温柔的爱护。所以,外甥既依附于舅父,但和他又存在着分隔。

但是,我们已经知道在这个例子中,戏谑关系的双方是不对称的。[①] 关系的不对称即不平等是指舅父接受外甥对自己的不敬,此处外甥位于优势地位,而且土著人也承认了这一点。因此,据说,在汤加人中,外甥是舅父的“首领”。朱诺德[②]就曾引用过聪加土著人的话:“同父异母的外甥是首领。他可以在

① 在某些社会中,舅父与外甥的关系是一种近于对称的平等关系。就像托雷斯海峡西部群岛那样。但是,虽然据说那里舅父和外甥可以互取对方的财产,却没有任何关于戏谑的材料。

② 《南非部落的生活》,第1卷,第252页。

Thus the joking relationship with the uncle does not merely annul the usual relation between the two genera tions, it reverses it. But while the superiority of the father and the father's sister is exhibited in the respect that is shown to them, the nephew's superiority to his mother's brother takes the opposite form of permitted disrespect.

It has been mentioned that there is a widespread tendency to feel that a man should show respect towards, and treat as social superiors, his relatives in the generation preceding his own, and the custom of joking with, and at the expense of, the maternal uncle clearly conflicts with this tendency. This conflict between principles of behaviour helps us to understand what seems at first sight a very extraordinary feature of the kinship terminology of the Thonga tribe and the VaNdau tribe in South-East Africa. Amongst the Thonga, although there is a term *malume* (= male mother) for the mother's brother, this relative is also, and perhaps more frequently, referred to as a grandfather (*kokwana*) and he refers to his sister's son as his grandchild (*ntukulu*). In the VaNdau tribe the mother's brother and also the mother's brother's son are called 'grandfather' (*tetekulu*, *literally* '*great father*') and their wives are called 'grandmother' (*mbiya*), while the sister's son and the father's sister's son are called 'grandchild' (*muzukulu*).

This apparently fantastic way of classifying relatives can be interpreted as a sort of legal fiction whereby the male relatives of the mother's lineage are grouped together as all standing towards an individual in the same general relation. Since this relation is one of privileged familiarity on the one side, and solicitude and indulgence on the other, it is conceived as being basically the one appropriate for a grandchild and a grandfather. This is indeed in the majority of human societies the relationship in which this pattern of behaviour most frequently occurs. By this legal fiction the mother's brother ceases to belong to the first ascending generation, of which it is felt that the members ought to be respected.

It may be worth while to justify this interpretation by considering another of the legal fictions of the VaNdau terminology. In all these south-eastern Bantu tribes both the father's sister and the sister, particularly the elder sister, are persons who must be treated with great respect.

舅父那儿随意放任自己。"两代人的正常关系不仅没有表现出来，反而被与舅父之间的戏谑关系破坏了，甚至是被颠覆了。但是，这种双方之间地位优越的表现形式也会有所不同，父亲及其姐妹们对晚辈的优越地位使他们得到了后者对他们的尊敬，而外甥对舅父的优越地位却以相反的方式表现出来，即舅父允许外甥对其不敬。

刚才提到过人们普遍认为，应当像对待社会的长者一样尊重上一辈的人。与舅父戏谑的习俗却明显地不符合这种普遍看法。但这种冲突的行为模式可以帮助我们理解某种存在于非洲东南部聪加部落和万道部落的怪异的亲属称谓。在聪加人中，*malume*（意思是男性母亲）用来称呼舅父，但对他更常用的称呼却是祖父，而舅父也将外甥称为孙子。在万道部落中，把舅父和舅父的儿子称作"祖父"（"大父亲"的意思），而他们的妻子被称作"祖母"，外甥和姑母之子都被称作"孙子"。

显然，这是种怪异的亲属分类方式，它可能是一种法律上的假设。按照这种方式，一个人在母方世系群中的男性亲属被视为同属一个亲属范畴，他对他们采用同一行为模式。他有亲近的特权，而母方的男性亲属对他则是关心和溺爱，双方之间就像祖孙之间的关系一样。在大多数人类社会中，最常发生戏谑关系的亲属之间确实存在这种模式。在这种法律假设下，舅父已不再被看做是父辈亲属的范畴，因为父辈是应该得到尊敬的人。

为了证实以上这种解释，也许值得考察万道人称谓制度的另一个法律假设。在这个称谓分类假设中姐妹被看做属于父辈亲属的范畴，从而会被给予明显的敬意。我们可以看到在所有这些

They are also both of them members of a man's own patrilineal lineage. Amongst the VaNdau the father's sister is called 'female father' (*tetadji*) and so also is the sister. ①Thus by the fiction of terminological classification the sister is placed in the father's generation, the one that appropriately includes persons to whom one must exhibit marked respect.

In the south-eastern Bantu tribes there is assimilation of two kinds of joking relatives, the grandfather and the mother's brother. It may help our understanding of this to consider an example in which the grandfather and the brother-in-law are similarly grouped together. The Cherokee Indians of North America, probably numbering at one time about 20,000, were divided into seven matrilineal clans. ② A man could not marry a woman of his own clan or of his father's clan. Common membership of the same clan connects him with his brothers and his mother's brothers. Towards his father and all his relatives in his father's clan of his own or his father's generation he is required by custom to show a marked respect. He applies the kinship term for 'father' not only to his father's brothers but also to the sons of his father's sisters. Here is another example of the same kind of fiction as described above; the relatives of his own generation whom he is required to respect and who belong to his father's matrilineal lineage are spoken of as though they belonged to the generation of his parents. The body of his immediate kindred is included in these two clans, that of his mother and his father. To the other clans of the tribe he is in a sense an outsider. But with two of them he is connected, namely with the clans of his two grandfathers, his father's father and his mother's father. He speaks of all the members of these two clans, of whatever age, as 'grandfathers' and 'grandmothers'. He stands in a joking relationship with all of them.

① For the kinship terminology of the VaNdau see Boas, 'Das Verwandtschafts system der Vandau', in *Zeitschrift f r Ethnologie*, 1922, *pp.* 41-51.

② For an account of the Cherokee see Gilbert, *in Social Anthropology of North American Tribes*, *pp.* 285-338.

东南部的班图部落中，一个人父亲的姐妹以及自己的姐妹，都属于他的父方世系群的范畴。她们尤其是姐姐们会得到极大的尊重。而万道人甚至还把父亲的姐妹和自己的姐妹都称为“女性父亲”。①

在东南部班图部落中，存在把祖父和舅父这两种可以有戏谑关系的亲属同化的现象。下面的例子也许会有助于我们更好的理解此现象，在这个例子中，祖父和姐夫和妹夫被认为是同一类亲属范畴。北美洲的切罗基印第安人，曾经有大约2万人，分为7个母系氏族。② 一个男人不能够娶自己氏族或其父亲氏族的女人。他与他的兄弟及他母亲的兄弟依靠同属一个氏族这个纽带联系起来。按照习俗，对他的父亲以及父亲氏族内的所有同辈和父辈的一代亲属他都应该表示敬意。他不但要称呼父亲的兄弟为“父亲”，而且还要这样称呼姑母的儿子。这里的例子与上面所描述的假设相同的是，对于和他同辈的父亲的母方世系群的亲属，他将他们划为和他父母同辈的亲属范畴，而且他必须尊重他们。和他关系很近的亲属都在他母亲的氏族和父亲的氏族中，在某种程度上，他对于其他氏族是个局外人。他和这些氏族中的两个存在联系，即祖父及外祖父的氏族。无论年龄大小，他都称这两个氏族中的所有成员为“祖父”和“祖母”，并与他们所有人都保持着戏

① 万道人的亲属称谓，可参见博厄斯：《万道人的亲属制度》，《民族学杂志》1922年，第41~51页。

② 请参见吉尔伯特的有关切罗基人的描写，载弗雷德·伊根编《北美部落的社会人类学》，第285~338页。

When a man marries he must respect his wife's parents but jokes with her brothers and sisters.

The interesting and critical feature is that it is regarded as particularly appropriate that a man should marry a woman whom he calls 'grandmother', i. e. a member of his father's father's clan or his mother's father's clan. If this happens his wife's brothers and sisters, whom he continues to tease, are amongst those whom he previously teased as his 'grandfathers' and 'grandmothers'. This is analogous to the widely spread organisation in which a man has a joking relationship with the children of his mother's brother and is expected to marry one of the daughters.

It ought perhaps to be mentioned that the Cherokee also have a one-sided joking relationship in which a man teases his father's sister's husband. The same custom is found in Mota of the Bank Islands. In both instances we have a society organised on a matrilineal basis in which the mother's brother is respected, the father's sister's son is called 'father' (so that the father's sister's husband is the father of a 'father'), and there is a special term for the father's sister's husband. Further observation of the societies in which this custom occurs is required before we can be sure of its interpretation. I do not remember that it has been reported from any part of Africa.

What has been attempted in this paper is to define in the most general and abstract terms the kind of structural situation in which we may expect to find well-marked joking relationships. We have been dealing with societies in which the basic social structure is provided by kinship. By reason of his birth or adoption into a certain position in the social structure an individual is connected with a large number of other persons. With some of them he finds himself in a definite and specific jural relation, i. e. one which can be defined in terms of rights and duties. Who these persons will be and what will be the rights and duties depend on the form taken by the social structure. As an example of such a specific jural relation we may take that which normally exists between a father and

谑关系。在切罗基人中,一个男人婚后虽然可以同妻子的兄弟姐妹开玩笑,但是,他必须尊重妻子的双亲。

这里,一个有趣的关键特征是:一个男人与他祖父氏族或外祖父氏族的一位女人的婚姻被认为是特别合适的,婚前他称这些女子为“祖母”。发生这种婚姻后,他可以开玩笑的对象并无变化,只是他们的亲属称谓发生了变化,以前那些被称呼为“祖父”和“祖母”的人现在是他妻子的兄弟姐妹。这种现象与一种普遍的社会结构很相似。在这种社会结构中,戏谑关系存在于这个男子与舅父的子女之间,并且大家也期待他能与舅父的一个女儿结婚。

应该说,在切罗基人和班克群岛的莫塔人中都能够发现一个男人可以取笑姑母的丈夫,而且他们之间的这种戏谑关系是单方面的。因为是以母系基础构建上述两个社会结构,从而在这种社会中,舅父受到尊重,姑母的儿子被称作“父亲”(姑母的丈夫就是“父亲”的父亲),另外还专有一个名词来称呼姑母的丈夫。对这种风俗确切的解释建立在对这种习俗依存的社会深入考察的基础上。但目前为止我还没看到过有这方面的文献。

本文一直致力于对存在明显戏谑关系的社会结构用最具有概括性和抽象性的术语来定义。在我们已经讨论过的一些社会结构中,存在下述关系:社会的亲属制度决定了这个社会的基本社会结构;而社会结构决定了社会中各个人的地位、他们之间的关系等。一个人由于出生或被收养从而获得一个确定的地位,也就与其他人发生联系,并与一些特定的人产生以各种权利和责任为表现形式的法律关系。与哪些人发生关系,他们之间又是怎样的权利和责任,这些都依赖于社会结构的特定形式。其中一种具体

son, or an elder brother and a younger brother. Relations of the same general type may be extended over a considerable range to all the members of a lineage or a clan or an age-set. Besides these specific jural relations which are defined not only negatively but also positively, i. e. in terms of things that must be done as well as things that must not, there are general jural relations which are expressed almost entirely in terms of prohibitions and which extend throughout the whole political society. It is forbidden to kill or wound other persons or to take or destroy their property. Besides these two classes of social relations there is another, including many very diverse varieties, which can perhaps be called relations of alliance or consociation. For example, there is a form of alliance of very great importance in many societies, in which two persons or two groups are connected by an exchange of gifts or services. ① Another example is provided by the institution of blood-brotherhood which is so widespread in Africa.

The argument of this paper has been intended to show that the joking relationship is one special form of alliance in this sense. An alliance by exchange of goods and services may be associated with a joking relationship, as in the instance recorded by Professor Labouret. ② Or it may be combined with the custom of avoidance. Thus in the Andaman Islands the parents of a man and the parents of his wife avoid all contact with each other and do not speak; at the same time it is the custom that they should frequently exchange presents through the medium of the younger married couple. But the exchange of gifts may also exist without either joking or avoidance, as in Samoa, in the exchange of gifts between the family of a man and the family of the woman he marries or the very similar exchange between a chief and his 'talking chief'.

---

① See Mauss, 'Essai sur le Don', *Ann ée Sociologique*, *Nouvelle* Séréie, tome I, pp. 30-186.

② *Africa*, Vol. II, p. 245.

的法律关系就表现在父子或兄弟之间正常存在的关系中。其他与之基本相同的各种关系的适用范围更广，甚至可以扩展到世系群、氏族群或年龄组的所有成员。具体法律关系的规定基本都是确定性的，某件事要么被肯定，即这件事可以做；要么被否定，即它不可以做。除此之外还有一些普通的法律关系，它们几乎全是关于禁止做什么的，而且涵盖的范围包括整个政治社会。例如杀人、伤害他人、夺取或毁坏他人的财产都是受到禁止的。除了以上这两种以法律关系表述的社会关系之外，还有另外一种社会关系，在其中有很多种关系类型，也许可以把它叫做联盟或同盟关系。一个例子就是，在许多社会中一种重要的联盟都是靠这些社会中个人或群体交换礼品或劳动联结而成的。① 另一个例子就是在非洲普遍存在的结拜兄弟的习俗。

本文一直致力于表明，戏谑关系在某种程度上说是联盟的一种特殊形式。通过交换物品及劳务所结成的联盟也许与戏谑关系有关，正像拉布雷教授提供的实例中记载的那样；②也许恰恰相反，与回避的风俗有关。例如在安达曼群岛，夫妻双方的父母之间既避免任何相互接触，也彼此不说话；同时习俗规定，他们应当经常交换礼品，当然是通过这对年轻夫妇之手。但是，相互交换礼物的现象也存在于无须戏谑或回避的关系下。如在萨摩亚，夫妻双方家庭之间的礼物交换或者与此非常相似的首领与其“说话首领”之间的礼物交换。

---

① 见莫斯：《论馈赠》，《社会学年刊》，新丛书系列第 1 卷，第 30 ~ 186 页。

② 《非洲》第 2 卷，第 245 页。

So also in an alliance by blood-brotherhood there may be a joking relationship as amongst the Zande;[1] and in the somewhat similar alliance formed by exchange of names there may also be mutual teasing. But in alliances of this kind there may be a relation of extreme respect and even of avoidance. Thus in the Yaralde and neighbouring tribes of South Australia two boys belonging to communities distant from one another, and therefore more or less hostile, are brought into an alliance by the exchange of their respective umbilical cords. The relationship thus established is a sacred one; the two boys may never speak to one another. But when they grow up they enter upon a regular exchange of gifts, which provides the machinery for a sort of commerce between the two groups to which they belong.

Thus the four modes of alliance or consociation, (1) through intermarriage, (2) by exchange of goods or services, (3) by blood-brotherhood or exchanges of names or sacra, and (4) by the joking relationship, may exist separately or combined in several different ways. The comparative study of these combinations presents a number of interesting but complex problems. The facts recorded from West Africa by Professor Labouret and Mademoiselle Paulme afford us valuable material. But a good deal more intensive field research is needed before these problems of social structure can be satisfactorily dealt with.

What I have called relations by alliance need to be compared with true contractual relations. The latter are specific jural relations entered into by two persons or two groups, in which either party has definite positive obligations towards the other, and failure to carry out the obligations is subject to a legal sanction. In an alliance by blood-brotherhood there are general obligations of mutual aid, and the sanction for the carrying out of these, as shown by Dr. Evans-Pritchard, is of a kind that can be called magical or ritual. In the alliance by exchange of gifts failure

① Evans-Pritchard, 'Zande Blood-brotherhood', *Africa*, Vol. VI, 1933, pp. 369-401.

戏谑关系也有可能存在于由结拜兄弟而建立的联盟中，例如在赞德人中；[①]也可能存在于那种由于通过交换名字而建立的略为相似的同盟中。但在后者中也许存在一种相互极为尊敬，甚至是回避的关系。因此，在澳大利亚南部的雅拉尔德人及其邻近的部落中，两个男孩子分属两个相离很远甚至有些敌对的群体，他们通过互换脐带结成同盟。通过这种方式建立的关系是神圣的，要求他们之间永远不能讲话。但，成年后就开始经常互换礼物，以此为他们所属的两个群体之间建立一种贸易机制。

我已谈到的四种同盟或联盟的模式是：(1)通过联姻结盟；(2)通过交换物品及劳务而结成的联盟；(3)通过结拜兄弟或交换名字或骶骨结成的同盟；(4)通过戏谑关系而结成的同盟。它们也许会独立存在，也许以不同的方式结合在一起。对这些结合方式的比较研究给我们提出了许多有趣而又复杂的问题。在这方面，拉布雷和马德穆瓦瑟勒·波尔默教授关于西非的文献非常有价值也很丰富。但是，还必须做更多深入的实地研究才能对这些社会结构问题得出令人满意的答案。

上述的联盟关系还要与真正的契约关系做一对比。契约关系是指具体的法律关系，在两人或两个群体之间，一方对另一方承担确定的义务，法律会制裁不履行应有义务的一方。在通过结拜兄弟建立的同盟关系中，两人之间是一般的互助性义务，通过巫术或某种仪式履行对这些义务的约束，这点伊文斯·普理查德曾经有过论述。在由交换礼物而建立的同盟中，同盟关系将会因

① 伊文斯－普里查德：《赞德人中的拜把兄弟》，《非洲》第6卷，1933年，第369～401页。

to fulfil the obligation to make an equivalent return for a gift received breaks the alliance and substitutes a state of hostility and may also cause a loss of prestige for the defaulting party. Professor Mauss[1] has argued that in this kind of alliance also there is a magical sanction, but it is very doubtful if such is always present, and even when it is it may often be of secondary importance.

The joking relationship is in some ways the exact opposite of a contractual relation. Instead of specific duties to be fulfilled there is privileged disrespect and freedom or even licence, and the only obligation is not to take offence at the disrespect so long as it is kept within certain bounds defined by custom, and not to go beyond those bounds. Any default in the relationship is like a breach of the rules of etiquette; the person concerned is regarded as not knowing how to behave himself.

In a true contractual relationship the two parties are conjoined by a definite common interest in reference to which each of them accepts specific obligations. It makes no difference that in other matters their interests may be divergent. In the joking relation-ship and in some avoidance relationships, such as that between a man and his wife's mother, one basic determinant is that the social structure separates them in such a way as to make many of their interests divergent, so that conflict or hostility might result. The alliance by extreme respect, by partial or complete avoidance, prevents such conflict but keeps the parties conjoined. The alliance by joking does the same thing in a different way.

All that has been, or could be, attempted in this paper is to show the place of the joking relationship in a general comparative study of social structure. What I have called, provisionally, relations of consociation or alliance are distinguished from the relations set up by common membership of a political society which are defined in terms of general obligations, of etiquette, or morals, or of law. They

① 'Essai sur le Don'.

为一方接受了礼物而没有做出同等的回报导致破裂，取而代之的是一种敌对状态，同时也可能使不履行义务的一方失去威望。莫斯教授[①]认为，在这种同盟中也存在一种巫术以约束履行义务的一方，但这种约束力是否永远存在，还是很令人置疑的。即使在它有效的时候，也常常处于次要地位。

在某些方面，戏谑关系与契约关系甚至表现得截然相反。双方之间的不敬、随便，甚至是放纵取代了一方对另一方所承担的义务，对它们的约束甚至宽松到，这些行为只需在习俗规定的范围之内，只要没有超越这一范围，就不得对这些行为动怒。在这种关系中，任何失信都像是违背了某种礼节；而失信的人则被视为很没有礼貌。

而在真正的契约关系中双方的联盟建立在一种明确的共同利益基础上，这个共同利益规定了双方应该接受的具体义务。而他们对于其他事情的不同利益，并不影响他们之间的联合。在戏谑关系和某些回避关系中有不同的方式，例如一位男子与其岳母，特定的社会结构把他们分隔开来，从而造成了许多不同的利益区别，由此可能带来二者之间的冲突和敌对。但通过极端尊重和部分或全面的回避建立起的同盟防止了这种冲突，从而使他们达成联盟。不过通过戏谑关系结成的同盟也会达到同样的效果。

这篇文章一直试图做或者说能试图做的，完全是以一种比较性的研究方式来展示戏谑关系在社会结构中的地位。此处我暂时用的同伴关系或同盟关系不同于那种由政治社会的共同成员之间构成的，根据一般义务和礼俗、或道德与法律确定的关系；它与真正的契

① 《论馈赠》。

are distinguished also from true contractual relations, defined by some specific obligation for each contracting party, into which the individual enters of his own volition. They are further to be distinguished from the relations set up by common membership of a domestic group, a lineage or a clan, each of which has to be defined in terms of a whole set of socially recognised rights and duties. Relations of consociation can only exist between individuals or groups which are in some way socially separated.

This paper deals only with formalised or standardised joking relations. Teasing or making fun of other persons is of course a common mode of behaviour in any human society. It tends to occur in certain kinds of social situations. Thus I have observed in certain classes in English-speaking countries the occurrence of horse-play between young men and women as a preliminary to courtship, very similar to the way in which a Cherokee Indian jokes with his 'grandmothers'. Certainly these unformalised modes of behaviour need to be studied by the sociologist. For the purpose of this paper it is sufficient to note that teasing is always a compound. of friendliness and antagonism.

The scientific explanation of the institution in the particular form in which it occurs in a given society can only be reached by an intensive study which enables us to see it as a particular example of a widespread phenomenon of a definite class. This means that the whole social structure has to be thoroughly examined in order that the particular form and incidence of joking relationships can be understood as part of a consistent system. If it be asked why that society has the structure that it does have, the only possible answer would lie in its history. When the history is unrecorded, as it is for the native societies of Africa, we can only indulge in conjecture, and conjecture gives us neither scientific nor historical knowledge. ①

---

① The general theory outlined in this paper is one that I have presented in lectures at various universities since 1909 as part of the general study of the forms of social structure. In arriving at the present formulation of it I have been helped by discussions with Dr. Meyer Fortes.

约关系也有区别，因为契约关系是由协议双方自愿遵守某些具体义务定义的；另外，这种关系又区别于那些由一整套社会认可的权力和责任约束，以家庭团体、世系群或氏族的共同成员资格为基础的各种关系。我所说的同伴关系只存在于个人和群体间，他们由于某种方式被分隔开来。

本文只论述形式化或标准化的戏谑关系。作为一种人类社会共同的行为模式，嘲弄或取笑他人更经常地出现在几种特定的社会制度中。我发现在说英语的国家的某些阶层中，有一种现象与切罗基印第安人嘲弄“祖母”的方式非常相似，他们把年轻男女之间相互嘲弄、开玩笑的行为当做是求爱的初期表现。当然，那些没有模式化的行为方式需要由社会学家来研究。能指出戏谑关系是友谊和敌对的结合物这一点，就已经达到了本文的目的。

要科学地解释在一个特定的社会中这种习俗的特殊表现形式，必须对其做深入的研究，在此基础上，我们才能把这种特殊表现形式视为某种普遍现象的一个特例。这就意味着，如果我们认为戏谑关系的特殊形式及其影响是统一体系的一部分，这个结论的得出就必须建立在对整个社会结构进行深入研究的基础上。对于为什么特定社会是它现在所表现的这种结构，只能去它的历史中搜寻答案。如果没有历史记录，例如非洲土著社会，我们只好任意猜测，然而这既不能产生科学知识也不能产生历史知识。①

① 本文论述的普遍性理论，作为社会结构形式总体研究的一部分，自1909年以来，曾在许多大学讲授过。此次的系统论述，也得益于与迈耶·福茨博士的探讨。

CHAPTER V

A Further Note On Joking Relationships[①]

'Professor Griaule's article on 'L'Alliance cathartique' in Africa of October 1948 raises a methodological point of considerable importance. If we wish to understand a custom or institution that we find in a particular society there are two ways of dealing with it. One is to examine the part it plays in the system or complex of customs and institutions in which it is found and the meaning that it has within this complex for the people themselves. Professor Griaule deals in this way with the custom by which the Bozo and the Dogon exchange insults with each other. He considers it as an element in a complex of customs, institutions, myths, and ideas to which the Dogon themselves refer by the term *mangou.* He shows us also what meaning the natives themselves attribute to this exchange of insults (p. 253). As a piece of analysis the article is admirable, and is a most important contribution to our growing knowledge of West African society.

But there is another method open to us, namely, to make a wide comparative study of all those types of social relationship in which two persons are by custom permitted, or even required, to use speech or behaviour which in other relationships would be grievously offensive. To the use of this method it would seem that Professor Griaule objects. Referring to what has already been written on the comparative study of what are called 'joking relationships' or *parentésà plaisanterie* he writes:

① Reprinted from *Africa*, Vol. XIX, 1949, pp. 133-140.

第五章　再论戏谑关系[①]

格里奥莱教授在1948年10月份的《非洲》杂志发表了一篇关于“导泻联盟”的文章，其中他提出了一个相当重要的方法论问题。有两种方法可以帮助我们理解存在于特定社会中的某种习俗或制度，第一种方法是通过考察这种习俗或制度在其所处的整个习俗和制度体系或这两者综合体中所起的作用，以及它对受制于习俗和制度综合体的人们的意义。沿着这个方法，格里奥莱教授研究了博佐人与多贡人相互侮辱的习俗。他认为这种习俗是由包括多贡人称为“曼戈”的习俗、制度、神话和观念结合在一起的统一体的一个组成部分，而且土著人关于这种相互侮辱的习俗有他们自己的理解（第253页）。作为一篇分析性文章，此文值得一看，并且相当有助于我们逐步增长西非社会方面的知识。

但是，我们还有另一种方法，即用广泛的对比性研究方法考察此种社会关系的所有类型。在此种社会关系中，双方由于习俗允许，甚至被要求使用在其他社会关系中被视为严重冒犯的语言或行为。格里奥莱教授似乎不接受采用这种方法。在提到对所谓

---

① 重印自《非洲》，卷19，第133～140页。

'Nous adoptons, vis – à – vis travaux parus sur cette question, une attitude négative.'

Ethnographers had reported from North America, Oceania, and Africa instances of a custom by which persons standing in certain relationships resulting either from kinship, or more usually from marriage, were permitted or required to behave towards one another in a disrespectful or insulting way at which no offence might be taken. Such relationships came to be called 'joking relationships', admittedly not a very good name. The most numerous and widespread examples of this custom were in the relationship of a man to the brothers and sisters of his wife. But it was also found in some instances between cross-cousins, between mother's brother and sister's son, and in a somewhat milder form between grandparents and grandchildren. There thus arose a problem of comparative sociology: What is there in all these relationships that makes this type of behaviour appropriate, meaningful, and functional?

One of the first facts that strikes the sociological enquirer is that the custom of 'joking' with the wife's brothers and sisters is very commonly associated with a custom of strict avoidance of the wife's mother, frequently of the wife's father, and more occasionally the wife's mother's brother. Since it is clear that the avoidance custom and the joking custom are direct contraries, or polar opposites, the problem immediately became one of dealing with both these types of custom. And this in turn made it necessary to consider certain other kinds of relationships.

I became interested in this whole set of problems in 1908 when I was trying to find an explanation of customs of avoidance in the Andaman Islands. There the parents of a man and the parents of his wife must avoid each other. Their relationship is described by the term *aka-yat*, from a stem meaning 'forbidden' and a prefix referring to the mouth, and, therefore, to speech. Persons in such a relationship might not speak to each other. On the other hand I was told that they will regularly send each other presents. The explanation given by the Andamanese is: 'They are great friends because their children have married.' This conception of avoidance relationships as relationships of friendship I have found elsewhere. Thus in Australia,

戏谑关系或亲属关系的比较性研究时,他写道:"对于那些有关此问题的文章,我们认为,应持消极的态度。"

有关北美、大洋洲、非洲的一些例子曾被民族学家报道过,这些例子表明,由于习俗允许、甚而要求处于在由亲属制度或更常见的婚姻关系中的人们相互不敬或彼此侮辱,而不能动怒。这种关系叫做"戏谑关系"。需要承认的是,这并不是一个很确切的名字。这种习俗最常见的例子表现在一个人与他妻子的兄弟姐妹的关系中,同时也可以在交表兄弟姐妹关系和舅父与外甥的关系中发现。在祖辈和孙辈的关系中也可以发现这种例证,不过它是以略为温和的形式表现出来的。因此,这里提出一个比较社会学问题:在所有的这些关系中,是什么使得这种行为方式变得适当、有意义,同时具有功能性?

社会学家们探询的首要事实之一是,与妻子的兄弟姐妹戏谑的习俗通常和严格回避岳母、经常回避岳父、有时也回避妻子的舅父等习俗联系在一起。因为显然回避习俗与戏谑习俗是相反的或截然不同的,因此问题就直接变成了怎样处理这两种习俗。而这又有必要反过来考虑其他几种关系。

从 1908 年起,当我试图解释安达曼群岛的回避习俗时,我便对这一系列问题感兴趣了。在安达曼群岛,男方父母与女方父母必须相互回避,他们的这种关系可以由术语"阿卡亚特"来形容。这个词是由一个意思为"禁止"的词根和一个与嘴有关系,因而也与说话有关系的前缀组成。在这种关系下人们彼此互不讲话。另一方面,我听说他们经常会互赠礼物。安达曼人的解释是"他们是最好的朋友,因为他们的儿女成婚了"。这种将回避关系的概念视为友谊关系的现象,我在其他地方也曾发现过。在澳大利

where a man carefully avoids all social contact with his wife's mother, I have more than once been told that she is the greatest friend he has since she has provided him with a wife. Again, the joking relationship is commonly referred to as one of friendship. 'I can tease my mother's brother and take his property because we are great friends; I am the son of his sister.' 'I can joke with my grandfather or grandmother, and they will joke with me because we are great friends.'

What does 'friendship' mean in these contexts? It is clearly something different from the relationship of solidarity and mutual help between two brothers or a father and son. On the basis of comparative analysis it seems to me that the assertion of 'friendship' means an obligation for the two persons not to enter into open quarrel or conflict with each other. It is sufficiently evident that one way of obviating open conflict between two persons is for them to avoid one another or treat each other with very marked respect. I think it is also fairly evident that a relationship in which insults are exchanged and there is an obligation not to take them seriously, is one which, by means of sham conflicts, avoids real ones.

This theory can be supported by reference to customs of other kinds, of which, to economise space, I will only mention two that are typical of one kind. In the Andamans I was told that two men who were initiated together at the same ceremony of initiation would be forbidden thereafter to speak to one another, but would regularly exchange gifts. Again the explanation was: 'They are great friends.' In South Australia there was a custom whereby two boys, born about the same time in two clans that were normally hostile, were united into a special relationship by the exchange of that portion of the umbilical cord which remains on the infant and later falls off. The two men who stand in this relationship may never speak to each other, but each may visit in safety the clan of the other carrying gifts to his friend and receiving gifts in exchange. Again the relationship is described as one of great friendship; through it each of the persons is safe in what would otherwise be hostile territory.

A careful examination of a great many instances from all over the world seems to me to justify the formulation of a general theory.

亚,男人很小心地避免与岳母有任何社会接触。并且我曾不只一次听他们说,岳母是他们最好的朋友,因为她使他们有了妻子。另外,戏谑关系经常被叫作友谊关系。“因为我们是最好的朋友,我可以取笑我的舅父,并且拿走他的财产;我还是他姐妹的儿子。”“我可以取笑我的祖父、祖母,他们也可以取笑我,因为我们是最亲密的朋友。”

在这些场景下,“友谊”是指什么呢?很明显,这种友谊关系与兄弟间或者父子之间的那种团结与互助是不同的。通过对比性分析,我认为,“友谊”是指一种责任,这种责任要求双方不得公开争吵或彼此产生冲突。显然,避免双方公开冲突的办法之一就是,双方相互回避或给予对方极大的尊重。我觉得,同样显然的是,在相互凌辱而又不得把这种凌辱当真的关系中,采取了伪装的冲突,避免了真正的冲突。

此理论可以通过参照其他习俗得到论证。为了节省文章篇幅,我将只讨论一种习俗中的两个典型例证。据说,在安达曼群岛,在同一个成年仪式上,举行成年礼的两个男人在以后的日子里禁止相互交谈,但他们应该经常交换礼物,解释同样是:“他们是亲密的朋友。”在澳洲南部,存在一种习俗,即在两个习惯上有敌对关系的氏族中几乎同时出生的两个男孩子,通过交换婴儿身上脱落下的那部分脐带而结成一种特殊关系。处于这种关系的两个男人永远不得相互交谈,但是双方都可安全地在另一方氏族内访问,携带礼物赠送对方并从对方收到礼物。在这里,这种关系又再一次地被描述为亲密的“友谊”关系,通过这种“友谊”关系任何一方都可在敌对区域内得到安全保障。

我认为,要想证实一种基本理论的系统解释,从全世界各地

But these special forms of 'friendship' can, of course, only be fully dealt with in terms of a study of forms of social relationship in general, and this is not the place in which to take up that very wide subject. Some social relationships are required by custom to be based on respect, of different degrees and expressed in different ways; others are such as to permit a certain degree of familiarity, and in extreme cases of licence. The rules of etiquette are one method of standardising these features of social relations. The respect required of a son to his father in many African tribes must be exhibited in this way. The avoidance relationship is in one sense an extreme form of respect, while the joking relationship is a form of familiarity, permitting disrespectful behaviour, and in extreme instances, licence. It is, for example, a relationship in which, in some cases, obscenity may be freely indulged in, as between the Dogon and the Bozo. Obscene talk, in all or most societies, is only permissible in ordinary social intercourse between persons standing in a specially familiar relationship. The prohibition against any reference to sexual matters before a father, and still more before a father-in-law, in many African societies, exemplifies this contrast between respectful and familiar or licentious behaviour.

The theory, of which I gave a brief outline in an earlier number of *Africa*① and to which M. Griaule adopts a negative attitude, starts from the position that the customs of avoidance or extreme respect towards the wife's parents, and of privileged 'joking' with the wife's brothers and sisters, can be regarded as the means of establishing and maintaining social equilibrium in a type of structural situation that results in many societies from marriage. In this situation we have two separate and distinct social groups, families or lineages, which are brought into connection with one another through the union

① *Africa*, Vol. XIII, No. 3, 1940, pp. 195-210. See Chapter IV.

区收集大量的例证做仔细的考察是十分必要的。但是当然这种特殊的"友谊"形式只有通过对总体社会关系研究后才能得到解释,并且这里不适宜讨论这样范围较广的问题。按照习俗,某些社会关系需要以对不同程度、不同表达方式的尊敬为基础;而另一些社会关系则允许一定程度的亲热,在极端的例子中甚至允许放肆。礼仪规则是使这些社会关系的特点标准化的一种方法。在非洲许多部落里儿子对父亲的尊敬必须以这种方式表现出来。回避关系,在某种意义上,也可以说是一种极端的尊敬,然而,戏谑关系却是一种包含有不敬的行为双方之间的亲热,甚至在极端的情况下还包含有放肆的成分。例如,在多贡人和博佐人中,存在戏谑关系的人之间有时甚至可以随意猥亵。但是在所有或大多数社会中,这种猥亵性的谈话只能出现在处于特殊亲密关系的人们中。在非洲许多社会中,在父亲面前,尤其是岳父面前不能谈论性方面的话题,这证实了尊敬关系与亲密关系或放纵关系之间的不同。

我曾在以前的《非洲》杂志中总结过,[①]M. 格里奥莱不接受的那个观点,是基于这样的一种见解:对岳父母的回避与极端尊敬的习俗以及有特权和妻子的兄弟姐妹开玩笑的习俗,可以看做是在许多社会由通婚所导致的某种结构性状态中建立和保持社会平衡的手段。

---

① 《非洲》,1940 年,卷 13,第 195 ~ 210 页。参见本书第四章。

of a man of one with a woman of the other. The husband is outside, and socially separated from, his wife's group. Through his relationship with her he is in an indirect or mediated relationship with individuals of her group. What is required for social equilibrium is that, as far as possible, he should not enter into conflict with his wife's group, but be obliged to maintain with that group or its members a 'friendly' relation. Both the avoidance customs and the 'joking' customs are the means by which this situation is socially regulated.

Why the difference, then, between the behaviour towards the wife's parents and that towards her brothers and sisters? The answer lies in the general principle, widely recognised, that towards relatives of the first ascending generation respect is required, whereas relations of familiarity and equality are appropriate between persons of the same generation. There are, of course, examples of exceptions to this rule, such as joking relations or privileged familiarity towards the father's sister's husband or the mother's brother.

Thus the special structural situation considered in this theory is one of groups which maintain their separateness, each having its own system of internal relationships between its members, and an indirect connection of a person of one group with the other group through a particular personal relation. In the instance of marriage the indirect relation is that of a man through his wife. The custom of a joking relationship with the mother's brother is found in societies in which an individual belongs to a patrilineal group, and therefore has an indirect relation to his mother's group through his mother. The widespread custom of relationships of familiarity with grandparents, often taking the form of a joking relationship (in Australia, Africa, North America, the Oraons of India), emphasises the relation of the two generations as being socially separated. The grandparents are thus placed in contrast with the relatives of the parents' generation, and the relation to one's own grandparent is an indirect one through a parent. The joking relationship between cross-cousins (Fiji, Ojibwa, etc.) is frequently a relation between possible relatives by marriage, but the relation is an indirect one through the mother or through the father's sister.

在这种状态下，有两种分离的而且不同的社会群体：家庭和世系群。他们通过一方的男人和另一方的女人之间的婚姻结成联盟。对于女方的家庭来说，男方是个局外人，并且在社会上与女方群体分离。由于他们的夫妻关系，男方与女方的亲属处于一种间接和中介人的关系。由于社会平衡的需要，男方不但要尽可能不与女方的亲属成员产生冲突，而且应有义务与女方群体及其所有成员保持友好关系。回避与戏谑习俗都是调节这种状态的社会手段。

那么，为何对待岳父母的行为与对待其妻子的兄弟姐妹的行为会有所不同呢？答案就在于被广泛承认的一般性原则中，即对父辈的亲属表示尊敬，而对待同辈的亲属则显示出亲昵与平等的关系，这样的行为是适当的。当然，这一原则也存在例外，正如对姑夫和舅父的戏谑关系或亲昵特权。

因此，这种理论讨论的是分离的各个团体之间的一种特殊结构状态，每个团体的成员之间都有其内部联系；并且，一个团体由于其中的一位成员通过一种特殊的个人关系而与其他团体有间接的联系。比如，在通婚的情形下，丈夫与其他团体的间接关系就是通过与妻子的婚姻构成的。存在与舅父有戏谑关系习俗的社会中，个人属于父系集团，他通过与母亲的关系而与母系集团保持间接的关系。那种分布广泛的与祖父母亲昵的习俗，经常采取戏谑关系的形式（如在澳大利亚、非洲、北美洲、以及印度的奥昂人），此习俗重视的是被社会分离的隔代人之间的关系。祖辈与父辈的地位关系形成了鲜明对照，自己与祖辈的关系是间接的，要通过父辈一代。交表亲之间（斐济、奥吉布瓦等等）的戏谑关系经常是姻亲之间的关系，但是这种关系是间接的，

An interesting crucial instance for the theory is provided by the Crow Indians, who have matrilineal clans. A man must be respectful to all the members of his father's clan; though he is not a member of that clan his relation to its members is one of close solidarity. In the other clans of the tribe there are to be found some men who are sons of men of his father's clan. They belong to clans that are separate and distinct, not only from his own clan but also from his father's clan. With such men, with whom his personal relation is an indirect one through his father's clan, he has a joking relationship; he may make offensive remarks to them or receive such from them without offence. In the Crow tribe this relationship has been developed into an instrument of social control of conduct, since the joking relative may call public attention to the shortcomings of his relative.

The Cherokee also had a system of matrilineal clans, and a man was required to show respect to all the members of his father's clan. But with the clans of his father's father and his mother's father he had only an indirect connection through a parent. He called all the women of these clans 'grandmother' and could be on a relationship of familiarity or joking with them. Since marriage with such a 'grandmother' was approved they were possible wives or sisters-in-law.

The theory that I have offered of joking relationships between persons related through marriage or by kinship is that they occur as social institutions in structural situations of a certain general kind in which there are two groups, the separateness of which is emphasised, and relations are established indirectly between a person in one group and the members or some of the members of the other. The relationship may be said to be one which expresses and emphasises both detachment (as belonging to separated groups) and attachment (through the indirect personal relation). These relationships of 'friendship', by avoidance or joking, contrast in a marked way with

要把母亲或姑母作为中介者。

此理论一个有趣且重要的例证是具有母系氏族制度的克劳印第安人的情况。一个男人必须尊重父系氏族的所有成员;并且,尽管此男子不属于父亲氏族的成员,但他与该氏族的所有成员都保持紧密的团结。在该部落的其他氏族中,可以发现一些男子是其父系氏族的男人的儿子。这些男子,无论是从自己的,还是从他们的父亲的氏族群来讲,都属于相互分离而又不同的氏族群。通过父亲的氏族,他与那些人建立了一种间接的个人关系,并与他们形成了戏谑关系。他可以对他们说冒犯性的语言,同时对于他们的冒犯性语言不予回敬。在克劳部落中,这种戏谑关系已经发展成为社会行为控制的工具,因为有戏谑关系的亲属们可以让公众关注自己亲属的缺点。

在切罗基人中,也存在着母系氏族制度,在此制度中,男子需要对其父系氏族的所有成员显示敬意。但是,对于男子的祖父的氏族及外祖父的氏族,他与他们是通过父母建立起一种间接的关系。他称这些氏族中所有的女人为“祖母”,并可以与她们有亲昵和戏谑的关系。因为与“祖母”结婚是得到允许的,因此她们都有可能成为他的妻子、嫂嫂或弟媳。

我认为,由婚姻或亲属制度而结成的人们之间的戏谑关系是以一种特定的、一般类型的结构状态中的社会习俗的形式出现的。在这种结构中,在分离性被加强的两个群体间的关系是由其中一方群体中的一名成员与另一方群体的成员或许多成员的关系而被间接地建立起来的。这种关系可以说是既分离(因为属于两个分离的群体)、又联合(通过间接的个人关系)。这些通过回避或戏谑而建立的“友谊关系”与那种团结关系形成了非常鲜明的

the relationships of solidarity, involving a complex system of obligations, that exist within a group such as a lineage or a clan. For the further development of the theory they need to be compared also with those relations which are set up, between persons belonging to different groups, by the regular exchange of gifts. Thus the theory is only one part of an attempt to deal systematically with the types of social relationship that are to be found in primitive societies.

The great majority of instances of joking relationships that were recorded by ethnographers were relationships between individuals connected through marriage or by kinship. Hence the reference to them in French as relations of *parenté* . But there were also found instances of a similar relation between groups of persons, by which a member of one group was permitted and expected to offer insulting or derogatory remarks to any member of the other. A good example is provided by the 'coyote' and 'wild cat' moieties of Californian tribes. More recently similarcu stoms have been reported from Africa (Northern Rhodesia, Tanganyika, West Africa)① in which this kind of relationship exists between two clans of a tribe or between two tribes. These obviously present a problem of a somewhat different kind. But it is obvious that any valid general theory of joking relationships must take into account these relations between groups.

Tribes and clans are distinct separated groups each maintaining its own identity and separateness. Within a clan the relations of its members are those of solidarity in the special sense in which I have been using that term in this note. Two clans may, in some instances, be united in a way in which there is a permanent union of solidarity between the clans as groups and the members thereof. On the other hand there may also be a relation between two clans of active or latent hostility. There is a third possibility, that between two particular clans there may be a relation neither of solidarity nor

① See Bibliography, p. 115.

对比，后者是指存在于像世系群或氏族群这样的群体中，并包含一套复杂责任的体系。为了能使该理论得到进一步发展，还需要把这些关系与由属于不同组群的个人之间的、通过经常互换礼物建立起的友谊关系进行比较。因而，此理论只对在原始社会中发生的几种社会类型进行了系统的尝试，此尝试是不完整的。

由民族学家记载的绝大部分有关戏谑关系的例证都发生在那些由联姻或亲属关系结成的亲属间。因此，在法语里，人们称之为亲属关系。但是，也可以发现一些例证，其中相似的关系发生在不同组群之间，即一组群的一个成员对另一组群的任何成员的污辱性或诽谤性的语言是被允许甚至被期盼的。加利福尼亚部落中的“土狼”和“野猫”两个半偶族就是很好的例子。据报道，最近非洲（北罗得西亚、坦葛尼喀、西非）[①]也存在类似的风俗。在那里，同一部落的两个氏族之间或两个部落之间，也存在这种戏谑关系。很明显，这些例证为我们提出了一个略微不同的问题。但是，显然，群体之间的这些关系都体现在关于戏谑关系的任何有效的一般性理论中。

部落和氏族是不同的、相互分离的群体。每个群体都具有一致性和与其他群体的分离性。在一个氏族内部，氏族中所有成员之间是一种团结关系。本文是在某种特殊意义上，使用团结这个词。在一些例证中，两个氏族以某种方式联合在一起，即通过作为群体的氏族之间，也就是两个氏族的成员之间的长久团结而联合。另一方面，也许在两个氏族间，也存在一种活跃的或潜

① 参见本章参考书目。

of hostility but of 'friendship' in which the separateness of the groups is emphasised, but open conflict between the groups or the members on the two sides is avoided by establishing a relation in which they may insult each other without giving or taking offence. This kind of thing is well illustrated in the account of the clans of the Tallensi given by Dr. Meyer Fortes. ① A similar relationship, whereby hostility is avoided, may exist between two tribes, as in the instances known from Tanganyika. ② It seems to me that in this way the joking relationship between clans and tribes recorded from Africa can be brought within the scope of a single theory that refers all instances of these relationships to a certain general type of structural situation. It should be made clear that what such a theory attempts to do is to deal with all the known examples of a certain recognisable type of institutionalised relationships in order to discover what common social feature makes this type of behaviour appropriate, meaningful, and functional.

It is evident that in one particular respect the relation between the Dogon and the Bozo is similar to the relations that have been described from other parts of Africa, namely, in the exchange of insults. There is no evidence that they are similar in other respects, and they certainly are not so in all. The relation is spoken of as an 'alliance', but it is something very different from an alliance between two nations which co-operate in fighting a war against another. The term 'alliance' is therefore not entirely suitable, nor have I been able to find a really suitable term. I have used the term 'friendship' and there is justification for this in the way in which native peoples themselves speak of friendship. In Australian tribes a man may have a 'friend', that is, a person with whom he has a special personal relationship. In one region a wife's own sister's husband, if he is not a near kinsman, is such a friend. In other regions a man may not select a 'friend' from amongst the men to whom he applies the classificatory

① Fortes, M., *The Dynamics of Clanship among the Tallensi*, London: Oxford University Press, 1945.

② See Bibliography, p. 115.

伏的敌对关系。第三种可能性是,在两个特定的氏族间,他们之间的关系既不是团结也不是敌对,而是“友谊”。在这种友谊关系中,两个群体间的分离性被加强,但是,两个群体或双方的成员间不会产生公开的冲突,这种冲突建立的基础是:双方成员可以彼此相互侮辱,但并不动怒。这种事实在迈耶·福茨博士对塔西兰诸氏族的描述中可以得到解释。[①] 坦葛尼喀的例证可以证明,在两个部落之间,也许存在类似的避免敌对的关系。[②] 因此,我认为,从这个角度分析,非洲的氏族和部落中的戏谑关系可以归到一种理论范围之内。这种理论将这些关系的所有例证都归为某种结构状态的一般类型中。这里,我要澄清的是,此理论旨在通过对某种公认的制度化关系所有已知例证的讨论,揭示到底是什么共同社会特征使这种行为变得适当、有意义,并且具有功能性。

显然,在某一特殊方面,即相互凌辱方面,多贡人与博佐人的关系与非洲其他一些部落的关系很相似。在其他方面,没有证据表明,他们有相似的关系,他们在整体上肯定是不同的。这种关系被说成是一种“联盟”,但这种联盟与两个国家联合起来与另一国家进行斗争的意义不同。因此,这里使用的“联盟”其实并不完全恰当,但我也实在找不到其他更恰当的词了。我在文章中用的“友谊”一词,是有根据的,因为土著人也称他们那种关系为友谊。在澳洲部落中,一男子也许有一个“朋友”,这朋友与他有特殊关系。在某个地区,妻子的姐夫或妹夫,如果不是近亲的话,可能就

① 迈耶·福茨:《塔兰西人氏族制度发展史》,伦教:牛津大学出版社,1945 年版。

② 参见本章参考书目。

term for 'brother'. Between 'brothers' relations are fixed by the kinship system. He may choose a man who stands to him in the classificatory relation of 'brother-in-law' but not his own brother- in-law. For brothers-in-law always necessarily belong to separated groups. There is a clear distinction made between friendship and relationships by kinship.

I am distinguishing, therefore, a certain class of what I call 'friendship' relations, from what I have called relations of 'solidarity' established by kinship or by membership of a group such as a lineage or clan. These terms are used only for the purposes of the present analysis because in this matter, as in so many others in social anthropology, no precise technical terms are yet available.

We may regard as one type of 'friendship' in this sense the relation set up between persons or groups on the basis of a continued exchange of goods and services. The world-wide custom of gift-exchange has to be considered in this connection. But there are other varieties; one group may bury the dead of the other or perform other ritual services. In North-West America one group would call in a 'friend' group to erect a totem-pole for them. A component of the relationship between groups is very commonly a certain amount and kind of opposition, meaning by that term socially controlled and regulated antagonism. The two groups may regularly engage in competitive games such as football. In *potlatch* in North America there is competition or rivalry in exchange of valuables. Social relations of friendly rivalry are of considerable theoretical importance. The universities of Oxford and Cambridge maintain a certain relation by competing regularly in rowing, football, etc. The joking relationship is thus one example of a wider kind; for it is a relation of friendship in which there is an appearance of antagonism, controlled by conventional rules.

The 'alliance' between the Dogon and the Bozo described and analysed by M. Griaule is clearly an example of what I have been referring to as 'friendship'. The Dogon and the Bozo are separate peoples

是这样一位朋友。在其他一些地区,一位男子是不允许从按分类称谓称作“兄弟”的男人中挑选“朋友”的。因为,“兄弟”间的关系是由亲属制度规定的。此男子从“姐夫或妹夫”中选择可以作为朋友的人选,但是他们并不是他自己的姐夫或妹夫。因为,姐夫或妹夫永远是其他群体中的成员。这种区分是存在于友情和亲情之间的。

因此,我把我称作有友好关系的一定阶层的人,与那些由亲属关系或像世系群或氏族的成员资格确立的“团结”关系的人,进行了区分。这些术语是为了目前的分析使用的,因为在这方面,正如在社会人类学其他领域一样,目前还没有专门术语可使用。

我们可以把两个人或两个群体之间由于持续交换礼物和服务建立起来的关系看做友谊关系的一种类型。遍布世界各地的交换礼物习俗可以根据这种关系来考察。但是,还有其他类型的友谊,如一个群体可以为另一群体埋葬死人或执行涉及利益的事务。在美国西北部,一个群体可以请另一群体为其建造图腾柱。不同群体之间关系的一个因素通常包含一定程度、一定种类的对抗,即那种受社会控制和调解的对抗。两个群体也许会经常从事一些具有竞争性的游戏,如踢足球。在北美的赠财宴上,在互赠贵礼时也存在着竞争或敌对关系。友好的社会敌对关系从理论上讲是非常重要的。牛津大学和剑桥大学经常通过举行划船、踢足球的运动来保持这种友好关系。因此,戏谑关系是友好泛化的例证,因为这是一种表面对抗,却受习俗规则主导的友谊关系。

M. 格里奥莱描述和分析的多贡人与博佐人之间的“联盟”显然是我说的“友谊关系”的一个例证。语言、生活方式的不同,

distinguished by language and by their mode of life. The prohibition against intermarriage maintains this separation by preventing the creation of relations of kinship between members of the two groups. The 'friendship' appears in the prohibition, under supernatural sanction, against the shedding of the blood of a member of the allied people, and in the regular exchange of gifts and services, for example, the services that individuals of one group perform in the ritual purification of those of the other. To these is added a 'joking relationship', the exchange of insults between members of the two groups. It is with this last feature that we are concerned here.

This alliance is conceived by the two peoples concerned in terms of their own cosmological system of myths and ideas, and M. Griaule's article is an important addition to the series of publications in which he and his co-workers have given the results of their investigation of this cosmology. It is in terms of these ideas that the Dogon interpret the exchange of insults. ① The exchange of insults is 'cathartic' because it rids the livers of both parties of impurities. M. Griaule has thus given us an ex planation of the exchange of insults between Dogon and Bozo by showing what meaning it has to the natives themselves and also by showing its interconnections within a complex system of institutions, ideas, and myths. He finds that the most important function of the alliance is to provide what he calls, for lack of a more suitable term, 'purification'. So, provisionally, he proposes to call this type of alliance, as found in an extensive region of Africa, 'cathartic alliance'. Doubtless he would not suggest that we should apply this name to the exchange of insults between clans among the Tallensi or Bemba, or between tribes in Tanganyika.

M. Marcel Mauss and I have both been seeking for many years to find a satisfactory general theory of what I have been calling relations of 'friendship' between separate groups of persons belonging to separate groups. One part of such a theory must be a study of prestations or exchanges of goods or services. Another must be a study of

---

① *Africa*, Vol. XVIII, No. 4, pp. 253-4.

使多贡人和博佐人成为两个不同的群体。由于禁止通婚的规定，即严禁两个族群的成员间出现任何的亲属关系，使两族群保持了分离。在这种超自然的制约下，“友谊”表现为严禁出现致使联盟群体成员发生流血冲突的事件，并经常互换礼物与劳务。例如，一族群中的一些成员可以为另一族群的成员举行洗罪礼仪。另外，他们之间还存在“戏谑关系”，即两族人相互凌辱。这里我们要关注的就是这最后一个特征。

两个相关族群对这种联盟的解释是基于他们各自对群体的宇宙观神话和观念的认知的。格里奥莱的这篇文章，对他以及他同事做的关于这种宇宙观的调查成果来说，是非常重要的补充。多贡人正是以这种观念诠释这种相互凌辱的习俗的。[①] 相互凌辱是一种“泻药”，因为它驱除了双方肝脏中的不洁之物。

M. 格里奥莱对多贡人与博佐人之间这种相互凌辱的习俗进行了解释。为了提供这种解释，他向我们展示了凌辱对两族人自身的意义，并阐释了习俗、观念、神话这套复杂体系的相互联系。他认为，这种联盟最重要的功能就是他所称的“净化”。由于找不到更恰当的词，所以这里用净化一词。因此，他建议暂时称这种在非洲分布极广泛的联盟形式为“导泻联盟”。毫无疑问，他并不建议在塔兰西人或本巴人氏族之间，或在坦葛尼喀部落之间相互凌辱的习俗中使用这一名词。

我和马赛尔·莫斯多年来一直在寻找一种比较令人满意的一般性理论，用于解释不同族群的人中所谓的“友谊关系”。对赠予或礼物和劳务互换的研究，以及对“戏谑关系”的研究必然包含

① 《非洲》，第 18 卷，第 4 期，第 253～254 页。

'joking relationships'. It is towards such studies that M. Griaule adopts, as he says, 'a negative attitude'. He suggests that to classify together the various examples of 'joking relationships' and to look for a general explanation, is like classifying together the ceremonies at which church bells are rung, such as funerals and weddings, calling them all *céré monies à cloches*. This is the question of methodology in social anthropology that seems to me so important. For M. Griaule seems to be questioning the scientific validity of the comparative method as a means of arriving at general theoretical interpretations of social institutions.

It is only by the use of a comparative method that we can arrive at general explanations. The alternative is to confine ourselves to particularistic explanations similar to those of the historians. The two kinds of explanation are both legitimate and do not conflict; but both are needed for the understanding of societies and their institutions. That the Dogon explain the exchange of insults as a means of purifying the liver does not prevent us from treating the Dogon institution as one example of a very widespread form of 'friendship' in which such exchange is a distinctive feature.

It is not a question of whether my theory, or any other general theory, of joking relationships is or is not satisfactory. It is the different question of whether such a general theory is possible, or whether attempts to arrive at one should be abandoned in favour of resting content with particularistic explanations.

The same question of methodology arises in connection with the conclusion of M. Griaule's article. He touches briefly on the need for an explanation of the Dogon-Bozo alliance 'en tant que systè me de groupes couplés et dont les deux parties ont des prérogatives et devoirs complé mentaires'. He finds the explanation in 'les fondements même de la métaphysique dogon. En effet, dès l'origine du monde, la règle était de gémelléité . Les êtres devaient naî tre par couple.' This is therefore a particularistic explanation in terms of Dogon ideas about twins.

Relations of this kind between paired groups are to be found in many parts of the world. Outstanding examples are provided by the moiety organisations of North and South America, Melanesia, and Australia.

在此理论中。据M·格里奥莱所说,他恰恰对这种研究持“消极态度”。他认为,通过把“戏谑关系”的各种例证归类寻求一个一般性解释,就像是将教堂中所有需要敲钟的礼仪,如葬礼、婚礼,统称为“敲钟仪式”一样。我认为这似乎是社会人类学中非常重要的方法论问题。因为,M·格里奥莱似乎对社会制度进行一般性理论解释的比较方法的科学有效性有所质疑。

我们只有通过对比方法才能得出一般性的解释。另一种选择是,如历史学家们做的那样,把我们自己局限于对个别事例的解释。两种方法都很合理,而且并不相互冲突;但使用这两种方法都需要我们对社会及社会制度有所理解。多贡人把相互凌辱作为净化肝脏手段的事实,并不会防碍我们把多贡人的这种制度看做是分布广泛的一种“友谊”的例证。这种相互凌辱的习俗只是“友谊”的一个鲜明特点。

问题不在于,是我的戏谑关系理论,还是其他的戏谑关系理论能否让大家满意;而在于,是否有可能建立这种一般理论,或者是否为了满足对个别事物的解释,而应该放弃尝试一般理论的建立。

M.格里奥莱文章的结论引起了同样的方法论问题。他简要地谈论了对多贡人与博佐人联盟解释的必要性,“因为在这种群体联盟制度中,双方享有共同权利,并承担着对权利起补充作用的义务”。他在“多贡人抽象观念的基础中”找到了解释。“事实上,关于世界的起源,其标志一直就是事物的二元结合。世界万物都应是成双出现的。”因而这就是多贡人对孪生概念做的解释。

在世界上许多地方都可以找到成对的族群间的那种关系。北美、南美、美拉尼西亚和澳大利亚的半偶族组织就是显著的例子。

The most usual way of representing this unity in duality, linking two groups into one society, is by pairs of opposites, such as heaven and earth, war and peace, red and white, land and water, coyote and wild cat, eaglehawk and crow. The underlying conception is therefore that of the union of opposites, as in the philosophy of Heraclitus. It was highly elaborated by the Chinese in the philosophy of *Yin* and *Yang*; *yang* and *yin* are male and female, day and night, summer and winter, activity and passivity, etc., and the dictum is that *yang* and *yin* together are required to make a unity or harmony (*tao*) as in the union of husband and wife, or the union of winter and summer to make a year.

The Dogon are therefore unusual when they represent the relation between paired groups by reference to human twins. But this can be seen to be only a special development of a conception that is very widespread in Africa, by which twins are regarded as a single entity divided into two parts. A comparative study of African customs concerning twins shows this co-nception developed in a number of different ways.

In the Dogon cosmology as recorded by M. Griaule and his associates the most fundamental conception of unity in duality seems to be not that of twin births but rather the opposition of the masculine and feminine principles, just as in the *yin* and *yang* of China. Human beings are born endowed with both principles and it is by operations of circumcision and clitoridectomy that they become truly male and female, so that there is again a Heraclitean union of opposites in the sexual union of husband and wife. One useful clue to the understanding of Dogon cosmological ideas, or certain of them, is the way in which this duality of male and female is combined with the duality in unity of twins. The latter form of duality corresponds to the number 2; the former to the opposition between 3, masculine symbol, and 4, feminine, which being added together give 7, the symbol of the complete being.

The symbolic representations of the Dogon present striking similarities to those found in other parts of the world besides West Africa. The basis of any scientific understanding of them must be such a particularistic study as is being made by M. Griaule and his co-workers; but it is suggested that it will need to be supplemented by a systematic

这种把两个族群连成一个社会的最通常的表现方法就是使用一对对立,如天与地、战争与和平、红与白、土与水、土狼与野猫、鹰与乌鸦。因此,这里隐含的概念就是对立统一,这与赫拉克利特的哲学相同。中国的阴阳哲学对此也有详细的阐述:阴和阳是指男性与女性、白天与黑夜、夏季与冬季、主动和被动,等等。他们断言,只有阴阳结合才能够成和谐(道),正如夫妻之合,或冬夏合为一年一样。

因此,从参照人类孪生现象来表现两个族群之间的关系这方面来说,多贡人非常与众不同。但是,这种认知可以看做是广泛流传于非洲的一种观念的特殊演变。这种观念认为双胞胎是同一实体中的两部分,有关非洲孪生习俗的对比性研究显示,这种观念已进化为许多不同的形式。

在M.格里奥莱及其助手记载的有关多贡人的宇宙观中,关于二元一体最根本的概念似乎不是孪生,而是男与女本性的对立,正如中国的阴性与阳性。人类天生具有两种本性,而只有通过做阴茎包皮和阴蒂表皮的切除手术,才能真正成为男人和女人。因此,这又体现了赫拉克利特的有关性结合的对立统一观念。理解多贡人宇宙观的所有观念及部分观念的一个很有用的线索是,懂得男女二元性和孪生二元性的结合方式。孪生二元性与数字2相一致;男女二元性表示,表示男性的数字3和表示女性的数字4对立,二者相加等于7,表示完整的人。

在西非以外的世界其他许多地区,都可以发现与多贡人极为相似的象征性表现手法。对这种象征性表现手法的任何科学解释必须基于对个体事例的研究,正如M.格里奥莱及其同事们那样。但是,还要尽可能广泛地以系统的比较研究为补充。人类不

comparative study extended as widely as possible. The conception of unity in duality has been used by man not only in the establishment of systems of cosmology but also in organising social structures. A comparative study of this, as of joking relationships, may be expected to aid in most important ways the understanding of the Dogon system which, without it, would seem to be only a peculiar product of a particular people.

仅用二元一体概念来建立他们的宇宙观体系，而且还以之来组织社会结构。正如对戏谑关系一样，对二元一体的概念同样需要对比研究，这对我们在对多责人体系的理解的重要方式上有很大的帮助。如果没有这种比较，我们只能把一种习俗、制度看做是某个特定民族的独特产物。

Bibliography

Fortes, M. *The Dynamics of Clanship among the Tallensi*. London Oxford University Press, 1945.

Moreau, R. E. 'The Joking Relationship (*utani*) in Tanganyika', *Tanganyika Notes and Records*, 12, 1941, pp. 1-10.

—'Joking Relationships in Tanganyika', *Africa*, Vol. XIV, No. 3, 1944, pp. 386-400.

Paulme, Denise. 'Parenté à plaisanteries et alliance par le sang en Afrique occidentale', *Africa*, Vol. XII, No. 4, 1939, pp. 433-44.

Pedler, F. J. 'Joking Relationships in East Africa', *Africa*, Vol. XIII, No. 2, 1940, pp. 170-3.

Radcliffe-Brown, A. R. 'On Joking Relationships', *Africa*, Vol. XII, No. 3, 1940, pp. 195-210.

Richards, A. I. 'Reciprocal Clan Relationships among the Bemba of N. Rhodesia', *Man*, Vol. XXXVII, p. 222, 1927.

Schapera, I. 'Customs relating to twins in South Africa', *fournal Afr. Soc.*, Vol. XXVI, cii, pp. 117-37.

参考书目:

福茨:《塔兰西人氏族制度发展史》,伦敦,牛津大学出版社1945年版

莫罗:《坦噶尼喀的戏谑关系》,载《坦噶尼喀笔记和报告》第1~10页,1941年出版

《坦噶尼喀的戏谑关系》,载《非洲》第14卷第3期,第386~400页,1944年

波尔默:《西非的亲属关系和家族联盟》,载《非洲》,第12卷第4期,第433~444页,1939年

佩德勒:《东非的戏谑关系》,载《非洲》,第13卷第2期,第170~173页,1940年

拉德克得夫-布朗:《论戏谑关系》,载《非洲》第12卷第3期,第195~210页,1940年

理查德:《北罗得西亚本马人中互惠的氏族关系》,载《人类》第37卷,第222页,1927年

斯查皮拉:《南非有关双胞胎的习俗》,载《非洲学会学报》第26卷,第117~137页,1937年

[英 汉 对 照]

西方学术经典文库

原始社会结构与功能

STRUCTURE AND FUNCTION
IN PRIMITIVE SOCIETY

[英] A.R.拉德克利夫-布朗 著

丁国勇 译

(二)

九 州 出 版 社
JIUZHOUPRESS

CHAPTER Ⅵ

The Sociological Theory Of Totemism [1]

There has been in the past some disagreement and discussion as to the definition of totemism. I wish to avoid as far as possible entering into any such discussion. The purpose of preliminary definitions in science is to mark off a class of phenomena for special study. A term is useful if and in so far as it brings together for our attention a number of phenomena which are in reality, and not merely in appearance, closely related to one another. It will be part of my thesis in this paper that however widely or narrowly we may define totemism, we cannot reach an understanding of the phenomena we so name unless we study systematically a much wider group of phenomena, namely, the general relation between man and natural species in mythology and ritual. It may well be asked if 'totemism' as a technical term has not outlived its usefulness.

It is necessary, however, to have some definition to guide and control our discussion. I shall use the term in the wider sense to apply wherever a society is divided into groups and there is a special relation between each group and one or more classes of objects that are usually natural species of animals or plants but may occasionally be artificial objects or parts of an animal. The word is sometimes used in a narrower sense and applied only when the groups in question are

① Reprinted from *Proceedings of the Fourth Pacific Science Congress*, Java, 1929.

第六章　图腾社会学理论[①]

一直以来都存在对图腾崇拜概念的不同意见及争论，但我希望我尽可能避免参与到这种争论之中。在科学领域中下定义的最初想法，是为了特别的研究目的而对不同现象进行分类。只要新术语可以将一些事实内在的现象联系起来，并得到我们的关注，那么该术语就是有用的。下面的论题是我在本文中要花费一定篇幅谈论的内容：不管是以广义还是狭义来定义图腾崇拜，除非我们系统研究范围宽泛的社会现象，即人与自然物种在巫术与礼仪上的普遍关系，否则我们不可能达到理解图腾崇拜的目的。而且，最好也要问一问作为一个专业术语，“图腾崇拜”是否仍具有效性。

然而，我们仍有必要给图腾崇拜下一个定义以引导和掌握我们对它的讨论。广义上说，图腾崇拜是指，整个社会可以被分为几个群体，每个群体与一个或多个物种之间存在特殊关系。这些物种通常是自然界的动物或植物，但有时也可能是人造物或是动物的某个部位。有时，也可以使用这个术语的狭义定义，即只有

① 重印自1929年爪哇《第四次太平洋科学大会论文集》。

clans, i. e. exogamous groups of which all the members are regarded as being closely related by descent in one line. I shall regard 'clan totemism' as only one variety of totemism, in the wider sense. ①

Even in the narrower sense of clan totemism, and still more in the wider sense, totemism is not one thing but is a general name given to a number of diverse institutions which all have, or seem to have, something in common. Thus even in the limited region of Australia, which has a single homogeneous culture throughout, there have been recorded a number of different varieties of totemism, and new varieties are being discovered by systematic researches now in progress.

In the south-east of the continent is found sex-totemism, i. e. an association of the two sex-groups, men and women, with two animal species. In the coastal districts of New South Wales, for example, the bat is the totem or animal representative of the men and the tree-creeper (*Climacteris sp.*) is that of the women.

In many parts of Australia the tribe is divided into two exogamous moieties, patrilineal in some regions, matrilineal in others. In some instances the moieties are named after species of animals, generally birds. Amongst such names are the following pairs: crow and white cockatoo, white cockatoo and black cockatoo, eaglehawk and crow, native companion and turkey, hill kangaroo and long-legged kangaroo. In other instances the meanings of the moiety names have not been discovered, and in some of them, at any rate, it seems certain that they are not animal names.

In many of the tribes that have this dual division, independently

① It is sometimes said that totemism has two aspects, a social aspect and a religious or ritual aspect. What is referred to as the 'social aspect' of totemism is simply the clan organisation. But exogamous clans similar in all essentials to totemic clans so far as economic or juridical functions go, can, as we well know, exist without totemism. The so-called 'social aspect' of clan totemism is simply the social aspect of the clan.

当刚才谈论到的那些组成社会的群体都是氏族时，例如在外婚制群体中，所有成员之间的联系纽带都是血缘关系时，该术语才会被使用。从广义上讲，我将只把“氏族图腾崇拜”看做是图腾崇拜中的一种。[①]

无论是从更为狭义的氏族图腾崇拜方面还是从更为宽泛的角度来讲，图腾崇拜都不是一个具体的表现形式，而只是一个概括性名称，只是用来代表那些存在或似乎存在某些共同之处的不同习俗。因此，记录显示在澳大利亚那些一向只保持着同种文化的有限区域内，却存在许多不同形式的图腾崇拜。而且，通过系统的考察，人们还在不断发现新形式的图腾崇拜。

性图腾崇拜存在于这个大陆东南部，所谓的性图腾崇拜是将两性群体，即男人和女人，分别与两种动物联系起来。例如，在新南威尔士的沿海地区，男性的图腾或代表男性的动物是蝙蝠，而女性的图腾或代表女性的动物则是攀树动物（尤其是已经成熟的这类动物）。

在澳大利亚许多地方，部落被划分为两个外婚制的半偶族，其中一些地方是父系半偶族，另一些是母系半偶族。在某些地方，半偶族的命名是以动物名称来表示的，通常是鸟的名称，下面是其中的几对名字：乌鸦和白鹦、白鹦和黑鹦、鹰和乌鸦、火鸡和土鸡、山袋鼠和长腿袋鼠。其他地区半偶族名称的意思还没有搞清

① 有人认为图腾崇拜具有两个方面的内容，一是社会方面，另一个是宗教或仪式方面。所谓图腾崇拜的“社会方面”只是指氏族组织，但我们知道，即使没有图腾崇拜，那些在诸如经济和司法等基本方面与图腾氏族相似的外婚制氏族也能存在。所谓氏族图腾崇拜的“社会方面”就是氏族的社会方面。

of whether the moieties are named after animals or not, there is a classification of animals and frequently of other natural objects whereby some are regarded as belonging to one moiety and others to the other.

Such moiety totemism, if we may use that term for any such association between the moiety and one or more natural species, is found in a number of different varieties in Australia, and still other varieties are found in Melanesia and in North America.

Over a large part of Australia the tribe is divided into four groups which have often been called 'classes' but which I prefer to call 'sections'. The easiest way to understand this division into four is to regard it as constituted by the intersection of a pair of patrilineal moieties and a pair of matrilineal moieties. ①

These sections are not as a rule named after species of animals, though there are one or two instances in which a section name is also the name of an animal. Thus Bandjur in Yukumbil is the name of a section and also of the native bear. In some tribes, however, there is a definite association between each section and one or more species of animal. Thus in the Nigena tribe of the Kimberley district of Western Australia the four sections are associated with four species of hawk. In some regions this association does not carry with it any prohibition against killing or eating the animal associated with one's own or any other section. In part of Queensland, however, each section has associated with it a number of species of animals and there is a rule that the members of a section may not eat the animals so associated with their section.

① If we denote the four sections as A, B, C, and D, the matrilineal moieties are A + C and B + D; the patrilineal moieties are A + D and B + C. Since a man may not marry within his own patrilineal moiety or within his own matrilineal moiety it will follow that a man of A can only marry a woman of B and their children must belong to section D, i. e. to the patrilineal moiety of the father (A) and to the matrilineal moiety of the mother (B).

楚,但其中--些肯定不是动物的名字。无论它们是否以动物的名字命名,在许多具有这种二元划分结构形式的部落中,都会对动物进行分类,也会对除动物以外的其他自然物种分类,并把这些种类分配给不同的半偶族。

如果我们用半偶族图腾崇拜术语表示半偶族与一个或更多自然物种之间的联系,那么可以发现,在澳洲的半偶族图腾崇拜是多种多样的。在美拉尼西亚和北美,也可以发现这种形式的其他变体。

在澳大利亚的大部分地方,通常部落都由四个群体组成,它们常叫做“不同的级别”,而我倾向于称它们“不同的组别”。要理解这种划分办法,最简单的方法是,把它们看做由一对父系半偶族和一对母系半偶族组成。①

这些组别的名字并不都以动物名字命名,也没有这方面的规定,尽管确实存在一两个组别的名字用的是动物的名字的情况。因而,在尤卡比尔语中,班甲既可能是指当地的熊,也可能说的是某一个组别。然而,每个组别与一个或更多动物之间存在确定联系的现象,确实可以在一些部落中发现。如,在西澳大利亚金伯利地区的尼基那部落中,它的四个组别就与四种鹰有关联。在一些地区中,这种关联并不意味着禁止猎杀或食用与组别相关联的动物。然而,在昆士兰的部分地区,有好几种动物和组别相关联,并且组别成员被严格规定绝对不允许食用与本组

① 我们若称这四个组别为 A、B、C 和 D 的话,母系半偶族是 A + C 和 B + D;父系半偶族是 A + D 和 B + C。由于一个男人不可能与本父系半偶族内部或本母系半偶族内部的女人通婚。这样,A 里的男人只能与 B 里的女人结婚,其孩子属于组别 D,即同时属于父系(A)的父系半偶族,也属于母系(B)的母系半偶族。

This ‘section totemism’ requires further investigation. We may distinguish, however, three varieties. In one each section has associated with it a single species of animal which is representative of the section in somewhat the same way as the sextotem is the representative of the sex-group. In a second variety each section stands in a special ritual relation to a certain limited number of species which may not be eaten by the members of the section. In the third variety a great number of species of animals are classified as belonging to one or other of the four sections but there is no rule against eating the animals belonging to one's own section. The one thing that is common to these varieties is that each section is differentiated from the others and given its own individuality by being associated with one or more animal species.

In some tribes the four sections are again sub-divided each into two parts, giving a division of the tribe into eight subsections. In some of these tribes there exist special associations between the subsections and certain natural species. Further investigation is needed before we can profitably discuss this subject.

If now we turn to clan-totemism we find a number of different varieties of this in Australia, too many, in fact, to be even enumerated in a short paper. Matrilineal clan totemism of different varieties occurs in three, or possibly four, separate areas in the east, north, and west of the continent. In Melville and Bathurst Islands there are three matrilineal phratries subdivided into twenty-two clans. Each clan is associated with one natural species, usually a species of animal or plant, though one or two clans have two totems and one has three. The assoiciation between the clan and its totem is apparently of very little importance in the life of the tribe. There is no prohibition against eating or using the totem, there are no totemic ceremonies, and totemism has

别有关联的动物。

我们仍需对这种“组别图腾崇拜”做进一步考察。到目前为止我们区分出三种类型:第一种类型,每个组别都对应单独一种动物,就像用性图腾代表性群体一样,也用此种动物代表这个组别;第二种类型,每个组别对应的动物种类为数不多,并且存在特殊礼仪关系,该组别的成员禁止食用这些物种;第三种类型,四个组别中的任一个都对应数量众多的动物,但是该组成员可以食用与本组对应的动物。这三种类型的共性是:每一组别都区别于其它组别,并且,每个组别通过与各自的一种或多种动物关联表现出自己的特性。

在一些部落中,把这四个组别中的每一个又划分为二个次组别,从而该部落就包含有八个次组别。在一些部落中,次组别也像组别一样与某些自然物种存在特殊关系。要深入讨论这个问题,需要对它做进一步深入考察。

现在如果我们继续回来讨论氏族图腾崇拜,会发现在澳大利亚存在氏族图腾崇拜的许多不同的变体种类。事实上,此种类数量之多,以至于不能够在本文逐一列举。母系氏族图腾崇拜的不同变体可以在澳大利亚大陆东、北、西各地大约三四个不同地区发现。在梅尔维尔和巴瑟斯特群岛存在三个母系部落分支,划分为22个氏族,每个氏族都与一个自然物种(通常,该物种是动物或植物)相联系,但也有崇拜一个以上图腾的现象,有一到二个氏族崇拜两个图腾,有一个氏族崇拜了三个图腾。因为部落中并没有关于禁止食用或使用图腾的规定,也不存在图腾仪式,并且图腾崇拜对巫术也没有多大影响,显然可以看出氏族与其图腾之间的关系在部落生活中并不是很重要。

little influence on the mythology.

The matrilineal clan totemism of some tribes of New South Wales, Victoria and South Australia seems to be of somewhat more importance. Here we find matrilineal moieties sometimes named totemically, sometimes not, and each moiety is divided into a number of clans. Each clan has one or more natural species regarded as belonging to it. Where there are several species associated with each clan, as is the case in many tribes, one of them is regarded as more important than the others and the clan is named after it. Throughout this region there is, so far as we know, no prohibition against killing or eating the totem.

Totemic ceremonial is apparently little developed nor have we any evidence of any elaborate totemic mythology connected with matrilineal totemism.

It should be noted that throughout Australia the most important group for social purposes is the horde, i. e. a small group occupying and owning a certain defined territory, and that the horde is normally strictly patrilineal. It follows that wherever there is a system of matrilineal totemic clans the clan consists of individuals scattered through a number of hordes. We thus get a double grouping of individuals. For most social purposes the individual is dependent on the local group, i. e. the horde, to which he is connected through his father, while at the same time he is also connected through his mother to a totemic group the members of which are scattered throughout the tribe.

Patrilineal totemism in Australia is more difficult to describe briefly than is matrilineal totemism. Where it exists the primary totemic group is usually the horde, i. e. the small patrilineal local group. In some regions the horde is a clan, i. e. it consists of close relatives in the male line and is therefore exogamous. But in a few regions the horde is not a clan in this sense.

母系氏族图腾崇拜，在新南威尔士、维多利亚和南澳大利亚的某些部落中似乎显得极为重要。我们发现，在这里，母系半偶族的名字有时是按图腾称呼，有时不是，并且每一个半偶族都被划分为几个氏族。每个氏族都拥有一个或几个属于它自己的自然物种。如果某个氏族和几个物种有对应联系，正如在许多部落中显示的那样，会认为其中一个物种在所有物种中最重要，同时以这个物种命名这个氏族。我们还没有发现这一地区存在禁止捕杀或食用图腾动物的规定。

很明显：图腾仪式在这里并没有发展起来，我们也找不到任何与母系图腾有关的详细的图腾神话的证据。

应该注意，在澳大利亚，队群是指占据并拥有一定范围领地的小群体，它们具有最重要的社会意义，并且它们一般都严格遵守父系制。因而，无论在哪儿，只要实行母系图腾氏族制度，这个氏族就只能是由分散在不同队群里的各个个体构成，从而我们可以看出存在一种个体的双重从属原则。出于整体社会意义上考虑，个体依赖于地域群体，即队群，他与这些队群的联系是依靠他与父亲的关系为中介的，同时，他又通过与母亲的关系这个中介，与母系图腾群体及其成员联系起来，这些成员分散在整个部落之中。

澳大利亚的父系图腾崇拜更复杂，描述起来要比母系图腾崇拜更困难。在父系图腾崇拜存在的地方，队群由小规模的地域父系群体组成，它是图腾群体的主要形式。而且队群在某些地区就是指一个氏族，并且是由按男方世系计算的亲属构成，因而是外婚制的。但是还有一些地区，队群指的不是这种意义上的氏族。

As an example of one variety of patrilineal totemism we may take the tribes at the mouth of the Murray River (Yaralde, etc.). Here each horde is a local clan and each clan has one or more species of natural object associated with it. There is no prohibition against eating the totem of one's clan, but it is regarded with some respect. There is no evidence of totemic ceremonial or of any elaborate totemic mythology. The function of the totem seems to be merely to act as the representative of the group.

Perhaps the most important, and certainly the most interesting, form of totemism in Australia is that to a brief consideration of which we now pass. This consists of a fourfold association between (1) the horde, i. e. the patrilineal local group, (2) a certain number of classes of objects, animals, plants, and other things such as rain, sun and hot weather, cold weather, babies, etc., (3) certain sacred spots within the territory of the horde, frequently water-holes, each one of which is specially associated with one or more of the 'totems' of the group, and (4) certain mythical beings who are supposed to have given rise to these sacred spots in the mythical period of the beginning of the world. This system of totemism is now being traced and studied in a number of variant forms over a very large part of the Australian continent. It was formerly known best from the centre of the continent, where, however, the Aranda have it in a somewhat modified or anomalous form. We now know that it exists or existed over a large part of Western Australia. Recently it has been discovered and studied in the Cape York Peninsula by Miss McConnel. At the beginning of this year I was able to demonstrate its former existence on the east coast of Australia in the north of New South Wales and in southern Queensland.

Where this type of totemism is found it is usually accompanied by a system of ceremonies for the increase of natural species. The members of the horde, or some of them, proceed to the totem centre or sacred spot connected with a natural species and

我们以墨累河发源处的部落(亚拉德等)为例,考察父系图腾崇拜的一个变体。在那里,每个队群就是由一个地域氏族构成,并且,它们都与一个或多个自然物种相对应。在氏族内部不存在禁止食用这些图腾物的规定,但要给予图腾一定的尊重。在那里还没有发现有关图腾典礼或图腾神话的证据。这里图腾的作用似乎只是这一群体的代表物而已。

在澳大利亚,我将要简单描述的这种图腾崇拜形式可以说是最重要的,当然也是最有趣的。这种图腾崇拜是由以下四种要素之间的联系构成:(1)队群,即父系地域群体。(2)一定数量的物种,如动物、植物和其他一些事物如雨水、太阳、酷暑、寒冬、婴儿等。(3)在队群地域之内的某些神圣地方,一般是水洞,每个地方都与一个或更多个群体的"图腾"有特殊联系。(4)某些神话人物,这些神圣地方就是由这些神话人物在创世纪之时创建的。人们正在澳大利亚的大部分地区追踪研究这种图腾崇拜体制的各种变体。在对大陆中部图腾崇拜的研究中,曾经对这种体系有过准确完整的阐述。但是,现在那里的阿兰达人的图腾形式已经稍有改变。现在我们知道,我描述的这种图腾崇拜体系曾经在西澳大利亚的许多地区存在过,而且在有些地区至今还能发现它的存在。例如就在最近,麦康奈尔小姐就曾在约克角半岛发现了这种体系,并研究了它。而且在今年初,我已经证明了,这种体系的早期形式曾经在新威尔士北部的澳大利亚东海岸和南昆士兰地区出现过。

在这种图腾崇拜出现的地区,通常会伴随一种为增加新的崇拜物而举行庆典的制度。也就是说,在与某种自然物种有关的图腾中心或神圣场所,队群中的全部或部分成员都赶来举行一个典

perform there a ceremony which is believed to result in an increase of that species. There is also an elaborate mythology dealing with the sacred totem centres and with the mythical beings who gave rise to them.

It may be noted that this kind of totemism may coexist in the same tribe with other kinds. Thus in the Dieri tribe it exists together with a system of matrilineal clan totemism. In some parts it coexists with section totemism.

Finally, we may note that in some parts of Australia there exists what is sometimes called individual or personal totemism. This is a special relation between an individual and some one or more species of animal. A good example is found in some tribes of New South Wales where every medicine-man has one or more of such personal totems. It is through his association with the animal species that he acquires his power to perform magic. Whether we call this totemism or not, it is quite evident that it is closely related to totemism and that any theory of totemism, to be satisfactory, must take it into account.

This brief and very incomplete survey of Australian institutions has shown us that special associations of groups or individuals with natural species exist in that region in a number of different forms. We find all gradations from a tribe with no form of totemism at all (such as the Bad of northern Dampier Land) through tribes such as the Melville Islanders where totemism of a simple form exists but is of comparatively little importance in the life of the tribe, to a tribe such as the Dieri which combines in a complex system two forms of totemism, one of matrilineal clans and the other of patrilineal hordes, with a highly elaborated totemic ritual and mythology. The only thing that these totemic systems have in common is the general tendency to characterise the segments into which society is divided by an association between each segment and some natural species or some portion

礼仪式,因为他们相信这种仪式能够增强这个物种的效力。另外,这里还附着一个内容丰富的神话,讲述了这个神圣的图腾中心和创建它的神话人物。

也许应该引起我们注意的是,这种图腾崇拜可以与其他种类的图腾崇拜共存于同一部落中。比如在迪埃里部落,它就与母系氏族图腾崇拜制度共存。在一些地区,它还可以和组别图腾崇拜同时存在。

最后,我们还要看到,所谓的个人或个体图腾崇拜也存在于澳大利亚的一些地区中。在这种图腾崇拜中,个体会与一个或多个物种发生特殊联系。在新南威尔士一些部落中,每位巫医都与一种或多种此类个人图腾物有关系。正是通过与动物的这种关系,才使他获得了显示巫术的能力。无论我们是否将它称呼为图腾崇拜,很明显,它与图腾崇拜的关系是密切的。而且,任何令人满意的图腾理论都必须考虑到这一点。

这种对于澳大利亚习俗制度的简单且并不完整的调查已向我们展示,群体或个人与当地的自然物种之间有特殊的关系,并且这种关系具有不同的表现形式。我们发现在不同的部落中,他们的图腾崇拜也有形式上的等级区别:有的部落不存在任何形式的图腾崇拜(例如丹皮尔半岛北部的巴德部落);在某些部落只有简单形式的图腾崇拜,而且对于部落的社会生活并无多少影响,就像梅尔维尔岛人那样;还有的部落图腾崇拜形式要复杂得多,例如迪埃里人,他们把母系氏族图腾崇拜与父系氏族图腾崇拜相结合,并与极其复杂的图腾仪式和神话传说紧密联系,形成了更为复杂的图腾崇拜形式。在以上的图腾崇拜形式中,有一点共同之处,即社会分支的划分依赖它

of nature. The association may take any one of a number of different forms.

In the past the theoretical discussion of totemism was almost entirely concerned with speculations as to its possible origin. If we use the word origin to mean the historical process by which an institution or custom or a state of culture comes into existence, then it is clear that the very diverse forms of totemism that exist all over the world must have had very diverse origins. To be able to speak of an origin of totemism we must assume that all these diverse institutions that we include under the one general term have been derived by successive modifications from a single form. There does not seem to me to be a particle of evidence to justify such an assumption. But even if we make it we can still only speculate as to what this original form of totemism may have been, as to the enormously complex series of events which could have produced from it the various existing totemic systems, and as to where, when, and how that hypothetical original form of totemism came into existence. And such speculations, being for ever incapable of inductive verification, can be nothing more than speculations and can have no value for a science of culture.

For sociology, or social anthropology, by which I understand the study of the phenomena of culture by the same inductive methods that are in use in the natural sciences, the phenomena of totemism present a problem of a different kind. The task of the inductive sciences is to discover the universal or the general in the particular. That of a science of culture is to reduce the complex data with which it deals to a limited number of general laws or principles. Approaching totemism in this way we may formulate the problem that it presents in the form of the question, 'Can we show that totemism is a special form of a phenomenon which is universal in human society and is therefore present in different forms in all cultures?'

The most important attempt to arrive at a sociological theory of totemism is that of the late Professor Durkheim in his work *Les Formes élémentaires de la Vie religieuse.* I think that that work is an important and permanent contribution to sociological theory, but that it does not

与自然中动植物或自然界的某些现象之间的联系。而且它们之间的这种联系有多种多样的表现形式。

过去对图腾崇拜理论的讨论,几乎全都与对图腾起源的猜测有关。如果我们用起源一词来表示一种体系、习俗或一种文化状态的产生过程,那么,存在于世界各地的不同图腾崇拜形式必定有不同的起源。要想说明图腾崇拜的起源,我们必须假设所有这些被我们用一个名称概括的不同制度,都是从一个单一形式经过不断的变化而来的。对我来说,似乎还没有任何合理的证据来证明这种假设。但,既使我们可以证明这种假设,我们也只能猜测这种图腾崇拜的原始形式,猜测它如何在那些大量复杂事件的促使下变成现有的图腾体系,以及对这种假设的图腾崇拜原始形式产生的地点、时间以及方式的设想。由于这种猜测永远不可能得到归纳性的验证,这些猜测也仅是猜测而已,对文化科学没有任何价值。

我认为,社会学或社会人类学的研究对象是文化现象,它采用的归纳方法与自然科学所采用的归纳方法很相似。然而,图腾崇拜现象研究的问题不同于上面所进行的猜测。归纳科学的任务是从特殊得到一般。在文化科学中的归纳,就是把研究的复杂数据简化为一定数量的普遍规则或原理。如果用这种方法来研究图腾崇拜,我们会问,“我们能否证明图腾崇拜是人类社会中普遍存在现象的一种特殊形式,因此对于不同文化就有相应的不同形式呢?”

作出最重要的尝试,形成图腾崇拜的社会学理论的,是已故的杜尔干教授,见于其著作《宗教生活的基本形式》。我认为杜尔干教授

provide a complete and satisfactory theory of totemism. I shall attempt to point out, in the briefest possible way, where Durkheim's theory seems to me to fail.

Durkheim speaks of the totem as being 'sacred' to the members of the group of which it is the totem. This is to use the term 'sacred' in a sense somewhat different from that which it has at the present day in English or even in French, and not even identical with, though somewhat nearer to, the meaning that *sacer* had in Latin. I prefer to use a term which is as free as possible from special connotations, and therefore instead of saying that the totem is sacred I find it preferable to say that there is a 'ritual relation' between persons and their totem. There exists a ritual relation whenever a society imposes on its members a certain attitude towards an object, which attitude involves some measure of respect expressed in a traditional mode of behaviour with reference to that object. Thus the relation between a Christian and the first day of the week is a typical example of a ritual relation.

Every society adopts, and imposes upon its members, towards certain objects, this attitude of mind and behaviour which I am calling the ritual attitude. There are, not only in different societies, but in the same society in different references, many different varieties of this attitude, but all the varieties have something in common. Moreover the ritual attitude may vary from a very indefinite one to a definite and highly organised one.

One of the important problems of sociology is therefore to discover the function of this universal element of culture and to formulate its laws. This general problem obviously includes a vast number of partial problems of which the problem of totemism is one. That problem may be stated as being that of discovering why in certain societies a ritual attitude towards a certain species of natural object is imposed upon the members of a particular social group. It is obvious that no solution of the lesser problem of totemism can be satisfactory unless it conforms with or is part of a general solution of the wider problem, i. e. a theory

的著作对社会学理论做出了不朽的重要贡献。但它并没有提出一个完整的、令人满意的图腾崇拜理论。我将以最简单的方式指出杜尔干理论的失败之处。

杜尔干认为,一个群体的崇拜物对该群体成员来说是“神圣”的。这里“神圣”一词的涵义与现代英语甚至是法语中这个词的词意有所不同,尽管与拉丁语 sacer 的意思相近,但也并不完全一样。我喜欢用一个尽可能不受特定涵义限制的术语,因而我倾向于用人们与他们的图腾间存在“仪式上的关系”,来替代“神圣的”。当一个社会强迫其成员对某一物体具有某种态度,而在这种态度中,包含着对那一物体表现出的传统行为模式的某种崇敬感,就会形成一种仪式关系。因而,可以说基督教徒与礼拜日之间的关系,就是这种仪式关系的典型例子。

每一个社会强迫其成员在思想和行为上对某种物体持有的态度,被我称为仪式态度。在不同的社会中这种仪式态度会有不同的表现形式,即便在同一社会的不同关系中表现方式也会有所不同。但是某些共性的因素,依然存在于这些不同形式之中。另外,这种仪式态度存在很多不同的形态,并可以由不确定的形态向确定的、高度组织性的形态演化。

因此,社会学的重要问题之一,就是发现文化普遍要素的功能,并且归纳出其规则。很显然,这个一般性的问题包含有许多小的问题,图腾崇拜的问题就是其中之一。那个问题可以这样描述:即研究为什么在某些社会中,崇拜某一自然物种的仪式态度能够强加给一个特定群体中的所有成员。显然,对于图腾崇拜这样一个较小问题的解释是建立在对上述基本仪式关系理论这个一般性问题研究成果之上的,二者互相联系,相辅相成,小问题是

of ritual relations in general.

With regard to the general problem Durkheim's theory is that the primary object of the ritual attitude is the social order itself, and that any thing becomes an object of that attitude when it stands in a certain relation to the social order. This general theory, with which I agree, obviously amounts to very little until we have succeeded in defining the more important types of relation to the social order which result in the object which stands in such a relation becoming an object of ritual attitude.

If I may restate in my own terms Durkheim's theory of totemism it is as follows. A social group such as a clan can only possess solidarity and permanence if it is the object of sentiments of attachment in the minds of its members. For such sentiments to be maintained in existence they must be given occasional collective expression. By a law that can be, I think, readily verified, all regular collective expressions of social sentiments tend to take on a ritual form. And in ritual, again by a necessary law, some more or less concrete object is required which can act as the representative of the group. So that it is a normal procedure that the sentiment of attachment to a group shall be expressed in some formalised collective behaviour having reference to an object that represents the group itself.

A typical example is to be found in our own society. National solidarity depends on a sentiment of patriotism in the minds of the nation. This sentiment, in conformity with the laws stated above, tends to find some of its chief expressions in reference to such concrete objects as flags, or kings and presidents, and such objects become in this way objects of the ritual attitude.

Part of a king's sacredness, whether in Africa or in Europe, is due to the fact that he is the representative of the national solidarity and unity, and the ritual that surrounds him is the means by which patriotic sentiments are maintained. In the same way in the flag we have an object which is 'sacred' because it is the concrete material representative or emblem of a social group and its solidarity.

一般性问题的有机组成部分。否则,得出的结果就不能令人满意。

上述一般性问题,在杜尔干看来,仪式态度的主要对象是社会秩序本身,而且任何与社会秩序存在一定关系的事物,都会成为态度的对象。我接受他的这个一般性的理论。但是在我们能够成功定义更重要的、与社会秩序有关的类型之前,这个理论的重要性并不大,因为正是由于社会秩序,才产生了那个作为仪式态度的对象而被置于这种关系中的事物。

用我自己的话表述杜尔干的图腾崇拜理论,就是:只有当像氏族这样的社会群体是其成员的情感和思想寄托对象时,该群体才能维持团结和永恒。要想让这种情感持续存在,它就必须得到偶尔的集体表达。我认为,根据那种显而易见的法则可以得到,所有有规律的社会情感的集体表达通常都会采取一种仪式的形式。同样,按照其他的法则,仪式中也多少需要一些具体的可以代表群体的物种。因此,一种正常程序是以一个代表群体本身的物体为参照,可以把集体行为具体化、形式化,从而用这样的方式来表达依附于一个群体的情感。

在我们的社会中可以找到这个理论的典型例子。国家的团结依赖于全国人民的爱国主义情感。这种情感与上述的规则相一致,往往会通过类似国旗、国王和总统那样的具体事物作为主要表现形式。因此,这些事物就变成了仪式态度的对象。

无论是在非洲还是欧洲,国王神圣性的原因一方面来自国王是一个国家团结和统一的代表,另一方面源于以国王为中心的仪式已成为保持爱国主义情感的手段。同样,国旗的神圣性也来源于此,即我们认为它是一个社会群体及其团结的具体实物性代表或标志。

Durkheim compares the totem of a clan with the flag of a nation. The comparison is valid, in a very general sense, for some forms of totemism, if not for all. But putting the comparison aside, the theory is that the totem is 'sacred' as Durkheim says, or is an object of ritual attitude, as I prefer to say, because it is the concrete representative or emblem of a social group. And the function of the ritual attitude towards the totem is to express and so to maintain in existence the solidarity of the social group.

With Durkheim's theory as stated above in my own terms I am in agreement, but I do not regard it as complete. In the first place it seems to me that totemism has other functions besides the one indicated above. Secondly, the theory so far as stated above does not explain why so many peoples in America, Asia, Africa and Australasia should select as emblems or representatives of clans or other social groups species of animals or plants. It is true that Durkheim offers an answer to this question, but it is an entirely unsatisfactory one. He regards as an essential part of totemism the use of totemic emblems or designs, i. e. figured representations of the totemic animal or plant, and suggests that the reason for selecting natural objects as emblems of social groups is because they are capable of being used in this way.

This hypothesis fails as soon as we apply it to the facts. In Australia no designs are made of the sex totems or of the totems of the moieties or sections, and even for clan totemism there are many tribes that do not make any representations of their totems. Totemic designs, which for Durkheim are so important or indeed so essential a part of totemism, are characteristic of central and northern Australia but not of the continent as a whole.

Moreover, the reason suggested for the selection of natural objects as emblems of social groups is of too accidental a character to give a satisfying explanation of an institution that is so widespread

杜尔干把氏族的图腾与国家的国旗进行了对比。这种对比从广义上讲,尽管并不是对所有图腾崇拜形式都有效,但对于某些形式的图腾崇拜是有效的。暂且不管这种对比,这种图腾理论告诉我们:无论是杜尔干认为的图腾是"神圣"的理论,还是我倾向于使用的图腾是仪式态度对象的说法,它都是社会群体的具体代表物或标志。人们对于图腾所持的仪式态度的作用,在于显示并进一步由此维系社会群体的团结。

我赞同以上用我的话表述出来的杜尔干的理论。但,我认为这些理论并不完整。首先,这种理论似乎让我觉得,它除了以上所述的功能外,并无其他功能。其次,以上所述的理论并没有解释为什么在美洲、亚洲、非洲和澳洲,如此之多的民族会选择动物或植物作为氏族或其他种类的社会群体的象征或代表物。当然,杜尔干为这个问题提供了解释,但是他的解释根本不能令人满意。他认为对图腾徽记或图案的运用是图腾崇拜的基本内容,即对图腾动植物图像的表达,并认为这些自然物种容易被使用的特性才是人们之所以选择它们作为社会群体的象征物的原因。

一旦我们运用这种假设来考察实际现象,它就会变得苍白无力。在澳洲,性图腾、半偶族图腾或组别图腾都没有图案,甚至在存在氏族图腾崇拜情形的很多部落中,也没有他们自己的图腾代表物。但对杜尔干来说,图腾图案是图腾崇拜的一个非常重要和根本的一部分。而这只是澳洲中部和北部的特征,并非是整个大陆的特征。

另外,对于选择自然物种作为社会群体徽记的原因,该项假设所提出的理论偶然性成分太强,因而并不能够对于广泛分布的

as totemism. There must surely be some much more important reason why all these peoples all over the world find it appropriate to represent social groups in this way by associating each one with some animal or plant.

This, then, is where I think Durkheim's theory of totemism fails. It implies that the totem owes its sacred or ritual character solely to its position as the emblem of a group. Now there are a number of peoples who have no form of totemism amongst whom we still find that natural species such as animals and plants are objects of ritual or of the ritual attitude expressed in mythology. And even amongst totemic peoples such as the Australian tribes the ritual customs relating to natural species are not all totemic. In other words the phenomena which we have agreed to denote by the term totemism are merely a part of a much larger class of phenomena which includes all sorts of ritual relations between man and natural species. No theory of totemism is satisfactory unless it conforms with a more general theory providing an explanation of many other things besides totemism. Durkheim's theory fails to do this.

In a great number, and I believe probably in all, of the societies where man depends entirely or largely on the hunting of wild animals and the collection of wild plants, whether they have any form of totemism or not, the animals and plants are made objects of the ritual attitude. This is done frequently, though perhaps not quite universally, in mythology, in which animal species are personified and regarded as ancestors or culture heroes. It is done also by a mass of customs relating to animals and plants. This system of ritual and mythological relations between man and natural species can be best studied in non-totemic peoples such as the Eskimo or the Andaman Islanders. In such societies we find that the relation between the society and the

图腾崇拜制度给予令人满意的解释。至于为什么世界上如此多的民族都认为恰当的表现每个社会群体只能通过把它们与某种动植物联系起来的方式,肯定存在某种更重要的原因可以解释它。

我认为这就是杜尔干图腾崇拜理论的不对之处。因为该理论认为,图腾具有神圣性或仪式性特点的唯一原因是由于它的社会群体徽记的地位。然而,有一些民族,它们不存在这种图腾崇拜的形式,但我们仍可以在这些民族中发现动物、植物这样的自然物种是他们的仪式对象,还可以发现他们通过神话表达的仪式态度描述的对象。甚至在澳洲部落中一些有图腾崇拜的民族中,那种与自然物种有关的仪式习俗也并不具有图腾性。也就是说,我们认可的可以用图腾崇拜这一术语表达的现象,只是组成更为广泛现象的一部分要素,这种广泛现象包括人与自然物种之间的各种仪式关系。除非能够提出一种既能解释图腾崇拜现象,又能解释图腾崇拜之外的其他现象的更加具有概括性的理论,否则任何有关图腾崇拜的理论都不会令人满意。这也就是我所说的杜尔干理论的不足之处。

在许多(我认为也许是所有的)完全或主要依赖打猎或采集为生的社会中,无论这些社会是否存在图腾崇拜形式,动植物都可成为仪式态度的对象。神话通常是将动植物仪式对象化的方式,尽管这种情况并不是很普遍。在神话中,动物被拟人化,并被看做是人类祖先或文化的渊源。这种仪式对象化也可以通过许多与动植物有关的习俗完成。那些不存在图腾崇拜的民族,如爱斯基摩人或安达曼群岛人,是研究人与自然物种之间的仪式和神话关系体制最理想的对象。因为,我们在这些社会中发现,社会与

natural species is a general one, all the most important animals and plants being treated as in some way sacred (either in ritual or in mythology) and some being regarded as more sacred than others, but any single species being equally sacred to every member of the whole community. The ritual attitude of the Andaman Islanders towards the turtle, of Californian Indians to the salmon, of the peoples of North America and northern Asia to the bear, constitutes a relation between the whole society and the sacred species.

Now totemism, I would suggest, arises from or is a special development of this general ritual relation between man and natural species. Let us assume for the moment that such a general ritual relation of man to nature is universal in hunting societies, as I believe it can be shown to be. When the society becomes differentiated into segmentary groups such as clans, a process of ritual specialisation takes place by which each segment acquires a special and particular relation to some one or more of the *sacra* of the community, i. e. to some one or more natural species. The totem of the clan or group is still sacred in some sense to the whole community, but is now specially sacred, and in some special way, to the segment of which it is the totem.

The process here suggested as the active principle in the development of totemism is one which I believe to be of great importance in social development, and which can be observed in other phenomena. Thus, to take only one example, and perhaps not the best, in the Roman Church the saints are sacred to all members of the church as a whole. But the church is segmented into local congregations and a congregation is often placed in a special relation to one particular saint to whom its chapel is dedicated. This is, I think, parallel to clan or group totemism. We might also draw a significant though not quite exact analogy between the patron saint of an individual and the personal totem or guardian animal of Australian and American tribes.

自然物种之间的关系是一种普遍存在的关系,所有最重要的动物和植物都被认为是神圣的(无论在仪式中还是在神话中),但是对于社会成员,一些物种可能被认为比另一些更神圣些。安达曼群岛人对乌龟的仪式态度、加利福尼亚印第安人对鲑鱼的态度、北美和南亚人对熊的态度分别构成了在他们所属的社会中整个社会与具有神圣性物种之间的关系。

现在,我会说,图腾崇拜发源于人与自然物种的那种普遍礼仪关系,或者是这种普遍礼仪关系的一个特殊发展。现在如果我们假设,人与自然的这种仪式关系在那些狩猎社会中是普遍现象,那么以下将是我对此假设的证明:把一个社会划分为像氏族这样的不同群体的过程,也就是产生一种使仪式趋向专门化的过程,通过这种过程,每一个群体都会与群体对应的一个或多个神圣物,即一种或多种自然物种产生独特的关系。在某种意义上,对于整个群体来说,氏族或群体的图腾仍具有神圣性,但对于崇拜这个图腾的社会分支来说,它更具有特殊的神圣性。

作为图腾崇拜发展中的一个有生命力的原理,我认为,该过程对于社会发展有极大的重要性,这一点在其他社会现象中也有所体现。我举个例子,这个例子也许不是最恰当的。在罗马教会中,对于整个教会成员来说,圣徒是神圣的。但教会又被划分为各个当地的教区教会,教区教会与某个特定的圣徒(当地一般为他修建教坛)之间存在特殊的关系。我认为,这与氏族或群体的图腾崇拜情况相同。我们还可以做一个有意义的,但并不十分准确的类比:即个人的守护神与个人图腾或澳洲、美洲一些部落的守护动物之间的类比。它们之间虽然分类并不完全相同,但还是有一定的相似性。

There is no space in this paper to discuss this process of ritual specialisation, and indeed any adequate treatment of the subject would require us to deal with the whole process of social differentiation and segmentation. I will refer to a single example that may help to illustrate the problem. Amongst the Eskimo of part of North America one of the most important features of their adaptation to their environment is the sharp division between winter and summer, and between the winter animals and the summer animals. There is a complex system of ritual relations between the society and all the most important of these animals and in this ritual the opposition between summer and winter is strongly expressed. Thus you may not eat reindeer meat (summer food) and walrus meat (winter food) on the same day. The Eskimo have made for themselves a segmentation into two groups, one consisting of all the persons born in the summer and the other of those born in the winter, and there is some slight ritual specialisation, the summer people being regarded as specially connected with the summer animals and the winter people with the winter animals. This is not quite totemism, but it is clearly related to it, and illustrates, I think, the process by which totemism arises.

In this way, I think, we can formulate a sociological theory of totemism which incorporates a great deal of Durkheim's analysis and is not open to the criticisms that can be levelled against Durkheim's own presentation. We start with the empirical generalisation that amongst hunting and collecting peoples the more important animals and plants and natural phenomena are treated, in custom and in myth, as being 'sacred', i. e. they are made, in various ways and in different degrees, objects of the ritual attitude. Primarily this ritual relation between man and nature is a general one between the society as a whole and its sacra. When the society is differentiated, i. e. divided into segments or social groups marked off from one another and each having its own solidarity and individuality, there comes into action a principle which is more widespread than totemism and is indeed an important part of the general process of social differentiation, a principle by which within the general relation of the society to its sacra there

由于篇幅限制,我不能对仪式专门化问题进行讨论。并且对此课题充分的研究,需要我们对社会演变及其分化的整个过程进行分析。我将举一个例子来解释仪式专门化问题,在北美洲爱斯基摩人中,他们适应环境的最重要的特征是,他们能准确区分冬季和夏季,习冬和习夏动物。此处存在着社会与所有最重要动物之间的一种复杂仪式关系。并且,在这个仪式中,夏季和冬季的对比被强烈地表现出来。因而,人们不可能在同一天,既吃驯鹿肉(夏季食物),又吃海象肉(冬季食物)。爱斯基摩人把自己分为两个群体,其中一个群体由出生于夏季的人组成,另一个群体则由出生于冬季的人组成,两个群体之间存在微小的仪式上的分化:夏季人与夏季动物存在特殊的联系;冬季人与冬季动物之间存在特殊的联系。虽然此现象并不能说成是图腾崇拜,但却与它有明显的关系。而且我认为可以用它来解释图腾崇拜产生的过程。

我认为,我们可以以这种方式构建一种关于图腾崇拜的社会学理论。该理论与杜尔干的分析有很大的共同之处,但不会像杜尔干提出的观点那样容易受到批评。我们先来看以下的经验总结:在狩猎和采集部落中,在习俗和神话上把最重要的动植物和猎物还有自然现象,看做是"神圣的",即以不同方式、不同程度把它们确定为仪式态度对象。人与自然的仪式关系主要是作为整体的社会与其神圣物之间的关系。"当一个社会可以被划分为不同的或具有各自团结形式和独立性的分支或群体时,一种比图腾崇拜分布还广的行为原则就产生了。这种行为原则是社会分化大过程中的一个重要组成部分。根据这个原则,另一种特殊关系,即每个群体或分支与一种或多种神圣物之间的关系,在社会

are established special relations between each group or segment and some one or more of those sacra.

This theory incorporates what I think is the most valuable part of Durkheim's analysis, in the recognition that the function of the ritual relation of the group to its totem is to express and so to maintain in existence the solidarity of the group. It gives moreover a reason, which can be shown, I think, to be grounded in the very nature of social organisation itself, for the selection of natural species as emblems or representatives of social groups.

Before leaving this part of the discussion I would like to touch on one further point. Durkheim, in reference to clan totemism, emphasises the clan and its solidarity. The totem, for him, is primarily the means by which the clan recognises and expresses its unity. But the matter is much more complex than this. The clan is merely a segment of a larger society which also has its solidarity. By its special relation to its totem or totems the clan recognises its unity and its individuality. This is simply a special example of the universal process by which solidarity is created and maintained by uniting a number of individuals in a collective relation to the same sacred object or objects. By the fact that each clan has its own totem there is expressed the differentiation and opposition between clan and clan. The kangaroo men not only recognise the bond that unites them as kangaroo men but also recognise their difference from the emu men and the bandicoot men and so on. But also the wider unity and solidarity of the whole totemic society is expressed by the fact that the society as a whole, through its segments, stands in a ritual relation to nature as a whole. This is seen very well in the system of increase ceremonies that is so widespread in Australia. Each group is responsible for the ritual care of a certain number of species by which the maintenance of that species is believed to be assured. For the tribe all these species are of importance, and the ceremonies are thus a sort of co-operative effort, involving a division of (ritual) labour, by which the normal processes of nature and the supply of food are provided for. One of the results of Durkheim's theory is that it over-emphasises the clan and clan solidarity.

与其神圣物的普遍关系之内建立起来。

这个理论承认了群体与其图腾之间的仪式关系主要是用来表现并维系群体的生存与团结的,这一点与我认为杜尔干分析中有价值的部分相同。另外,这个理论也提供了说明社会组织本身性质的理由,进而说明了选择自然物种作为社会群体的象征或代表物的原因。

在结束这部分讨论之前,我还要提及另一个问题。关于氏族图腾崇拜,杜尔干强调氏族及其团结。对他来说,图腾的主要作用是作为氏族认识并表现其统一性的手段。但是,问题要复杂得多。氏族只是那种同样拥有社会团结,并且规模更大的社会的一个组成部分。氏族的统一性和不同个性是通过它与一个或多个图腾间的特殊关系逐渐表现出的,这种表现方式只是社会普遍发展过程的一个例子罢了。在这个过程中,与一个或多个氏族图腾崇拜对象之间具有相同联系的个体被氏族这个纽带联结起来,并通过这种方式确立和维系氏族的团结。每个氏族都拥有其各自的图腾,因而以此为标志,氏族之间的划分与对比就表现出来了。例如具有袋鼠崇拜的群体,不但认识到他们与袋鼠之间的关系,而且还意识到他们与那些崇拜鸸鹋和崇拜袋狸群体之间的不同之处。但是,整个图腾社会更坚实和广泛的统一是通过整个社会的行为表现的,虽然是一部分,对于自然整体的关系来说,表现为礼仪关系。如在澳大利亚流行的增殖典礼体系中就可以看见这种现象。在这里,任何一个群体都必须对某个物种给予仪式上关注,这是他们的义务。这些物种正是通过群体的这种关注,得到了持续。所有物种对这些部落而言,都非常重要,因此需要人们共同举行仪式。它涉及到劳动的分配(仪式性的),通过这种典礼,自然界的正常划分类别和食物的正常供给都得到了具体的规定。杜尔

Totemism does more than express the unity of the clan; it also expresses the unity of totemic society as a whole in the relations of the clans to one another within that wider unity.

The result of my argument, if it is valid, is to substitute for the problem of totemism another problem. The question that now demands an answer is, 'Why do the majority of what are called primitive peoples adopt in their custom and myth a ritual attitude towards animals and other natural species?' My aim in this paper has simply been to exhibit as exactly as possible in a brief space the relation of the problem of totemism to this wider problem.

It is obvious that I cannot attempt in a mere conclusion to a paper to deal with this subject of the relation in myth and ritual of man and nature. I attempted some years ago to deal with it in reference to the customs and beliefs of one non-totemic people, the Andaman Islanders. As a result of that and other investigations I was led to formulate the following law: Any object or event which has important effects upon the well-being (material or spiritual) of a society, or any thing which stands for or represents any such object or event, tends to become an object of the ritual attitude.

I have given reasons for rejecting Durkheim's theory that in totemism natural species become sacred because they are selected as representatives of social groups, and I hold, on the contrary, that natural species are selected as representatives of social groups, such as clans, because they are already objects of the ritual attitude on quite another basis, by virtue of the general law of the ritual expression of social values stated above.

In modern thought we are accustomed to draw a distinction between the social order and the natural order. We regard society as consisting of certain human beings grouped in a social structure under certain moral principles or laws, and we place over against the society its environment, consisting of geographical features, flora and fauna, climate with its seasonal changes, and so on, governed by natural law.

干的观点过于强调了氏族和氏族的团结。但是,图腾崇拜表现出的不只是氏族的团结,还有整个图腾社会的团结,即表现了这个图腾社会整体与其内部各个氏族有着紧密的关系,并且处于更为广泛的团结之中。

如果我对这个问题得出的结论是有效的,那么该结论会代替图腾崇拜问题而转化为另一个问题。现在需要回答的问题是:"为什么大多数所谓的原始民族在他们的习俗和神话中对动物和其他自然物种采用一种仪式态度?"本文的主旨在于用简短的篇幅尽可能准确地展现图腾崇拜问题与这一更广泛问题间的关系。

我在本文中不能够对人与自然之间的神话和仪式关系问题简单下结论。若干年前,我为了研究这个问题,曾考察了安达曼群岛人(一个非图腾民族)的习俗和信仰。通过对该民族的调查和其他研究的结果,我总结出以下规则:任何对社会的人(物质的或精神的)有重要影响的事物和事件,或任何能够代表或表现这个事物或事件的东西,都会变成仪式态度的对象。

我反对杜尔干的理论,因为他认为,在图腾崇拜中,自然物种是由于它们被选为社会群体的代表才变得神圣。相反,我认为,之所以像氏族这样的群体会选择自然物种作为他们的代表,是由于这些自然物种已经成为了仪式态度的对象,这一理论是以下述的有关社会价值仪式表达的总体规则为基础的。

在现代观念中,我们习惯于划分社会秩序和自然秩序。我们把社会看作是由属于同一社会结构的某些人构成的,这些人受一定的法律原则或道德准则支配,并认为社会环境与社会是相对应的。而社会环境是由受自然法则支配的地理特征、植物和动物种类以及随季节变化的气候等等组成的。

For certain purposes this contrast of society and environment, of man and nature, is a useful one, but we must not let it mislead us. From another and very important point of view the natural order enters into and becomes part of the social order. The seasonal changes that control the rhythm of social life, the animals and plants that are used for food or other purposes, these enter into and become an essential part of the social life, the social order. I believe that it can be shown that it is just in so far as they thus enter into the social order that natural phenomena and natural objects become, either in themselves, or through things or beings that represent them, objects of the ritual attitude, and I have already tried to demonstrate this so far as the Andaman Islanders are concerned. Our own explicit conception of a natural order and of natural law does not exist amongst the more primitive peoples, though the germs out of which it develops do exist in the empirical control of causal processes in technical activities. For primitive man the universe as a whole is a moral or social order governed not by what we call natural law but rather by what we must call moral or ritual law. The recognition of this conception, implicit but not explicit, in ritual and in myth is, I believe, one of the most important steps towards the proper understanding not only of what is sometimes called 'primitive mentality' but also of all the phenomena that we group vaguely around the term religion. ①

A study of primitive myth and ritual from this point of view is, I think, very illuminating. In Australia, for example, there are innumerable ways in which the natives have built up between themselves and the phenomena of nature a system of relations which are essentially similar to the relations that they have built up in their social structure between one human being and another.

---

① A more precise way of stating the view I am here suggesting is that in every human society there inevitably exist two different and in a certain sense conflicting conceptions of nature. One of them, the naturalistic, is implicit everywhere in technology, and in our twentieth century European culture, with its great development of control over natural phenomena, has become explicit and preponderant in our thought. The other, which might be called the mythological or spiritualistic conception, is implicit in myth and in religion, and often becomes explicit in philosophy.

为了某些目的,这种社会与环境、人与自然的对比是非常有用的,但我们不可以让这种对比误导我们。从另一个非常重要的角度来看,自然秩序可以融入社会秩序中,并成为社会秩序的一部分。例如,控制社会生活节奏的季节变化,被人们用来当食物或其他目的动物和植物等等,都进入了人类社会生活并成为社会秩序的重要组成部分。我们认为,这些事实说明了,正是由于自然秩序对社会秩序的融入,以它们自己或通过代表它们的人或物为中介,自然现象或自然物体才转化为仪式态度涉及的对象。我曾在安达曼岛人的例子中证明了这一观点。在较为原始的民族中明显没有总结出我们目前定义的关于自然秩序和自然法规的清晰概念,尽管那些民族在受经验控制的技术活动的固定过程中已经开始孕育这些概念了。宇宙就是道德或社会秩序,在原始人类看来,它并不受自然原则控制,而是受所谓的道德或仪式法则控制。我相信,对这种概念(无论隐含的还是显现的)的认识,不但是准确理解所谓的仪式和神话中的“原始心智”的非常重要的步骤之一,而且对于理解我们统称为宗教①的所有现象也非常重要。

我认为,从这一角度对原始神话和仪式进行研究能够给人启发。例如,在澳大利亚,土著人用很多种方法在自己与自然现象之间建立一种关系体制,这种体制与他们在社会结构中建立的人与人之间的关系基本相似。

---

① 更准确地表述我提出的观点就是:每个人类社会都必然保持两种不同的,甚至是相对立的自然观。一种是自然主义的观点,它隐含在所有的技术中,在我们20世纪的欧洲文化中,在控制自然现象方面取得的巨大发展使它得到了外显,并占据了我们的思想中的主导地位。另一种可被称为神话学的或唯灵论的观点,暗含于神话和宗教中,但常常在哲学中被外显出来。

I can do no more than mention examples. One is the personification of natural phenomena and of natural species. A species of animal is personified, i. e. treated for certain purposes as if it were a human being, and in the mythology such personified species are regarded as ancestors or culture heroes. The function of this process of personification is that it permits nature to be thought of as if it were a society of persons, and so makes of it a social or moral order. Another of the processes by which, in Australia, the world of nature is brought within the social order is to be found in the systems of classification of natural species, existing in a number of diverse forms in different parts of the continent with this one thing in common to them all, that the more important natural species are so classified that each one is regarded as belonging to a certain social group, and occupying a specific position in the social structure.

Although there is always a danger in short formulas I think it does not misrepresent Australian totemism to describe it as a mechanism by which a system of social solidarities is established between man and nature. The mechanism has been worked out in many different ways, and much more elaborately in some than in others, but everywhere it possesses this character.

The suggestion I put forward, therefore, is that totemism is part of a larger whole, and that one important way in which we can characterise this whole is that it provides a representation of the universe as a moral or social order. Durkheim, if he did not actually formulate this view, at any rate came near to it. But his conception seems to have been that the process by which this takes place is by a projection of society into external nature. On the contrary, I hold that the process is one by which, in the fashioning of culture, external nature, so called, comes to be incorporated in the social order as an essential part of it.

Now the conception of the universe as a moral order is not confined to primitive peoples, but is an essential part of every system of religion. It is, I think, a universal element in human culture. With the question of why this should be so I cannot now attempt to deal.

I may summarise what I have tried to say as follows: A sociological

对此我还要举一些例子。其中一个是将自然现象和自然物种拟人化的例子。一种动物被拟人化,即为了某些目的把这种动物看做人类。在神话中,它们是作为人类的祖先和文化的起源出现的。这种拟人化的物种在人类研究或文化过程中的功能在于:自然界被假想为人类社会,进而使它拥有社会秩序或道德秩序。在澳大利亚,这种拟人化过程的功能还表现在把自然界带入社会秩序中,这一点可以在其自然物种分类体系中找到。以不同形式分布于大陆很多地区的这些自然物种都被同样带进了社会秩序之中,并且,对于那些较重要的自然物种,人们对之进行了划分,每个物种属于某一特定群体,并在社会结构中占有一定的位置。

尽管用简短的公式研究问题总是存在一定的危险性,但我认为把澳大利亚图腾崇拜描述成一种社会团结体系,这种说法并不是一种误导。许多人对这种机制有不同的描述,有些人描述得更为具体些,但在各种各样的描述中它都具有这种特点。

因此,我提出的观点是:图腾崇拜是一个更大范围整体中的一部分,我们辨别这个整体的一个重要方法是看它是否把宇宙看做是一种道德或社会秩序。尽管杜尔干事实上并没有提出此观点,但无论怎样,他的观点已经与此非常接近。但他似乎强调这是一个将社会投射到外部自然的过程。与之相反,我的观点却是:在这样一个文化形成过程中,外部自然与社会秩序结合,并成为了社会秩序的一部分。

现在来看,把宇宙作为一种道德秩序概念不仅局限于原始民族中,它是所有宗教体制的重要组成部分。我认为这是人类文化的普遍因素。至于为什么是这样,我目前还不能给予回答。

以下是我对以上陈述观点进行的总结:图腾崇拜的社会学理

theory of totemism must be able to show that totemism is simply a special form taken in certain definite conditions by an element or process of culture that is universal and necessary. Durkheim's attempt to provide such a theory fails in certain important respects. We can, however, incorporate a good deal of Durkheim's analysis in a theory which rests on the same general hypothesis of the nature and function of ritual or the 'sacred'.

Finally, my argument has brought out something of the con ditions in which this universal element of culture is most likely to take the form of totemism. These are (1) dependence wholly or in part on natural productions for subsistence, and (2) the existence of a segmentary organisation into clans and moieties or other similar social units. The Andamanese and the Eskimo have (1) but not (2), and they have no totemism though they have the material out of which totemism could easily be made. There are, of course, apparent exceptions to this generalisation, in some of the tribes of Africa, America and Melanesia. The detailed examination of these, which of course cannot be undertaken in a brief paper, really serves, I believe, to confirm the rule.

I would not be understood to maintain the view that totemism, or rather the different institutions which in different parts of the world we call by this general term, have arisen independently of one another. I think that it is very likely. But it does not matter for the sociologist, at any rate in the present state of our knowledge. If anyone wishes to believe that all the existing forms of totemism have come into existence by a process of what is rather unsatisfactorily called 'diffusion' from a single centre, I have no objection. I would point out that totemism has not spread everywhere, or evenly, and that it has not survived equally in all regions. It is sufficient for my argument if we can say that it is only where certain other features of culture are present that totemism is likely to be accepted by a people when it is brought to them from outside, or is likely to remain in active existence after it has been introduced.

论必须可以证明，图腾崇拜只是一个普遍和必要的文化成分或过程在某些特定条件下所采用的一种特殊方式。杜尔干对于这一理论的总结在一些重要方面是失败的。然而，我们可以把杜尔干大量的理论分析与一个对仪式或神圣物的性质和功能有相同假设的理论结合到一起。

我在文章的最后讨论了构成这种普遍文化成分的主要图腾崇拜形式的条件。它们是：(1)为了生存而全部或部分依赖于自然界物产；(2)存在氏族、半偶族或其他类似的拆和组织。对于第一个条件，安达曼人和爱斯基摩人都拥有，但是却没有第二个条件，而且尽管他们拥有那些容易构成图腾崇拜的物质条件，但他们却没有产生图腾崇拜这种仪式。这个总结显然还存在一些例外，譬如，它们就存在于非洲、美洲和美拉尼西亚的某些部落中。我认为，通过对这些部落的细致研究，必然会进一步证实这种规则。但是，由于篇幅关系，我不能在此对其进行细致探讨。

请大家不要误以为我同意以下观点，即：图腾崇拜，或所有我们用图腾崇拜这个概括性的术语指代的存在于全世界的不同风俗，是独立发展而来的。我认为，此种现象也许存在，但是，从我们目前积累的知识来看，我们不能说它与社会学家们有关系。我不反对那些观点，即认为现有的图腾崇拜形式是从单一的图腾中心，并经过那种“扩散”（这个称呼并非令人满意）过程导致的结果。但是，我要说的是，图腾崇拜没有扩散到世界的各个角落，并且在每个地区表现出的形式也各不相同。然而，我们可以承认，如果一些地区存在其他地区的文化特征，那么图腾崇拜就可能被当地人接受，并有可能继续在此地区延续。对于我的理论来说，这就足够了。

CHAPTER VII

Taboo[1]

The purpose of this lecture, which you have done me the honour of inviting me to deliver, is to commemorate the work of Sir James Frazer, as an example of life-long single-minded devotion to scientific investigation and as having contributed, in as large a measure as that of any man, to laying the foundations of the science of social anthropology. It therefore seems tome appropriate to select as the subject of my discourse one which Sir James was the first to investigate systematically half a century ago, when he wrote the article on 'Taboo' for the ninth edition of the *Encyclopaedia Britannica*, and to the elucidation of which he has made many successive contributions in his writings since that time.

The English word 'taboo' is derived from the Polynesian word 'tabu' (with the accent on the first syllable). In the languages of Polynesia the word means simply 'to forbid', 'forbidden', and can be applied to any sort of prohibition. A rule of etiquette, an order issued by a chief, an injunction to children not to meddle with the possessions of their elders, may all be expressed by the use of the word tabu.

The early voyagers in Polynesia adopted the word to refer to prohibitions of a special kind, which may be illustrated by an example. Certain things such as a newly-born infant, a corpse or the person of a chief are said to be tabu. This means that one should, as far as possible,

① The Frazer Lecture, 1939.

第七章　禁忌[①]

能够得到你们的邀请来做此次演讲，我感到非常的荣幸。本次演讲的目的是纪念詹姆斯·弗雷泽爵士的著作。他的著作不但是他终身坚定不移地致力于科学研究的成果，而且也为奠定社会人类学的基础做出了重要贡献。因此，我觉得选择詹姆斯·弗雷泽爵士在半个世纪前开创并进行过系统研究的领域作为讲演的主题是合适的。当时，他正在为大不列颠百科全书撰写题为“禁忌”的词条。在那之后，他又对该文做了多次修订。

英语中的“禁忌”一词可以在波利尼西亚语“tabu”一词中追溯其根源（重音在第一音节）。在波利尼西亚语中，此词的意思只是“在禁止”、“被禁止”，可用于各种行为类型的禁止。礼仪的规则、酋长颁布的命令、禁止孩童干涉比其年龄大者的财产的指令，都可以用“tabu”一词来表达。

波利尼西亚的一些早期航海者采用这个词表示一种特殊的禁律，我们用一个例子说明。就像新生婴儿、尸体、首领等等东西，据说都是被禁止的。这就意味着，某人应该尽可能避免与他们接

① 1939 年的“弗雷泽讲座”。

avoid touching them. A man who does touch one of these tabu objects immediately becomes tabu himself. This means two things. In the first place a man who is tabu in this sense must observe a number of special restrictions on his behaviour; for example, he may not use his hands to feed himself. He is regarded as being in a state of danger, and this is generally stated by saying that if he fails to observe the customary precautions he will be ill and perhaps die. In the second place he is also dangerous to other persons—he is tabu in the same sense as the thing he has touched. If he should come in contact with utensils in which, or the fire at which, food is cooked, the dangerous influence would be communicated to the food and so injure anyone who partook of it. A person who is tabu in this way, as by touching a corpse, can be restored to his normal condition by rites of purification or desacralisation. He is then said to be *noa* again, this term being the contrary of tabu.

Sir James Frazer has told us that when he took up the study of taboo in 1886 the current view of anthropologists at the time was that the institution in question was confined to the brown and black races of the Pacific, but that as a result of his investigations he came to the conclusion that the Polynesian body of practices and beliefs 'is only one of a number of similar systems of superstition which among many, perhaps all the races of men have contributed in large measure, under many different names and with many variations of detail, to build up the complex fabric of society in all the various sides or elements of it which we describe as religious, social, political, moral and economic'.

The use of the word taboo in anthropology for customs all over the world which resemble in essentials the example given from Polynesia seems to me undesirable and inconvenient. There is the fact already mentioned that in the Polynesian language the word tabu has a much wider meaning, equivalent to our own word 'forbidden'. This has produced a good deal of confusion in the literature relating to Polynesia owing to the ambiguity resulting from two different uses

触。任何人按触了这些禁忌的东西也会立刻成为禁忌人物。这意味着两种情况:一方面一个属于这种意义的禁忌人物,必须遵守某些行为上的限制,例如,他不可以用自己的手吃饭;而且此人还会被看做处于一种危险状态,即如果他不能遵守这种习俗的警告,他就会生病,可能还会死去。第二方面,对其他人而言,他具有一定的危险性。他与所接触过的禁忌物,具有同等意义的禁忌性。如果此人接触了用来煮食的器皿或炊火,那么这种危险性就会传播到食物上,进而会对分享食物的人造成伤害。诸如因为接触尸体等等情况而成为的禁忌人物,可以通化净化仪式或驱邪仪式恢复到正常状态。这时,他就被说成是“返真”了。返真是与禁忌相对的。

詹姆斯·弗雷泽爵士曾告诉我们,当他于1886年开始对禁忌问题研究时,当时流行在人类学家中的观点是:禁忌习俗只局限于太平洋沿岸的棕种人和黑种人中。但他经过调查研究所得出的结论是:波利尼西亚人对禁忌的行为和信仰“只是这种迷信体系中的一个特殊例子。在大多数民族中,甚至可能是在所有的民族中,这些迷信体系都曾经出现过,只不过对它们的称呼或它们的表现形式不同罢了。它们是在社会生活的各个方面以及各组成部分之间建立复杂社会网络的主要推动因素。社会生活的各个方面以及各组成部分包括宗教、社会、政治、道德和经济等等领域”。

禁忌一词在人类学中是指那种分布于全世界的,与上述波利尼西亚例子本质相似的习俗。这一说法并不令我满意,而且也不适用。上面已经提过一种事实:即禁忌一词在波利尼西亚语中,具有更广泛的概念,它等同于我们自己语言中的“禁止”一词。由于对同一词的两种用法的混淆,所以研究波利尼西亚禁

of the same word. You will have noticed that I have used the word taboo (with the English spelling and pronunciation) in the meaning that it has for anthropologists, and tabu (with the Polynesian spelling and pronunciation) in special reference to Polynesia and in the Polynesian sense. But this is not entirely satisfactory.

I propose to refer to the customs we are considering as 'ritual avoidances' or 'ritual prohibitions' and to define them by reference to two fundamental concepts for which I have been in the habit of using the terms 'ritual status' and 'ritual value'. I am not suggesting that these are the best terms to be found; they are merely the best that I have been able to find up to the present. In such a science as ours words are the instruments of analysis and we should always be prepared to discard inferior tools for superior when opportunity arises.

A ritual prohibition is a rule of behaviour which is associated with a belief that an infraction will result in an undesirable change in the ritual status of the person who fails to keep to the rule. This change of ritual status is conceived in many different ways in different societies, but everywhere there is the idea that it involves the likelihood of some minor or major misfortune which will befall the person concerned.

We have already considered one example. The Polynesian who touches a corpse has, according to Polynesian belief, undergone what I am calling an undesirable change of ritual status. The misfortune of which he is considered to be in danger is illness, and he therefore takes precautions and goes through a ritual in order that he may escape the danger and be restored to his former ritual status.

Let us consider two examples of different kinds from contemporary England. There are some people who think that one should avoid spilling salt. The person who spills salt will have bad luck. But he can avoid this by throwing a pinch of the spilled salt over his shoulder. Putting this in my terminology it can be said that spilling salt produces an undesirable change in the ritual status of the person who does so, and that he is restored to his normal or previous ritual status by the positive rite of throwing salt over his shoulder.

忌的文献产生了很多混乱。你将会注意到,我会把“taboo”(英语的拼写和发音)主要当做人类学家的术语。而把“tabu”(波利民西亚语拼写和发音)一词用于特指波利尼西亚以及和波利尼西亚有关的涵义。但这种作法还是不能完全令人满意。我提出,把我们正在考察的这些有关禁忌的习俗用“仪式性回避”或“仪式性禁限”来代替,而用“仪式状态”和“仪式价值”这两个我习惯使用的概念定义它。但,我并不认为这些是最恰当的术语,它们只是目前我所能找到的最恰当的术语而已。术语对于我们的科学研究来说,只是分析的工具而已。因此,我们应该时刻做好摒弃旧术语,采用更恰当的新术语的准备。

仪式性禁限指的是一种行为规则,它与一种信仰紧密相联,即任何人如果违反了这个规则都会导致他的仪式状态发生不好的变化。在不同的社会中,这种仪式状态的变化会采取不同的方式,但有一个基本的理念是认为会有或大或小的不幸降临到那人身上。

我们前面已经研究过的一个例子指出,根据波利尼西人的信仰,任何一个接触尸体的波利尼西亚人都会体验到我说的那种仪式状态发生不好的改变的过程。他将要面临的不幸是疾病。因此,他必须小心翼翼,并经历一种仪式以便能够逃脱这一危险,恢复到其原有的仪式状态。

让我们从当代英国中举一个不同的例子。人们认为,人们应该避免撒盐,撒了盐的人会有厄运。但是这种厄运可以通过将撒掉的盐捡起一撮从自己肩上扔过的方式得到避免。用我的术语解释就是:撒盐会使某人的仪式状态恶化;而这种主动地把盐从自己肩上扔过去的行为方式,使得此人可以恢复自己的正常或原

A member of the Roman Catholic Church, unless granted a dispensation, is required by his religion to abstain from eating meat on Fridays and during Lent. If he fails to observe the rule he sins, and must proceed, as in any other sin, to confess and obtain absolution. Different as this is in important ways from the rule about spilling salt, it can and must for scientific purposes be regarded as belonging to the same general class. Eating meat on Friday produces in the person who does so an undesirable change of ritual status which requires to be remedied by fixed appropriate means.

We may add to these examples two others from other societies. If you turn to the fifth chapter of Leviticus you will find that amongst the Hebrews if a 'soul' touch the carcase of an unclean beast or of unclean cattle, or of unclean creeping things, even if he is unaware that he does so, then he is unclean and guilty and has sinned. When he becomes aware of his sin he must confess that he has sinned and must take a trespass offering—a female from the flock, a lamb or a kid of the goats—which the priest shall sacrifice to make an atonement for the sin so that it shall be forgiven him. Here the change in ritual status through touching an unclean carcase is described by the terms 'sin', 'unclean' and 'guilty'.

In the Kikuyu tribe of East Africa the word *thahu* denotes the undesirable ritual status that results from failure to observe rules of ritual avoidance. It is believed that a person who is *thahu* will be ill and will probably die unless he removes the *thahu* by the appropriate ritual remedies, which in all serious cases require the services of a priest or medicine man. Actions which produce this condition are touching or carrying a corpse, stepping over a corpse, eating food from a cracked pot, coming in contact with a woman's menstrual discharge, and many others. Just as among the Hebrews a soul may unwittingly be guilty of sin by touching in ignorance the carcase of an unclean animal, so amongst the Kikuyu a man may become *thahu* without any voluntary act on his part. If an elder or a woman when coming out of the hut slips and falls down on the ground, he or she is *thahu* and lies

有的仪式状态。

按照罗马天主教教规,除非获得特许,否则教徒是不允许在星期五和大斋期的日子吃肉的。如果教徒不遵守这一戒律,他就是罪人,他需要通过忏悔来获得宽恕,就像对待他所犯的其他罪过那样。从科学的角度讲撒盐的例子和这个例子可以被归为一类,尽管它们表面看起来有很大不同。教徒在星期五吃肉会给他带来仪式状态的不良变化,而这一变化又需要通过恰当的手段来补偿。

除了这些例子,我们还可以在其他社会中选出二个例子。如果你翻到《利未记》的第五章,你会看到,在希伯来人中,不管有意还是无意,只要一个人接触到不洁的野兽、畜牧的尸体或爬行动物的尸体,他就会变得不洁,而且有罪。当他意识到这一点以后,必须以忏悔和献牲的方式赎罪,所谓献牲就是献出一头母羊羔,或一只山羊。然后,牧师会以牺牲这些祭品的方式来为他赎罪。这里,可以用"罪孽"、"不洁"和"负罪"等术语来描述由于接触不洁的动物尸体而使某人仪式状态发生的改变。

在东非的吉库尤部落中,"*thahu*"一词用来表示由于没有遵守仪式性回避规则而导致仪式状态的恶化。这一地区的人们认为,除非一个 *thahu* 人通过采用一些适当的仪式性补偿措施,否则他就会生病也许还会死去。导致这种恶化状况的行为包括:接触或搬运尸体、跨过尸体、食用破罐子里的食品、接触女人经血等等。与希伯来人无意中接触不洁动物尸体会负罪一样,吉库尤人任何非自愿的行为也会使他们成为 *thahu*。比如说如果当一位老人或一位妇女从茅屋出去时摔倒在地上,那么他或她就

there until some of the elders of the neighbourhood come and sacrifice a sheep. If the side-pole of a bedstead breaks, the person lying on it is *thahu* and must be purified. If the droppings of a kite or crow fall on a person he is *thahu*, and if a hyaena defaecates in a village, or a jackal barks therein, the village and its inhabitants are *thahu.*

I have purposely chosen from our society two examples of ritual avoidances which are of very different kinds. The rule against eating meat on Friday or in Lent is a rule of religion, as is the rule, where it is recognised, against playing golf or tennis on

Sunday. The rule against spilling salt, I suppose it will be agreed, is non-religious. Our language permits us to make this distinction very clearly, for infractions of the rules of religion are sins, while the non-religious avoidances are concerned with good and bad luck. Since this distinction is so obvious to us it might be thought that we should find it in other societies. My own experience is that in some of the societies with which I am acquainted this distinction between sinful acts and acts that bring bad luck cannot be made. Several anthropologists, however, have attempted to classify rites into two classes, religious rites and magical rites.

For Emile Durkheim the essential distinction is that religious rites are obligatory within a religious society or church, while magical rites are optional. A person who fails in religious observances is guilty of wrong-doing, whereas one who does not observe the precautions of magic or those relating to luck is simply acting foolishly. This distinction is of considerable theoretical importance. It is difficult to apply in the study of the rites of simple societies.

Sir James Frazer defines religion as 'a propitiation or conciliation of superhuman powers which are believed to control nature and man', and regards magic as the erroneous application of the notion of causality. If we apply this to ritual prohibitions, we may regard as belonging to religion those rules the infraction of which produces a

成了 *thahu*。并且,在他或她邻居中的老者过来祭献一只羊前,他或她要一直躺在那里。另外一个人还可能因为躺在一张断了腿的床上而成为 *thahu*,他也要像刚才那样净化。同样,从天而降的风筝和乌鸦也会把一个人变为 *thahu*。而在村庄里狂吠的鬣狗,或嚎叫的豺狼,都可以使整个村庄及其村民变成 *thahu*。

我已经有意识地从我们社会中挑出两个类型完全不同的仪式回避例子。不许在星期五或大斋期吃肉的禁令是种宗教戒律,这与某些地方在周日不许打高尔夫球性质是一样的。而不许撒盐的禁令,是非宗教性的,我想这个观点会被大家赞同。我们的语言可以让我们将这一区别划分得很清楚,因为违反宗教的行为是招致罪孽的,而那些非宗教的回避是与好运和厄运相连的。由于这种区分对我们而言十分明显,所以我们认为这种区分在其他社会也可能找得到。就我自身的经验而言,在一些我熟知的社会中致使罪孽的行为和带来好、厄运的行为是不能加以区分的。另外,一些人类学家正试图将这些仪式分为两类:宗教仪式和巫术仪式。

对杜尔干来说,这两种仪式最本质的区别是,宗教仪式在宗教社会或教会中具有强制性,而巫术仪式却是随意的。任何违反宗教规定的人都犯有不法行为,然而,如果某人没有遵守与巫术或与运气有关的警告,那么此人仅仅是被视为愚笨而已。虽然在理论上这种区分具有相当重要的意义,但是,在简单社会的仪式研究中却难以应用。

詹姆斯·弗雷泽爵士把宗教定义为“可以操控自然界与人类的超人力量对人的抚慰与安抚”,而巫术则是对因果关系概念的错误应用。如果我们把这一概念应用于仪式禁限,以下行为可以划

change of ritual status in the individual by offending the superhuman powers, whereas the infraction of a rule of magic would be regarded as resulting immediately in a change of ritual status, or in the misfortune that follows, by a process of hidden causation. Spilling salt, by Sir James Frazer's definition, is a question of magic, while eating meat on Friday is a question of religion.

An attempt to apply this distinction systematically meets with certain difficulties. Thus with regard to the Maori Sir James Frazer states that 'the ultimate sanction of the taboo, in other words, that which engaged the people to observe its commandments, was a firm persuasion that any breach of those commandments would surely and speedily be punished by an *atua* or ghost, who would afflict the sinner with a painful malady till he died'. This would seem to make the Polynesian taboo a matter of religion, not of magic. But my own observation of the Polynesians suggests to me that in general the native conceives of the change in his ritual status as taking place as the immediate result of such an act as touching a corpse, and that it is only when he proceeds to rationalise the whole system of taboos that he thinks of the gods and spirits—the *atua*—as being concerned. Incidentally it should not be assumed that the Polynesian word *atua* or *otua* always refers to a personal spiritual being.

Of the various ways of distinguishing magic and religion I will mention only one more. For Professor Malinowski a rite is magical when 'it has a definite practical purpose which is known to all who practise it and can be easily elicited from any native informant', while a rite is religious if it is simply expressive and has no purpose, being not a means to an end but an end in itself. A difficulty in applying this criterion is due to uncertainty as to what is meant by 'definite practical purpose'. To avoid the bad luck which results from spilling salt is, I suppose, a practical purpose though not very definite. The desire to please God in all our actions and thus escape some period of Purgatory is perhaps definite enough, but Professor Malinowski

分为属于宗教范围之内：由于对戒律的违犯使神灵受到冒犯从而带来个人仪式状态的劣变；而那种由于对超人力量的冒犯引起的某人仪式状态的劣变或遭受厄运，可以被划到巫术范围之内。根据詹姆斯·费雷泽爵士的定义，撒盐是巫术问题，然而，在星期五食肉则是宗教问题。

试图对这种区分的系统应用会遇到一些问题。譬如，詹姆斯·弗雷泽爵士在谈到毛利人的禁忌时说："对禁忌的最终制裁，也就是说让人们遵守戒律的力量，是严厉地劝信人们，任何破坏戒律的行为一定会并且立即会受到神灵或鬼的惩罚。神灵或鬼会让这个罪人饱受疾病的折磨直到死去。"这似乎使人觉得波利尼西亚人的禁忌属于宗教范畴而不是巫术。通过对波利尼西亚人的考察，我认为，波利尼西亚人一般把他们仪式状态的变化看做是像接触尸体这样的行为导致的结果，而只有当他们能够对整个禁忌体系合理分析时，他才会想到有神鬼的存在。顺便提一下，我们不应该认为波利尼西亚语中 *atua* 或 *otua* 总是用来指神灵。

在区分巫术和宗教的各种方法中，我还要论述一种。对马林诺夫斯基教授来说，"当一种仪式存在某种明确的实践目的时，并且这种实践目的能被实践者所熟知，而且也能被当地人在回答问询时轻易说出时"，这种仪式就是巫术仪式；然而，当一种仪式形式没有任何目的，也不是为达到某一目的手段，而只是一种形式，那它就是宗教仪式。运用这一标准的难度在于"明确的实践目的"涵义其实并不明确。我认为，躲避由于撒盐而导致的厄运，就是一种不明确的实践目的。而人们企图用一切行为来取悦上帝，以求免去赎罪的苦难的愿望则是相当明确的。可马林诺夫斯基

may regard it as not practical. What shall we say of the desire of the Polynesian to avoid sickness and possible death which he gives as his reason for not touching chiefs, corpses and newly-born babies?

Seeing that there is this absence of agreement as to the definitions of magic and religion and the nature of the distinction between them, and seeing that in many instances whether we call a particular rite magical or religious depends on which of the various proposed definitions we accept, the only sound procedure, at any rate in the present state of anthropological knowledge, is to avoid as far as possible the use of the terms in question until there is some general agreement about them.

Certainly the distinctions made by Durkheim and Frazer and Malinowski may be theoretically significant, even though they are difficult to apply universally. Certainly, also, there is need for a systematic classification of rites, but a satisfactory classification will be fairly complex and a simple dichotomy between magic and religion does not carry us very far towards it.

Another distinction which we make in our own society within the field of ritual avoidances is between the holy and the unclean. Certain things must be treated with respect because they are holy, others because they are unclean. But, as Robertson Smith and Sir James Frazer have shown, there are many societies in which this distinction is entirely unrecognised. The Polynesian, for example, does not think of a chief or a temple as holy and a corpse as unclean. He thinks of them all as things dangerous. An example from Hawaii will illustrate this fundamental identity of holiness and uncleanness. There, in former times, if a commoner committed incest with his sister he became *kapu* (the Hawaiian form of tabu). His presence was dangerous in the extreme for the whole community, and since he could not be purified he was put to death. But if a chief of high rank, who, by reason

教授却认为它没有什么实际意义。那么,波利尼西亚人通过告诫自己不可以接触首领、尸体和新生婴儿来避免疾病及可能带来的死亡这一现象,又如何解释呢?

考虑到在巫术和宗教的定义方面,及两者区别的本质方面存在不一致的意见,又考虑到在很多情况下,我们主要依赖接受的定义判断某种仪式为巫术性的还是宗教性的。所以就现在的人类学知识状态而言,唯一可采用的程序,是在我们达成总的共识之前尽可能避免使用一些有歧义的术语。当然由杜尔干、弗雷泽和马林诺夫斯基所做的区分具有非常重要的理论意义,虽然这些区分还很难被普遍应用。同时,有必要对各种仪式进行系统分类,但令人满意的分类制度是相当复杂的。不过这种巫术仪式和宗教仪式简单二分法可能带来的分歧并不会对我们的研究有较大影响。

在我们社会的仪式回避领域中,我们需要做的是划分圣洁和不洁。一些东西因为圣洁而必须给予尊敬,而另一些东西必须得到尊重却恰恰是因为他们是不洁的。但是正如罗伯逊·史密斯和詹姆斯·弗雷泽爵士向我们证明的,对于这种圣洁与不洁的划分,很多社会都没有认可。例如,波利尼西亚人并没有首领和寺庙是圣洁的,而尸体是不洁之物的想法。波利尼西亚人认为这些事物都是危险的。夏威夷的例子也可以说明圣洁和不洁的基本同一性。

在以前的夏威夷地区,一个平民与其姐妹的乱伦关系,会使他成为 *Kapu*(禁忌的夏威夷语形式)。整个群体都会将他的存在视为最大的危险。并且,由于他已经不能够被净化了,所以只能处死他。但是,如果一个地位很高的酋长(当然,由于他的地位关

of his rank was, of course, sacred (*kapu*), married his sister he became still more so. An extreme sanctity or untouchability attached to a chief born of a brother and sister who were themselves the children of a brother and sister. The sanctity of such a chief and the uncleanness of the person put to death for incest have the same source and are the same thing. They are both denoted by saying that the person is *kapu*. In studying the simpler societies it is essential that we should carefully avoid thinking of their behaviour and ideas in terms of our own ideas of holiness and uncleanness. Since most people find this difficult it is desirable to have terms which we can use that do not convey this connotation. Durkheim and others have used the word 'sacred' as an inclusive term for the holy and the unclean together. This is easier to do in French than in English, and has some justification in the fact that the Latin sacer did apply to holy things such as the gods and also to accursed things such as persons guilty of certain crimes. But there is certainly a tendency in English to identify sacred with holy. I think that it will greatly aid clear thinking if we adopt some wide inclusive term which does not have any undesirable connotation. I venture to propose the term 'ritual value'.

Anything—a person, a material thing, a place, a word or name, an occasion or event, a day of the week or a period of the year—which is the object of a ritual avoidance or taboo can be said to have ritual value. Thus in Polynesia chiefs, corpses and newly-born babies have ritual value. For some people in England salt has ritual value. For Christians all Sundays and Good Friday have ritual value, and for Jews all Saturdays and the Day of Atonement. The ritual value is exhibited in the behaviour adopted towards the object or occasion in question. Ritual values are exhibited not only in negative ritual but

系,他是神圣的)与其姐妹结婚,那么他也会成为一个 *Kapu*。如果某个酋长是一对同胞兄妹结婚后生的孩子,而且这对同胞兄妹又是另一对同胞兄妹结婚所生的子女,那么,这个酋长就具有极端的尊严和不可触犯性。这种酋长的圣洁和由于乱伦而被处死的那个人的不洁来自同一根源,并且同属一类事情,都可以用 *Kapu* 来指称他们。在研究较为简单的社会时,我们应当小心避免用我们关于圣洁和不洁的观点来考察他们的思维和行为,这是很关键的。由于大多数人认为做到这一点很难,所以我们最好用一些不含这种意思的术语。杜尔干和其他一些人用"神圣"一词来概括圣洁和不洁。这种用法对于法语来说要比英语容易,原因是拉丁词 sacer 的确既可以用来指如上帝这样的事物,也可以指如罪人这样的可恶之人。但是,当然英语中存在将神圣和圣洁这两个词之间建立一致性的趋势。我想,如果我们采用一些不包含此意的,更加具有概括性的术语,会有助于我们的思考。我要大胆提出一个术语,即"仪式价值"。

所有的事物——无论是一个人、一个物体、一个地方、一个词,还是一个名字、一个场所或事件、一周中的一天或一年中一段时期——这些只要是仪式回避或禁忌的对象,它就可以被说成是具有仪式价值。那么首领、尸体和新出生婴儿对于波利尼西亚来说,就具有仪式价值。而在英国,盐对于某些人来说也具有仪式价值。对于基督教徒来说具有仪式价值的是,比如所有的礼拜日、耶稣受难日等等;而所有的礼拜六和赎罪日却是对犹太人具有仪式价值的日子。仪式价值在刚才提到的人们对物体或场合的行为中都有所体现。负面仪式和正面仪式

also in positive ritual, being possessed by the objects towards which positive rites are directed and also by objects, words or places used in the rites. A large class of positive rites, those of consecration or sacralisation, have for their purpose to endow objects with ritual value. It may be noted that in general anything that has value in positive ritual is also the object of some sort of ritual avoidance or at the very least of ritual respect.

The word 'value', as I am using it, always refers to a relation between a subject and an object. The relation can be stated in two ways by saying either that the object has a value for the subject, or that the subject has an interest in the object. We can use the terms in this way to refer to any act of behaviour towards an object. The relation is exhibited in and defined by the behaviour. The words 'interest' and 'value' provide a convenient shorthand by which we can describe the reality, which consists of acts of behaviour and the actual relations between subjects and objects which those acts of behaviour reveal. If Jack loves Jill, then Jill has the value of a loved object for Jack, and Jack has a recognisable interest in Jill. When I am hungry I have an interest in food, and a good meal has an immediate value for me that it does not have at other times. My toothache has a value to me as something that I am interested in getting rid of as quickly as possible.

A social system can be conceived and studied as a system of values. A society consists of a number of individuals bound together in a network of social relations. A social relation exists between two or more persons when there is some harmonisation of their individual interests, by some convergence of interest and by limitation or adjustment of divergent interests. An interest is always the interest of an individual. Two individuals may have similar interests. Similar interests do not in themselves constitute a social relation; two dogs may have a similar interest in the same bone and the result may be a dog-fight. But a society cannot exist except on the basis of a certain measure of similarity in the interests of its members. Putting this in terms of value,

都能表现出仪式价值，而且正面仪式直接指向的对象，只要是在仪式中使用过的东西如器物、词语、场所等，也具有仪式价值。不过像献祭或使某事物神化这样的正面仪式，需要赋予祭物以仪式价值来达成其目的。要注意的是，一般具有正面仪式价值的东西，同样也是某种仪式回避的对象。

“价值”一词，正如我使用的那样，一般是指主体与客体之间的关系。这种关系可以用两种方式陈述：一种方式是客体对主体有一定的价值；另一种方式是主体对客体有兴趣。我们可以用这一术语来描述对客体的任何行为。主客体之间的关系体现在行为中，并由行为规定。使用“兴趣”和“价值”可以为我们提供方便、简略的表达方式，我们可以用它们来描述那种由各种行为动作及其所指示的主客体的真实关系构成的现实。如果杰克爱吉尔，那么吉尔就具有被杰克所爱的客体的价值，并且显然杰克对吉尔也感兴趣。当我感到饥饿时，我对食物感兴趣，那么一顿丰盛的大餐对我来说就具有在其他情况下没有的直接价值。牙痛病对我也有一定的价值，因为我对如何尽快解除这种病痛感兴趣。

一种社会体系可以被认为是一种价值体系，而且可以这样研究它。一个社会的组成要素是那些构成复杂社会关系网络的若干个体。当两个或更多的个人，通过限制或调整他们的兴趣，最后达到兴趣的融合时，他们之间就会有一种社会关系产生。所谓兴趣总是指某一个人的兴趣，两个人之间只会存在相似的兴趣，但相似的兴趣本身并不能构成一种社会关系。两只狗之间对一根骨头产生相似兴趣的结果只会使它们打架，但一个社会存在的基础是建立在其成员兴趣相似度之上的。从价

the first necessary condition of the existence of a society is that the individual members shall agree in some measure in the values that they recognise.

Any particular society is characterised by a certain set of values—moral, aesthetic, economic, etc. In a simple society there is a fair amount of agreement amongst the members in their evaluations, though of course the agreement is never absolute. In a complex modern society we find much more disagreement if we consider the society as a whole, but we may find a closer measure of agreement amongst the members of a group or class within the society.

While some measure of agreement about values, some similarity of interests, is a prerequisite of a social system, social relations involve more than this. They require the existence of common interests and of social values. When two or more persons have a common interest in the same object and are aware of their community of interest a social relation is established. They form, whether for a moment or for a long period, an association, and the object may be said to have a social value. For a man and his wife the birth of a child, the child itself and its well-being and happiness or its death, are objects of a common interest which binds them together and they thus have, for the association formed by the two persons, social value. By this definition an object can only have a social value for an association of persons. In the simplest possible instance we have a triadic relation; Subject 1 and Subject 2 are both interested in the same way in the Object and each of the Subjects has an interest in the other, or at any rate in certain items of the behaviour of the other, namely those directed towards the object. To avoid cumbersome circumlocutions it is convenient to speak of the object as having a social value for any one subject involved in such a relation, but it must be remembered that this is a loose way of speaking.

It is perhaps necessary for the avoidance of misunderstanding to add that a social system also requires that persons should be objects

值的角度阐述的话，一个社会存在的基础就是，社会的个体成员对他们认识的价值的某种程度的一致性。

任何一个社会的道德、美学、经济等方面的价值决定了这个社会的基本特征。在一个简单的社会结构中，其成员价值体系一致性的程度很高，当然这种一致性不会是绝对的。在一个复杂的现代社会中，对于一个作为整体来考虑的社会，我们会发现价值体系存在着很多歧义，但是，在这个社会的某个群体内部或某一阶层，我们又会发现较多的一致性。

尽管在价值观上某种程度的一致性和兴趣的相似性是构成社会制度的前提条件，但社会关系是构成社会制度更重要的前提。这些社会关系的基础是共同利益和共同社会价值。当两个或者更多的人对某一客体具有共同的兴趣，并且彼此之间认识到了这种兴趣共同性时，一种社会关系便建立起来了。他们建立起了一种联合，无论这种联合是暂时的还是长期的，并且，他们共同感兴趣的客体也可以说具有一定的社会价值。对于一位男子及其妻子来说，他们孩子的出生、孩子本身及其健康、幸福或死亡是他们共同关心的兴趣所在，他们因此而联合在一起，这些客体对于他们两个建立起的联合就具有一定的社会价值。根据这个定义，客体针对人们的联合才具有一定的社会价值。我们可以在最简单的例子中看到一种三位一体的关系，即主体 1 与主体 2 都以同种方式对某一客体感兴趣，两个主体之间又相互感兴趣，至少一主体对另一主体与它感兴趣的客体间的相互行为感兴趣。为了避免叙述过于冗长，简而言之就是，客体对涉及到这一关系之中的任何一个主体都具有社会价值。但要注意，这种说法并不严谨。

为了避免产生误解，也许有必要向大家补充说明：一种社会

of interest to other persons. In relations of friendship or love each of two persons has a value for the other. In certain kinds of groups each member is an object of interest for all the others, and each member therefore has a social value for the group as a whole. Further, since there are negative values as well as positive, persons may be united or associated by their antagonism to other persons. For the members of an anti-Comintern pact the Comintern has a specific social value.

Amongst the members of a society we find a certain measure of agreement as to the ritual value they attribute to objects of different kinds. We also find that most of these ritual values are social values as defined above. Thus for a local totemic clan in Australia the totem-centres, the natural species associated with them, i. e. the totems, and the myths and rites that relate thereto, have a specific social value for the clan; the common interest in them binds the individuals together into a firm and lasting association.

Ritual values exist in every known society, and show an immense diversity as we pass from one society to another. The problem of a natural science of society (and it is as such that I regard social anthropology) is to discover the deeper, not immediately perceptible, uniformities beneath the superficial differences. This is, of course, a highly complex problem which will require the studies begun by Sir James Frazer and others to be continued by many investigators over many years. The ultimate aim should be, I think, to find some relatively adequate answer to the question—*What is the relation of ritual and ritual values to the essential constitution of human society*? I have chosen a particular approach to this study which I believe to be promising—to investigate in a few societies studied as thoroughly as possible the relations of ritual values to other values including moral and aesthetic values. In the present lecture, however, it is only one small part of this study in which I seek to interest you—the question of

体制也需要人们成为其他人的兴趣客体。处于友情、爱情关系中的两个人,互相都对对方具有一定价值。而某种群体的每个成员都可以被当做其他成员的兴趣客体,因此,对于整个群体来说他们都有一定的社会价值。另外,除了存在正面价值,还会相应地存在负面价值,因此人们之间的联合也许是建立在一种对立关系之上。比如,第三国际对于那些反对它的国家来说,就拥有一种特定的社会价值。

在一个社会的成员中,我们发现他们对不同种类的客体赋予的仪式价值存在一定程度的一致性。我们还发现,上述定义的社会价值是大多数仪式价值的组成要素。因此,在澳大利亚的一个土著图腾氏族中,那些具有特定社会价值的对象主要有:图腾中心、与图腾中心相联系的一些自然物种也就是氏族图腾,以及与此有关的神话和仪式。对这些客体产生的共同兴趣,把每个人结合在一起成为一个坚固的、永久的联盟。

所有已知的社会都具有仪式价值,并且表现出极大的多样性。社会自然科学(我把社会人类学看做是这种学科)的任务就是,通过表面的区别来发现其深层次的、不能被立即感知的内在统一性。当然,对于这个极度复杂的问题,在詹姆斯·弗雷泽爵士等学者所做的开创性工作之后,还需要更多研究者们更长时间的探索。我认为,研究的最终目的就是为这个问题——即怎样来定义人类社会基本构成与仪式价值之间的关系——提供足够的答案。我为此选择了一个我认为能够解决它的独特方法——在几个已经被研究过的社会里,尽可能全面深入地考察仪式价值与其他价值(包括道德和美学价值)的各种关系。今天的演讲中,正是属于我想让你们感兴趣的这个研究的一小部分——仪式价值和

a relation between ritual values and social values.

One way of approaching the study of ritual is by the consideration of the purposes or reasons for the rites. If one examines the literature of anthropology one finds this approach very frequently adopted. It is by far the least profitable, though the one that appeals most to common sense. Sometimes the purpose of a rite is obvious, or a reason may be volunteered by those who practise it. Sometimes the anthropologist has to ask the reason, and in such circumstances it may happen that different reasons are given by different informants. What is fundamentally the same rite in two different societies may have different purposes or reasons in the one and in the other. The reasons given by the members of a community for any custom they observe are important data for the anthropologist. But it is to fall into grievous error to suppose that they give a valid explanation of the custom. What is entirely inexcusable is for the anthropologist, when he cannot get from the people themselves a reason for their behaviour which seems to him satisfactory, to attribute to them some purpose or reason on the basis of his own preconceptions about human motives. I could adduce many instances of this from the literature of ethnography, but I prefer to illustrate what I mean by an anecdote.

A Queenslander met a Chinese who was taking a bowl of cooked rice to place on his brother's grave. The Australian in jocular tones asked if he supposed that his brother would come and eat the rice. The reply was 'No! We offer rice to people as an expression of friendship and affection. But since you speak as you do I suppose that you in this country place flowers on the graves of your dead in the belief that they will enjoy looking at them and smelling their sweet perfume.'

So far as ritual avoidances are concerned the reasons for them may vary from a very vague idea that some sort of misfortune or ill-luck, not defined as to its kind, is likely to befall anyone who fails to observe the taboo, to a belief that non-observance will produce some quite specific and undesirable result. Thus an Australian aborigine told me that if he spoke to any woman who stood in the relation of

社会价值的关系问题。

研究仪式的一种方法是考察进行仪式的目的和原因。如果有人查阅过人类学方面的文献,那么就会发现这种方法经常被采用。尽管这种方法吸引了很多人,但到目前为止,这种方法的成就还很小。有时举行仪式的目的很明显,有时,仪式的原因会通过仪式参加者的情况表现出来。有时,人类学家们需要询问仪式的原因,此时,不同的受问者会提供不同的答案。两个不同社会中的完全相同的仪式也许是由不同的原因造成的。对于人类学家来说,某一群体中的成员对于我们遵守的任何习俗给出的原因都是非常重要的数据。但是,如果简单地认为他们的解释是正确的话,那就犯了极严重的错误。对人类学家来说最不可原谅的就是,当人们无法解释对他们来说似乎是合理的行为时,人类学家们便基于自己对人类动机的了解对此行为的目的或原因进行猜测。我可以从民族学文献中举出很多有关这种现象的例子,下面就举一件有趣的事。

一位昆士兰人看到中国人将一碗熟米饭放在其兄弟的坟旁边。这位澳洲人开玩笑地问,他是不是料想他的兄弟会来把米饭吃掉。那位中国人回答:“不！供米饭是表达我们的友情和感情。如果像你说的那样,那么我猜想,在这个国家,你把花放在已故之人的墓旁,也相信他们会来欣赏花的美丽、品味花的芬芳吧。”

就不同的仪式回避而言,它们的起因也许与那种模糊不清的概念有所区别,这个概念认为,任何不遵守禁忌的人都会遭受某种不确定的不幸或厄运,并且违反禁忌的行为将会产生某种特殊的、难以想象的后果。因而,一位澳洲土著人告诉我,他的头发会

mother-in-law to him his hair would turn grey. ①

The very common tendency to look for the explanation of ritual actions in their purpose is the result of a false assimilation of them to what may be called technical acts. In any technical activity an adequate statement of the purpose of any particular act or series of acts constitutes by itself a sufficient explanation. But ritual acts differ from technical acts in having in all instances some expressive or symbolic element in them.

A second approach to the study of ritual is therefore by a consideration not of their purpose or reason but of their meaning. I am here using the words symbol and meaning as coincident. Whatever has a meaning is a symbol and the meaning is whatever is expressed by the symbol. But how are we to discover meanings? They do not lie on the surface.

There is a sense in which people always know the meaning of their own symbols, but they do so intuitively and can rarely express their understanding in words. Shall we therefore be reduced to guessing at meanings as some anthropologists have guessed at reasons and purposes? I think not. For as long as we admit guess-work of any kind social anthropology cannot be a science. There are, I believe, methods of determining, with some fair degree of probability, the meanings of rites and other symbols.

There is still a third approach to the study of rites. We can consider the effects of the rite—not the effects that it is supposed to produce by the people who practise it but the effects that it does actually

① In case it may be thought that this is an inadequate supernatural punishment for a serious breach of rules of proper behaviour a few words of explanation are necessary. Grey hair comes with old age and is thought to be usually associated with loss of sexual potency. It is thus premature old age with its disadvantages but without the advantages that usually accompany seniority that threatens the man who fails to observe the rules of avoidance. On the other hand when a man's hair is grey and his wife's mother has passed the age of child-bearing the taboo is relaxed so that the relatives may talk together if they wish.

因他与处于岳母关系上的任何一位女人讲话，而变得灰白。①

在仪式行为中寻求仪式的起因是一种非常普遍的做法，而且这是吸取所谓技术活动的做法，其假设是认为这两种活动是相同的。在任何一项活动中，对任一行为或一系列行为目的的充分描述本身就是在提供充分的解释。但仪式活动与技术活动的不同之处在于，所有仪式活动中都不得包含某些表达性或象征性因素。

因此，对仪式进行研究的第二种方法，是不考察其活动目的或原因，而是其意义。这里，我要使用符号和意义这两个并列存在的词。任何有意义的东西都是一种符号，同时任何意义都由符号来表现。

但是，我们怎样才能发现其中的意义呢？意义并不存在于仪式活动的表面。然而，人们总是有一种感觉，即在直觉上他们知道自己的符号具有的意义，但是却不能够用语言表达出来。那么我们就应该像一些人类学家猜测原因和目的一样，来猜测意义吗？我不这样认为。因为我们必须承认，对于社会人类学的任何猜测都是不科学的。我相信，会存在确定仪式意义和其他一些符号意义的方法。

我们还有第三种研究仪式的方法。我们可以考察仪式带来的影响——并不是执行仪式活动的人们所希望仪式产生的

① 为了避免认为这是因严重违反正常行为规范而导致的不适当的超自然力的惩罚，我认为有必要在这里解释一下。随年龄增长头发也会变灰白，但它也常被看成是失去性功能的象征。因此，少白发并不代表那种跟随年资增长而具有的优势，而是表示那种因为违反回避规则而带来的威胁的劣势。然而，在一个男人的头发已灰白，而他丈母娘也已超出生育年龄条件下，这种禁忌的限制就会被放宽，因而，这类亲戚只要愿意就可以自由交谈。

produce. A rite has immediate or direct effects on the persons who are in any way directly concerned in it, which we may call, for lack of a better term, the psychological effects. But there are also secondary effects upon the social structure, i. e. the network of social relations binding individuals together in an ordered life. These we may call the socialeffects. By considering the psychological effects of a rite we may succeed in defining its psychological function; by considering the social effects we may discover its social function. Clearly it is impossible to discover the social function of a rite without taking into account its usual or average psychological effects.

But it is possible to discuss the psychological effects while more or less completely ignoring the more remote sociological effects, and this is often done in what is called 'functional anthropology'.

Let us suppose that we wish to investigate in Australian tribes the totemic rites of a kind widely distributed over a large part of the continent. The ostensible purpose of these rites, as stated by the natives themselves, is to renew or maintain some part of nature, such as a species of animal or plant, or rain, or hot or cold weather. With reference to this purpose we have to say that from our point of view the natives are mistaken, that the rites do not actually do what they are believed to do. The rain-making ceremony does not, we think, actually bring rain. In so far as the rites are performed for a purpose they are futile, based on erroneous belief. I do not believe that there is any scientific value in attempts to conjecture processes of reasoning which might be supposed to have led to these errors.

The rites are easily perceived to be symbolic, and we may therefore investigate their meaning. To do this we have to examine a considerable number of them and we then discover that there is a certain body of ritual idiom extending from the west coast of the continent to the east coast with some local variations. Since each rite has a myth associated with it we have similarly to investigate the meanings of the myths. As a result we find that the meaning of any single rite becomes clear in the light of a cosmology, a body of ideas and beliefs about nature and human society, which, so far as its most general features are

影响,而是仪式实际产生的影响。仪式对那些参与其中的人们有切身的或直接的影响,由于缺乏更适合的术语,我们称这种影响为心理效应。但是,仪式还会对社会结构,即把每个人联系在一个有秩序的生活下的社会关系网,产生第二级的影响。我们称之为社会效应。通过考察仪式的心理效应,我们可以成功地确定其心理功能;通过考察仪式的社会效应,我们可以提示其社会功能。很明显,我们对仪式社会功能的揭示是以考察仪式的一般或普遍的心理效应为前提的。但是,在讨论其心理效应时,多多少少会忽视,甚至可能完全忽视较为间接的社会效应,这在所谓"功能人类学"中经常发生。

我们假定,现在想要考察在大部分澳洲部落中分布极为广泛的一种图腾仪式。举行这些仪式,正如土著人所说,就是为了恢复或保持大自然中存在的某些现象,例如某种动物或植物、雨水、冷热天气等。根据这些仪式的目的,我们不得不说,从我们的角度看,这些土著人错了;事实上,这些仪式并不能带来他们所希望的结果。我们认为,求雨典礼并不能真正给他们带来降雨。尽管是出于某种目的执行这些典礼仪式,但由于是建立在错误信仰的基础上,所以这是徒劳的。我认为对产生这些错误的推理过程进行猜测,没有任何科学价值。

由于仪式的符号性很容易看出,所以,我们可以考察其意义。在对大量仪式活动考察之后,我们发现带有一些地方色彩的仪式习语体系,它们存在于从东岸到西岸的整个大陆。由于仪式与神话之间的紧密联系,在同样对这些神话的意义研究之后,我们发现,任何一个仪式的意义,按照他们的宇宙观来看,即从他们关于自然和人类社会的观点和信仰的角度分析都会变得十分清晰。

concerned, is current in all Australian tribes.

The immediate psychological effects of the rites can be to some extent observed by watching and talking to the performers. The ostensible purpose of the rite is certainly present in their minds, but so also is that complex set of cosmological beliefs by reference to which the rite has a meaning. Certainly a person performing the rite, even if, as sometimes happens, he performs it alone, derives therefrom a definite feeling of satisfaction, but it would be entirely false to imagine that this is simply because he believes that he has helped to provide a more abundant supply of food for himself and his fellow-tribesmen. His satisfaction is in having performed a ritual duty, we might say a religious duty. Putting in my own words what I judge, from my own observations, to express what the native feels, I would say that in the performance of the rite he has made that small contribution, which it is both his privilege and his duty to do, to the maintenance of that order of the universe of which man and nature are interdependent parts. The satisfaction which he thus receives gives the rite a special value for him. In some instances with which I am acquainted of the last survivor of a totemic group who still continues to perform the totemic rites by himself, it is this satisfaction that constitutes apparently the sole motive for his action.

To discover the social function of the totemic rites we have to consider the whole body of cosmological ideas of which each rite is a partial expression. I believe that it is possible to show that the social structure of an Australian tribe is connected in a very special way with these cosmological ideas and that the maintenance of its continuity depends on keeping them alive, by their regular expression in myth and rite.

Thus any satisfactory study of the totemic rites of Australia must be based not simply on the consideration of their ostensible purpose and their psychological function, or on an analysis of the motives of the individuals who perform the rites, but on the discovery of their meaning and of their social function.

It may be that some rites have no social function. This may be the case with such taboos as that against spilling salt in our own

就其最普遍的特征而言,澳洲所有部落都存在这种宇宙观。

对仪式的直接心理效应的考察,可以通过观察以及与仪式执行者交谈这两种方式进行。在仪式执行者的头脑之中当然会存在仪式的直接目的,不过其中也夹杂着使仪式具有意义的一系列复杂的宇宙观概念。

即使通常只有一个人单独举行仪式,这个人也可以从仪式中获得满足感。如果认为此人的满足感只是源于相信他的行动会给自己及他的同族人提供更充足的食物,那就完全错了。

他的满足感来源于他执行了一种仪式责任,我们可以称之为宗教责任。依据我的观察,我认为此人在执行仪式时的感受是:他有权利也有责任为维护人与自然相互依存的宇宙的秩序做出贡献。因而,他得到的满足感使仪式对他具有一种特别的价值。在那些最后幸存下来的我熟悉的图腾群体中,那里的人仍旧独自地继续举行图腾仪式,很明显,正是这种满足感成为了他采取这种行为的唯一动力。

为实现揭示图腾仪式社会功能的目的,我们必须对整个宇宙观体系进行考察,其中的每一种仪式都是对整个宇宙观体系认识的部分反映。我相信,从存在于澳大利亚部落的神话和仪式有规律地描述他们的宇宙观念的行为中,可以看出他们的社会结构与这些宇宙观概念之间的联系方式十分独特,并且这些宇宙观概念是社会结构得以延续的决定因素。

因此,有关澳大利亚图腾仪式的任何令人满意的研究,必须赖以的基础,不仅是研究仪式的直接目的及其心理功能,或者是分析举行仪式的人的动机,而且还要发现其意义及社会功能。

也许,有些仪式并没有任何社会功能。这与发生在我国的关

society. Nevertheless, the method of investigating rites and ritual values that I have found most profitable during work extending over more than thirty years is to study rites as symbolic expressions and to seek to discover their social functions. This method is not new except in so far as it is applied to the comparative study of many societies of diverse types. It was applied by Chinese thinkers to their own ritual more than twenty centuries ago.

In China, in the fifth and sixth centuries B. C., Confucius and his followers insisted on the great importance of the proper performance of ritual, such as funeral and mourning rites and sacrifices. After Confucius there came the reformer Mo Ti who taught a combination of altruism—love for all men—and utilitarianism. He held that funeral and mourning rites were useless and interfered with useful activities and should therefore be abolished or reduced to a minimum. In the third and second centuries B. C., the Confucians, Hsün Tze and the compilers of the *Li Chi* (Book of Rites), replied to Mo Ti to the effect that though these rites might have no utilitarian purpose they none the less had a very important social function. Briefly the theory is that the rites are the orderly (the *Li Chi* says the beautified) expression of feelings appropriate to a social situation. They thus serve to regulate and refine human emotions. We may say that partaking in the performance of rites serves to cultivate in the individual sentiments on whose existence the social order itself depends.

Let us consider the meaning and social function f an extremely simple example of ritual. In the Andaman Islands when a woman is expecting a baby a name is given to it while it is still in the womb. From that time until some weeks after the baby is born nobody is allowed to use the personal name of either the father or the mother; they can be referred to by teknonymy, i. e. in terms of their relation to the child. During this period both the parents are required to abstain from eating certain foods which they may freely eat at other times.

I did not obtain from the Andamanese any statement of the purpose or reason for this avoidance of names. Assuming that the act is

于禁止撒盐的禁忌情况相同。然而,在过去 30 多年的工作中,我发现研究仪式和仪式价值最有效的一个方法就是,把仪式作为符号表达来研究,从而揭示其社会功能。但此方法除了可以应用于许多不同社会的对比性研究之外,并没有什么新意。因为这个方法早在两千多年前就被中国的思想家应用于他们的仪式研究中了。

公元前五六世纪,在中国,孔子及其追随者们强调恰当举行仪式的重要性,例如,丧葬仪式、哀悼仪式及祭祀仪式。自孔子之后,改革者墨子提倡一种利他主义——爱所有的人——与功利主义的结合。他认为,举行丧葬和哀悼仪式是无用的,并且干扰了一些有用的活动,因此,应该取消这类仪式或将其限制到最小范围内。公元前二三世纪,儒家学者荀子和《礼记》一书的作者们对墨子的观点加以反驳,认为尽管这些仪式也许没有任何实用目的,但是,它们或多或少都有很重要的社会功能。简单地说,荀子认为,仪式是那些符合社会规范之感情的条理化(《礼记》称之为美化),因而,这些仪式是用来调节和净化人的感情的。我们可以说,参加仪式活动可以改善人的感情,而社会秩序则建立在这些感情之上。

让我们考察一个极端简单的仪式的意义和社会功能。在印度安达曼群岛,当一个女人期待生一个小孩,她就先把小孩的名字起好,尽管孩子还在腹中。自那时起,一直到孩子出生几个星期后,任何人不允许使用孩子父亲或母亲的名字。人们可以通过关系称呼法,即根据自己与孩子的关系来决定如何称呼这个孩子的父母。一些在平时可以吃的食物,孩子的父母在这一时期也不能食用。

对于安达曼人为何要回避名字以及这样做的目的,我从他们

symbolic, what method, other than that of guessing, is there of arriving at the meaning? I suggest that we may start with a general working hypothesis that when, in a single society, the same symbol is used in different contexts or on different kinds of occasions there is some common element of meaning, and that by comparing together the various uses of the symbol we may be able to discover what the common element is. This is precisely the method that we adopt in studying an unrecorded spoken language in order to discover the meanings of words and morphemes.

In the Andamans the name of a dead person is avoided from the occurrence of the death to the conclusion of mourning; the name of a person mourning for a dead relative is not used; there is avoidance of the name of a youth or girl who is passing through the ceremonies that take place at adolescence; a bride or bridegroom is not spoken of or to by his or her own name for a short time after the marriage. For the Andamanese the personal name is a symbol of the social personality, i. e. of the position that an individual occupies in the social structure and the social life. The avoidance of a personal name is a symbolic recognition of the fact that at the time the person is not occupying a normal position in the social life. It may be added that a person whose name is thus temporarily out of use is regarded as having for the time an abnormal ritual status.

Turning now to the rule as to avoiding certain foods, if the Andaman Islanders are asked what would happen if the father or mother broke his taboo the usual answer is that he or she would be ill, though one or two of my informants thought it might perhaps also affect the child. This is simply one instance of a standard formula which applies to a number of ritual prohibitions. Thus persons in mourning for a relative may not eat pork and turtle, the most important flesh foods, and the reason given is that if they did they would be ill.

那里还没有得到任何有价值的资料能够对此解释。假设此行为是具有符号性的，那么除了猜测之外，还有什么方法可以研究出这个禁忌的意义呢？我建议我们可以先提出一个可行的基本假设，即在一个单独的社会中，当同一种符号被用于不同的情境或不同的场合时，其间一定会有一些意义上的共同要素，通过对这些不同符号用法的对比，我们就可以揭示这个共同的要素是什么。我们在研究没有文字记录的语言时，为揭示词和词素意义就曾采用过这种有效的方法。

在安达曼人中，有很多场合都需要回避名字：从某个人死到哀悼结束，他的名字需要避讳；为死者亲属作哀悼的那个人的名字也不能够使用；一位年轻小伙或一位姑娘在自己的成人礼上，也应该回避使用自己的名字；新郎和新娘在婚后的一段短时期内，也不能被提及姓名。对于安达曼人来说，一个人的名字是其社会人格的符号，而社会人格是指一个人在社会结构和社会生活中占有的位置。回避个人姓名是一种对符号的认知，即认识到此人那时在社会生活中并没有处于正常的位置。我要补充说明的是，当一个人名字被暂停使用，说明此人只是暂时地处于一种不正常的仪式状态。

我们把话题转向有关回避某些食物的规则。当安达曼人被问道，如果他的双亲违反禁忌，会发生什么样的情况。通常的回答就是其父亲或母亲会生病，尽管我的几个被调查者认为有时也会影响到孩子。这种回答只是许多仪式禁忌的标准回答中的一例。例如，为亲属做哀悼的人们不可以食用猪肉和甲鱼，尤其不能吃新鲜食物，原因和上述一样，一旦他们吃了这些食物，就会生病。

To discover the meaning of this avoidance of foods by the parents we can apply the same method as in reference to the avoidance of their names. There are similar rules for mourners, for women during menstruation, and for youths and girls during the period of adolescence. But for a full demonstration we have to consider the place of foods in Andamanese ritual as a whole, and for an examination of this I must refer to what I have already written on the subject.

I should like to draw your attention to another point in the method by which it is possible to test our hypotheses as to the meanings of rites. We take the different occasions on which two rites are associated together, for example the association of the avoidance of a person's name with the avoidance by that person of certain foods, which we find in the instance of mourners on the one hand and the expectant mother and father on the other. We must assume that for the Andamanese there is some important similarity between these two kinds of occasions—birth and death—by virtue of which they have similar ritual values. We cannot rest content with any interpretation of the taboos at childbirth unless there is a parallel interpretation of those relating to mourners. In the terms I am using here we can say that in the Andamans the relatives of a recently dead person, and the father and mother of a child that is about to be, or has recently been, born, are in an abnormal ritual status. This is recognised or indicated by the avoidance of their names. They are regarded as likely to suffer some misfortune, some bad luck, if you will, unless they observe certain prescribed ritual precautions of which the avoidance of certain foods is one. In the Andaman Islands the danger in such instances is thought of as the danger of illness. This is the case also with the Polynesian belief about the ritual status of anyone who has touched a corpse or a newly-born baby. It is to be noted that for the Polynesians as well as for the Andamanese the occasion of a birth has a similar ritual value to that of a death.

The interpretation of the taboos at childbirth at which we arrive by studying it in relation to the whole system of ritual values of the Andamanese is too complex to be stated here in full. Clearly, however,

对上述有关父母禁止食用某些食物的意义的讨论,也可以参照研究回避使用名字的方法。另外对哀悼者、月经中的妇女及青春期中的男女也可以使用相似的研究方法。但是,对这个问题的充分证明,就不得不把这些食物在整个安达曼仪式中所处的位置也考虑进来。要想对此进行考察,还需要参考我在前面讨论过的问题。

对这个方法,我还要说明一点,以便可以猜测我们关于仪式意义的假设。在有些场合中,两个仪式可以联系在一起,例如,某个场合既要求回避提及某人的名字,而同时此人又正在忌食某些食物。这个人如果既是个哀悼者,同时又是临产父母,就是这样的例子。我们必须假设,对于安达曼人来说,肯定有某种相似性存在于这两个不同的场合——出生与死亡——之间,从而使它们具有相似的仪式价值。因此我们对生育禁忌的任何满意的解释,都要以对有关哀悼者仪式的相应的解释为前提。根据我在这里的说法,我们可以说,在安达曼人中,刚刚死去亲人的人们和即将成为父母或刚刚成为父母的人们,他们的仪式状态都是不正常的。对他们名字的回避就显示了这种不正常的仪式状态。人们认为,如果这些人不遵守规定的仪式警告(忌讳食用一些食物就是警告之一),他们很可能会遭遇一些不幸和厄运。在安达曼岛,使某人面临生病的危险就是这些不幸或厄运的表现。在波利尼西亚人中,接触尸体或新生婴儿的人也被认为处于和上述安达曼人相同的仪式状态。应该注意的是,对于波利尼西亚人和安达曼人来说,出生的场合与死亡的场合具有相同的仪式价值。

对产婴禁忌的解释是建立在对产婴与安达曼人的整个仪式价值体系关系研究的基础之上的,但由于问题的复杂性,因而我

they express, in accordance with Andamanese ritual idiom, a common concern in the event. The parents show their concern by avoiding certain foods; their friends show theirs by avoiding the parents' personal names. By virtue of these taboos the occasion acquires a certain social value, as that term has been defined above.

There is one theory that might seem to be applicable to our example. It is based on a hypothesis as to the psychological function of a class of rites. The theory is that in certain circumstances the individual human being is anxious about the outcome of some event or activity because it depends to some extent on conditions that he cannot control by any technical means. He therefore observes some rite which, since he believes it will ensure good luck, serves to reassure him. Thus an aeronaut takes with him in a plane a mascot which he believes will protect him from accident and thus carries out his flight with confidence.

The theory has a respectable antiquity. It was perhaps implied in the *Primus in orbe deos jecit timor* of Petrbnius and Statius. It has taken various forms from Hume's explanation of religion to Malinowski's explanation of Trobriand magic. It can be made so plausible by a suitable selection of illustrations that it is necessary to examine it with particular care and treat it with reasonable scepticism. For there is always the danger that we may be taken in by the plausibility of a theory that ultimately proves to be unsound.

I think that for certain rites it would be easy to maintain with equal plausibility an exactly contrary theory, namely, that if it were not for the existence of the rite and the beliefs associated with it the individual would feel no anxiety, and that the psychological effect of the rite is to create in him a sense of insecurity or danger. It seems very unlikely that an Andaman Islander would think that it is dangerous to eat dugong or pork or turtle meat if it were not for the existence of a specific body of ritual the ostensible purpose of which is to protect him from those dangers. Many hundreds of similar instances could

在这里不加以详细的陈述。然而,很明显地可以从安达曼人的仪式习惯中看出他们对这一事件表现出的共同关注。例如,父母通过避讳某些食物而表示他们的关注;父母的朋友通过回避使用这对父母的名字来表示他们的关注。依靠这些禁忌,仪式场合获得了某种上述规定的社会价值。

有一种理论似乎很适用于我们的例子,它是以一种与仪式的心理功能有关的假设为基础的。这个理论认为,在一些情况下,个人对于某些在某种程度上他无法通过技术手段操控的事件或活动的产生感到焦虑,所以,他不得不遵守某种仪式,因为他认为这种仪式会给他带来好运并且使他得到慰藉。比如,飞行员在飞行时会带上一个吉祥物。他相信此吉祥物会保护他远离灾难,并增加飞行的自信。

这个理论非常古老。它也许早在彼得罗纽斯和斯特休斯的著作 *Primus in orbe deos fecit timor* 中就已有所暗示,也曾以各种不同形式出现在从休莫对宗教的解释到马林诺夫斯基对特罗布里恩人巫术的解释的过程中。一些经过适当挑选的例证使得这个理论看起来如此有道理,以至于我们有必要对其进行仔细检验,并持有合理的置疑态度。因为,我们总是有可能被最终证明是没有根据的理论的合理性欺骗。

我认为,对某些仪式来说,一种完全相反的理论也可以容易地从同样合理的解释得出。也就是说要不是存在着仪式及与仪式相关的一些信仰,那么,人们就不会觉得焦虑,人们的不安全感和危险感觉事实上来自于仪式所产生的心理效应。因而,如果不存在那种其直接目的是为了使安达曼人免受危险的仪式体系的话,安达曼人就很可能不会认为吃儒艮肉、猪肉或龟肉是危险的。

be mentioned from all over the world.

Thus, while one anthropological theory is that magic and religion give men confidence, comfort and a sense of security,① it could equally well be argued that they give men fears and anxieties from which they would otherwise be free—the fear of black magic or of spirits, fear of God, of the Devil, of Hell.

Actually in our fears or anxieties as well as in our hopes we are conditioned (as the phrase goes) by the community in which we live. And it is largely by the sharing of hopes and fears, by what I have called common concern in events or eventualities, that human beings are linked together in temporary or permanent associations.

To return to the Andamanese taboos at childbirth, there are difficulties in supposing that they are means by which parents reassure themselves against the accidents that may interfere with a successful delivery. If the prospective father fails to observe the food taboo it is he who will be sick, according to the general Andamanese opinion. Moreover, he must continue to observe the taboos after the child is safely delivered. Further, how are we to provide a parallel explanation of the similar taboos observed by a person mourning for a dead relative?

The taboos associated with pregnancy and parturition are often explained in terms of the hypothesis I have mentioned. A father, naturally anxious at the outcome of an event over which he does not have a technical control and which is subject to hazard, reassures himself by observing some taboo or carrying out some magical action. He may avoid certain foods. He may avoid making nets or tying knots, or he may go round the house untying all knots and opening any locked or closed boxes or containers.

I wish to arouse in your minds, if it is not already there, a suspicion that both the general theory and this special application of it do

---

① This theory has been formulated by Loisy, and for magic has been adopted by Malinowski.

类似于这样的例子在全世界很多地方都可能找到。

因此,尽管一种人类学理论认为巫术和宗教会给人们带来自信、慰籍和安全感,①但人们同样认为它也带来了不安和焦虑,否则,他们就从——对黑巫术的恐惧、对灵魂的恐惧、对上帝的恐惧、对魔鬼的恐惧和对地狱的恐惧——中逃脱出来。

实际上,我们的希望和不安以及焦虑一样,都受到我们生活的社会制约。并且,很大程度上是通过对希望和不安的共同分享和承担,也就是我所说的对于事件和不测的共同关注,才暂时地或永久地把人类联系到一起。

让我们把话题转到有关安达曼人产婴的禁忌。很难想象父母遵循这些禁忌是为了躲避那些可能干扰顺产的因素。根据安达曼人的普遍说法,如果一位将要成为父亲的人没能遵守食物禁忌他就会生病,而且,直到孩子安全出生,他都应该一直遵守这些禁忌。但是,相似的禁忌在一个人去哀悼死去的亲属时也要遵守,我们该对这一现象如何解释呢?

与怀孕和分娩有关的禁忌通常是根据我提供的那个假设解释。一位父亲对于自己无法进行技术操控的事情,自然是很不安的,他通常会很害怕,只有通过遵守一些禁忌或举行某种巫术行为来安慰自己。他有可能回避食用一些食物,或者停止结网搓绳,打开房屋四周所有的绳结以及所有锁着的或关着的盒子或容器。

如果大家没有疑问的话,我想提醒你们,这个理论概括以及

① 卢瓦西确立了这个理论;马林诺夫斯基采纳了其有关巫术的那部分理论。

not give the whole truth and indeed may not be true at all. Scepticism of plausible but unproved hypotheses is essential in every science. There is at least good ground for suspicion in the fact that the theory has so far been considered in reference to facts that seem to fit it, and no systematic attempt has been made, so far as I am aware, to look for facts that do not fit. That there are many such I am satisfied from my own studies.

The alternative hypothesis which I am presenting for consideration is as follows. In a given community it is appropriate that an expectant father should feel concern or at least should make an appearance of doing so. Some suitable symbolic expression of his concern is found in terms of the general ritual or symbolic idiom of the society, and it is felt generally that a man in that situation ought to carry out the symbolic or ritual actions or abstentions. For every rule that *ought* to be observed there must be some sort of sanction or reason. For acts that patently affect other persons the moral and legal sanctions provide a generally sufficient controlling force upon the individual. For ritual obligations conformity and rationalisation are provided by the ritual sanctions. The simplest form of ritual sanction is an accepted belief that if rules of ritual are not observed some undefined misfortune is likely to occur. In many societies the expected danger is somewhat more definitely conceived as a danger of sickness or, in extreme cases, death. In the more specialised forms of ritual sanction the good results to be hoped for or the bad results to be feared are more specifically defined in reference to the occasion or meaning of the ritual.

The theory is not concerned with the historical origin of ritual, nor is it another attempt to explain ritual in terms of human psychology; it is a hypothesis as to the relation of ritual and ritual values to the essential constitution of human society, i. e. to those invariant general characters which belong to all human societies, past, present and future. It rests on the recognition of the fact that while in animal societies social coaptation depends on instinct, in human societies it depends upon the efficacy of symbols of many different kinds. The

这一理论的特殊应用并没有为我们提供真理,也许它根本就不是真实的。对于合理的但并未证实的假设持怀疑态度,对每门科学来说都是最关键的。而且我们至少有理由对它进行怀疑,因为理论一向都是根据与其吻合的事实得到证明的。据我所知还没有人对那些与这一理论不符的事实进行过系统的考察。然而,在我的研究中,我却发现许多这类让我满意的证据。

以下是我提出需要考虑的另一个假设。在一个特定的社会中,一位将要成为父亲的人应当对某些事件的发生给予关注或至少要表现出他的这种关注。根据这个社会的一般仪式符号习俗,我们可以发现一些恰当的符号表现方式。处于这一状况下的男子一般都应该执行一些符号的或仪式性的行为或禁忌。务必要遵守的每一条规则都必须有某种约束力或合理性,而且道德和法律制裁也会有效地约束那些显然会影响他人的行为,同时仪式制裁也为仪式义务提供了一致性和合理性。仪式制裁最简单的形式就是使人们相信,如果不遵守某种规则,他们就将面临某种意想不到的厄运。在许多社会中,一般认为这种厄运是疾病,但在最严重的情况下也可能带来死亡。在比较成熟的仪式制裁形式中,人们所期待的好运和畏惧的厄运的内容是根据仪式具体的场合或仪式的意义确定的。

此理论既不是从历史起源的角度,也不是从人类心理学角度来解释仪式,而是一种有关仪式和仪式价值与人类社会基本构成之间关系的假说。人类社会的基本构成是指所有人类社会过去、现在和未来的永远不变的那些普遍特征。这一理论的基础建立在如下事实之上,即在动物社会中,是动物本能决定了它们的社会形式,而在人类社会中,社会依赖于许多不同种类的符号的

theory I am advancing must therefore, for a just estimation of its value, be considered in its place in a general theory of symbols and their social efficacy.

By this theory the Andamanese taboos relating to childbirth are the obligatory recognition in a standardised symbolic form of the significance and importance of the event to the parents and to the community at large. They thus serve to fix the social value of occasions of this kind. Similarly I have argued in another place that the Andamanese taboos relating to the animals and plants used for food are means of affixing a definite social value to food, based on its social importance: The *social* importance of food is not that it satisfies hunger, but that in such a community as an Andamanese camp or village an enormously large proportion of the activities are concerned with the getting and consuming of food, and that in these activities, with their daily instances of collaboration and mutual aid, there continuously occur those inter-relations of interests which bind the individual men, women and children into a society.

I believe that this theory can be generalised and with suitable modifications will be found to apply to a vast number of the taboos of different societies. My theory would go further for I would hold, as a reasonable working hypothesis, that we have here the primary basis of all ritual and therefore of religion and magic, however those may be distinguished. The primary basis of ritual, so the formulation would run, is the attribution of ritual value to objects and occasions which are either themselves objects of important common interests linking together the persons of a community or are symbolically representative of such objects. To illustrate what is meant by the last part of this statement two illustrations may be offered. In the Andamans ritual value is attributed to the cicada, not because it has any social importance itself but because it symbolically represents the seasons of the year which do have importance. In some tribes of Eastern Australia the god Baiame is the personification, i. e. the symbolical representative, of the moral law of the tribe, and the rainbow-serpent (the Australian equivalent of the Chinese dragon) is a symbol representing growth and fertility in nature. Baiame and the rainbow-serpent in their turn are represented by the figures of earth which are made on the sacred ceremonial ground of the initiation ceremonies and at which rites are performed. The reverence that the Australian shows to the image of Baiame

效应。因此，为了公正地评价我在此提出的理论，就必须考察此理论在有关符号及其社会效应的基本理论中所处的位置。

和产婴禁忌相关的这种标准化象征形式是为了强制人们承认这一事件对于父母以及整个社会具有的意义和重要性。因而，这些禁忌本身就是这种仪式的社会价值的表现。同样，我在别处曾说过，在安达曼人中那些关于可当做食物的动植物的禁忌为食物赋予了社会价值。从社会意义上来说，食物并非仅用来充饥，它的意义在于在类似安达曼的营地或村庄中，人们的大部分活动都是围绕食物的获得与消耗展开的。通过人们之间日常的合作与互助，就会不断出现一些利益的相互联系，正是这种联系把每一个男女老幼联系到一起，组成一个社会。

我认为，这个理论在经过适当地归纳和修正后，可以运用到许多不同社会的禁忌中去。作为一种合理的、可行的假设，我的理论能够被进一步地扩展。因为，我认为我们已经证明了所有仪式的主要基础，进而也证明了宗教和巫术的主要基础。然而它们仍旧需要加以区分。根据该理论进行推理，仪式的主要基础赋予了事物、场合以仪式价值。由共同兴趣联系起来的社区中的人们既把这些事物和场合看做这些共同兴趣的对象，也把它们当做这些对象的象征性代表。对上述论点的最后一部分的意思，我用两个例子加以说明。在安达曼人中，蝉所以被赋予仪式价值，并不是因为它本身具有任何社会重要性，它的重要性来自于可以象征性地代表季节。在澳大利亚东部的一些部落中，把拟人化的巴亚马神当做部落道德法规的象征性代表，而把云中之蛇（相当于中国的龙）当做自然界中生长繁殖的象征性代表。巴亚马神和云中之蛇都是由在神圣的创世典礼场所中创造出来的已存

or towards his name is the symbolic method of fixing the social value of the moral law, particularly the laws relating to marriage.

In conclusion let me return once more to the work of the anthropologist whom we are here to honour. Sir James Frazer, in his *Psyche's Task* and in his other works, set himself to show how, in his own words, taboos have contributed to build up the complex fabric of society. He thus initiated that functional study of ritual to which I have in this lecture and elsewhere attempted to make some contribution. But there has been a shift of emphasis. Sir James accounted for the taboos of savage tribes as the application in practice of beliefs arrived at by erroneous processes of reasoning, and he seems to have thought of the effects of these beliefs in creating or maintaining a stable orderly society as being accidental. My own view is that the negative and positive rites of savages exist and persist because they are part of the mechanism by which an orderly society maintains itself in existence, serving as they do to establish certain fundamental social values. The beliefs by which the rites themselves are justified and given some sort of consistency are the rationalisations of symbolic actions and of the sentiments associated with them. I would suggest that what Sir James Frazer seems to regard as the accidental results of magical and religious beliefs really constitute their essential function and the ultimate reason for their existence.

NOTE:

The theory of ritual outlined in this lecture was first worked out in 1908 in a thesis on the Andaman Islanders. It was written out again in a revised and extended form in 1913 and appeared in print in 1922. Unfortunately the exposition contained in *The Andaman Islanders* is evidently not clear, since some of my critics have

在的生物的形象代表的。对巴亚马的形象及其名称的崇拜这种象征性方法对澳大利亚人来说，目的是为了确定道德法则，尤其是与婚姻有关的法则的社会价值。

最后，让我们再次回到我们崇敬的人类学家詹姆斯·弗雷泽爵士的著作上来，在他的《灵魂的重任》和其他著作中，他用自己的观点阐明了在建立复杂的社会网络中禁忌所起的作用。因此是他首先提倡对仪式进行功能性研究，而在其他场合及本次演讲中我也希望能对此做出一点贡献。但我们两人研究的侧重点有所不同。在詹姆斯爵士看来，把在错误推理过程产生的信仰应用在实践中，是禁忌产生的原因，并且他似乎认为这些信仰对创造和保持一个稳定有序的社会的影响只是偶然的。而我认为，原始人的正面和负面的仪式之所以存在并能够持续下去，原因是这些仪式只是一个有序社会维持其生存的机制的一部分。它们的作用是建立某种根本的社会价值。这些信仰不仅给予仪式的合法形式，并保持了仪式的连贯性，它们还是象征行为以及与之相关的情感的理性结果。在詹姆斯·弗雷泽爵士看来似乎是由巫术和宗教信仰的偶然结果带来的东西，在我看来却真正构成了这些信仰的基本功能和最终存在的原因。

附注：

本次演讲所概括的仪式理论，早在 1908 年一篇有关安达曼岛人的论文中就已完成。经过 1913 年的修改和扩充，发表于 1922 年。很不幸，我在《安达曼群岛人》一文中所做的阐释现在看来显然论述得并不清楚，因为对此持批评态度的人看来并没有理解这个理论。例如，他们一直认为我所

failed to understand what the theory is. For example, it has been assumed that by 'social value' I mean 'utility'.

The best treatment of the subject of value with which I am acquainted is Ralph Barton Perry's *General Theory of Value*, 1926. For the Chinese theory of ritual the most easily accessible account is in chapter xiv of Fung Yu-lan's *History of Chinese Philosophy*, 1937. The third chapter, on the uses of symbolism, of Whitehead's *Symbolism, its Meaning and Effect*, is an admirable brief introduction to the sociological theory of symbolism.

One very important point that cold not be dealt with in the lecture is that indicated by Whitehead in the following sentence – 'No account of the uses of symbolism is complete without the recognition that the symbolic elements in life have a tendency to run wild, like the vegetation in a tropical forest.'

说的“社会价值”是“效用”的意思。

拉尔夫·巴顿·佩里于1926年发表的《价值的一般理论》一文是对我熟悉的有关价值论题的最好论述。关于中国仪式的理论,参阅冯友兰1937年出版的《中国哲学史》的第14章,非常方便。怀特海在《象征,它的意义和效用》的第三章,讨论了象征的使用,这一章中简介了象征的社会学理论。

在本次演讲中,有一点我没有提到,但怀特海的几句话可以对此加以说明:“生活中的象征性成分就像热带雨林中的植物那样随意蔓延,只有认识到了这一点,我们才能够彻底地解释象征的运用。”

CHAPTER Ⅷ

Religion And Society ①

The Royal Anthropological Institute has honoured me with an invitation to deliver the Henry Myers Lecture on the rôle of religion in the development of human society. That is an important and complex subject, about which it is not possible to say very much in a single lecture, but as it is hoped that this may be only the first of a continuing series of lectures, in which different lecturers will each offer some contribution, I think that the most useful thing I can do is to indicate certain lines along which I believe that an enquiry into this. problem can be profitably pursued.

The usual way of looking at religions is to regard all of them, or all except one, as bodies of erroneous beliefs and illusory practices. There is no doubt that the history of religions has been in great part a history of error and illusion. In all ages men have hoped that by the proper performance of religious actions or observances they would obtain some specific benefit: health and long life, children to carry on their line, material well-being, success in hunting, rain, the growth of crops and the multiplication of cattle, victory in war, admission of their souls after death to a paradise, or inversely, release by the extinction of personality from the round of reincarnation. We do not believe that the rainmaking rites of savage tribes really produce rain. Nor do we believe that the initiates of the ancient mysteries did actually attain through their initiation an immortality denied to other men.

When we regard the religions of other peoples, or at least those

① The Henry Myers Lecture, 1945.

第八章　宗教与社会[①]

皇家人类学会邀请我来做“亨利·迈耶斯讲座”，我感到非常荣幸。本次讲座的主题是宗教在人类社会发展中的角色。这是一个非常重要而且复杂的主题，我不可能在一次讲座中对此进行全部论述。但是，我希望这只是一系列讲座中的第一场，并且以后每场讲座都会为这个主题做出一些不同的论述。我想，目前我对这一主题能够做到的最有意义的事就是首先对它提出一个框架，沿着它继续进行深入探讨会使我们收益颇丰。

研究宗教问题的通常做法是，把所有的宗教或大部分宗教看做是错误的信仰和虚幻行为的体现。毫无疑问，在很大程度上，宗教的历史就是错误和虚幻的历史。无论在什么年代，执行适当的宗教行为或仪式在人们看来都能够带来以下他们所期待的特定利益：健康长寿、家族延续、物质富裕、狩猎成功、风调雨顺、五谷丰登、畜牧兴旺、战争胜利、死后升天和超凡脱俗等。但是我们不相信原始部落的求雨仪式真的能带来降雨；同样也不相信古代神秘社团的入会仪式就能为其成员带来别人都没有的长生不老。

如果我们认为其他民族的宗教，或至少是我们称之为原始部

---

① “亨利·迈耶斯讲座”，1945 年。

of what are called primitive peoples, as systems of erroneous and illusory *beliefs*, we are confronted with the problem of how these beliefs came to be formulated and accepted. It is to this problem that anthropologists have given most attention. My personal opinion is that this method of approach, even though it may seem the most direct, is not the one most likely to lead to a real understanding of the nature of religions.

There is another way in which we may approach the study of religions. We may entertain as at least a possibility the theory that any religion is an important or even essential part of the social machinery, as are morality and law, part of the complex system by which human beings are enabled to live together in an orderly arrangement of social relations. From this point of view we deal not with the origins but with the social functions of religions, i. e. the contribution that they make to the formation and maintenance of a social order. There are many persons who would say that it is only *true* religion (i. e. one's own) that can provide the foundation of an orderly social life. The hypothesis we are considering is that the social function of a religion is independent of its truth or falsity, that religions which we think to be erroneous or even absurd and repulsive, such as those of some savage tribes, may be important and effective parts of the social machinery, and that without these 'false' religions social evolution and the development of modern civilisation would have been impossible.

The hypothesis, therefore, is that in what we regard as false religions, though the performance of religious rites does not actually produce the effects that are expected or hoped for by those who perform or take part in them, they have other effects, some at least of which may be socially valuable.

How are we to set to work to test this hypothesis? It is of no use thinking in terms of religion in general, in the abstract, and society in the abstract. Nor is it adequate to consider some one religion, particularly if it is the one in which we have been brought up and about which we are likely to be prejudiced one way or another. The only method is the experimental method of social anthropology, and that

落的宗教,是错误的和虚幻的信仰的体系时,那么摆在我们面前的问题就是:这些信仰是如何形成并被人们所接受的?人类学家们已经对这个问题给予了最多的关注。我个人的观点是,尽管这一问法看起来似乎是最直接的,但它并不一定能够真正地理解宗教的本质。

对于宗教研究我们还可以遵循另一种方法。它要求我们这样来理解宗教,即把它看做和道德、法律一样,是社会机器的一个重要或关键的组成部分,它们共同组成了这个复杂的体系。正是通过宗教,才使人们一起在一种有序的社会关系下生活。从这一点来看,我们所要关注的就不再是宗教的起源,而是其社会功能,即宗教对社会秩序的形成与维护所做的贡献。很多人说,他们的有序社会生活只能构建于真正的宗教(即他们自己的宗教)之上。而我们所提出的假设是:宗教的社会功能独立于宗教的真实和虚幻之外,那些我们认为是错误的甚至是荒谬和令人厌恶的宗教,如一些原始部落中的宗教,也许是社会结构重要及有效的组成部分,如果没有这些“荒谬”的宗教存在,社会的进化和现代文明的发展也许就不可能产生。

因此,我们提出的假设是:对于我们认为是荒谬的那些宗教来说,尽管执行宗教仪式在事实上并没有给执行者或参与仪式的人们带来他们期望或希望的那种结果,但是它却有一些其他的影响,至少其中的一些影响具有社会价值。

那么,这一假设应该如何论证呢?用抽象的方法来理解一般意义的宗教是没有用处的,这种方法也不能用之于理解社会;而且把它单纯用之于某一具体宗教也是不适当的,尤其不能用于我们生长在其中、并对之存有偏见的宗教。唯一的方法就是采用社

means that we must study in the light of our hypothesis a sufficient number of diverse particular religions or religious cults in their relation to the particular societies in which they are found. This is a task not for one person but for a number.

Anthropologists and others have discussed at length the question of the proper definition of religion. I do not intend to deal with that controversial subject on this occasion. But there are some points that must be considered. I shall assume that any religion or any religious cult normally involves certain ideas or beliefs on the one hand, and on the other certain observances. These observances, positive and negative, i. e. actions and abstentions, I shall speak of as rites.

In European countries, and more particularly since the Reformation, religion has come to be considered as primarily a matter of belief. This is itself a phenomenon which needs to be explained, I think, in terms of social development. We are concerned here only with its effects on the thinking of anthropologists. Among many of them there is a tendency to treat belief as primary: rites are considered as the results of beliefs. They therefore concentrate their attention on trying to explain the beliefs by hypotheses as to how they may have been formed and adopted.

To my mind this is the product of false psychology. For example, it is sometimes held that funeral and mourning rites are the result of a belief in a soul surviving death. If we must talk in terms of cause and effect, I would rather hold the view that the belief in a surviving soul is not the cause but the effect of the rites. Actually the cause – effect analysis is misleading. What really happens is that the rites and the justifying or rationalising beliefs develop together as parts of a coherent whole. But in this development it is action or the need of action that controls or determines belief rather than the other way about. The actions themselves are symbolic expressions of sentiments.

会人类学的实验方法,即根据我们的假设,系统地综合研究各种不同的宗教及宗教崇拜和它们各自赖以存在的社会。这个工作并非一人能力所及,它需要许多人的共同努力。

人类学家和其他一些学者曾详细地讨论过如何给宗教下一个合适的定义,我在此并不想加入到这个争论之中。但是,我需要对几点问题加以说明。我认为,通常来说,在任何宗教或宗教崇拜中不仅包含一些观念和信仰,同时也有一些惯例的成分在其中。不论是正面的还是负面的惯例,即无论是行为还是禁忌,我都称之为仪式。

在欧洲国家,尤其是基督教改革运动之后,宗教主要被作为一个信仰问题来看待。对这个现象,我认为应该依据社会发展来解释,但是我们却只是从宗教如何影响人类学家的思想这个角度考虑这个问题。在一些人类学家看来,宗教信仰是基本的、首要的,而宗教仪式是宗教信仰的产物。因此,他们集中精力试图通过假设来解释有关宗教信仰是如何形成及怎样被人们采纳的。

依我的观点,这是一种伪心理学的产物。例如,人们通常认为正是因为人们信奉了灵魂永存,才导致了特定的葬礼和哀悼仪式的产生。但是如果我们非要在这两者之间讨论出个因果来的话,我倒宁愿认为,它们之间的关系恰恰相反,灵魂永存的信仰不是产生那些仪式的原因,而是它们的结果。其实,因果关系分析法经常会误导人。实际上,仪式和这些合理的信仰都是作为连贯整体的一部分同时发展起来的。在这一发展过程中,起控制和决定作用的正是这种行为或行为的需要,而不是别的东西。行为本身就是一种对情感的象征性表达。

My suggestion is that in attempting to understand a religion it is on the rites rather than on the beliefs that we should first concentrate our attention. Much the same view is taken by Loisy, who justifies his selection of sacrificial rites as the subject of his analysis of religion by saying that rites are in all religions the most stable and lasting element, and consequently that in which we can best discover the spirit of ancient cults. ①

That great pioneer of the science of religion, Robertson Smith, took this view. He wrote as follows:

In connection with every religion, whether ancient or modern, we find on the one hand certain beliefs, and on the other certain institutions, ritual practices and rules of conduct. Our modem habit is to look at religion from the side of belief rather than that of practice; for, down to comparatively recent times, almost the only forms of religion seriously studied in Europe have been those of the various Christian Churches, and all parts of Christendom are agreed that ritual is important only in connection with its interpretation. Thus the study of religion has meant mainly the study of Christian beliefs, and instruction in religion has habitually begun with the creed, religious duties being presented to the learner as flowing from the dogmatic truths he is taught to accept. All this seems to us so much a matter of course that, when we approach some strange or antique religion, we naturally assume that here also our first business is to search for a creed, and find in it the key to ritual and practice. But the antique religions had for the most part no creed; they consisted entirely of institutions and practices. No

---

① 'Les rites étant dans toutes les religions l'élément le plus consistant et le plus durable, celui, par conséquent, où se découvre le mieux l'esprit des cultes anciens.'—*Essai historique sur le Sacrifice*, Paris, 1920, p. 1.

我认为,要想理解宗教,首先要研究各种仪式,而不是各种信仰。卢瓦西对此的看法和我基本相同。在他看来,在所有的宗教中,最具有稳定性和持久性的因素是仪式。从对仪式的研究中,我们可以得到关于古代崇拜的最本质的内容。① 正是由于这一原因,他才把祭祀仪式作为其宗教分析的主题。

承认这一观点的还有罗伯逊·史密斯,他是宗教科学领域的伟大开拓者,他写到:

我们发现,无论是在古代还是现代,任何一个宗教不仅与一定的信仰相联系,而且还与一定的习俗、仪式活动和行为准则发生关系。在以上这两个方面,信仰方面似乎是我们现代宗教研究习惯于关注的,而其习俗方面则经常被忽视。这种现象的原因大概是因为到现代为止,在欧洲被深入研究过的所有宗教形式几乎都是各种基督教。在所有的基督教徒看来,仪式的意义是与宗教的阐释联系在一起的。因此,对基督教信仰的研究就构成了欧洲宗教研究的主要内容;从各种信条和宗教义务中不仅派生出了宗教教义,而且这些信条和义务也正是通过教义向入教者灌输的,教诲他们把它接受为教条真理。当我们对某种奇特或古老的宗教进行研究时,我们似乎会因为以上原因而理所当然地认为,我们研究的首要任务就是认真研究教义并从中发现重要的仪式和习惯。但是,惯例和习俗构成了大部分古代宗教基本内容,这些宗教并无明确的教义。事实上,人们一般是不会受没有被赋予意

---

① “在所有宗教中仪式最稳定并保持得最持久,因而,通过仪式可以更透彻地揭示古代崇拜的精髓。”——《献祭史论》,巴黎,1920 年,第 1 页。

doubt men will not habitually follow certain practices without attaching a meaning to them; but as a rule we find that while the practice was rigorously fixed, the meaning attached to it was extremely vague, and the same rite was explained by different people in different ways, without any question of orthodoxy or heterodoxy arising in consequence. In ancient Greece, for example, certain things were done at a temple, and people were agreed that it would be impious not to do them. But if you asked why they were done you would probably have had several mutually contradictory explanations from different persons, and no one would have thought it a matter of the least religious importance which of these you chose to adopt. Indeed, the explanations offered would not have been of a kind to stir any strong feeling; for in most cases they would have been merely different stories as to the circumstances under which the rite first came to be established, by the command or by the direct example of the god. The rite, in short, was connected not with dogma but with a myth. ①

... It is of the first importance to realise clearly from the outset that ritual and practical usage were, strictly speaking, the sum – total of ancient religions. Religion in primitive times was not a system of belief with practical applications; it was a body of fixed traditional practices to which every member of society conformed as a matter of course. Men would not be men if they agreed to do certain things without having a reason for their action; but in ancient religion the reason was not first formulated as a doctrine and then expressed in practice, but conversely, practice preceded doctrinal theory. Men form general rules of conduct before they begin to express general principles in words; political institutions are older than political theories, and in like manner religious institutions are older than religious theories. This analogy is not arbitrarily chosen, for in fact the parallelism in ancient society between religious and political institutions is complete. In each sphere great importance was attached to form and

---

① W. Robertson Smith, *Lectures on the Religion of the Semites*, 1907, pp. 16-17.

义的习惯制约的。但即使是有严格的行为模式的习惯，也经常会被发现其意义仍是含糊不清的。同时，同一仪式对于不同的人来说又会得出不同的解释，但不会导致所谓的正教与异教的后果。例如，在古希腊，一个寺庙里可能会举行多种教事。人们普遍认为，如不这样做的话就会冒犯神灵。但对于这种做法的原因，不同的人会给我们许多相互矛盾的回答，并且没有一个人会认为这种做法具有我们所解释的那些宗教意义。事实上，在他们的解释中未包含使人产生强烈情绪感情的内容，因为，这些解释在绝大多数情况下，只不过是一些涉及仪式初创的不同说法，这些说法认为，是依照神的或神的化身的旨意创立这些仪式的。总之，与仪式相关的并不是教义，而是神话。①

……严格地说，整个古代宗教的全部内容就是在仪式上和实践上的用途，从一开始就认识到这一点是很重要的。在原始社会中，不能认为宗教是可以直接应用到实际中去的信仰体系，它是一个约定俗成的传统习俗实体。全部的社会成员都会自觉遵守这一实体。如果人类的行为没有任何动因，那么也就不能称之为人类了。但在古代宗教中，并不是开始就把这种动因看成为一种教义，然后再通过行为将它表现出来的。与此相反，是行为在教义理论之先。人们自己行为准则的形成是先于用语言和文字表达的一般性原理的，如政治制度就总是早于政治理论；同样，宗教制度也先于宗教理论出现。进行这种类推不是没有根据的，因为，宗教制度在古代社会中与政治制度是完全相同的。形式和习惯

① 威廉·罗伯逊·史密斯 1907 年的《关于闪族宗教的讲演录》第 16 ~17 页。

precedent, but the explanation why the precedent was followed consisted merely of a legend as to its first establishm'ent. That the precedent, once established, was authoritative did not appear to require any proof. The rules of society were based on precedent, and the continued existence of the society was sufficient reason why a precedent once set should continue to be followed.①

The relative stability of rites and the variability of doctrines can be illustrated from the Christian religions. The two essential rites of all Christian religions are baptism and the eucharist, and we know that the latter solemn sacrament is interpreted differently in the Orthodox Church, the Roman Church and the Anglican Church. The modern emphasis on the exact formulation of beliefs connected with the rites rather than on the rites themselves is demonstrated in the way in which Christians have fought with and killed one another over differences of doctrine.

Thirty-seven years ago (1908), in a fellowship thesis on the Andaman Islanders (which did not appear in print till 1922), I formulated briefly a general theory of the social function of rites and ceremonies. It is the same theory that underlies the remarks I shall offer on this occasion. Stated in the simplest possible terms the theory is that an orderly social life amongst human beings depends upon the presence in the minds of the members of a society of certain sentiments, which control the behaviour of the individual in his relation to others. Rites can be seen to be the regulated symbolic expressions of certain sentiments. Rites can therefore be shown to have a specific social function when, and to the extent that, they have for their effect to regulate, maintain and transmit from one generation to another sentiments on which the constitution of the society depends. I ventured to suggest as a general formula that religion is everywhere an expression in one form or another of a sense of dependence on a power outside ourselves, a power which we may speak of as a spiritual or moral power.

① op. cit., p. 20.

在任何地区都会被认为包含有某些重要的意义，但对于为什么这种习惯能够继承下来，要想解释清楚就只能借助于有关它如何形成的传说了。习惯的权威性是与它的建立联系在一起的，这几乎是毫无疑问的。社会秩序构建于习惯的基础之上，社会能够延续发展的事实就充分证明了为什么习惯一旦建立，就可延续下去。①

在基督教中可以很明显地看到宗教仪式的相对稳定性和教义的相对易变性这两种倾向。在基督教中洗礼和圣餐是两个最基本的仪式，可我们知道圣餐在东正教、天主教和新教中，却有着不尽相同的含义。在现代，人们更多强调的是如何准确阐述那些与仪式有关的信仰，而不注重对仪式本身的深入研究。基督教徒由于教义的不同而相互迫害就可以充分地说明这一点。

37 年前(1908 年)，我的一篇有关安达曼群岛人的论文(此篇文章直到 1922 年才出版)曾获得了奖学金，在这篇论文中，简单阐明了有关仪式和典礼的一般性理论。这一理论也是我今天要演讲的主要内容。这个理论用最简单的话说就是：社会成员头脑中的某些情感不仅是人们有序的社会生活的决定因素，而且它还控制着个体与他人之间的行为。对这些情感的有规则的象征性表现就产生了仪式。因此，仪式特定的社会功能就表现在它对这些社会情感的作用方式上，仪式对这些社会构成所依赖的社会情感在某种程度上起着调节、维持和代代传承的作用。因此，我冒昧地提出一个普遍公式，即无论宗教在哪里，它只是人们对自身以外力量的一种依赖感的不同体现，我们称这种力量为精神或道德力量。

① 同上书，第 20 页。

This theory is by no means new. It is to be found in the writings of the philosophers of ancient China. It is most explicit in the teachings of Hsün Tzŭ who lived in the third century B. C., and in the *Book of Rites* (the Li Chi), which was compiled some time later. The Chinese writers do not write about religion. I am doubtful if there is in Chinese any word which will convey just what we understand by the word religion. They write about li, and the word is variously translated as ceremonial, customary morality, rites, rules of good manners, propriety. But the character by which this word is written consists of two parts, of which one refers to spirits, sacrifice and prayer, and the other originally meant a vessel used in performing sacrifices. We may therefore appropriately translate li as 'ritual'. In any case what the ancient philosophers are chiefly concerned with are the rites of mourning and sacrificial rites.

There is no doubt that in China, as elsewhere, it was thought that many or all of the religious rites were efficacious in the sense of averting evils and bringing blessings. It was believed that the seasons would not follow one another in due order unless the Emperor, the Son of Heaven, performed the established rites at the appropriate times. Even under the Republic a reluctant magistrate of a *hsien* may be compelled by public opinion to take the leading part in a ceremony to bring rain. But there developed among the scholars an attitude which might perhaps be called rationalistic and agnostic. For the most part the question of the efficacy of rites was not considered. What was thought important was the social function of the rites, i. e. their effects in producing and maintaining an orderly human society.

In a text that is earlier than Confucius we read that 'sacrifice is that through which one can show one's filial piety and give peace to the people, pacify the country and make the people settled. ... It is through the sacrifices that the unity of the people is strengthened' (*Ch'u Y*, *II*, 2).

You know that one of the major points of the teaching of Confucius was the importance of the proper performance of rites. But it is said of Confucius that he would not discuss the super-

这一理论的内容并无太多的新意。我们在古代中国的哲学家们的著作中就可以发现这个理论。生活在公元前三世纪的荀子对这一理论就有清晰的阐述,这一点可以在他的学说中以及稍后一些时代编纂的《礼记》一书中发现。中国的学者从没写过宗教的问题。我很怀疑中国文字中有没有一个词与我们所理解的宗教一词的含义是一样的。他们只写有关"礼"的问题,并且"礼"一词可以翻译为典礼、习俗道德、仪式、礼貌规则和礼节等等。但是,"礼"这个词的汉字写法由两部分构成,它的含义从构词法看来一部分是指精神、祭祀和祈祷,另一部分原意是指举行祭祀用的器皿。因此,我们可以把这个字恰当地翻译成"礼仪"。不管怎样,哀悼仪式及祭祀仪式是那些古代哲学家们最为关注的对象。

无疑,与在其他地方一样,在中国,人们认为许多或所有的宗教仪式都是很灵验的,具有辟邪和给人们带来好运的功能。在古代,人们认为,除非皇帝也就是天子在适当的时候执行某种传统的仪式,否则四季将不会按照应有顺序变换。即使是在民国时期,县长也必须顺应公众舆论而带头执行求雨仪式。但是,在一些学者中发展出了一种唯理主义或不可知论的观点。这种观点产生的大部分原因是由于他们没有考虑仪式的应验问题,他们认为重要的是仪式的社会功能,即对产生和维护有序的人类社会的影响。

在孔子之前,曾有一篇文章这样写道:"通过祭祀,人们可以表示出他们的孝心,给他人带来平安,国泰民安……通过祭祀使人民加强团结。"(《楚语》第二卷,第二页)

孔子的主要思想之一是正确实施礼仪。但据说他并不讨论

natural.① In the Confucian philosophy, music and ritual are considered as means for the establishment and preservation of social order, and regarded as superior to laws and punishments as means to this end. We take a very different view of music, but I may remind you that Plato held somewhat similar ideas, and I suggest that an anthropological study of the relations between music (and dancing) and religious rituals would provide some interesting results. In the *Book of Rites* one section (the *Yüeh Chi*) is concerned with music. The third paragraph reads:

The ancient kings were watchful in regard to the things by which the mind was affected. And so they instituted ceremonies to direct men's aims aright; music to give harmony to their voices; laws to unify their conduct; and punishments to guard against their tendencies to evil. The end to which ceremonies, music, punishments and laws conduct is one; they are the instruments by which the minds of the people are assimilated, and good order in government is made to appear. ②

The view of religion that we are here concerned with might be summed up in the following sentence from the *Book of Rites*, 'Ceremonies are the bond that holds the multitudes together, and if the bond be removed, those multitudes fall into confusion.'

The later Confucian philosophers, beginning with Hsün Tzü, paid attention to the ways in which rites, particularly the mourning and sacrificial rites, performed their function of maintaining social order. The chief point of their theory is that the rites serve to 'regulate' and 'refine' human feelings. Hsün Tzü says:

Sacrificial rites are the expressions of man's affectionate longings. They represent the height of altruism, faithfulness, love and reverence. They represent the completion of propriety and refinement. ③

Of the mourning rites Hsün Tzü says:

---

① *Analects*, VII, 20. Waley translates this passage as: 'The Master never talked of prodigies, feats of strength, disorders or spirits.'

② Legge's translation. An alternative translation of the last sentence would be: 'Rites, music, punishments, laws have one and the same end, to unite hearts and establish order.'

③ The translations from Hsün Tzü are those of Fung Yu Lan and are quoted from his *History of Chinese Philosophy*, Peiping, 1937.

超自然的东西。[1] 在孔子的哲学思想中,建立和维护社会秩序应当通过音乐和仪式,而法律和惩罚则是低一等的手段。我们对音乐抱有的观点不同于孔子,但是,我要提醒你们,柏拉图却有与他相似的观点。我认为,从人类学角度研究音乐(和舞蹈)与宗教仪式的关系会为我们提供一些有趣的结果。在《礼记》一书中,其中一部分讲的是与音乐有关的内容,第三段是这样写的:

古代的国王十分关注那些陶冶人们心灵的事物。因而创建了仪式以使人们朝向正确目标;用音乐使人们声音和谐;以法律统一他们的行为;依惩罚震慑他们的恶行。仪式、音乐、惩罚和法律都是为一个共同目的服务的,不外乎就是使人们同心协力,从而达到良好政治秩序。[2]

我在这里所关注的有关宗教的观点可以用《礼记》中的话作为概括:“礼仪是将民众联结起来的纽带,如果这个纽带丧失了,民众就会陷于混乱。”

孔子之后,以荀子为首的一些儒家学者们,开始重视仪式,尤其是哀悼和祭祀仪式在维护社会秩序方面所起的作用。他们的主要观点是,仪式可以用来“调节”和“净化”人们的感情。荀子说:

祭祀,就是人们用于表达情性的仪式。它代表着无私、忠诚、爱戴和尊敬的极致,以及臻于完美的礼节和优雅。[3]

关于哀悼仪式,荀子说:

---

① 在《论语》第7卷第20页,韦利将这段话译为:“圣人从不谈及天才、神力的伟绩、混乱或神灵。”

② 理雅各译本。对最后一句的另一个译本为“仪式、音乐、惩罚、法律都有一个同样的目的,即统一心灵从而建立秩序”。

③ 有关荀子的译文转引自冯友兰的《中国哲学史》北平,1937年。

The rites (li) consist in being careful about the treatment of life and death. Life is the beginning of man, Death is the end of man. When the end and beginning are both good, the way of humanity is complete. Hence the Superior Man respects the beginning and venerates the end. To make the end and beginning uniform is the practice of the Superior man, and is that in which lies the beauty of *li* and standards of justice (*i*). For to pay over-attention to the living and belittle the dead would be to respect them when they have knowledge and disrespect them when they have not ……

The way of death is this: once dead, a person cannot return again. [It is in realising this that] the minister most completely fulfils the honour due to his ruler, and the son the honour of his parents.

Funeral rites are for the living to give beautified ceremonial to the dead; to send off the dead as if they were living; to render the same service to the dead as to the living; to the absent as to the present; and to make the end be the same as the beginning……

Articles used in life are prepared so as to be put into the grave, as if [the deceased] were only moving house. Only a few things are taken, not all of them. They are to give the appearance, but are not for practical use……Hence the things [such as were used] in life are adorned, but not completed, and the 'spiritual utensils' are for appearance but not use……①

Hence the funeral rites are for no other purpose than to make clear the meaning of death and life ,to send off the ead with sorrow and reverence ,and when the end comes,to prepare for storing the body away……Service to the living is beautifying their beginnign;sending

① Fung Yu Lan translates by the term 'spiritual utensils' the Chinese *ming ch'i*, which Legge in the following passage from the *Book of Rites* translates as 'vessels to the eye of fancy': 'Confucius said, "In dealing with the dead, if we treat them as if they were entirely dead, that would show a want of affection, and should not be done; or, if we treat them as if they were entirely alive, that would show a want of wisdom, and should not be done. On this account the vessels of bamboo [used in connection with the burial of the dead] are not fit for actual use; those of earthenware cannot be used to wash in; those of wood are incapable of being carved; the lutes are strung, but not evenly; the pandean pipes are complete, but not in tune; the bells and musical stones are there, but they have no stands. They are called vessels to the eye of fancy; that is [the dead] are thus treated as if they were spiritual intelligencies." ' Legge, *The Sacred Books of China*, Part III, The Lî Kî, I-X, Oxford, 1885, p. 148.

对待生死的慎重态度构成了仪式(礼)。人始于生,而终于死。能够善始善终,就可以是人生的圆满。所以君子敬始而慎终。保持始终如一,这是君子的实践,是礼之美和正义的标准(义)的所在。重生而轻死,就是对可知的事情给予重视,而轻视那些不可知的事情……

死亡遵循人死不能复生的规律(正是由于认识到这一点),大臣们会对其君主给予极高的尊崇,儿子也会极力敬重他的父母。

葬礼是生者为死者举行的美化仪式;犹如送别生者一样来送别死者;犹如侍奉生者一样来侍奉死者;犹如对待未亡者一样来对待已亡者;使开端与终结相一致…

把一些生活用具与死者一起埋葬,这就像(死者)搬家一样。这些随葬的生活用具并不是包括所有的,而仅仅是其中的一部分。而且这些随葬品也只是仅具形貌,并不是为了能被真正的使用……因此,生时的器物并不是全部被放弃,精神器物注重的仅是形貌,而不是实用……①

因此举行葬礼不过是为了申明生死的意义,怀着哀伤和敬重的感情送别死者,安放好死者的遗体……为生者服务是为了美化

---

① 冯友兰把汉语中的“明器”翻译为“精神器物”,理雅各在下面引自《礼记》的章节中将之译为“想象性器物”:孔子说:在对待死者时,如果完全把死者当成死者,这就是缺乏仁爱的表现,不可为之;如果完全把死者当成生者,这是缺乏智慧的表现,不可为之。因此,竹制的器物[丧葬所用]并不适于实际使用;陶制的器物并不能用来洗涮,木制的器物不能经受雕刻;琵琶张了弦器,但不均匀;竽笙是完整的,但不能成调;有钟磬但无架位摆放。这些器物被称作想象的器物;这也就是说,[死者]被当成了神灵——理雅各:《中国的圣书》第三编(《礼记》1~10卷)第148页,牛津,1885年版。

off the dead is beautifying their end. When the end and the beginning are both attended to, the service of the filial son is ended and the way of the Sage is completed. Slighting the dead and over-emphasising the living is the way of Mo (Tzǔ). ① Slighting the living and over-attention to the dead is the way of superstition. Killing the living to send off the dead is murder. ② The method and manner of li and standards of justice (*i*) is to send off the dead as if they were alive, so that in death and life, the *end* and the beginning, there is nothing that is not appropriate and good. The Confucian does this.

The view taken by this school of ancient philosophers was that religious rites have important social functions which are independent of any beliefs that may be held as to the efficacy of the rites. The rites gave regulated expression to certain human feelings and sentiments and so kept these sentiments alive and active. In turn it was these sentiments which, by their control of or influence on the conduct of individuals, made possible the existence and continuance of an orderly social life.

It is this theory that I propose for your consideration. Applied, not to a single society such as ancient China, but to all human societies, it points to the correlation and co-variation of different characteristics or elements of social systems. Societies differ from one another in their structure and constitution and therefore in the customary rules of behaviour of persons one to another. The system of sentiments on which the social constitution depends must therefore vary in correspondence with the difference of constitution. In so far as religion has the kind of social function that the theory suggests, religion must also vary in correspondence with the manner in which the society is constituted. In a social system constituted on the basis of nations which make war on one another, or stand ready to do so, a well-developed sentiment of patriotism in its members is essential to maintain a strong nation. In such circumstances patriotism or national feeling may be given support

---

① Mo Tzǔ was a philosopher who criticised the mourning rites as being wasteful.

② Referring to the ancient practice of human sacrifice at the burial of important persons.

他们的开端,送别死者则是为了美化他们的终结。侍奉了开端和终结,孝道的义务即告完成,圣人之道亦告完备。墨(子)倡导轻死而重生;[1]迷信则教人轻生而重死。用杀生者来殉葬死者,这是谋杀。[2] 把死者当做生者来送别,使生与死、始与终都和谐美好,这是礼和正义伦理(义)的方式和方法,也是儒家所为。

这一古代哲学流派持有的观点是:宗教仪式具有独立于信念之外重要的社会功能,这一功能可以叫做是仪式的功效。仪式规范了人们的情感和情绪的表达方式,从而使人们的情感得以存在并保持活跃。而且,正是因为人们的行为在这些情感的控制和影响之下,才使得一个有序的社会生活得以存在和持续。

我现在引领你们考察的正是这个理论。这个理论并不是只能被应用于如古代中国那样的某个单个的社会,而且可以把它应用于全人类社会。它还指出了存在于许多社会体系中不同特点和不同因素之间的相互联系和互相变化。由于不同社会之间结构和构成成分的差异,因而,不同社会的人们之间的习惯性行为规则也有所不同。所以,社会构成所依赖的情感体系也会相应地有所区别。由于宗教具有该理论所提出的社会功能,所以宗教必定也因其社会构成方式的不同而有所差异。如果一个社会体系的基础是建立在一个彼此正在打仗或准备打仗的民族国家之上的,那么在这个社会体系中保持国家强大的主要因素应该是在其成员中的那种高度的爱国主义情绪。在这种情况下,宗教也许会为那种爱国主义情绪提供支持。例如,当以色列的人民在约书亚

① 墨子是一个哲学家,他批评丧礼太浪费。

② 指古代在重要人物举行葬礼时用活人为他陪葬。

by religion. Thus the Children of Israel, when they invaded the land of Canaan under the leadership of Joshua, were inspired by the religion that had been taught to them by Moses and was centred upon the Holy Tabernacle and its rites.

War or the envisaged possibility of war is an essential element in the constitution of great numbers of human societies, though the warlike spirit varies very much from one to another. It is thus in accordance with our theory that one of the social functions of religion is in connection with war. It can give men faith and confidence and devotion when they go out to do battle, whether they are the aggressors or are resisting aggression. In the recent conflict the German people seem to have prayed to God for victory not less fervently than the people of the allied nations.

It will be evident that to test our theory we must examine many societies to see if there is a demonstrable correspondence of the religion or religions of any one of them and the manner in which that society is constituted. If such a correspondence can be made out, we must then try to discover and as far as possible define the major sentiments that find their expression in the religion and at the same time contribute to the maintenance of stability in the society as constituted.

An important contribution to our study is to be found in a book that is undeservedly neglected by anthropologists, *La Citéantique*, by the historian Fustel de Coulanges. It is true that it was written some time ago (1864) and that in some matters it may need correction in the light of later historical research, but it remains a valuable contribution to the theory of the social function of religion.

The purpose of the book is to show the point-by-point correspondence between religion and the constitution of society in ancient Greece and Rome, and how in the course of history the two changed together. It is true that the author, in conformity with the ideas of the nineteenth century, conceived this correlation between two sets of social features in terms of cause and effect, those of one

的带领下进入伽南时，鼓舞他们的就是由摩西传授的宗教精神，并因此团结在圣犹太教及其仪式的周围。

许多的人类社会，尽管他们对于战争的好恶程度各不相同，都会面临与其他社会组织之间的战争和爆发战争的可能性，这种情况可以说是社会的基本构成要素。所以依照我们的理论，宗教的社会功能也会有和战争相关的一方面。不管是侵略战争还是抵抗侵略的战争，当人们准备去战斗时，宗教信仰会使人保持忠诚、对己方充满自信并随时准备牺牲自己。在近代的战争中，德国人更强烈地希望上帝能保佑他们取得胜利，在这点上他们似乎比同盟国的人民虔诚一些。

显然，我们必须要对许多社会进行考察，以检验我们的理论，看看我们的理论是否能正确地反映社会的宗教及这些社会的构成方式。如果存在我们理论与现实的一致性，那我们就必须努力研究，来尽可能揭示那些由宗教展现的主要情感，并且确定它们对维持社会稳定所做的贡献。

法国历史学家菲斯泰尔·德·库朗热所写《古代城邦》一书为我们的研究做出了极大贡献，人类学家都不应该忽视此书。尽管这本书已经出版了很长一段时间了，而且它在某些方面还需要参照后来的历史研究进行一些修订，但是，它对于宗教的社会功能理论研究来说仍旧是非常有价值的一部著作。

在这本书中作者要说明的是在古希腊和古罗马，社会构成与宗教之间的密切联系，以及它们是如何在历史进程中共同发展变化的。与十九世纪人类学家们的观点相同，此书的作者把这两种社

set being thougt of as the cause producing those of the other set. The men of the ancient world, so the argument runs, came to hold certain beliefs about the souls of the dead. As the result of their beliefs they made offerings at their tombs.

Since the dead had need of food and drink it appeared to be a duty of the living to satisfy this need. The care of supplying the dead with sustenance was not left to the caprice or to the variable sentiments of of men; it was obligatory. Thus a complete religion of the dead was established, whose dogmas might soon be effaced, but whose rites endured until the triumph of Christianity. ①

It was a result of this religion that ancient society came to be constituted on the basis of the family, the agnatic lineage and the gens, with its laws of succession, property, authority and marriage.

A comparison of beliefs and laws shows that a primitive religion constituted the Greek and Roman family, established marriage and paternal authority, fixed the order of relationship, and consecrated the right of property and the right of inheritance. This same religion, after having enlarged and extended the family, formed a still larger association, the city, and reigned in that as it had reigned in the family. From it came all the institutions, as well as all the private law, of the ancients. It was from this that the city received all its principles, its rules, its usages and its magistracies. But, in the course of time, this ancient religion became modified or effaced, and private law and political institutions were modified with it. Then came a series of revolutions, and social changes regularly followed the development of knowledge. ②

---

① The Ancient City (trans. Willard Small), p. 23.

② op cit., p. 12.

会特征之间的关系也看成是一种因果关系,其中一种社会特征是引起另一种社会特征的原因。如果按照此理论推理,就是:正是因为古代人对已经死去的人的灵魂持有的某种信念,才驱使他们到墓前奉献祭品。

由于认为死者也需要食物与饮料,那么活着的人就有义务去满足死者。活着的人认为给死者提供生计需求品,是他们必须坚持的、不能动摇的情感,也是一种义务。这样,一个关于死者的宗教就建立了。这种宗教的教义的存在也许没有多长时间,但其仪式却持续到了基督教的繁荣时期。①

也正是由于宗教的原因,才使得以家庭、父系团体和氏族为基础建立起了古代的社会,并同时产生了继承法、财产、权力和婚姻等法律。

对比信仰与法律,我们可以发现,原始宗教建立了古希腊和古罗马的家庭,明确了婚姻制及父系权力,构建了亲属之间的关系,并建立起了财产权和继承权制度。同样,还是这一宗教,在家庭基础上进行扩大和发展以后,使更大的城邦统一体得以建立。城邦和家庭的相同之处在于,它们的统治形式是一样的。在这一基础上,相继建立了古代人的整套制度以及私法。在此基础上,城邦有了原则、规则、习惯及其行政长官。不过,古代宗教在整个的发展过程中是逐步得到修正或削弱的,与此同时,私法和政治机构也得到了修正。随后,一系列的革命相继发生,而且随着知识的发展社会也发生了有规律的变化。②

---

① 《古代城邦》,威拉德·斯莫尔译,第23页。

② 《古代城邦》,威拉德·斯莫尔译,第12页。

In his final paragraph the author writes:

We have written the history of a belief. It was established and human society was constituted. It was modified, and society underwent a series of revolutions. It disappeared and society changed its character. ①

This idea of the primacy of belief and of a causal relation in which the religion is the cause and the other institutions are the effect is in accordance with a mode of thought that was common in the nineteenth century. We can, as I indeed do, completely reject this theory and yet retain as a valuable and permanent contribution to our subject a great deal of what Fustel de Coulanges wrote. We can say that he has produced evidence that in ancient Greece and Rome the religion on the one side and the many important institutions on the other are closely united as interdependent parts of a coherent and unified system. The religion was an essential part of the constitution of the society. The form of the religion and the form of the social structure correspond one with the other. We cannot, as Fustel de Coulanges says, understand the social, juridical and political institutions of the ancient societies unless we take the religion into account. But it is equally true that we cannot understand the religion except by an examination of its relation to the institutions.

A most important part of the religion of ancient Greece and Rome was the worship of ancestors. We may regard this as one instance of a certain type of religion. A religious cult of the same general kind has existed in China from ancient times to the present day. Cults of the same kind exist to-day and can be studied in many parts of Africa and Asia. It is therefore possible to make a wide comparative study of this type of religion. In my own experience it is in ancestor-worship that we can most easily discover and demonstrate the social function of a

① Op cit ,p. 529.

在最后一段，作者这样写到：

我们已论述了信仰的历史。人类社会在信仰建立的基础上，也逐步发展形成；而且随着对信仰的不断修正，社会也相应发生了一系列的变革；并且社会的特点也会随着信仰的消失，发生某些变化。①

以信仰为首要地位，以宗教为起因，以其他体制为结果的因果关系的思维模式，在十九世纪是非常普遍的。我们可以，正如我确实已经做的那样，完全抛弃这一理论，而把菲斯泰尔·德·库朗热的观点作为对我们的研究主题的一个有价值且永久的贡献保留下来。我们可以说，菲斯泰尔·德·库朗热已经证明了，在古希腊和古罗马，宗教和其他许多重要的体系，作为一个相互联系的统一的整体中相互依赖的部分而紧密结合在一起。在构成社会的诸多要素中，宗教是其中一个重要的组成部分，宗教的形式和社会结构的形式彼此相互对应。宗教与社会构成各要素之间相辅相成，在它们之间正如菲斯泰尔·德·库朗热所说的，除非我们把宗教这一社会构成要素考虑进去，否则我们不可能理解古代社会的社会、司法和政治制度；同样，如果不考察宗教与其他社会制度之间的关系，我们也不可能真正懂得宗教。

祖先崇拜是构成古希腊和古罗马宗教的一个最重要的组成部分，它是宗教的一种类型。从中国的古代到现代，都可以发现与之相似的宗教崇拜的例子的存在。而且在非洲和亚洲的许多地区，这种宗教崇拜也延续至今。所以，用比较研究的方法对这种宗教形式进行研究在理论上是可行的。根据我的经验，祖先崇

① 同上书，第529页。

religious cult.

The term 'ancestor-worship' is sometimes used in a wide, loose sense to refer to any sort of rites referring to dead persons. I propose to use it in a more limited and more precisely defined sense. The cult group in this religion consists solely of persons related to one another by descent in one line from the same ancestor or ancestors. In most instances descent is patrilineal, through males. But in some societies, such as the Bakongo in Africa and the Nayar in India, descent is matrilineal, and the cult group consists of descendants of a single ancestress. The rites in which the members of the group, and only they, participate have reference to their own ancestors, and normally they include the making of offerings or sacrifices to them.

A particular lineage consists of three or more generations. A lineage of four or five generations will normally be included as a part in one of six or seven generations. In a well-developed system related lineages are united into a larger body, such as the Roman gens, or what may be called the clan in China. In parts of China we can find a large body of persons, numbering in some instances as much as a thousand, all having the same name and tracing their descent in the male line from a single ancestor, the founder of the clan. The clan itself is divided into lineages.

A lineage, if it is of more than three or four generations, includes both living persons and dead persons. What is called ancestor-worship consists of rites carried out by members of a larger or smaller lineage (i. e. one consisting of more or fewer generations) with reference to the deceased members of the lineage. Such rites include the making of offerings, usually of food and drink, and such offerings are sometimes interpreted as the sharing of a meal by the dead and the living.

拜本身以及它对宗教崇拜的社会功能的显示，表现得最为明显，也最容易被我们所揭示。

“祖先崇拜”这个术语经常被用来泛指任何一种有关死去的人的仪式。我认为应该把这一术语加以限制并进行准确地定义。因为进行这种宗教仪式的群体的成员都具有同一祖先，或者他们都是同一血缘中几个直系亲属的后代。在大多数情况下，这种世系是父系的，不过也有的世系是母系的，例如在一些像非洲的巴孔戈、印度的纳亚尔这样的社会中，并且在这些母系社会里，参加祭祀的群体成员都是单一女祖先的后代。仪式一般包括对祖先的供奉或祭祀，只有这个群体的成员才能参与这些仪式，并且只能对自己的祖先举行这些仪式。

一般来说，典型的世系群是由三代或更多代人构成的。如果一个世系群由四代或五代人构成，那么它一般包括在一个由六代或七代人构成的世系群之中。随着社会体系的高度发展，会出现一些更大的由相互关联的世系群联合形成的组织，例如古罗马的氏族或我们所说的中国的家族。在中国的一些地区，我们可以发现由上千人构成的大家族，他们同属一个姓氏，并且依靠同祖的男性血缘延续。在家族中所有和家族同姓的人都源于一个共同的祖先，他是这个家族的缔造者。随着家族的不断繁衍，它本身又会被分成几个世系群。

如果一个世系群由三到四代或更多代的人组成，那么实际上就把活着的人和死去的人都包括进去了。所谓的祖先崇拜是指由大的或小的世系群的成员，即代数较多的世系群或代数较少的世系群的成员，为世系群中已死去的人举行的仪式。这类仪式包括供奉，供品通常包括食物和酒，通常认为这种供奉能让死去的

In such a society, what gives stability to the social structure is the solidarity and continuity of the lineage, and of the wider group (the clan) composed of related lineages. For the individual, his primary duties are those to his lineage. These include duties to the members now living, but also to those who have died and to those who are not yet born. In the carrying out of these duties he is controlled and inspired by the complex system of sentiments of which we may say that the object on which they are centred is the lineage itself, past, present and future. It is primarily this system of sentiments that is expressed in the rites of the cult of the ancestors. The social function of the rites is obvious: by giving solemn and collective expression to them the rites reaffirm, renew and strengthen those sentiments on which the social solidarity depends. We have no means of studying how an ancestor-worshipping society comes into existence, but we can study the decay of this type of system in the past and in the present. Fustel de Coulanges deals with this in ancient Greece and Rome. It can be observed at the present time in various parts of the world. The scanty information I have been able to gather suggests that the lineage and joint-family organisation of some parts of India is losing something of its former strength and solidarity and that what we should expect as the inevitable accompaniment of this, a weakening of the cult of ancestors, is also taking place. I can speak with more assurance about some African societies, particularly those of South Africa. The effect of the impact of European culture, including the teaching of the Christian missionaries, is to weaken in some individuals the sentiments that attach them to their lineage. The disintegration of the social structure and the decay of the ancestral cult proceed together.

Thus for one particular type of religion I am ready to affirm that the general theory of the social function of religions can be fully demonstrated.

A most important contribution to our subject is a work of Emile Durkheim published in 1912. The title is *Les Formes élémentaires*

人和活着的人共同分享膳食。

在这类社会中,社会结构稳定的基础就是建立在世系群和那个更大组织(氏族)的团结和延续上。对于个人而言,他的主要责任就是对他所属的世系群的责任。这些责任的对象既包括世系群中活着的成员,也包括已死的成员和未出生的成员。在履行这些责任的同时,一直会有一个复杂的情感体系控制他、鼓舞他。在祖先崇拜仪式中,这些情感得到了具体的体现,进入这些情感视野的是世系群的过去、现在和未来。因此,仪式的社会功能就能明显地看出来:情感通过仪式得到了庄重和统一的表达,从而再次肯定、更新和加强了社会稳定所依赖的那些情感。

我们没有办法研究拥有祖先崇拜仪式的社会是如何产生的,但是,我们可以对其在过去和现在的衰落进行研究,就像菲斯泰尔·德·库朗热对古罗马和古希腊做的那样。目前,在世界各地都可以观察到这种现象。从我收集到的不多的资料可以看出,印度一些地区的世系群和联合家庭组织正在逐渐丧失其原有的活力和稳定性。同时,我们预计的伴随这一现象不可避免产生的那种对祖先崇拜的削弱也得到了证实。我可以很肯定地说,非洲一些社会,尤其是南非的那些社会也存在这种情况。由于欧洲文化的冲击,包括基督教徒传教的影响,使人们依附于其世系群的那种情感会逐渐被削弱。而且,我们可以看到,社会结构的瓦解和祖先崇拜的衰落是同时进行的。

因此,我会很肯定地说,有关宗教社会功能的一般性理论在特定的宗教类型的层面上,可以得到充分的证明。

埃米尔·杜尔干在1912年发表的著作对于我们所研究的课题具有重大的贡献,书名是《宗教生活的基本形式》,

de la Vie religieuse, but the sub-title reads: *La Systè me totèmique en Australie*, It is worth while mentioning that Durkheim was a pupil of Fustel de Coulanges at the Ecole Normale Supèrieure and that he himself said that the most important influence on the development of his ideas about religion was that of Robertson Smith.

Durkheim's aim was to establish a general theory of the nature of religion. Instead of a wide comparative study of many religions, he preferred to take a simple type of society and carry out an intensive and detailed analysis, and for this purpose he selected the aboriginal tribes of Australia. He held the view that these tribes represent the simplest type of society surviving to our own times, but the value of his analysis is in no way affected if we refuse to accept this view, as I do myself.

The value of Durkheim's book is as an exposition of a general theory of religion which had been developed with the collaboration of Henri Hubert and Marcel Mauss, starting from the foundations provided by Robertson Smith. Durkheim's exposition of this theory has often been very much misunderstood. A clear, though very brief, statement of it is to be found in the Introduction written by Henri Hubert in 1904 for the French translation of the *Manuel d'Histoire des Religions* of Chantepie de la Saussaye. But it is not possible on this occasion to discuss this general theory. I wish only to deal with one part of Durkheim's work, namely his theory that religious ritual is an expression of the unity of society and that its function is to 're-create' the society or the social order by reaffirming and strengthening the sentiments on which the social solidarity and therefore the social order itself depend.① This theory he tests by an examination of the totemic

① op cit., pp. 323, 497 and elsewhere.

副标题为《澳大利亚图腾体系》。需要提及的是，埃米尔·杜尔干在巴黎高等师范学校曾是菲斯泰尔·德·库朗热的学生，但是，他本人说，罗伯逊·史密斯对他的宗教思想发展影响最大。

杜尔干希望他的研究能够建立一个关于宗教本质的普遍理论。他的研究方法是，不对各种宗教进行广泛的对比性研究，而是倾向于挑选一个简单类型的社会，并对之进行深入细致的分析。所以，他把澳大利亚土著部落作为他的研究对象。他认为，澳大利亚土著部落可以代表在我们时代的那些依然存在的最简单的社会类型。虽然我们有些人不能接受他的观点，我就是这样，但是他的分析的价值却不会受到一点点的影响。

杜尔干那本有关宗教的一般性理论著作是由罗伯逊·史密斯的思想发展而来，又由亨利·胡贝尔和马塞儿·莫斯的补充而进一步延伸。不过，杜尔干关于这一理论的阐述也经常被别人误解。亨利·胡贝尔就曾在1904年为钱特皮·德·拉·索塞耶的《宗教史手册》的法文译本作序时，对此有过简短明确的描述。但是，我不能在这里对这个理论详尽讨论，而只想对下面将要述及的，只是杜尔干理论一小部分的内容进行研究。在我将要讨论的部分里，他的理论观点是：宗教仪式是社会团结的表现，它的功能表现在，通过对情感的强调来“重塑”社会或社会秩序，而这些情感是一个社会中团结和秩序的依靠。[①] 他的这一理论也

① 该书第323~497页及其他地方。

ritual of the Australians. For while Frazer regarded the totemic rites of the Australian tribes as being a matter of magic, Durkheim treats them as religious because the rites themselves are sacred and have reference to sacred beings, sacred places and sacred objects.

In 1912 very much less was known about the Australian aborigines than is known at present. Some of the sources used by Durkheim have proved to be unreliable. The one tribe that was well known, through the writings of Spencer and Gillen and Strehlow—the Aranda—is in some respects atypical. The information that Durkheim could use was therefore decidedly imperfect. Moreover, it cannot be said that his handling of this material was all that it might have been. Consequently there are many points in his exposition which I find unacceptable. Nevertheless, I think that Durkheim's major thesis as to the social function of the totemic rites is valid and only requires revision and correction in the light of the more extensive and more exact knowledge we now have. ① The beings to which the Australian cult refers are commonly spoken of as 'totemic ancestors', and I have myself used the term. But it is somewhat misleading, since they are mythical beings and not ancestors in the same sense as the dead persons commemorated in ancestor-worship. In the cosmology of the Australian natives the cosmos, the ordered universe, including both the order of nature and the social order, came into existence at a time in the past which I propose to speak of as the World-Dawn, for this name corresponds to certain ideas that I have found amongst the aborigines of some tribes. This order (of nature and of society) resulted from the doings and adventures of certain sacred beings. These beings, whom I shall call the

---

① For a criticism of some points in Durkheim's work, see 'The Sociological Theory of Totemism' in this volume.

根据他对澳大利亚图腾仪式的研究而得到验证。尽管弗雷泽认为澳大利亚图腾仪式只是一种巫术，但是，杜尔干还是把它们看做是具有宗教性质的。因为他认为，仪式本身就是神圣的，并且与神灵、圣地和圣物有关。

和现在相比，我们在 1912 年时对澳大利亚土著人的了解还远远不够。现在已经证实，杜尔干所使用的一些资料来源是不可靠的。我们通过斯宾塞、吉伦和斯特洛对阿兰达部落的描述，已经掌握了很多关于它的情况，而且知道，在某些方面来说这一部落的例子并不典型。因此，杜尔干为我们提供的信息很可能是不准确的。另外，他所收集的材料也并不完整。从而，我发现他的理论的某些方面是不能被我接受的。然而我还是认为，关于图腾仪式的社会功能，杜尔干的大部分观点还是有效的，只是需要在我们现在掌握的更为广泛准确的知识的基础上，对其做些修正。①

澳大利亚人通常用“图腾祖先”来指称他们崇拜的人，我也曾使用过该术语。但这种说法有点令人误解，因为他们用它来代表所崇拜的神话人物，与我们在祖先崇拜中纪念已故的人并非属于同种意义。根据澳大利亚土著人的宇宙观，他们认为宇宙和有序的世界，既包括自然界的秩序也包括社会秩序，都是在过去某个时期内同时产生的。我称那一时期为“世界的初始”，因为这一叫法与我发现的一些土著人的观点相一致。这种秩序（自然的和社会的秩序）是某些神圣人物的行为和冒险的结果。这些神圣人

① 有关杜尔干著作中应加批评的观点，请见本书第六章“图腾的社会学理论”。

Dawn Beings, are the totemic ancestors of ethnological literature. The explanations of topographical features, of natural species and their characteristics, and of social laws, customs and usages are given in the form of myths about the happenings of the World-Dawn.

The cosmos is ruled by law. But whereas we think of the laws of nature as statements of what invariably does happen (except, of course, in miracles), and of moral or social laws as what ought to be observed but are sometimes broken, the Australian does not make this distinction. For him men and women ought to observe the rules of behaviour that were fixed for all time by the events of the World-Dawn, and similarly the rain ought to fall in its proper season, plants should grow and produce fruit or seed, and animals should bear young. But there are irregularities in human society and in nature.

In what I shall venture to call the totemic religion of the Australian aborigines, there are two main types of ritual. One of these consists of rites carried out at certain spots which are commonly referred to as 'totem centres'. A totem centre is a spot that is specially connected with some species of object, most commonly with a particular species of animal or plant, or with an aspect of nature such as rain or hot weather. Each centre is associated with one (or occasionally more than one) of the Dawn Beings. Frequently the Being is said to have gone into the ground at this spot. For each totem centre there is a myth connecting it with the events of the World-Dawn. The totem centre, the myth connected with it and the rites that are performed there, belong to the local group that owns the territory within which the totem centre lies. Each totem centre is thought of as containing, in a rock or a tree or a pool of water or a heap of stones, what we may perhaps call the life-spirit or life-force of the totem species.

The rites performed at the totem centre by the members of the local group to which it belongs, or under their leadership and direction, are thought to renew the vitality of this life-spirit of the species. In

物，我称他们为“初始物”，就是民族学文献中所指的图腾祖先。对于地貌特征、自然物种及其特点、社会法则、习俗和风俗等等这些现象，我们把它们与初始事件有关的神话联系起来加以解释。

宇宙是由法规支配的。尽管我们对自然法规和道德以及社会法规的定义加以区别，把前者看做是对必然发生事情的陈述（当然，除了奇迹之外），而把后者看做是对我们有时可能会违反、但应当遵守的规则的陈述。但是，澳大利亚人并不对其进行区分。对澳大利亚人来说，任何事物都应遵守一定的规则。在他们看来，无论男女都应该时刻遵守世界初始事件规定的行为准则；同样地，天应该在适当的季节下雨，植物应当生长、结果实，动物应当繁殖后代。但是，总有一些不规则的事情在人类社会和大自然中存在。

在所谓的澳大利亚土著人的图腾宗教中有两种主要的仪式类型。其中一种是由一些仪式构成，这些仪式通常在那些被认为是“图腾中心”的地点举行。“图腾中心”是一个地点，这个地点与某个物种有特殊的联系，大多数情况是与某种动植物，或是与大自然的某一部分，如雨水或炎热的天气相联系。每一个图腾中心都和通常认为是存在于这个中心地下的一个（偶尔也多于一个）“初始物”相对应，而且还对应于一个关于初始事件的神话。哪个地方群体拥有了这块领土，也就相应拥有了这里的图腾中心、与此中心相关的神话以及在这里举行的仪式。每一个图腾中心都被认为包含某个图腾物种的神灵或生命力，它们也许存在于石头里、树里、池塘里或石群里。

地方群体的成员认为，通过在属于自己的，或在自己统辖下的图腾中心举行仪式，会使这个物种的神灵恢复活力。例如在澳

eastern Australia the totem centre is spoken of as the 'home' or 'dwelling-place' of the species, and the rites are called 'stirring up'. Thus, the rite at a rain totem centre brings the rain in its due season, that at a kangaroo totem centre ensures the supply of kangaroos, and that at the baby totem centre provides for the birth of children in the tribe.

These rites imply a certain conception, which I think we can call specifically a religious conception, of the place of man in the universe. Man is dependent upon what we call nature: on the regular successions of the seasons, on the rain falling when it should, on the growth of plants and the continuance of animal life. But, as I have already said, while for us the order of. nature is one thing and the social order another, for the Australian they are two parts of a single order. Well-being, for the individual or for the society, depends on the continuance of this order free from serious disturbance. The Australians believe that they can ensure this continuance, or at least contribute to it, by their actions, including the regular performance of the totemic rites.

In the rites that have been described, each group takes care (if we may so express it) of only a small part of nature, of those few species for which it owns totem centres. The preservation of the natural order as a whole therefore depends on the actions of many different groups.

The social structure of the Australian natives is based on two things: a system of local groups, and a system of kinship based on the family. Each small local group is a closed patrilineal descent group; that is, a man is born into the group of his father and his sons belong to his group. Each group is independent and autonomous. The stability and continuity of the social structure depends on the strong solidarity of the local group.

Where there existed the totemic cult which I have just described

大利亚东部，人们称图腾中心为物种的“家”或“居住之地”，而将这些仪式称为对它们的“激活”。因此，不同的图腾中心会具有不同的功能：如果在雨水图腾中心举行仪式，就会在预期的时间下雨；如果在袋鼠图腾中心举行仪式，就会保证袋鼠的繁殖；如果在婴儿图腾中心举行仪式，就会给本部落带来更多的婴儿。

这些仪式中隐含着某种人在宇宙中所处地位的概念，我们可以具体称之为宗教概念。人类依赖于大自然：依赖于四季的规律交替，依赖于它的风调雨顺，依赖于动植物的生生不息。但是，正如我所说的，对于我们来说，自然界的秩序和社会秩序是互不相同的事物。然而，对于澳大利亚人来说，它们是同一秩序的两个组成部分。对于每个人及社会来说，这种秩序的稳定、持续以及没有外来的严重干扰是他们幸福的决定因素。澳大利亚人相信，他们的行为，包括举行日常的图腾仪式，是这种秩序持续的保证，至少也会对这种持续做出贡献。

在我们所描述的那些仪式中，每一个群体只关注自然界的一小部分（如果可以对其如此表达的话），即其图腾中心对应的为数不多的物种。因此，对于整个自然界的秩序，维持它们就要取决于许多不同群体的行为。

澳大利亚土著人的社会结构是以两种体系为基础的：地方群体体系和以家庭为基础的亲属体系。每一个小的地方群体都是按父系方式组成的封闭家族群体，也就是说，每个男子出生后就属于其父亲的群体，而此男子的儿子又属于他的群体。并且每个群体都是独立和自治的。地方团体的坚固的团结性是他们所属的社会结构的稳定性和延续性的决定因素。

如果某个群体存在我刚刚所描述的图腾崇拜，那么就可称此

(and it existed over a very large part of Australia), each local group was a cult group. The totemic ritual served to express the unity and solidarity of the group and its individuality and separation from other groups by the special relation of the group to its *sacra*: the totem centre or centres, the Dawn Beings associated with them, the myths and songs referring to those Beings, and the totems or species connected with the centres. This aspect of the social function of totemism was emphasised, and I think somewhat over-emphasised, by Durkheim.

There is, however, another aspect, for while the local totemic groups are separate individual and continuing social entities, they are also part of a wider social structure. This wider structure is provided by the kinship system. For an individual in Australian native society, every person with whom he has any social contact is related to him by some bond of kinship, near or distant, and the regulation of social life consists essentially of rules concerning behaviour towards different kinds of kin. For example, a man stands in very close relation to his mother's local group and, in many tribes, in a very close relation to its *sacra*: its totems, totem centres and totemic rites.

While Australian totemism separates the local groups and gives each an individuality of its own, it also links the groups together. For while each group is specially connected with certain parts of the natural order (e. g. with rain, or with kangaroo) and with certain of the Beings of the World-Dawn, the society as a whole is related through the totemic religion to the whole order of nature and to the World-Dawn as a whole. This is best seen in another kind of totemic cult, part of which consists of sacred dramas in which the performers impersonate various Dawn Beings. Such dramatic dances are only performed at those religious meetings at which a number of local groups come together, and it is on these occasions that young men are initiated

群体为一个图腾崇拜群体。图腾仪式的内涵十分丰富,它可以用来表达群体的统一性、团结性和它的个性;它还可以通过展示群体与其神圣物之间的特殊关系,即群体与一个图腾中心或几个图腾中心、与初始物、与和初始物有关的神话或歌曲、与图腾中心有关联的图腾或物种之间的特殊关系,从而使各个群体相互区别。杜尔干已经对图腾这方面的社会功能给予强调,但我认为,他对此有些过于强调了。

尽管地方图腾群体作为个体是独立的和持续存在的,但是,它们也作为一个组成部分属于更大的由亲属体系构成的社会结构。因此,图腾崇拜的社会功能还存在着另一个方面。在澳大利亚土著社会中,对于每一个人来说,和任何一个与他有社会关系的人之间肯定都是通过某种亲属关系联系到一起的,他们的亲属关系或近或远,而对不同亲属类别的行为规则就构成了主要的社会生活规则。例如,一位男子与其母方的地方群体有着很亲密的关系,那么在很多部落中,他也会与这个群体的神圣物(即部落的图腾)、图腾中心和图腾仪式,产生很密切的关系。

尽管澳大利亚图腾崇拜把不同的地方群体加以区分,并且赋予每个群体以独立的个性,但它同时也将这些群体联系到一起。因为每一个群体都与自然秩序的某一部分(即与雨水或袋鼠)以及与某些初始物之间存在特别的联系,所以各个群体组成的社会作为一个整体就通过图腾宗教与整个自然秩序和整个初始世界联系起来。在另一种图腾崇拜中可以明显看出这种关系的存在。这种图腾崇拜是由神戏构成,人们扮演着各种各样神戏中的初始物。只有在许多地方群体聚集到一起,参加宗教集会时才举行这类神戏,同时,也只有在这种场合下,年轻小伙才可以正

into manhood and into the religious life of the society.

Australian society is not merely a collection of separate local groups; it is also a body of persons linked together in the kinship system. Australian totemism is a cosmological system by which the phenomena of nature are incorporated in the kinship organisation. When I was beginning my work in Australia in 1910, a native said to me, '*Bungurdi* (kangaroo) [is] my *kadja* (elder brother).' This simple sentence of three words gives the clue to an understanding of Australian totemism. The speaker did not mean that individuals of the kangaroo species are his brothers. He meant that to the kangaroo species, conceived as an entity, he stood in a social relation analogous to that in which a man stands to his elder brother in the kinship system. I am sorry that there is not time on this occasion to expound this thesis more fully.

The account I have just given of Australian totemism differs considerably from that given by Durkheim. But far from contradicting, it confirms Durkheim's fundamental general theory as to the social function of the totemic religion of Australia and its rites. The two kinds of totemic cult are the demonstration, in symbolic action, of the structure of Australian society and its foundations in a mythical and sacred past. In maintaining the social cohesion and equilibrium, the religion plays a most important part. The religion is an intrinsic part of the constitution of society. I have dwelt, if only cursorily, with two types of religion: ancestor-worship and Australian totemism. In both of them it is possible to demonstrate the close correspondence of the form of religion and the form of the social structure. In both it is possible to see how the religious rites reaffirm and strengthen the sentiments on which the social order depends. Here then are results of some significance for our problem. They point to a certain line of investigation. We can and should examine other religions in the light of the results already reached. But to do this we must study religions

式步入成年，并且进入社会的宗教生活。

澳大利亚社会不但是分离的地方群体的集合，而且是人们根据亲属制度联合到一起的一个团体。在澳大利亚图腾崇拜这种宇宙观体系中，自然现象与亲属组织得以相互结合。当我于1910年在澳大利亚开始我的考察工作时，一位土著人告诉我说："*Bungurdi*（袋鼠）[是]我的 *Kadia*（兄长）。"这个只有两三个字构成的句子为我理解澳大利亚的图腾崇拜提供了线索。这位土著人并不是真的说袋鼠这个物种是他的兄弟，而是把袋鼠这个物种看做是一个实体，并认为他与袋鼠的关系类似于在亲属关系体系中他与他哥哥的关系。由于时间关系，我不能在此对这一话题进行详细论述，我感到十分抱歉。

我刚才对澳大利亚图腾崇拜的描述与杜尔干的理论大相径庭。但这两种观点并不是相互对立的，它与杜尔干的有关澳大利亚图腾宗教及其仪式的社会功能的一般性理论是相一致。通过象征性的行为，澳大利亚社会的结构及其早期的神话和神圣的基础，在这两种图腾崇拜中得到展示。宗教在维系社会的团结、持续和平衡方面起着重要的作用，它是社会构成中固有的一个组成部分。

我已经粗略谈论过两种形式的宗教，即祖先崇拜和澳大利亚图腾崇拜。我们能够发现它们之间密切的宗教形式和社会结构形式的关系。从这两种宗教形式中可以看出宗教仪式是如何肯定并强化了社会情感的，这种情感决定了社会秩序。这里存在我们研究该问题的意义所在，它们指出了我们研究的确切方向，在受到我们研究成果的启发之下，我们应该能够研究其他宗教。要做到这一点，我们必须研究处于"运动"中的宗教。当人们积极参与

in action; we must try to discover the effects of active participation in a particular cult, first the direct effects on the individual and then the further effects on the society of which these individuals are members. When we have a sufficient number of such studies, it will be possible to establish a general theory of the nature of religions and their rôle in social development.

In elaborating such a general theory it will be necessary to determine by means of comparative studies the relations between religion and morality. There is only time to refer very briefly here to the question of religion and morality. As representing a theory that seems to be widely held, I quote the following passages from Tylor:

One great element of religion, that moral element which among the higher nations forms its most vital part, is indeed little represented in the religion of the lower races. ①

The comparison of savage and civilised religions brings into view by the side of a deep-lying resemblance in their philosophy, a deep-lying contrast in their practical action on human life. So far as savage religion can stand as representing natural religion, the popular idea that the moral government of the universe is an essential tenet of natural religion simply falls to the ground. Savage animism is almost devoid of that ethical element which to the educated modern mind is the very mainspring of practical religion. Not, as I have said, that morality is absent from the life of the lower races. Without a code of morals, the very existence of the rudest tribe would be impossible; and indeed the moral standards of even savage races are to no small extent well-defined and praiseworthy. But these ethical laws stand on their own ground of tradition and public opinion, comparatively independent of the animistic beliefs and rites which exist beside them. The lower animism is not immoral, it is

---

① Tylor, *Primitive Culture*, 3rd ed., 1891, Vol. I, p. 427.

具体的宗教仪式时,我们一定要首先发现这种参与对个人的影响,然后再进一步发现对这些个人所在社会的影响。当我们进行了足够的研究之后,就可以建立一个宗教本质及它们在社会发展中所起角色的概括性理论。

要详细阐述这个概括性理论,对比研究宗教和道德间的关系是很必要的。由于时间有限,我们只能简要地提一下宗教和道德的关系。我以下引用泰勒著作中的一些篇章来介绍一个似乎被广泛接受的理论:

道德成分作为宗教的一个重要成分,已经在那些先进民族中成为关键的组成部分,但几乎还没有在低级种族的宗教中显示出来。①

如果比较野蛮的宗教和文明的宗教的话,我们会得出如下的结论:在哲学思想上两者存在深刻的相似性,但它们在对人类生活实际的作用方面又存在着明显的区别。如果我们认为野蛮宗教是自然宗教的代表,那么,那种流行的观点,即认为宇宙受制于道德是自然宗教的最基本特点,就站不住脚。伦理成分几乎不存在于野蛮人的万物有灵论中,而受过教育的现代人,却把它当做宗教实践的主要动因。但是,正如我曾提到的,低级种族也并不是不存在道德。如果道德准则不存在的话,即使连最粗野的部落想生存下去都将是不可能的。实际上,就算是在野蛮种族中,它们也在相当程度上明确规定了要遵守的道德标准,并且这些道德标准也是值得赞赏的。但是,这些伦理法则建立于自己的传统和公众舆论基础之上,如果加以比较的话,它和万物有灵论以及

① 泰勒:《原始文化》第三版,1891 年,第 1 卷第 427 页。

unmoral……The general problem of the relation of morality to religion is difficult, intricate, and requiring immense array of evidence. 1[①] I agree with Tylor that the problem of the relation of morality to religion is difficult and intricate. But I wish to question the validity of the distinction he makes between the religions of savage sand those of civilised peoples, and of his statement that the moral element 'is little represented in the religion of the lower races'. I suspect that when this view is held it often means only that in the 'lower races' the religion is not associated with the kind of morality which exists in contemporary Western societies. But societies differ in their systems of morals as in other aspects of the social system, and what we have to examine in any given society is the relation of the religion or religions of that society to their particular system of morality.

Dr. R. F. Fortune, in his book on Manus religion, has challenged the dictum of Tylor. [②] The religion of Manus is what may be called a kind of spiritualism, but it is not ancestor-worship in the sense in which I have used the term in this lecture. The Manus code of morals rigidly forbids sexual intercourse except between husband and wife, condemns dishonesty and insists on the conscientious fulfilment of obligations, including economic obligations, towards one's relatives and others. Offences against the moral code bring down on the offender, or on his household, punishment from the spirits, and the remedy is to be found in confession and reparation for wrong.

Let us now reconsider the case of ancestor-worship. In the societies which practise it, the most important part of the moral code is that which concerns the conduct of the individual in relation to his lineage and clan and the individual members thereof. In the more usual form of ancestor-worship, infractions of this code fall under religious or

---

① op cit., Vol. II, p. 360.

② R. F. Fortune, *Manus Religion*, Philadelphia, 1935, pp. 5 and 356. Dr. Fortune's book is a useful contribution to the study of the social function of religion and deals with a religion of a very unusual type.

与此相关的仪式没有什么关系。不能说低级的万物有灵论是不道德的,实际上它与道德无关……道德与宗教的关系非常难以解释,十分复杂,论证它需要有丰富的论据。①

泰勒认为道德和宗教之间关系的问题是困难而棘手的,在这一点上我是同意他的观点的。但他把宗教区分为野蛮宗教和文明宗教,并认为"在低等种族中只存在少量的道德因素",在这一点上我是持怀疑态度的。我对此表示质疑,并认为这种观点仅仅是指,在"低等"种族中宗教是与当代西方社会的道德没有联系的。但是正如社会系统的其他方面,社会在各自道德体系上也是不同的。在任何一个特定社会中我们都必须得研究其中的一个或多个宗教与它们独特道德体系的关系。

福琼博士在他的一本关于马努人宗教的书中,对泰勒的观点提出了质疑。② 马努人的宗教可以称作是一种唯灵论,但不是我在演讲中所指的祖先崇拜意义上的。马努人的道德准则严格禁止夫妇之外的性关系、谴责不忠行为、坚持尽责地履行职责,包括对亲属和其他人履行经济职责。触犯道德准则会降罪于触犯者或其家人,惩罚是来自于精神上的,只能通过忏悔和补救错误来获得拯救。

现在让我们看看祖先崇拜这个例子。在祖先崇拜的社会,道德准则最重要的部分是关于个人行为与世系群的关系,与氏族间的关系及与其氏族中的其他人之间的关系。在更加普遍的祖先崇

---

① 同上书,第2卷,第360页。

② 福琼,《马努斯宗教》,费城,1935年,第5页、第356页。该书对宗教社会功能的研究做出了有益的贡献,并研究了罕见的宗教类型。

supernatural sanctions, for they are offences against the ancestors, who are believed to send punishment.

Again we may take as an example of the lower races the aborigines of Australia. Since the fundamental social structure is a complex system of widely extended recognition of relations of kinship, the most important part of the moral code consists of the rules of behaviour towards kin of different categories. One of the most immoral actions of which a man can be guilty is having sexual relations with any woman who does not belong to that category of his kinsfolk into which he may legally marry.

The moral law of the tribe is taught to young men in the very sacred ceremonies known as initiation ceremonies. I will deal only with the Bora ceremonies, as they are called, of some of the tribes of New South Wales.

These ceremonies were instituted in the time of the World-Dawn by Baiame, who killed his own son Daramulun (sometimes identified with the sacred bull-roarer) and on the third day brought him back to life. As the ceremony is conducted, the initiates all 'die' and are brought back to life on the third day. ①

On the sacred ceremonial ground where these initiations take place there is usually an image of Baiame made of earth, and sometimes one of Baiame's wife. Beside these images sacred rites are shown to the initiates, and sacred myths about Baiame are recounted.

Now Baiame instituted not only the initiation ceremonies, which are, amongst other things, schools of morals for young men, but also the kinship system with its rules about marriage and behaviour towards different categories of kin. To the question, 'Why do you observe

---

① The suggestion has been made that we have here the influence of Christianity, but that opinion can be dismissed. The idea of ritual death and rebirth is very widespread in religion, and the three-day period is exemplified every month in every part of the world by the death and resurrection of the moon.

拜的情况下，如果触犯了道德准则，人们就认为他们会受到宗教或超自然力的惩戒，因为他们冒犯了祖先神灵，他们相信是这些祖先降下了惩罚。

让我们再次把澳大利亚土著的低等种族作为例子。因为该社会基本的社会结构是复杂的，它是一种对于亲属关系的广泛延伸的认同，在这样的社会中，最重要的道德准则包括对与其不同亲属的行为规则。令一个人感到有罪的最不道德的行为就是与不属于他的合法通婚的亲属范围内的人发生性关系。

这种部落的道德准则在神圣的仪式中，如我们所知道的成人礼仪式上被传授给年轻人。在此我将列举布拉典礼，也就是他们所说的在新南威尔士的一些部落举行的这种仪式。据说这些仪式是在世界初始日由巴亚马创立的。巴亚马杀了自己的儿子达拉姆伦（有时他被认为是神圣的吼牛者），并于第三日把他救活。在进行此仪式时参加者都会“死去”，第三天获得重生。①

在神圣的举行成人仪式的场地上，总会有一座由泥做成的巴亚马塑像，有时也会放置巴亚马其中一个妻子的塑像。在神圣的塑像边，参加者观看了神圣的仪式，并听到神圣的巴亚马神话。

巴亚马不但设立了成年礼，为向年轻人传授道德观念提供一种手段是成年礼最重要的一个功能；而且还规定了亲属关系制度，在这个制度中包含了婚姻法规和对不同亲属范畴的亲戚的行

---

① 有人认为这里可能存在基督教的影响，但这一说法可不予理会。仪式性死亡与生还的理念在宗教中很普遍，但三天生还期的确定，是根据世界各地月亮的消失与复出计算的。

these complex rules about marriage?' the usual answer is, 'Because Baiame established them'. Thus Baiame is the divine law-giver, or, by an alternative mode of expression, he is the personification of the tribal laws of morality.

I agree with Andrew Lang and Father Schmidt that Baiame thus closely resembles one aspect of the God of the Hebrews. But Baiame gives no assistance in war as Jehovah did for the children of Israel, nor is Baiame the ruler or controller of nature, of storms and seasons. That position is held by another deity, the Rainbow-Serpent, whose image in earth also appears on the sacred ceremonial ground. The position held by Baiame is that of the Divine Being who established the most important rules of morality and the sacred ceremonies of initiation.

These few examples will perhaps suffice to show that the idea that it is only the higher religions that are specially concerned with morality, and that the moral element is little represented in the religions of the lower races, is decidedly open to question. If there were time I could provide instances from other parts of the world.

What makes these problems complex is the fact that law, morality and religion are three ways of controlling human conduct which in different types of society supplement one another, and are combined, in different ways. For the law there are legal sanctions, for morality there are the sanctions of public opinion and of conscience, for religion there are religious sanctions. A single wrongful deed may fall under two or three sanctions. Blasphemy and sacrilege are sins and so subject to religious sanctions; but they may also sometimes be punished by law as crimes. In our own society murder is immoral; it is also a crime punishable by death; and it is also a sin against God, so that the murderer, after his sudden exit from this life at the hands of

为规则。如果你要问:“为什么你们要遵守这些复杂的婚姻法规?”你通常得到的答案是:“因为这是巴亚马建立的。”因而,巴亚马就被看成了是神圣的制法者,或者换句话说,他就代表了部落的道德法规。

我同意安德雷·兰和施密特神父的观点,他俩认为,巴亚马与希伯来人的上帝在某些方面很相似。但是,二者又有不同:巴亚马并没有像耶和华帮助犹太人的后代那样,在战争方面给予帮助;他也没有成为自然界如暴风雨、季节的供给者或控制者。那些职位是由另一个神——雨中之蛇,占据着,并且在神圣典礼场所也有此神的雕像。巴亚马的地位与神的地位很相似,是他们建立了最重要的道德法规和神圣的成年礼法规。

我们质疑过下面这个观点,它认为只有较高级的宗教才会与道德存在某种特殊的联系,而在低级的民族的宗教里,几乎没有体现任何的道德因素。这些例子也许有助于说明,我们的质疑是有根据的。如果时间允许,我会再从世界其他地区挑选一些例子来说明此观点。

控制人类行为的因素主要包括法律、道德和宗教三个方面,它们在不同社会中以不同方式相互补充、相互结合。正是这些因素,才使得这些问题变得更为复杂。因为在法律方面存在法律制裁,在道德方面有公共舆论和良心的约束力,在宗教方面有宗教处罚。而且它们又互为补充、互相联系在一起,一种简单的错误行为就有可能受到两种或三种惩罚。亵渎和渎圣行为是一种罪孽,因此要受到宗教制裁,但有时也会作为一种罪行而受到法律制裁。在我们的社会中,谋杀是不道德的,会作为一种犯罪而被处以死刑,但它也是触犯上帝的罪孽。因此,谋杀犯在被处以死

the executioner, must face an eternity of torment in the fires of Hell.

Legal sanctions may be brought into action in instances where there is no question of morality or immorality, and the same is true of religious sanctions. It is held by some of the Fathers or doctors of the Christian churches that an upright and virtuous life devoted to good works will not save a man from Hell unless he has attained grace by accepting as true the specific doctrines taught by a church.

There are different kinds of religious sanctions. The penalty for sin may be conceived simply as alienation from God. Or there may be a belief in rewards and punishments in an after-life. But the most widespread form of the religious sanction is the belief that certain actions produce in an individual or in a community a condition of ritual pollution, or uncleanness, from which it is necessary to be purified. Pollution may result from things done unintentionally and unwittingly, as you may see from the fifth chapter of the Book of Leviticus. One who unwittingly has touched any unclean thing, such as the carcase of an unclean beast, is guilty and has sinned and must bear his iniquity. He must make a sacrifice, a trespass offering, by which he may be cleansed from his sin.

Ritual uncleanness does not in itself involve moral condemnation. We read in the twelfth chapter of the same Book of Leviticus that the Lord instructed Moses that a woman who has borne a male child shall be unclean for seven days and her purification must continue for a further three and thirty days, during which she shall touch no hallowed thing, nor come into the sanctuary. If the child she bears is female, the first period of uncleanness is to be two weeks and the period of purification threescore-and-six days. Thus, it is polluting, but no one can suppose that it is immoral, to bear a child, and more polluting if the child is female than if it is male.

The opposite of pollution or sinfulness is holiness. But holiness comes not from leading an honest and upright life, but from religious exercises, prayer and fasting, the performance of penance, meditation and the reading of sacred books. In Hinduism the son of a Brahmin is born holy; the son of a leather-worker is born unclean.

刑后,必须在地狱的火中永受折磨。

在与道德问题无关的一些例子中,人们也许会采用法律制裁。同理,宗教制裁也是一样。基督教的一些神父和长老认为,只有当一个人把教堂里传授的信条看做真理时,他才可以获得美德。否则,即使他为人正直并且投身于有德行的工作,也不会把他从地狱中拯救出来。

存在着不同种类的宗教制裁,使远离上帝就是一种简单的对罪孽的惩罚;或者是一种有关来生报应或惩罚的信仰。但是,分布最广的宗教制裁,是使某人或整个群体处于一种仪式污染或不洁的状态,只有通过一种赎罪的方式才可以驱除这种状态。当然这种仪式污染可能是由于不经意或不小心的行为引起的,有关这方面的例子可以在《利未记》第十五章中找到。如果一个人接触了不洁之物,如龌龊的动物的死尸,他就会变得有罪,而且他必须通过赎罪祭的方式来净化自己。

仪式不洁本身并不涉及道德上的谴责。《利未记》第十二章是这样讲的:上帝指示摩西说,生育了男孩的女人,有 7 天是不洁的,需要进行 3 到 30 天的净化。在此期间,她不可以接触任何圣物,也不许靠近圣所。如果她生的是女孩,就会使不洁期延长为 2 周,相应的净化期也变为 66 天。因而,生育孩子被看做是不洁的行为,而且生育女孩比生育男孩更为不洁。但是,没有人认为这是不道德的行为。

与不洁和有罪相对的是圣洁。圣洁的源头是一些宗教活动,它并不来自诚实、正直的生活,而是来自祈祷与斋戒、忏悔、沉思、阅读圣典等。在印度教中,婆罗门的子孙生来就是圣洁的,而皮匠的子孙则天生就是不洁的。

The field covered by morality and that covered by religion are different; but either in primitive or in civilised societies there may be a region in which they overlap.

To return to our main topic, a writer who has dealt with the social function of religions on the basis of a comparative study is Loisy, who devotes to the subject a few pages of the concluding chapter of his valuable *Essai historique sur le Sacrifice*. ① Although he differs from Durkheim in some matters, his fundamental theory is, if not identical, at any rate very similar to that of the earlier writer. Speaking of what he calls the sacred action (*l' action sacrée*), of which the most characteristic form is the rite of sacrifice, he writes:

We have seen its rlôe in human societies, of which it has maintained and strengthened the social bonds, if indeed it has not contributed in a large measure to creating them. It was, in certain respects, the expression of them; but man is so made that he becomes more firmly fixed in his sentiments by expressing them. The sacred action was the expression of social life, of social aspirations, it has necessarily been a factor of society……

Before we condemn out of hand the mirage of religion and the apparatus of sacrifice as a simple waste of social resources and forces, it is proper to observe that, religion having been the form of social conscience, and sacrifice the expression of this conscience, the loss was compensated by a gain, and that, so far as purely material losses are concerned, there is really no occasion to dwell on them. Moreover the kind of sacred contribution that was required, without real utility as to the effect that was expected from it, was an intrinsic part of the system of renunciations, of contributions which, in every human society, are the condition of its equilibrium

① 1920, pp. 531-40.

道德与宗教所覆盖的领域有所不同,但是不论在原始社会还是在文明社会,二者覆盖的领域都会出现重叠的部分。

现在回到我们的主题上来。有一位学者曾在比较研究的基础上对宗教的社会功能这一主题进行了详尽的分析,这位学者就是卢瓦西。他有一本很有价值的书名为《献祭史论》,在这本书的结论这一章中,他用了几页的篇幅来论述这一主题。[①] 尽管他与杜尔干在某些问题的观点上不同,但是他的基本观点与早期的学者如果不是完全一样,也是很相似的。他认为献祭是他所称的“神圣行为”(*l' action sacrée*),的最典型的形式,在谈到这一点时他说道:

我们已经注意到了在人类社会中它所起的作用,即使不能说它成功地创造出社会规范,但是,至少可以认为它维护和加强了这些规范。在一定的程度上,神圣行为可以作为社会规范的具体表现。但人总是用情感的表达来实现情感的固化。神圣行为不仅是社会生活的具体表现,而且还是社会命脉的具体体现,可以肯定地说它是社会的一个要素。

在把虚幻的宗教及献祭行为看做是一种社会资源和力量的浪费而加以指责之前,我们应看到,由于社会良心以宗教为一种基本形式,同时献祭为这种良心的具体表现,从而所得弥补了所耗。而且对于单纯的物质形式的损耗,人们一般很少介意。而且,人们并不奢求从这种被要求做出的神圣奉献中获得实际的效益,而仅仅是把它当做抛弃私欲、崇尚奉献的体系中的一个内在组成部分。而对于任何社会来说,抛弃私欲和崇尚奉献都是维持

① 《献祭史论》1920 年版,第 531 ~ 540 页。

and its conservation. [1]

But besides this definition of the social function in terms of social cohesion and continuity, Loisy seeks for what he calls a general formula (*formuleég nérale*) in which to sum up the part that religion has played in human life. Such a formula is useful so long as we remember that it is only a formula. The one that Loisy offers is that magic and religion have served to give men confidence.

In the most primitive societies it is magic that gives man confidence in face of the difficulties and uncertainties, the real and imaginary dangers with which he is surrounded.

A la merci des élé ments, des saisons, de ce que la terre lui donne ou lui refuse, des bonnes ou des mauvaises chances de sa chasse ou de sa pêche, aussi du hasard de ses combats avec ses semblables, il croit trouver le moyen de régulariser par des simulacres d'action ces chances plus ou moins incertaines. Ce qu'il fait ne sertà rien par rapport au but qu'il se propose, mais il prend conriance en ses entreprises et en lui-même, il ose, et c'est en osant que réellement il obtient plus ou moins ce qu'il veut. Confiance rudimentaire, et pour une humble vie; mais c'est le commencement du courage moral. [2]

This is the same theory that was later developed by Malinowski in reference to the magical practices of the Trobriand Islanders.

At a somewhat higher stage of development, 'when the social organism has been perfected, when the tribe has become a people, and this people has its gods, its religion, it is by this religion itself that the strength of the national conscience is measured, and it is in the service of national gods that men find a pledge of security in the present,

---

① op cit., pp. 535-7.

② op cit., p. 533.

社会平衡和永存的条件。①

卢瓦西除了根据社会内聚力和社会连续性来定义社会功能之外,他正在试图寻找一个一般性的公式,用这条公式来总结宗教在人类生活中所起的作用。只要铭记住这条公式,那么它对我们就会有些作用。这个总体性公式是:巫术和宗教被用来鼓舞人们的自信。

在大多数原始社会中,当人们在面临困难与不安,被真正的危险或假想的危险困扰时,总是由巫术来为人们提供信心。

置身于复杂的自然现象中,例如四季轮回,获得良田或受困于灾难,狩猎、捕鱼可能遇上的好坏运气,以及能否战胜这些自然现象等等,人们相信,施行某些巫术就可以找到怎样卜测控制运气的方法。虽然这些行为本身与他们希望的实现并无联系,但当事人所在的群体以及他们自己却可以从这些实践中树立信心,从而获得某些勇气。而正是这种勇气,一定程度上满足了他们的欲望。在原始民族中,这些信念显示为规则,从而作为道德伦理的开端。②

后来,马林诺夫斯基参考特罗布里安人的巫术活动对此理论做了进一步发展。

当社会发展到某种较高级的阶段时,即"当社会机制得到完善,部落已演变成一个民族,并且拥有其自身的神灵和宗教时,正是通过宗教本身,民族意识的力量才可以得到衡量;同时,也正是在民族神灵的庇护下,人们才可以为自身目前的安全性和未来的

---

① 同上书,第535~537页。

② 同上书,第533页。

of prosperity in the future. The gods are as it were the expression of the confidence that the people has in itself; but it is in the cult of the gods that this confidence is nourished. ①

At a still higher stage of social development, the religions which give men a promise of immortality give him thereby an assurance which permits him to bear courageously the burdens of his present life and face the most onerous obligations. 'It is a higher and more moral form of confidence in life②.'

To me this formula seems unsatisfactory in that it lays stress on what is only one side of the religious (or magical) attitude. I offer as an alternative the formula that religion develops in mankind what may be called a sense of dependence. What I mean by this can best be explained by an example. In an ancestor-worshipping tribe of South Africa, a man feels that he is dependent on his ancestors. From them he has received his life and the cattle that are his inheritance. To them he looks to send him children and to multiply his cattle and in other ways to care for his wellbeing. This is one side of the matter; on his ancestors he *can* depend. The other side is the belief that the ancestors watch over his conduct, and that if he fails in his duties they will not only cease to send him blessings, but will visit him with sickness or some other misfortune. He cannot stand alone and depend only on his own efforts; on his ancestors he *must* depend.

We may say that the beliefs of the African ancestor-worshipper are illusory and his offerings to his gods really useless; that the dead of his lineage do not really send him either blessings or punishments. But the Confucians have shown us that a religion like ancestor-worship can be rationalised and freed from those illusory beliefs that we call superstition. For in the rites of commemoration of the ancestors it is sufficient that the participants should express their reverential gratitude

---

① Loc cit.

② Op cit., P534.

繁荣找到一种保证。人们对自身信心的外在表现就是神灵。而对神灵的崇拜也正是培养这种信心的土壤。"①

而在社会发展至一个更为高级的时期时,承诺给人们带来不朽的宗教会教导人们去勇敢地承担目前生活的负担,去面对最繁重的责任。"这是一种对生活的更为高级和更为道德的自信形式。"②

对我来说,这个公式是不能让人满意的,因为它过分强调了宗教(或巫术)态度中的一个方面。而我的观点是:宗教培养了人类的某种依赖感。我用一个例子可以最清晰地说明我的这个观点。在南非的一个存在祖先崇拜的部落中,一位男子会认为他对祖先是具有依赖性的。并且,他认为,是祖先赋予了他生命,给他留下了牲畜。他渴望祖先可以赐予他满堂子孙、成群的牛羊,同时关照他的幸福和健康。这是人类依赖祖先的一个方面。另一个方面是,人们认为,他们的行为受到祖先的监督,如果没有履行自己的职责,祖先就不会赋予其任何祝福,反而会使他们病魔缠身,或给他带来一些不幸。人类不能独自依靠其自身的努力,而必须依赖他们的祖先。

我们可以这么说,非洲人的祖先崇拜通常是虚幻的,并且他们的祭祀也的确是无用的。世系群中已故的人们并不能够真正的带给他们任何幸福或惩罚。但是,孔子学说已经向我们证明,像祖先崇拜这样的宗教可以被理性化,并且脱离我们所说的那种虚幻性。由于在祖先悼念仪式上,参与者们应该向那些赋予他们

① 同上书,第533页。

② 《献祭史论》,第534页。

to those from whom they have received their life, and their sense of duty towards those not yet born, to whom they in due course will stand in the position of revered ancestors. There still remains the sense of dependence. The living depend on those of the past; they have duties to those living in the present and to those of the future who will depend on them.

I suggest to you that what makes and keeps a man a social animal is not some herd instinct, but the sense of dependence in the innumerable forms that it takes. The process of socialisation begins on the first day of an infant's life and it has to learn that it both *can* and *must* depend on its parents. From them it has comfort and succour; but it must submit also to their control. What I am calling the sense of dependence always has these two sides. We can face life and its chances and difficulties with confidence when we know that there are powers, forces and events on which we can rely, but we must submit to the control of our conduct by rules which are imposed. The entirely asocial individual would be one who thought that he could be completely independent, relying only on himself, asking for no help and recognising no duties.

I have tried to present to you a theory of the social function of religion. This theory has been developed by the work of such men as Robertson Smith, Fustel de Coulanges, Durkheim, Loisy. It is the theory that has guided my own studies for nearly forty years. I have thought it worth while to indicate that it existed in embryo in the writings of Chinese philosophers more than twenty centuries ago.

Like any other scientific theory it is provisional, subject to revision and modification in the light of future research. It is offered as providing what seems likely to be a profitable method of investigation. What is needed to test and further elaborate the theory is a number of systematic studies of various types of religion in relation to social systems in which they occur.

I will summarise the suggestions I have made:

生命的祖先们表示他们的尊敬,并向没有出生的人表示一种责任感,所以,他们将来也会处于祖先的位置受到下辈人的尊敬。这里仍然存在一种依赖感,即活着的人对已故人的依赖,同时,他们对现在活着的人有责任,对未来将要依赖他们的下一代人也有责任。

我认为,使人类具有社会性的并不是某种群聚本性,而是人类所拥有的不同形式的依赖性。婴儿出生的第一天也就是人类社会化过程的开始,在这个过程中,他必须逐渐意识到他可以并且必须依赖其双亲。他可以从双亲那里得到慰籍和帮助,但他同时也必须听命于他们。这两方面的含义在我所说的依赖性中总是存在的。当我们意识到在生活中有些东西,例如权力、力量和事件可以依赖时,我们就有了面对生活及其机遇和困难的自信。但同时,我们也必须服从那些控制我们行为的规则。所以,那种所谓完全的非社会的个人通常是那种自认为是完全独立,只靠自己,而不需要别人帮助,从而也不承担任何责任的人。

我现在向你们论述的是有关宗教的社会功能的理论。罗伯特·史密斯、菲斯泰尔·德·库朗热、杜尔干及卢瓦西等人对这一理论都分别进行了发展。我认为有必要提及的一点是,这个理论的萌芽早在20多个世纪前的中国的哲学家们的著作中就已经出现。

该理论与其他的理论一样,其真理性都是相对的,需要根据不断的调查研究加以不断的更新。不过,此理论似乎可以作为一种有效的调查研究方法。如果要对这个理论进行检测和进一步深化,我们需要对与这种体制有关的各种宗教类型进行大量的系统化研究。

以下是我提出的几点建议:

1. To understand a particular religion we must study its effects. The religion must therefore be studied *in action*.

2. Since human conduct is in large part controlled or directed by what have been called sentiments, conceived as mental dispositions, it is necessary to discover as far as possible what are the sentiments that are developed in the individual as the result of his participation in a particular religious cult.

3. In the study of any religion we must first of all examine the specifically religious actions, the ceremonies and the collective or individual rites.

4. The emphasis on belief in specific doctrines which characterises some modern religions seems to be the result of certain social developments in societies of complex structure.

5. In some societies there is a direct and immediate relation between the religion and the social structure. This has been illustrated by ancestor-worship and Australian totemism. It is also true of what we may call national religions, such as that of the Hebrews or those of the city states of Greece and Rome. ① But where there comes into existence a separate independent religious structure by the formation of different churches or sects or cult-groups within a people, the relation of religion to the total social structure is in many respects indirect and not always easy to trace.

6. As a general formula (for whatever such a formula may be worth) it is suggested that what is expressed in all religions is what I have called the sense of dependence in its double aspect, and that it is by constantly maintaining this sense of dependence that religions perform their social function.

---

① '...among the ancients what formed the bond of every society was a worship. Just as a domestic altar held the members of a family grouped about it, so the city was the collective group of those who had the same protecting deities, and who performed the religious ceremony at the same altar.' Fustel de Coulanges, op cit., p. 193.

1. 我们只有研究宗教产生的影响,才能真正的了解这种宗教。因此,我们必须在实际的社会生活及其运行中研究宗教。

2. 由于人类的行为在很大程度上是由我们所称的情感所控制和指引,因此,有必要尽可能地对人们在参与某种宗教崇拜时所产生的情感加以揭示。

3. 在对任何一种宗教进行研究时,首先,我们要考察其特定的宗教行为、仪式及整体或个人仪式。

4. 对某种信仰的信条的强调,是现代宗教的特征。这种现象似乎是复杂的社会结构中社会发展的结果。

5. 在一些社会中,宗教与社会之间存在着直接的关系。这种直接关系可以通过祖先崇拜和澳大利亚图腾崇拜得以解释。而且在我们所称的民族宗教中也能发现这种关系,例如在希伯来人的宗教中或在古希腊城邦以及古罗马的一些城市中的宗教。[1] 但是,如果在同一民族内,由于不同的教会、教派或不同的群体崇拜形成了不同的独立的宗教结构,会造成在这个民族内部,宗教与整个社会结构的关系从很多方面来讲都体现出间接性,并且不容易追溯的情况。

6. 作为一个普遍性公式(无论其价值多大)表明:所有宗教表达的都是一种我认为的双方面的依赖感,并且正是通过对依赖感的不断维持,宗教才可以发挥其社会功能。

---

① "……在古代人中,每个社会依靠共同的崇拜这个纽带相互联结。就如同家庭成员聚合在祭坛一样,城邦也是一个拥有共同保护神的集体。他们在同一圣坛下举行宗教典礼。"—菲斯泰尔·德·库朗热,《古代城邦》,第193页。

CHAPTER Ⅸ

On The Concept Of Function In Social Science[①]

The concept of function applied to human societies is based on an analogy between social life and organic life. The recognition of the analogy and of some of its implications is not new. In the nineteenth century the analogy, the concept of function, and the word itself appear frequently in social philosophy and sociology. So far as I know the first systematic formulation of the concept as applying to the strictly scientific study of society was that of Emile Durkheim in 1895. (*Règles de la Mé thode Sociologique.*)

Durkheim's definition is that the 'function' of a social institution is the correspondence between it and the needs (*besoins* in French) of the social organism. This definition requires some elaboration. In the first place, to avoid possible ambiguity and in particular the possibility of a teleological interpretation, I would like to substitute for the term 'needs' the term 'necessary conditions of existence', or, if the term 'need' is used, it is to be understood only in this sense. It may be here noted, as a point to be returned to, that any attempt to apply this concept of function in social science involves the assumption that there *are* necessary conditions of

---

① This paper, which is based on comments that I made on a paper read by Dr. Lesser to the American Anthropological Association, is reprinted from the *American Anthropologist*, Vol. XXXVII, p. 3, 1935, where it accompanied Dr. Lesser's paper.

第九章 论在社会科学中功能的内涵[①]

功能这个概念被运用到人类社会中，是基于社会生活和有机体生活的相似性。对于这种相似性的认可和对其含义的理解，已有人探索过。19 世纪，在哲学和社会学领域，相似性、功能这个概念以及概念本身屡屡被提及。据我所知，在 1895 年埃米尔·杜尔干做出了关于这个概念的系统阐述，该阐述被应用到严格的社会科学研究中。

杜尔干的定义是这样的，社会体制的功能旨在使该体制和社会组织的需求之间取得一致。此定义需要做进一步的分析。首先，为了避免可能出现的不明确性，尤其避免应用目的论来解释的可能性，我想用"存在的必要条件"来代替定义中的"需求"。否则，如果非要使用"需求"这个词，也只能把理解局限在这个词本身。在此应该指出，将功能这个概念应用到社会科学中去的任何一次尝试都会涉及到关于人类社会存在的必然条件的假设，正如对动物机体存在条件所作的假设一样。并且，这种人类社会存在

① 这篇文章是以对莱塞博士投给美国人类学协会的一篇署名文章做的评论为基础写成，重印自 1935 年《美国人类学家》第 37 卷第 3 页，当时是与莱塞博士的文章一同发表的。

existence for human societies just as there are for animal organisms, and that they can be discovered by the proper kind of scientific enquiry.

For the further elucidation of the concept it is convenient to use the analogy between social life and organic life. Like all analogies it has to be used with care. An animal organism is an agglomeration of cells and interstitial fluids arranged in relation to one another not as an aggregate but as an integrated living whole. For the biochemist, it is a complexly integrated system of complex molecules. The system of relations by which these units are related is the organic structure. As the terms are here used the organism is *not* itself the structure; it is a collection of units (cells or molecules) arranged in a structure, i. e. in a set of relations; the organism *has* a structure. Two mature animals of the same species and sex consist of similar units combined in a similar structure. The structure is thus to be defined as a set of relations between entities. (The structure of a cell is in the same way a set of relations between complex molecules, and the structure of an atom is a set of relations between electrons and protons.) As long as it lives the organism preserves a certain continuity of structure although it does not preserve the complete identity of its constituent parts. It loses some of its constituent molecules by respiration or excretion; it takes in others by respiration and alimentary absorption. Over a period its constituent cells do not remain the same. But the structural arrangement of the constituent units does remain similar. The process by which this structural continuity of the organism is maintained is called life. The life-process consists of the activities and interactions of the constituent units of the organism, the cells, and the organs into which the cells are united.

As the word function is here being used the life of an organism is conceived as the *functioning* of its structure. It is through and by the continuity of the functioning that the continuity of the structure is preserved. If we consider any recurrent part of the life-process, such as respiration, digestion, etc., its *function* is the part it plays in, the contribution it makes to, the life of the organism as a whole. As the

的必然条件会被彻底的科学探索发现。

对这个概念的进一步阐述,可以将社会生活简洁地比喻成机体生命。我们必须小心谨慎地运用这种相似性,正如进行其他相似性比较一样。动物机体是细胞和间质液的融合,但这些细胞和间质液并不是作为一种融合体而是作为一个生命体整体排列联系在一起的。对于生物化学家而言,这是一个有关合成分子的联合的综合体系。将这些个体联系起来的各种系统关系是一个有机组织。正如这里使用的其他术语,机体并不是指组织结构本身,它是位于组织内部,即位于一套关系中的单位个体(细胞或者分子)的集合。机体就含有组织结构。同种类、同性别的两只成年动物是由相似的单位个体构成的,该单位个体包含有相似的组织结构。因此,组织结构可以定义为各个实体之间的一系列关系(细胞的组织结构相似于合成分子间的一系列联系,原子的组织结构就是质子和电子之间的一系列联系)。只要机体存在,就会维持组织结构的连续性,尽管它无法维持其构成部分的全部特性。机体会因呼吸或排泄而失去一些构成分子;也会因呼吸和营养物质的吸收而吸收其他的分子。一段时期之后,其组成细胞将完全不同。但是,构成单位个体的组织结构排列会保持相似性。这种维持机体组织结构连续性的过程被称为生命。构成机体的个体单位、细胞以及细胞结合形成的器官,它们之间的活动和相互作用构成了生命的过程。

由于这里使用了功能这个概念,因此机体的生命被认为是其组织结构的机能。通过机能的连续性来维持组织结构的连续性。如果考虑生命过程的任何一个循环部分,例如,呼吸、消化等,这些循环部分的功能就是指其所起到的作用,以及对整个机体的生命过

terms are here being used a cell or an organ has an *activity* and that activity has a *function*. It is true that we commonly speak of the secretion of gastric fluid as a 'function' of the stomach. As the words are here used we should say that this is an 'activity' of the stomach, the 'function' of which is to change the proteins of food into a form in which these are absorbed and distributed by the blood to the tissues. ① We may note that the function of a recurrent physiological process is thus a correspondence between it and the needs (i. e. necessary conditions of existence) of the organism.

If we set out upon a systematic investigation of the nature of organisms and organic life there are three sets of problems presented to us. (There are, in addition, certain other sets of problems concerning aspects or characteristics of organic life with which we are not here concerned.) One is that of morphology—what kinds of organic structures are there, what similarities and variations do they show, and how can they be classified? Second are the problems of physiology—how, in general, do organic structures function, what, therefore, is the nature of the lifeprocess? Third are the problems of evolution or development—how do new types of organisms come into existence?

To turn from organic life to social life, if we examine such a community as an African or Australian tribe we can recognise the existence of a social structure. Individual human beings, the essential units in this instance, are connected by a definite set of social relations into an integrated whole. The continuity of the social structure, like that of an organic structure, is not destroyed by changes in the units. Individuals may leave the society, by death or otherwise; others may enter it. The continuity of structure is maintained by the process of social life, which consists of the activities and interactions of the individual human beings and of the organised groups into which they

① The insistence on this precise form of terminology is only for the sake of the analogy that is to be drawn. I hare no objection to the use of the term function in physiology to denote both the activity of an organ and the results of that activity in maintaining life.

程做出的贡献。正如这里使用的术语,细胞或器官进行着某种活动,而且这种活动具有某种功能。我们常常提到胃液是胃功能的分泌物,用此处的话,我们应当说,这个活动就是肠胃活动,该活动的功能就是将食物中的蛋白质转化成一种可被吸收的形式,并由血液分布到各个组织。① 可以注意到,循环性生理过程的功能就是在功能和机体需要(即存在的必要条件)之间达到一致。

如果我们对生物体特性和有机体生命过程进行一系列的调查研究,就会发现三个问题(另外,还有一系列关于有机体生命过程的特性的问题,我们没有注意到)。其中之一是形态学——关于有机体组织结构的类型、它们之间的相似性和变异性以及如何分类的问题。第二,关于生理学的问题——有机体的组织结构如何发挥作用及生命过程的实质。第三,关于进化和发展的问题——新型生物体的衍生。

从有机体生命谈到社会生活,如果我们对非洲或澳大利亚部落这样的社团进行研究,就能意识到社会组织结构的存在。个人,作为这次调查中的基本单位,通过一定的社会关系联系起来而形成完整的整体。正如有机体组织的连续性一样,社会结构的连续性并不会因为单位个体的变化而被摧毁。个人会因死亡或其他原因离开社会,同时也会有其他人融入其中。社会结构的连续性是通过社会生活过程维系的,个人行为及人与人之间的相互作用构成了社会生活;另外,由个人构成的团体组织的活动及相互作用也是社会生活的一部分。社会生活在这里被定义为社会组

---

① 为了以下的类比,必须准确应用术语。我不反对在生理学中使用功能这个术语来表示器官的活动和这种活动维持生命过程的作用。

are united. The social life of the community is here defined as the *functioning* of the social structure. The *function* of any recurrent activity, such as the punishment of a crime, or a funeral ceremony, is the part it plays in the social life as a whole and therefore the contribution it makes to the maintenance of the structural continuity.

The concept of function as here defined thus involves the notion of a *structure* consisting of a *set of relations* amongst *unit entities*, the *continuity* of the structure being maintained by a *lifeprocess* made up of the *activities* of the constituent units.

If, with these concepts in mind, we set out on a systematic investigation of the nature of human society and of social life, we find presented to us three sets of problems. First, the problems of social morphology—what kinds of social structures are there, what are their similarities and differences, how are they to be classified? Second, the problems of social physiology—how do social structures function? Third, the problems of development—how do new types of social structure come into existence?

Two important points where the analogy between organism and society breaks down must be noted. In an animal organism it is possible to observe the organic structure to some extent independently of its functioning. It is therefore possible to make a morphology which is independent of physiology. But in human society the social structure as a whole can only be *observed* in its functioning. Some of the features of social structure, such as the geographical distribution of individuals and groups can be directly observed, but most of the social relations which in their totality constitute the structure, such as relations of father and son, buyer and seller, ruler and subject, cannot be observed except in the social activities in which the relations are functioning. It follows that a social morphology cannot be established independently of a social physiology.

The second point is that an animal organism does not, in the course of its life, change its structural type. A pig does not become a hippopotamus. (The development of the animal from germination to maturity is not a change of type since the process in all its stages is typical for the species.) On the other hand a society in the course of its history can and does change its structural type without any breach of continuity.

织结构的功能。任何循环性行为活动,如对罪行的惩罚、葬礼,其功能都是指该行为在社会生活中发挥的作用以及在维持组织结构连续性过程中所做的贡献。

这里定义的功能概念涉及了组织结构和其连续性问题。其中,不同个体之间的关系构成了组织结构,而其连续性则是通过由各个要素的行为活动构成的生活过程维持的。如果在这些概念的基础上,我们进行关于人类社会和社会生活实质的系统调查,就会发现三个问题。第一,关于社会形态学的问题,包括社会组织结构的类型、异同点以及分类方法。第二,关于社会生理学的问题,也就是社会组织结构所起的作用。第三,关于发展进步的问题,即新型的社会组织结构的衍生。

我们必须注意到有机体和人类社会的两个不同点。首先,在动物有机体内部,我们可以在不考虑有机体功能的情况下,对其组织结构进行观察。因此,形态学的研究可以独立于生理学。但是,对于人类社会而言,作为整体的社会组织结构仅仅可以通过功能来评述。社会组织结构的一些特征,例如个人和团体的地理分布情况,可以得到直接的考察。但是,构成组织结构的大多数社会关系,例如父子、买卖及统治者与被统治者之间的关系,却无法得到观察,只有通过这些关系在社会活动中所起的作用来进行研究。也就是说,社会形态学的建立并不能完全独立于生理学。

第二个不同点指的是,动物有机体在生命过程中无法改变组织结构类型。猪永远不可能变成河马(从幼崽到成年,动物的发展过程并不会改变,因为发展过程的所有阶段都是这一物种独有的)。另一方面,在历史发展过程中,社会可以在不破坏连续性的前提下改变其组织结构类型。

By the definition here offered 'function' is the contribution which a partial activity makes to the total activity of which it is a part. The function of a particular social usage is the contribution it makes to the total social life as the functioning of the total social system. Such a view implies that a social system (the total social structure of a society together with the totality of social usages in which that structure appears and on which it depends for its continued existence) has a certain kind of unity, which we may speak of as a functional unity. We may define it as a condition in which all parts of the social system work together with a sufficient degree of harmony or internal consistency, i. e. without producing persistent conflicts which can neither be resolved nor regulated. ①

This idea of the functional unity of a social system is, of course, a hypothesis. But it is one which, to the functionalist, it seems worth while to test by systematic examination of the facts.

There is another aspect of functional theory that should be briefly mentioned. To return to the analogy of social life and organic life, we recognise that an organism may function more or less efficiently and so we set up a special science of pathology to deal with all phenomena of disfunction. We distinguish in an organism what we call health and disease. The Greeks of the fifth century B. C. thought that one might apply the same notion to society, to the city-state, distinguishing conditions of *eunomia*, good order, social health, from *dysnomia*, disorder, social illhealth. In the nineteenth century Durkheim, in his application of the notion of function, sought to lay the basis for a scientific social pathology, based on a morphology and a physiology. ② In his works, particularly those on suicide and the division of labour, he attempted to find objective criteria by which to judge

---

① Opposition, i. e. organised and regulated antagonism, is, of course, an essential feature of every social system.

② For what is here called dysnomia Durkheim used the term anomia (*anomie* in French). This is to my mind inappropriate. Health and disease, eunomia and dysnomia, are essentially relative terms.

根据这里给出的关于“功能”的定义，它是指部分行为对整体行为所做出的贡献。一种具体社会惯例的功能就是指其在整个社会体系运转时在全部社会生活中发挥的作用。这种观点表明，一种社会体系（一个社会的全部组织结构以及社会惯例的总和，其中，社会惯例包括组织结构，而组织结构为了保持其连续存在依赖于社会惯例）具有某种一致性，我们可以将其称为功能的一致性。这种一致性是指，在一定条件下，社会体系的所有部分以高度的和谐性和内部的连贯性共同运转，例如，不会出现永久的既无法解决又无法控制的冲突。①

当然，关于社会体系的功能一致性观点只是一种假设。但是，对于功能主义者而言，以事实为依据，进行系统的调查研究来检验这种一致性，是有价值的。

我们将对功能理论的另外一方面进行简要的说明介绍。为了重新回到社会生活和有机体生命过程相似的话题，我们承认有机体功能的有效性，所以我们建立了独特的病理学来解决所有的功能紊乱现象，以对我们所说的健康和病态的有机体进行区分。公元前5世纪的希腊人认为，我们应该把同样的主张应用到社会和城邦，把良好的秩序及健康的社会状态同无序状态及病态社会区分开。在19世纪，杜尔干应用功能这个想法时，试图将形态学和生理学作为社会病理学的科学基础。② 在他的著作中，尤其是关于自杀和劳动力的著作中，他努力尝试去寻找一种客观的标准来判断

① 显然，对抗作为组织和有规则的敌对，也是每个社会体系的基本特征。

② 此处的动乱杜尔干用“反常”（法语中的 *anomie*）这一术语来表示，我认为并不恰当。健康和疾病、安定和动乱在词语上基本上是对应关系。

whether a given society at a given time is normal or pathological, eunomic or dysnomic. For example, he tried to show that the increase of the rate of suicide in many countries during part of the nineteenth century is symptomatic of a dysnomic or, in his terminology, anomic, social condition. Probably there is no sociologist who would hold that Durkheim really succeeded in establishing an objective basis for a science of social pathology. ①

In relation to organic structures we can find strictly objective criteria by which to distinguish disease from health, pathological from normal, for disease is that which either threatens the organism with death (the dissolution of its structure) or interferes with the activities which are characteristic of the organic type. Societies do not die in the same sense that animals die and therefore we cannot define dysnomia as that which leads, if unchecked, to the death of a society. Further, a society differs from an organism in that it can change its structural type, or can be absorbed as an integral part of a larger society. Therefore we cannot define dysnomia as a disturbance of the usual activities of a social type (as Durkheim tried to do).

Let us return for a moment to the Greeks. They conceived the health of an organism and the eunomia of a society as being in each instance a condition of the harmonious working together of its parts. ② Now this, where society is concerned, is the same thing as what was considered above as the functional unity or inner consistency of a social system, and it is suggested that for the degree of functional unity of a particular society it may be possible to establish a purely objective criterion. Admittedly this cannot be done at present; but the science of human society is as yet in its extreme infancy. So that it may be that we should say that, while an organism that is attacked by a virulent disease will react thereto, and, if its reaction fails, will die,

---

① I would personally agree in the main with the criticisms of Roger Lacombe (*La Méthode Sociologique de Durkheim*, 1926, ch. IV) on Durkheim's general theory of social pathology, and with the criticisms of Durkheim's treatment of suicide presented by Halbwachs, *Les Causes du Suicide*.

② See, for example, the Fourth Book of Plato's *Republic*.

一个特定的社会在特定的时期是正常还是病态的，是有序的还是无序。例如，在 19 世纪，自杀比例上升，他认为这是社会秩序紊乱的表现。可能，社会学家并不认为杜尔干在建立社会病理科学的客观基础方面取得了成功。①

关于有机体的组织结构，我们可以找到严格的客观标准。通过这些标准，可以对疾病和健康、病态和正常状态加以区分，因为疾病可以将有机体致死（分散其组织结构）或者对这种有机体特有的行为活动产生干扰。但是，社会消亡和动物死亡不可同日而语，因此，如果没有经过证实，我们不能将紊乱状态定义为导致社会灭亡的原因。另外，社会与有机体的不同还在于，社会可以改变其组织结构的形式或者社会可以作为一部分被较大团体吸收。因此，我们不能将紊乱状态视为社会通常行为活动的干扰因素。

接下来我们会对希腊人的观点加以讨论。他们认为有机体的健康状态和社会的有序状态是使其各个部分共同和谐运转的条件。② 社会所关注的内容，与被视为功能和谐或社会制度内部连贯性的内容是相同的。对于考虑特殊社会功能性和谐的程度问题，设定一种纯粹的客观标准是可能实现的。但是，必须承认的是，目前尚无法做到这一点，人类社会科学尚处于初级阶段。因此，可以说，如果受到病毒的侵害，有机体就会做出相应的反

① 我个人基本同意罗歇·拉孔布对杜尔干的社会病理学的一般原理所做的批评和阿尔瓦歇尔在《自杀原因》中对于杜尔干的自杀论所做的批评。

② 其例参阅柏拉图《理想国》的第 4 本书 。

a society that is thrown into a condition of functional disunity or inconsistency (for this we now provisionally identify with dysnomia) will not die, except in such comparatively rare instances as an Australian tribe overwhelmed by the white man's destructive force, but will continue to struggle toward some sort of eunomia, some kind of social health, and may, in the course of this, change its structural type. This process, it seems, the 'functionalist' has ample opportunities of observing at the present day, in native peoples subjected to the domination of the civilised nations, and in those nations themselves. ①

Space will not allow a discussion here of another aspect of functional theory, viz. the question whether change of social type is or is not dependent on function, i. e. on the laws of social physiology. My own view is that there is such a dependence and that its nature can be studied in the development of the legal and political institutions, the economic systems and the religions of Europe through the last twenty-five centuries. For the preliterate societies with which anthropology is concerned, it is not possible to study the details of long processes of change of type. The one kind of change which the anthropologist can observe is the disintegration of social structures. Yet even here we can observe and compare spontaneous movements towards reintegration. We have, for instance, in Africa, in Oceania, and in America the appearance of new religions which can be interpreted on a functional hypothesis as attempts to relieve a condition of social dysnomia produced by the rapid modification of the social life through contact with white civilisation.

The concept of function as defined above constitutes a 'working hypothesis' by which a number of problems are formulated for investigation. No scientific enquiry is possible without some such formulation

---

① To avoid misunderstanding it is perhaps necessary to observe that this distinction of eunomic and dysnomic social conditions does not give us any evaluation of these societies as 'good' or 'bad'. A savage tribe practising polygamy, cannibalism, and sorcery can possibly show a higher degree of functional unity or consistency than the United States of 1935. This objective judgment, for such it must be if it is to be scientific, is something very different from any judgment as to which of the two social systems is the better, the more to be desired or approved.

应，否则，该有机体会死亡；但是，一个陷入功能性不和谐或非连续性状态（与紊乱状态等同）的社会却不会消亡（但是也存在一些例外，比如澳大利亚部落被白人所征服），而是仍然努力继续维持良好的秩序，保持社会的健康状态，并且可能在这个过程中改变其组织结构的类型。在这个过程中，功能主义学家似乎有充分的机会研究目前的社会、臣服于文明民族的当地种族，以及这些文明民族本身。①

因为篇幅有限，本文不会涉及到功能理论的另外一个方面，即，从社生理学的规则来看，社会类型的转换是否依赖于功能。我个人的观点是社会类型的转换依赖于功能，对于其性质的研究，可以纵观过去25个世纪以来欧洲在法律政治制度、经济体制及宗教方面的发展。对于人类学家所关注的前文明社会，不可能去对其漫长发展过程中形式转换的细节一一进行研究。人类学家所关注的唯一变化是社会组织结构的解体，尽管我们可以对自发的重组过程进行研究和比较。例如，在非洲、大洋洲和美洲，我们掌握了新宗教的表现，以功能主义的假想来看，该宗教试图通过与白人文明的接触，来减轻由于高度改变的社会生活导致的社会无序状态。

上文所定义的功能概念包含了一个“功能假设”，通过该假设确立了一系列有待调查的问题。如果没有功能假设的公式化，将

① 为不引起歧义，或许有必要明确，辨别社会状况的安定与动乱和评论社会的好坏不是一回事。一个实行多偶婚、具有食人习俗和盛行巫术的野蛮部落所表现出来的功能协调或和谐性的程度可能会比1935年的美国高。客观的评价（科学来自于客观）并不是判断哪种社会制度更可取，更值得人们向往和赞同。

of working hypotheses. Two remarks are necessary here. One is that the hypothesis does not require the dogmatic assertion that everything in the life of every community has a function. It only requires the assumption that it *may* have one, and that we are justified in seeking to discover it. The second is that what appears to be the same social usage in two societies may have different functions in the two. Thus the practice of celibacy in the Roman Catholic Church of today has very different functions from those of celibacy in the early Christian Church. In other words, in order to define a social usage, and therefore in order to make valid comparisons between the usages of different peoples or periods, it is necessary to consider not merely the form of the usage but also its function. On this basis, for example, belief in a Supreme Being in a simple society is something different from such a belief in a modern civilised community.

The acceptance of the functional hypothesis or point of view outlined above results in the recognition of a vast number of problems for the solution of which there are required wide comparative studies of societies of many diverse types and also intensive studies of as many single societies as possible. In field studies of the simpler peoples it leads, first of all, to a direct study of the social life of the community as the functioning of a social structure, and of this there are several examples in recent literature. Since the function of a social activity is to be found by examining its effects upon individuals, these are studied, either in the average individual or in both average and exceptional individuals. Further, the hypothesis leads to attempts to investigate directly the functional consistency or unity of a social system and to determine as far as possible in each instance the nature of that unity. Such field studies will obviously be different in many ways from studies carried out from other points of view, e. g. the ethnological point of view that lays emphasis on diffusion. We do not have to say that one point of view is better than another, but only that they are different, and any particular piece of work should be judged in reference to what it aims to do.

If the view here outlined is taken as one form of 'functionalism', a few remarks on Dr. Lesser's paper become permissible. He

无法进行任何科学探索。这里有两点要注意。第一,该假设并不要求对每个社会的每种生活所具有的功能进行教条式的评述,它只是假设,每种事物都可能有其功能,所以我们有必要把它揭示出来。第二,在两个不同社会中,两种看起来等同的社会习俗发挥的作用是不同的。因此,当今罗马天主教的独身行为与早期基督教的独身行为,在功能上有很大不同。换句话说,为了定义一种社会习俗,及为了将不同民族和不同时期的习俗进行有效的比较,不仅要考虑到习俗的形式还要考虑到其功能。在此基础上,一个初级社会与一个现代文明社会,对上帝的信仰是完全不同的。

接受功能假设或如上所陈述的观点就要承认一系列问题的存在,这些问题的解决要求对不同类型的社会进行广泛的对比研究,同时,也要对尽可能多的单一社会进行集约型分析。对较初级民族所进行的分析,首先,会导致对社会生活的直接研究,这种研究要求我们把该社会的生活看做是一个社会结构的运转。在近期文献中有很多这方面的实例。因为社会活动的功能是通过其对个体产生的影响而被检验的,因此这些研究是针对一般个体或针对一般和特殊个体进行的。另外,该假设促进了对社会制度功能连续性或和谐性的直接调查研究,同时也促进确定每个实例中和谐性的特质。这一领域的研究会与从其他角度进行的研究在很多方面有显著的不同之处,例如,人种学就重视传播扩散。我们没有必要认为一种观点优于另外一种,它们只是不同而已,并且任何一项工作都应该通过其目标来评判。

如果这里概述的观点被认为是“功能主义”的一种形式,则我们可以对莱塞博士的文章加以评述。他提出了功能性和非功能

makes reference to a difference of ' content ' in functional and non-functional anthropology. From the point of view here presented the ' content ' or subject-matter of social anthropology is the whole social life of a people in all its aspects. For convenience of handling it is often necessary to devote special attention to some particular part or aspect of the social life, but if functionalism means anything at all it does mean the attempt to see the social life of a people as a whole, as a functional unity.

Dr. Lesser speaks of the functionalist as stressing ' the psychological aspects of culture ' , I presume that he here refers to the functionalist ' s recognition that the usages of a society work or ' function ' only through their effects in the life, i. e. in the thoughts, sentiments and actions of individuals.

The ' functionalist ' point of view here presented does therefore imply that we have to investigate as thoroughly as possible all aspects of social life, considering them in relation to one another, and that an essential part of the task is the investigation of the individual and of the way in which he is moulded by or adjusted to the social life.

Turning from content to method Dr. Lesser seems to find some conflict between the functional point of view and the historical. This is reminiscent of the attempts formerly made to see a conflict between sociology and history. There need be no conflict, but there is a difference.

There is not, and cannot be, any conflict between the functional hypothesis and the view that any culture, any social system, is the end-result of a unique series of historical accidents. The process of development of the race-horse from its five-toed ancestor was a unique series of historical accidents. This does not conflict with the view of the physiologist that the horse of today and all the antecedent forms conform or conformed to physiological laws, i. e. to the necessary conditions of organic existence. Palaeontology and physiology are not in conflict. One ' explanation ' of the race-horse is to be found in its history—how it came to be just what it is and where it is. Another and entirely independent ' explanation ' is to show how the horse is a special exemplification of physiological laws. Similarly one ' explanation ' of a social system will be its history, where we know it—the

性人类学在内容上的差异。依照此观点,社会人类学的主题或内容是指人类全部社会生活的各个方面。为方便处理,有必要将注意力集中在社会生活的特殊方面,但是,如果功能主义意味着社会生活的各个方面,那么它就要试图将人类的社会生活视为一个整体,一个功能统一体。

莱塞博士提到功能主义者强调"文化的心理方面因素",我认为,他所指的是功能主义者对于一项社会工作或功能的习俗的认识,这些认识仅仅是通过习俗对社会生活,即对思想、情操、个人行为产生的影响获得。

这里提到的"功能主义者"的观点意味着我们必须要彻底调查社会生活的各个方面并考虑它们的相互影响。而且,这项任务的实质性部分是对个体的调查,以及该个体是如何被塑造或适应社会生活的。

从内容到方法,莱塞博士似乎发现了功能主义观点与历史观点之间的冲突。这使人想起了,人们曾经试图探索社会学和历史学之间冲突。事实上,并不存在冲突,只是有差异而已。

任何文化、社会体系是一系列独特历史事件的归宿,这种观点和功能主义假设并不存在冲突。源于五趾马的赛马的发展过程是历史事件中的特例。这并不与生理学家的观点相悖,他们认为现在的马和马的先祖在发展过程中都是遵循生理学基本规律的,例如,它们都要适应有机体存在的必要条件。古生物学和生理学的观点并不是冲突的。关于赛马的"解说"可以在其历史发展中得到考证——它是如何产生的、为何物及在何处。另一种完全不关联的"解释"是要表明,为何这种马成了研究生理学规律的特殊范例。同样,对于一种社会体系的"解释"也可追溯其历史

detailed account of how it came to be what it is and where it is. Another 'explanation' of the same system is obtained by showing (as the functionalist attempts to do) that it is a special exemplification of laws of social physiology or social functioning. The two kinds of explanation do not conflict, but supplement one another. ①

The functional hypothesis is in conflict with two views that are held by some ethnologists, and it is probably these, held as they often are without precise formulation, that are the cause of the antagonism to that approach. One is the 'shreds and patches' theory of culture, the designation being taken from a phrase of Professor Lowie② when he speaks of 'that planless hodge-podge, that thing of shreds and patches called civilisation'. The concentration of attention on what is called the diffusion of culturetraits tends to produce a conception of culture as a collection of disparate entities (the so-called traits) brought together by pure historical accident and having only accidental relations to one another. The conception is rarely formulated and maintained with any precision, but as a half-unconscious point of view it does seem to control the thinking of many ethnologists. It is, of course, in direct conflict with the hypothesis of the functional unity of social systems.

---

① I see no reason at all why the two kinds of study—the historical and the functional—should not be carried on side by side in perfect harmony. In fact, for fourteen years I have been teaching both the historical and geographical study of peoples under the name of ethnology in close association with archaeology, and the functional study of social systems under the name of social anthropology. I do think that there are many disadvantages in mixing the two subjects together and confusing them. See 'The Methods of Ethnology and Social Anthropology' (*South African Journal of Science*, 1923, pp. 124-47).

② *Primitive Society*, p. 441. A concise statement of this point of view is the following passage from Dr. Ruth Benedict's 'The Concept of the Guardian Spirit in North America' (*Memoirs*, American Anthropological Association, 29, 1923), p. 84: 'It is, so far as we can see, an ultimate fact of human nature that man builds up his culture out of disparate elements, combining and recombining them; and until we have abandoned the superstition that the result is an organism functionally interrelated we shall be unable to see our cultural life objectively, or to control its manifestations' I think that probably neither Professor Lowie nor Dr. Benedict would, at the present time, maintain this view of the nature of culture.

的发展,从何处得知它——关于它如何产生、为何物及在何处的详细说明。对同一体系的另一种“解释”可以通过说明该体系是社会生理学或社会功能学规律的特殊范例获得(正如功能主义者努力的那样)。这两种解释并不相互冲突,它们互为补充。[①]

功能假设与人种学者所持的两种观点是相悖的,可能是他们所持有的观点没有明确的表达方法,这也是导致对立的一种原因。一种是关于文化的“碎片与补丁”理论,这一名称源自罗维教授,[②]他曾说过:“那种杂乱的混合物,那种由各种碎片和补丁构成的东西被称作文明。”将注意力集中在文化特性的传播上,势必会产生一种文化观念,这种观念是迥然不同的实体(即特性)的结合,该实体通过纯粹的历史事件联系在一起并且互相之间仅仅存在非本质属性的关系。这种观点的形成和维持缺乏准确度,但是作为一种半无意识的观点,它似乎支配着许多人种学者的思想。当然,这种观点与社会制度功能统一体假设之间的冲突是直接的。

---

① 我不认为历史研究和功能研究不能和谐共处。事实上,我这14年来一直是在民族学名义下,和考古学紧密结合以讲授民族历史学和地理学研究,在社会人类学名义下,讲授社会制度的功能研究。但我也认为不加区分地把这两个学科混合起来也很不合适。参见“民族学的方法和社会人类学的方法”,载《南非科学杂志》,1923年,第124~147页。

② 《初民社会》,第441页。鲁思·本尼迪克特博士曾简述过这个观点,载于《北美洲的守护神观念》第84页(载美国人类学协会《纪要》,1923年,第29期):“就我们所知,有关人性的一个根本事实是,在不断合并那些毫无关系的成分的基础上构建其文化;如果我们不放弃认为文化是一个功能上相互关联的有机体的迷信,我们就不能客观地认识我们的文化生活,不能把握它的各种表现。”我想,在今天,无论是罗维教授还是本尼迪克特博士都会转变对文化的性质的这种看法。

The second view which is in direct conflict with the functional hypothesis is the view that there are no discoverable significant sociological laws such as the functionalist is seeking. I know that some two or three ethnologists say that they hold this view, but I have found it impossible to know what they mean, or on what sort of evidence (rational or empirical) they would base their contention. Generalisations about any sort of subject matter are of two kinds: the generalisations of common opinion, and generalisations that have been verified or demonstrated by a systematic examination of evidence afforded by precise observations systematically made. Generalisations of the latter kind are called scientific laws. Those who hold that there are no laws of human society cannot hold that there are no generalisations about human society because they themselves hold such generalisations and even make new ones of their own. They must therefore hold that in the field of social phenomena, in contradistinction to physical and biological phenomena, any attempt at the systematic testing of existing generalisations or towards the discovery and verification of new ones, is, for some unexplained reason, futile, or, as Dr. Radin puts it, 'crying for the moon'. Argument against such a contention is unprofitable or indeed impossible.

第二种与功能假设有直接冲突的观点是，他们认为并不存在功能主义者正在探询的有意义的社会学法则。据我所知，有二到三名人种学家持有这种观点，但是，我发现很难理解他们的意图或者他们如何支持自己的观点（理性分析后的，还是经验主义的证据）。关于主题的概述有两种：一为普通观点的概述，另一种是通过系统的证据调查来核实或验证的概述，而且这些证据是由准确的观察体系提供的。其中，后者被称作科学规律。认为不存在人类社会规律的科学家们，不能无视人类社会概述的存在，因为他们自己就支持这种概述甚至加以更新。因此，他们必须坚持认为在与物理学和生理学相对照的社会学领域，任何试图以系统的方法证实现存概述或者探索并验证新概述的努力，都是无效的，或者，像雷丁博士所说的那样是“对着月亮哭泣”。针对这一论点的辩论是徒劳的或者甚至是不可能的。

CHAPTER X

On Social Structure[①]

It has been suggested to me by some of my friends that I should use this occasion to offer some remarks about my own point of view in social anthropology; and since in my teaching, beginning at Cambridge and at the London School of Economics thirty years ago, I have consistently emphasised the importance of the study of social structure, the suggestion made to me was that I should say something on that subject.

I hope you will pardon me if I begin with a note of personal explanation. I have been described on more than one occasion as belonging to something called the 'Functional School of Social Anthropology' and even as being its leader, or one of its leaders. This Functional School does not really exist; it is a myth invented by Professor Malinowski. He has explained how, to quote his own words, 'the magnificent title of the Functional School of Anthropology has been bestowed by myself, in a way on myself, and to a large extent out of my own sense of irresponsibility'. Professor Malinowski's irresponsibility has had unfortunate results, since it has spread over anthropology a dense fog of discussion about 'functionalism'. Professor Lowie has announced that the leading, though not the only, exponent of functionalism in the nineteenth century was Professor Franz Boas. I do not think that there is any sense, other than the purely chronological one, in which I can be said to be either the follower of Professor Boas or the predecessor of Professor Malinowski. The statement that I am a

---

① Presidential Address to the Royal Anthropological Institute. Reprinted from the *Journal of the Royal Anthropological Institute*, Vol. LXX, 1940.

第十章　论社会结构[①]

一些朋友曾建议我，应该利用这次机会提出关于社会人类学的一些个人观点。自从 30 年前在剑桥和伦敦经济学院开始教学生涯，我就不断强调研究社会结构的重要性，在朋友们的盛情建议下，我决定就这个题目发表一下我的看法。

如果一开始我就表示个人的见解，希望大家能够原谅。多数情况下，大家认为我属于"社会人类学的功能学派"，并视我为学科领袖或是其中之一。事实上，功能学派并不是真实存在的，它是由马林诺夫斯基教授虚构出来的。我们引用马林诺夫斯基教授的原话，他曾经解释自己如何"授予社会人类学的功能学派这个响亮的名字，其实在很大程度上，是出于不负责任的想法"。马林诺夫斯基教授的不负责任产生了令人遗憾的后果，因为这在人类学领域掀起了关于"功能主义"讨论的狂潮。罗维教授认为，在 19 世纪功能主义的主要代表人物是弗朗斯·博厄斯教授，尽管他并不是唯一的。如果仅仅按照年代的顺序排列，可以说我是博厄斯教授的追随者或是马林诺夫斯基教授的前辈，但是我认为这毫

---

① 此文是在皇家人类学会上所作的"会长演说"。重印自《皇家人类学会杂志》第 70 卷(1940 年)。

'functionalist' would seem to me to convey no definite meaning.

There is no place in natural science for 'schools' in this sense, and I regard social anthropology as a branch of natural science. Each scientist starts from the work of his predecessors, finds problems which he believes to be significant, and by observation and reasoning endeavours to make some contribution to a growing body of theory. Co-operation amongst scientists results from the fact that they are working on the same or related problems. Such co-operation does not result in the formation of schools, in the sense in which there are schools of philosophy or of painting. There is no place for orthodoxies and heterodoxies in science. Nothing is more pernicious in science than attempts to establish adherence to doctrines. All that a teacher can do is to assist the student in learning to understand and use the scientific method. It is not his business to make disciples.

I conceive of social anthropology as the theoretical natural science of human society, that is, the investigation of social phenomena by methods essentially similar to those used in the physical and biological sciences. I am quite willing to call the subject 'comparative sociology', if anyone so wishes. It is the subject itself, and not the name, that is important. As you know, there are some ethnologists or anthropologists who hold that it is not possible, or at least not profitable, to apply to social phenomena the theoretical methods of natural science. For these persons social anthropology, as I have defined it, is something that does not, and never will, exist. For them, of course, my remarks will have no meaning, or at least not the meaning I intend them to have.

While I have defined social anthropology as the study of human society, there are some who define it as the study of culture. It might perhaps be thought that this difference of definition is of minor importance. Actually it leads to two different kinds of study, between which it is hardly possible to obtain agreement in the formulation of problems.

无意义。“我是一名功能主义者”这样的声明对我而言不具有任何特殊的含义。

在自然科学领域,“功能学派”没有任何地位可言,我本人将社会人类学看做是自然科学的一个分支。每一位科学家都是在前人工作的基础上进行调查研究的,他们发现他们自己认为有意义的问题,并通过观察和逻辑推理,为整个理论体系的发展做出贡献。从事相同或者相关课题研究的科学家之间需要相互协作。这种合作并不会形成学派,如果真的是这样的话,就会出现哲学学派或绘画学派。在科学领域内,传统学说和异端学说毫无地位。在这个领域内,最不良的影响莫过于试图妄想接受对教条主义的顶礼膜拜。老师所能做的就是帮助学生学习理解并运用科学方法。建立学派并不是老师的职责。

我将社会人类学视为关于人类社会的理论性自然科学,它对社会现象进行调查研究所采用的方法,在本质上与物理学和生物学采用的方法相似。如果有同仁响应的话,我愿意将这门学科称为“比较社会学”。重要的是学科本身,而不是它的命名。众所周知,一些人种学家或人类学家认为,将自然科学的理论研究方法运用到社会现象的研究上,是不可能的,至少是无回报可言的。对于这些科学家来讲,社会人类学,如我所定义的,并不存在,并且将永远不会存在。当然,他们会认为,我的评论是毫无意义的,或者至少他们无法理解我的真正意图。

我已将社会人类学定义为对人类社会的研究,而其他人将其定义为对文化的研究。或许,大家认为定义上的差异并不重要。事实上,这种差异会导致两种不同类型的研究,并且这两种研究类型很难在问题的表达上达成共识。

For a preliminary definition of social phenomena it seems sufficiently clear that what we have to deal with are relations of association between individual organisms. In a hive of bees there are the relations of association of the queen, the workers and the drones. There is the association of animals in a herd, of a mother-cat and her kittens. These are social phenomena; I do not suppose that anyone will call them cultural phenomena. In anthropology, of course, we are only concerned with human beings, and in social anthropology, as I define it, what we have to investigate are the forms of assoiation to be found amongst human beings.

Let us consider what are the concrete, observable facts with which the social anthropologist is concerned. If we set out to study, for example, the aboriginal inhabitants of a part of Australia, we find a certain number of individual human beings in a certain natural environment. We can observe the acts of behaviour of these individuals, including, of course, their acts of speech, and the material products of past actions. We do not observe a 'culture', since that word denotes, not any concrete reality, but an abstraction, and as it is commonly used a vague abstraction. But direct observation does reveal to us that these human beings are connected by a complex network of social relations. I use the term 'social structure' to denote this network of actually existing relations. It is this that I regard it as my business to study if I am working, not as an ethnologist or psychologist, but as a social anthropologist. I do not mean that the study of social structure is the whole of social anthropology, but I do regard it as being in a very important sense the most fundamental part of the science.

My view of natural science is that it is the systematic investigation of the structure of the universe as it is revealed to us through our senses. There are certain important separate branches of science, each of which deals with a certain class or kind of structures, the aim being to discover the characteristics of all structures of that kind. So atomic physics deals with the structure of atoms, chemistry with the structure of molecules, crystallography and colloidal chemistry with the structure of crystals and colloids, and anatomy and physiology with the structures of organisms. There is, therefore, I suggest, place

社会现象的最初的定义似乎清晰地表达了,我们所必须要涉及的是个体生物体之间的联合关系。在蜂箱内,体现了蜂王、工蜂和雄峰之间的联合关系。在动物群中,存在着动物之间的联合,如猫妈妈和小猫之间的联合。这些都是社会现象,我认为不会有人将其称为文化现象。当然,人类学仅仅关注人类,但是在社会人类学领域,正如我所定义的,我们要研究的是人类之间联合的形式。

我们接下来讨论社会人类学家所关注的具体事实。例如,我们对澳大利亚部分土著居民进行研究,发现在某种自然环境中生活着一定数量的人类。我们可以观察这些个体的行为活动,当然包括他们的语言行为以及过去活动中产生的物质产品。我们不会去研究所谓的“文化”,因为“文化”这个词蕴涵的是抽象的概念,无法表示具体的、真实的存在,我们常常用它指代模糊的、抽象的事物。但是直接的观察研究显示,人类是通过复杂的社会关系网络联系在一起的。这里使用术语“社会结构”来表示这个实际存在的关系网络。如果作为社会人类学家,而不是作为人种学者或心理学者,我会将“社会结构”视为我的科研任务。这并不是说,社会结构的研究是社会人类学的全部,但是我确实将其看做这门学科中最有意义和最基础的一部分。对于自然科学,我的态度是对宇宙万物的结构进行系统调查是必须的,因为我们是通过感官来接触它们的。自然科学拥有很多重要的独立的分支,每一个分支都涉及到对某种结构的研究,目的是为了发现该类型结构的所有特性。因此,原子物理学是关于原子结构的研究,化学是关于分子的研究,结晶学和胶质化学是关于晶体和胶质结构的研究,而解剖学和生理学是以有机体结构作为研究对象的。所以我

for a branch of natural science which will have for its task the discovery of the general characteristics of those social structures of which the component units are human beings.

Social phenomena constitute a distinct class of natural phenomena. They are all, in one way or another, connected with the existence of social structures, either being implied in or resulting from them. Social structures are just as real as are individual organisms. A complex organism is a collection of living cells and interstitial fluids arranged in a certain structure; and a living cell is similarly a structural arrangement of complex molecules. The physiological and psychological phenomena that we observe in the lives of organisms are not simply the result of the nature of the constituent moleules or atoms of which the organism is built up, but are the result of the structure in which they are united. So also the social phenomena which we observe in any human society are not the immediate result of the nature of individual human beings, but are the result of the social structure by which they are united.

It should be noted that to say we are studying social structures is not exactly the same thing as saying that we study social relations, which is how some sociologists define their subject. A particular social relation between two persons (unless they be Adam and Eve in the Garden of Eden) exists only as part of a wide network of social relations, involving many other persons, and it is this network which I regard as the object of our investigations.

I am aware, of course, that the term 'social structure' is used in a number of different senses, some of them very vague. This is unfortunately true of many other terms commonly used by anthropologists. The choice of terms and their definitions is a matter of scientific convenience, but one of the characteristics of a science as soon as it has passed the first formative period is the existence of technical terms which are used in the same precise meaning by all the students of that science. By this test, I regret to say, social anthropology reveals itself as not yet a formed science. One has therefore to select for oneself, for certain terms, definitions which seem to be the most convenient for the purpose of scientific analysis.

There are some anthropologists who use the term social structure to refer only to persistent social groups, such as nations, tribes and clans,

建议设立一门自然科学的分支，该分支以发掘由人类为组成单位的这些社会结构的总体特性作为主要任务。

社会现象组成了独特的自然现象。这些现象都是通过某种方式由真实存在的社会结构联系到一起的，它们或是在社会结构中体现出来或是源于社会结构。一个复杂有机体是活细胞和形成空隙的流体以某种结构结合在一起形成的，同样，一个活细胞是原子结构排列的联合体。我们观察到的关于有机体生命的生理学或心理学现象，并不仅仅产生于构成有机体的原子或分子的特性，而且还产生于将原子或分子联合起来的组织结构的特性。因此，同理可知，我们观察到的任何人类社会的社会现象，并不是直接源于个体特性，而是源于将个体结合到一起的社会结构。

值得注意的是，对社会结构的研究同对社会关系的研究并不完全一致，一些社会学家常常利用这种差异性来定义学科题目。两个人之间的特定社会关系（伊甸园中的亚当和夏娃的关系例外）存在于包含其他许多人的广泛的社会关系网络之中，我便将这种社会关系作为我们调查研究的对象。

当然，据我所知，“社会结构”包含多种含义，其中一些非常模糊。人类学家经常使用的一些术语也存在同样的问题。术语和定义的选择是出于科学上的便捷，但是如果一门科学度过了最初的成型阶段，那么该门科学的特点之一就是其既有的专门术语须在准确的意义上被其所有研究者沿用。很遗憾地告诉大家，这一验证过程表明社会人类学尚未成为一门成熟的学科。因此，对于某种术语，定义的选择还是因人而异，视情况而定的。

有一些人类学家用社会结构仅仅指代稳固存在的社会团体，例如民族、部落、宗族，这些团体仍然保留着自身的连续性和一致

which retain their continuity, their identity as individual groups, in spite of changes in their membership. Dr. Evans-Pritchard, in his recent admirable book on the Nuer, prefers to use the term social structure in this sense. Certainly the existence of such persistent social groups is an exceedingly important aspect of structure. But I find it more useful to include under the term social structure a good deal more than this.

In the first place, I regard as a part of the social structure all social relations of person to person. For example, the kinship structure of any society consists of a number of such dyadic relations, as between a father and son, or a mother's brother and his sister's son. In an Australian tribe the whole social structure is based on a network of such relations of person to person, established through genealogical connections.

Secondly, I include under social structure the differentiation of individuals and of classes by their social role. The differential social positions of men and women, of chiefs and commoners, of employers and employees, are just as much determinants of social relations as belonging to different clans or different nations.

In the study of social structure the concrete reality with which we are concerned is the set of actually existing relations, at a given moment of time, which link together certain human beings. It is on this that we can make direct observations. But it is not this that we attempt to describe in its particularity. Science (as distinguished from history or biography) is not concerned with the particular, the unique, but only with the general, with kinds, with events which recur. The actual relations of Tom, Dick and Harry or the behaviour of Jack and Jill may go down in our field note-books and may provide illustrations for a general description. But what we need for scientific purposes is an account of the form of the structure. For example, if in an Australian tribe I observe in a number of instances the behaviour towards one another of persons who stand in the relation of mother's brother and sister's son, it is in order that I may be able to record as precisely as possible the general or normal form of this relationship, abstracted from the variations of particular instances, though taking account of those variations.

性,尽管成员发生了变化。埃文斯－普里查德博士在他近期出版的令人拍案叫绝的论述努尔人的著作中使用了社会结构的这一层含义。当然,稳定的社会团体的存在是社会结构非常重要的方面。但是,我认为社会结构包括的内容远不止于此。

首先,我将社会中人与人间的关系视为社会结构的一部分。例如,任何社会的血族关系都包括像父亲和儿子、舅舅和外甥这种双重关系。在澳大利亚部落,整个社会结构是通过谱系关系建立在人与人之间关系的网络之上的。

第二,我认为社会结构还包括因社会分工不同而产生的个体差异和阶级差异。男人和女人、领导和普通民众、雇主和职员的不同社会地位,同样是社会关系的决定性因素,就像他们属于不同的宗族或民族那样。在对社会结构的研究中,我们所关注的具体事实是真实存在的关系,这种关系在某一时期将特定的人类连接起来。

关于这方面我们可以进行直接的调查。但是我们并不是要关注其特殊性。科学(与历史和传记有所不同)注重的不是特殊性、唯一性,而是全面性、多样性,以及反复发生的事件。汤姆、迪克和亨利之间的实际关系或杰克和吉尔的行为将记录在我们的工作日记中,并且会成为概括性描述的例证。但是,从科学研究的意图上考虑,我们需要的是对结构形态的记录。例如,如果在澳大利亚部落的一些事例中,我观察了存在于舅舅和外甥间的这种人与人的相互关系行为,我会尽可能准确地记录下由特殊事例的变化概括出来的这种关系的一般或正常的形态,但是我们会考虑到其中的某些变化。

This important distinction, between structure as an actually existing concrete reality, to be directly observed, and structural form, as what the field-worker describes, may be made clearer perhaps by a consideration of the continuity of social structure through time, a continuity which is not static like that of a building, but a dynamic continuity, like that of the organic structure of a living body. Throughout the life of an organism its structure is being constantly renewed: and similarly the social life constantly renews the social structure. Thus the actual relations of persons and groups of persons change from year to year, or even from day to day. New members come into a community by birth or immigration; others go out of it by death or emigration. There are marriages and divorces. Friends may become enemies, or enemies may make peace and become friends. But while the actual structure changes in this way, the general structural form may remain relatively constant over a longer or shorter period of time. Thus if I visit a relatively stable community and revisit it after an interval of ten years, I shall find that many of its members have died and others have been born; the members who still survive are now ten years older and their relations to one another may have changed in many ways. Yet I may find that the kinds of relations that I can observe are very little different from those observed ten years before. The structural form has changed little.

But, on the other hand, the structural form may change, sometimes gradually, sometimes with relative suddenness, as in revolutions and military conquests. But even in the most revolutionary changes some continuity of structure is maintained.

I must say a few words about the spatial aspect of social structure. It is rarely that we find a community that is absolutely isolated, having no outside contact. At the present moment of history, the network of social relations spreads over the whole world, without any absolute solution of continuity anywhere. This gives rise to a difficulty which I do not think that sociologists have really faced, the difficulty of defining what is meant by the term 'a society'. They do commonly talk of societies as if they were distinguishable, discrete entities, as, for example, when we are told that a society is an organism. Is the British Empire a society or a collection of societies? Is a Chinese

结构作为真实存在的有形实体,可对其进行直接研究,它与实地考察工作者所描述的结构形态之间的差别,经过长时间对社会结构连续性的考虑将会更加清晰。这种连续性不像建筑物那样是静止的,它是一种动态的连续,类似于活体的有机结构的连续。在有机体生命的整个过程中,其结构一直在不断地更新。同理,社会生活也在不断地更新社会结构。因此,人与人、团体与团体之间的关系年年不同,甚至日日不同。社会成员因生老病死或者移民而不断发生变化,并且,结婚和离异事件不断发生。朋友有可能成为敌人,敌人之间也可能和平相处甚至成为朋友。社会结构就是以这种方式发生变化的,但是,总的社会结构形态的相对稳定会在较长的时间或较短的时间内得以保持。这样的话,如果我参观一个相对稳定的社区,并且相隔十年之后再次去参观那个社区,会发现社会成员已经因生老病死改变了许多;仍然健在的成员比十年前苍老了许多,并且他们之间的关系较十年前也有了某种程度的变化。然而,我会发现这次观察到的种种关系与十年前的观察相差无几,而且社会结构形态也只是发生了很小的变化。

但是,另一方面,结构形态的变化,有时候循序渐进,有时候像革命和军事征服那样相对突然。但在最革命性的变革中,社会结构的连续性也仍然存在。

我要谈谈社会结构的空间方面。我们很难找到一种绝对孤立的和外界毫无联系的社团。在当今的历史时期,社会关系的网络遍布全世界,在任何地方都不存在完全绝对的连续性。这就产生了如何定义"社会"的困难,我想社会学家从未面临过这种困难。他们常常讨论的社会问题让人觉得好像社会是可辨别的、离散的实体,例如,就像我们被告知社会是一个有机体一样。大英

village a society, or is it merely a fragment of the Republic of China?

If we say that our subject is the study and comparison of human societies, we ought to be able to say what are the unit entities with which we are concerned.

If we take any convenient locality of a suitable size, we can study the structural system as it appears in and from that region, i. e. the network of relations connecting the inhabitants amongst themselves and with the people of other regions. We can thus observe, describe, and compare the systems of social structure of as many localities as we wish. To illustrate what I mean, I may refer to two recent studies from the University of Chicago, one of a Japanese village, Suye Mura, by Dr. John Embree, and the other of a French Canadian community, St. Denis, by Dr. Horace Miner.

Closely connected with this conception of social structure is the conception of 'social personality' as the position occupied by a human being in a social structure, the complex formed by all his social relations with others. Every human being living in society is two things: he is an individual and also a person. As an individual, he is a biological organism, a collection of a vast number of molecules organised in a complex structure, within which, as long as it persists, there occur physiological and psychological actions and reactions, processes and changes. Human beings as individuals are objects of study for physiologists and psychologists. The human being as a person is a complex of social relationships. He is a citizen of England, a husband and a father, a bricklayer, a member of a particular Methodist congregation, a voter in a certain constituency, a member of his trade union, an adherent of the Labour Party, and so on. Note that each of these descriptions refers to a social relationship, or to a place in a social structure. Note also that a social personality is something that changes during the course of the life of the person. As a person, the human being is the object of study for the social anthropologist. We cannot study persons except in terms of social structure, nor can we study social structure except in terms of the persons who are the units of which it is composed.

帝国是一个社会还是社会的联合体？一个中国村庄是一个社会，还是中华民国的个体部分？

如果说我们的课题是对人类社会作研究和比较，那么我们所关注的就是单位实体。

如果我们选择任一规模恰当又不方便的地域，我们就可以根据其表现出来的和来自这个地区以外的情况来研究它的结构体系，例如，将当地居民联系到一起的关系网络，以及与其他地区居民的关系网络。这样，我们可以观察、记录、比较尽可能多的居民群体的社会结构体系。为了阐释我所说的，我想列举芝加哥大学的两项最新研究成果，一个是约翰·恩布里博士对日本须惠村进行的考察；另一个是霍勒斯·迈纳对加拿大法语社区圣丹尼进行的考察。

与社会结构概念紧密相连的是社会特性概念，就像在社会结构中人类所占据的位置那样，所有的联合体均是由相互之间的社会关系形成的。每一个生活在社会中的人都具有两面性：他既是个体又是个人。作为个体，他是生物机体，是由千万个分子结合所形成的复杂机体，只要生物体存在，在其体内就会发生生理和心理上的活动、反应、过程和变化。作为个体的人类是生理学家和心理学家的研究对象。作为个人来讲，他体现了复杂的社会关系。他可以是英国公民、丈夫、父亲、砖匠、卫理公会派教徒、某选区的选民、工会成员、工党拥护者等等。可以看到，其中的任何一种描述都是指一种社会关系，或者指社会结构的某个结点。还可以看到，在人的生命过程中，社会特性会随之变化。作为个人，人类是社会人类学的研究对象。我们既不能依照社会结构研究个人，也不能依照构成社会结构的个人研究社会结构。

If you tell me that an individual and a person are after all really the same thing, I would remind you of the Christian creed. God is three persons, but to say that He is three individuals is to be guilty of a heresy for which men have been put to death. Yet the failure to distinguish individual and person is not merely a heresy in religion; it is worse than that; it is a source of confusion in science.

I have now sufficiently defined, I hope, the subject-matter of what I regard as an extremely important branch of social anthropology. The method to be adopted follows immediately from this definition. It must combine with the intensive study of single societies (i. e. of the structural systems observable in particular communities) the systematic comparison of many societies (or structural systems of different types). The use of comparison is indispensable. The study of a single society may provide materials for comparative study, or it may afford occasion for hypotheses, which then need to be tested by reference to other societies; it cannot give demonstrated results.

Our first task, of course, is to learn as much as we can about the varieties, or diversities, of structural systems. This requires field research. Many writers of ethnographical descriptions do not attempt to give us any systematic account of the social structure. But a few social anthropologists, here and in America, do recognise the importance of such data and their work is providing us with a steadily growing body of material for our study. Moreover, their researches are no longer confined to what are called 'primitive' societies, but extend to communities in such regions as Sicily, Ireland, Japan, Canada and the United States.

If we are to have a real comparative morphology of societies, however, we must aim at building up some sort of classification of types of structural systems. That is a complex and difficult task, to which I have myself devoted attention for thirty years. It is the kind of task that needs the co-operation of a number of students and I think I can number on my fingers those who are actively interested in it at the present time. Nevertheless, I believe some progress is being made. Such work, however, does not produce spectacular results and a book

如果你认为个体和个人是同一事物，那么我会用基督徒的信条来提示你。上帝是三个人，[1]但是如果说他是三个个体，就犯了足以致死的异端邪说罪。然而，不能将个体和个人区分开来，并不仅仅是宗教上的异教，更严重的是，它是科学概念混乱的根源。

但愿我已经清晰地定义了我认为重要的社会人类学分支的主题。我们采用的研究方法将源于该定义。它必须把对某一社会的深入调查研究（某一特定社区值得研究的结构体系）和对多个社会的系统对比（或者不同类型的结构体系对比）结合起来。对比方法的使用是必不可少的。对个别社会的研究可以为对比研究提供素材，或者它可以为假设提供机会，这种假设可以参照其他社会加以检验，但是对比方法无法得出论证性的结果。

当然，我们的首要任务就是尽可能多的了解结构体系的多样性或者差异性。这需要现场调查研究。许多人种学学者的记录并没有为我们提供任何关于社会结构的系统解释。但是，这里的和美洲的一些社会人类学家确实承认该数据资料的重要性，并且他们的工作为我们的研究提供了大量有效的素材。更重要的是，他们的研究不再局限于"原始"社会，而是扩展到如下领域，如西西里、爱尔兰、日本、加拿大和美国。

如果我们要真正掌握一种社会对比形态，我们必须致力于构建结构系统分类类型。这是一项复杂和艰巨的任务，我本人已经致力于这项研究达30年之久。这是一项需要多名学者共同合作才能进行的研究，目前对这项工作真正感兴趣的人屈指可数。然而，我相信这项研究工作正在取得很大的进步。当然，这种研究工作不会产生引人注目的成绩，关于这一学科的书籍也不会成为人

〔1〕 圣父、圣子、圣灵三位同体。

on the subject would certainly not be an anthropological best-seller.

We should remember that chemistry and biology did not become fully formed sciences until considerable progress had been made with the systematic classification of the things they were dealing with, substances in the one instance and plants and animals in the other.

Besides this morphological study, consisting in the definition, comparison and classification of diverse structural systems, there is a physiological study. The problem here is: How do structural systems persist? What are the mechanisms which maintain a network of social relations in existence, and how do they work? In using the terms morphology and physiology, I may seem to be returning to the analogy between society and organism which was so popular with medieval philosophers, was taken over and often misused by nineteenth century sociologists, and is completely rejected by many modern writers. But analogies, properly used, are important aids to scientific thinking and there is a real and significant analogy between organic structure and social structure.

In what I am thus calling social physiology we are concerned not only with social structure, but with every kind of social phenomenon. Morals, law, etiquette, religion, government, and education are all parts of the complex mechanism by which a social structure exists and persists. If we take up the structural point of view, we study these things, not in abstraction or isolation, but in their direct and indirect relations to social structure, i. e. with reference to the way in which they depend upon, or affect, the social relations between persons and groups of persons. I cannot do more here than offer a few brief illustrations of what this means.

Let us first consider the study of language. A language is a connected set of speech usages observed within a defined speech-community. The existence of speech-communities and their sizes are features of social structure. There is, therefore, a certain very general relation between social structure and language. But if we consider the special characteristics of a particular language—its phonology, its morphology and even to a great extent its vocabulary—there is no direct connection of either one-sided or mutual determination between these and the special characteristics of the social structure of the community within

类学的畅销书。

我们应该记得在化学和生物学对它们研究的物质或动植物所做的分类取得相当的进展以前,它们尚未成为成熟的科学。

形态学是对不同结构体系的定义、对比和分类进行研究的科学,生理学亦是如此。存在的问题是:结构体系如何存在?什么是维持社会关系网络的机制,以及它如何运行?在使用形态学和生理学这两个术语之前,我想再讨论一下社会和有机体之间的相似性,对于中世纪的哲学家而言,这是一个热门话题,19 世纪的社会学家常常滥用这种相似性,而现代学者完全拒绝这种相似性。但是,如果能够适当地运用这种相似性,将会成为科学思考的重要辅助手段,并且在有机体结构和社会结构之间确实存在着重要的相似性。在我定义的社会生理学领域,我们不仅对社会结构而且对社会现象感兴趣。道德、法律、礼节、宗教、政府和教育均属于社会结构赖以生存和维持的复杂机制的一部分。如果我们要采纳这种结构的观点,就不能以抽象或者孤立的方式,而是得从与社会结构的直接和间接关系方面进行研究,例如,关于它们所依赖的或影响的人与人、人群与人群之间的社会关系形式。这里我只能对其做简要的说明。

首先,我们将讨论有关语言的研究学习。语言是可以在特定语言社区内观察到的语词用法的结合体系。语言社区的存在及其规模是社会结构的特征。因此,在社会结构和语言之间存在着非常普遍的联系。但是,如果考虑特定语言的特殊特征——其语音体系、词态学甚至词汇——那么在这种语言和使用这种语言的社区结构的特性之间并不存在单方面的或者相互决定的直接联系。我们可以很容易想象到,两个社会的社会结构相似,但语言

which the language is spoken. We can easily conceive that two societies might have very similar forms of social structure and very different kinds of language, or vice versa. The coincidence of a particular form of social structure and a particular language in a given community is always the result of historical accident. There may, of course, be certain indirect, remote interactions between social structure and language, but these would seem to be of minor importance. Thus the general comparative study of languages can be profitably carried out as a relatively independent branch of science, in which the language is considered in abstraction from the social structure of the community in which it is spoken.

But, on the other hand, there are certain features of linguistic history which are specifically connected with social structure. As structural phenomena may be instanced the process by which Latin, from being the language of the small region of Latium, became the language of a considerable part of Europe, displacing the other Italic languages, Etruscan, and many Celtic languages; and the subsequent reverse process by which Latin split up into a number of diverse local forms of speech, which ultimately became the various Romance languages of today.

Thus the spread of language, the unification of a number of separate communities into a single speech-community, and the reverse process of subdivision into different speech-communities, are phenomena of social structure. So also are those instances in which, in societies having a class structure, there are differences of speech usage in different classes.

I have considered language first, because linguistics is, I think, the branch of social anthropology which can be most profitably studied without reference to social structure. There is a reason for this. The set of speech usages which constitute a language does form a system, and systems of this kind can be compared in order to discover their common general, or abstract, characters, the determination of which can give us laws, which will be specifically laws of linguistics.

Let us consider very briefly certain other branches of social anthropology and their relation to the study of social structure. If we take the social life of a local community over a period, let us say a year, we can observe a certain sum total of activities carried out by the persons who compose it. We can also observe a certain apportionment of these activities, one person doing certain things, another doing others. This apportionment of activities, equivalent to what is sometimes called the social division of labour, is an important feature of the social structure. Now activities are

不同,反之亦然。在某个社区内,某一种社会结构和特定语言的吻合常常是历史事件的结果。当然,社会结构和语言之间存在某种间接的和细微的相互作用,但是这些作用似乎及其微小。因而,语言的一般对比研究可以看做是科学的一个相对独立的分支来进行,可以将语言和使用该语言的社区结构分离出来考虑。

但是,另一方面,语言学历史的一些特征与社会结构有着确切的联系。拉丁语从拉丁姆地区的语言演变成欧洲绝大地区的语言从而代替了其他语言如意大利语、埃特鲁斯坎语以及各种克尔特语,这一过程可以证明语言是一种结构现象。但是,在接下来的过程中,从拉丁语中分化出一系列地方的语言形式,这些语言就是现在的罗曼诺语言。

语言的传播、若干个独立社区联合成一个语言社区以及相反的分化过程都属于社会结构现象。在任何社会都存在阶级结构,不同的阶级结构语言惯用法不同,这同样属于社会结构现象。

我最先讨论语言,因为我认为,语言学作为社会人类学的分支,可以不参照社会结构而对其进行有效的研究。对此我将加以解释。构成语言的惯用法确实形成了一套体系,并且为了探索其共同的概括性或抽象性的特征可以将这一类型的体系加以比较,这样可以为我们提供一些规则,尤其是语言学规则。

我们简单讨论一下社会人类学的其他分支及其与社会结构研究的关系。如果对一个地方社区的社会生活观察一段时间,假设时间为一年,我们可以观察到构成该社区人群的一系列行为活动。同时我们还可以获得关于对这些行为的分配,即不同个体所从事的活动具有的差异性。行为的分配类似于我们所说的社会劳动分工,它是社会结构的一个重要特征。现在,人们从事

carried out because they provide some sort of' ' gratification ' , as I propose to call it, and the characteristic feature of social life is that activities of certain persons provide gratifications for other persons. In a simple instance, when an Australian blackfellow goes hunting, he provides meat, not only for himself, but for his wife and children and also for other relatives to whom it is his duty to give meat when he has it. Thus in any society there is not only an apportionment of activities, but also an apportionment of the gratifications resulting therefrom, and some sort of social machinery, relatively simple or, sometimes, highly complex, by which the system works.

It is this machinery, or certain aspects of it, that constitutes the special subject-matter studied by the economists. They concern themselves with what kinds and quantities of goods are produced, how they are distributed (i. e. their flow from person to person, or region to region), and the way in which they are disposed of. Thus what are called economic institutions are extensively studied in more or less complete abstraction from the rest of the social system. This method does undoubtedly provide useful results, particularly in the study of complex modern societies. Its weaknesses become apparent as soon as we attempt to apply it to the exchange of goods in what are called primitive societies.

The economic machinery of a society appears in quite a new light if it is studied in relation to the social structure. The exchange of goods and services is dependent upon, is the result of, and at the same time is a means of maintaining a certain structure, a network of relations between persons and collections of persons. For the economists and politicians of Canada the potlatch of the Indians of the north-west of America was simply wasteful foolish ness and it was therefore forbidden. For the anthropologist it was the machinery for maintaining a social structure of lineages, clans and moieties, with which was combined an arrangement of rank defined by privileges.

Any full understanding of the economic institutions of human societies requires that they should be studied from two angles. From one of these the economic system is viewed as the mechanism by which goods of various kinds and in various quantities are produced, transported and transferred, and utilised. From the other the economic system is a set of relations between persons and groups which maintains, and is maintained by, this exchange or circulation of goods and

某种行为活动，因为它们能产生“满足感”，就像我所说的那样；并且社会活动的特点就是某一个人的行为活动能为他人创造满足感。举一个简单的例子，一名澳洲土人去打猎，他猎取的肉不仅用来自己食用，而且还可供他的妻子、孩子及其他亲戚食用。对于他来说，将获得的肉分给他人是他的责任。因此，在任何社会中不仅存在行为的分配而且存在由此产生的满足感的分配，以及支撑社会体系运转的社会机制，有的相对简单，有的却高度复杂。

社会机制或者其某一方面构成了经济学家的主要研究课题。他们关注物质生产的种类和数量及其分配问题（如，在个人之间，还是在地区之间流通）和支配方式。因此，我们对所说的经济制度做的广泛的研究都是在几乎完全脱离其他社会体系下的情况进行的。毫无疑问这种方法提供了有效的研究成果，尤其有益于对复杂的现代社会的研究。但是当我们将其运用到所说的原始社会的商品交换中去时，其缺点就开始表现出来。

如果从社会结构角度对一个社会的经济机制进行研究，其前景将会一片光明。商品和服务的交换依赖于某种结构，同时也是维持该结构的一种手段，人与人之间或者群体之间的关系网便构成了这种结构。加拿大的经济学家和政治家认为，美洲西北部印第安人的赠财宴是一种愚蠢的浪费行为，因此加以禁止。可是，人类学家又认为这却是维持世系群、氏族以及半偶族社会结构的一种机制，并且该机制与特权者制定的等级排列结合起来。

需要从两个角度对人类社会的经济制度进行研究，才能充分理解其内涵。其一，经济制度被看做是支配不同种类和数量商品生产、运输、调度和使用的机制。其二，经济制度代表了人与人之间、群体之间的一系列关系，并且保证受制于商品和服务的交换

services. From the latter point of view, the study of the economic life of societies takes its place as part of the general study of social structure.

Social relations are only observed, and can only be described, by reference to the reciprocal behaviour of the persons related. The form of a social structure has therefore to be described by the patterns of behaviour to which individuals and groups conform in their dealings with one another. These patterns are partially formulated in rules which, in our own society, we distinguish as rules of etiquette, of morals and of law. Rules, of course, only exist in their recognition by the members of the society; either in their verbal recognition, when they are stated as rules, or in their observance in behaviour. These two modes of recognition, as every field-worker knows, are not the same thing and both have to be taken into account. .

If I say that in any society the rules of etiquette, morals and law are part of the mechanism by which a certain set of social relations is maintained in existence, this statement will, I suppose, be greeted as a truism. But it is one of those truisms which many writers on human society verbally accept and yet ignore in theoretical discussions, or in their descriptive analyses. The point is not that rules exist in every society, but that what we need to know for a scientific understanding is just how these things work in general and in particular instances.

Let us consider, for example, the study of law. If you examine the literature on jurisprudence you will find that legal institutions are studied for the most part in more or less complete abstraction from the rest of the social system of which they are a part. This is doubtless the most convenient method for lawyers in their professional studies. But for any scientific investigation of the nature of law it is insufficient. The data with which a scientist must deal are events which occur and can be observed. In the field of law, the events which the social scientist can observe and thus take as his data are the proceedings that take place in courts of justice. These are the reality, and for the social anthropologist they are the mechanism or process by which certain definable social relations between persons and groups are restored, maintained or modified. Law is a part of the machinery by which a certain social structure is maintained. The system of laws of a particular society can only be fully understood if it is studied in relation to the social structure, and inversely the understanding of the social

或流通。从第二种观点来看,对社会经济生活的研究属于一般的社会结构研究范畴。

社会关系只能通过参照相关人群的互惠行为来观察和记录。因此,社会结构形式便通过个体和群体处理相互关系时所遵循的行为方式来记录社会结构形式。这些行为活动有一部分是依照我们所处社会的礼节、道德和法律的规则来形成的。当然,规则只有被社会成员认同才存在,只要它们被宣布为规则,人们即可能在口头上承认它或者在行为上遵循它。每个实地工作者都清楚,这两种认同方式截然不同,而且二者都必须加以考虑。

如果我说,在任何社会,礼节、道德和法律的规则属于维持某种现存社会关系的机制的一部分,我想这种观点将被视做真理。但是许多社会人类学者在口头上认可的真理却在理论讨论或描述分析时遭到了忽视。问题的关键并不是每个社会都存在规则,而在于我们必须要科学地理解这些规则如何在一般和特定事例中发挥作用。

我们以法律为例讨论一下这个问题。如果查看法学文献,会发现对大部分法律制度的研究几乎完全脱离同属于一个社会的其他制度。对法学家而言这无疑是进行专业研究最便捷的方法。但是这远远不足以对法律实质进行科学探索。科学家必须要处理的资料是那些已经发生并且可以观察的事件。在法律领域,社会科学家能够观察并视之为资料的是发生在审判法庭上的程序。这些程序都是真实的,并且社会人类学家认为它们是重建、维持或改正可定义的社会关系所必需的机制或程序。法律是维持社会结构的机制的一个部分。一个特定社会的法律体系只有参照社会结构来研究才能被充分理解,反过来,对社会结构的理解

structure requires, amongst other things, a systematic study of the legal institutions.

I have talked about social relations, but I have not so far offered you a precise definition. A social relation exists between two or more individual organisms when there is some adjustment of their respective interests, by convergence of interest, or by limitation of conflicts that might arise from divergence of interests. I use the term 'interest' here in the widest possible sense, to refer to all behaviour that we regard as purposive. To speak of an interest implies a subject and an object and a relation between them. Whenever we say that a subject has a certain interest in an object we can state the same thing by saying that the object has a certain value for the subject. Interest and value are correlative terms, which refer to the two sides of an asymmetrical relation.

Thus the study of social structure leads immediately to the study of interests or values as the determinants of social relations. A social relation does not result from similarity of interests, but rests either on the mutual interest of persons in one another, or on one or more common interests, or on a combination of both of these. The simplest form of social solidarity is where two persons are both interested in bringing about a certain result and co-operate to that end. When two or more persons have a *common interest* in an object, that object can be said to have a *social value* for the persons thus associated. If, then, practically all the members of a society have an interest in the observance of the laws, we can say that the law has a social value. The study of social values in this sense is therefore a part of the study of social structure.

It was from this point of view that in an early work I approached the study of what can conveniently be called ritual values, i. e. the values expressed in rites and myths. It is perhaps again a truism to say that religion is the cement which holds society together. But for a scientific understanding we need to know just how it does this, and that is a subject for lengthy investigations in many different forms of society.

As a last example let me mention the study of magic and witchcraft, on which there is an extensive anthropological literature. I would point to Dr. Evans-Pritchard's work on the Zande as an illuminating example of what can be done when these things are systematically

也需要对法律制度进行系统的研究。

我们已经讨论过社会关系,但是目前还没有给出确切的定义。社会关系存在于两个或多个单独有机体之间,即有机体各自的利益通过利益共同化或因利益分歧而导致的有限冲突进行协调。“利益”这个词含义广泛,这里指被视为具有目的性的所有行为。提及利益,就会涉及到主体客体及其相互关系。当我们说主体对客体有某种利益时,也可以说客体对主体具有某种价值。利益和价值是相互关联的术语,用来指不对称关系的两个方面。

所以对于社会结构的研究会直接引出对利益及价值的研究,而这种利益及价值又是社会关系的决定因素。社会关系不是来源于相似利益而是存在于人们之间的相互利益或者是一个或多个共同利益,要么就是来源于以上两者的共同作用。社会稳定性最简单的形式存在于两个人都对将要产生的特定结果有兴趣,并为达到该目的而共同合作。当两个或两个以上的人对某客体产生共同兴趣,那么可以说该客体对于与其相关联的人具有社会价值。如果社会所有成员对于遵守法律有共同兴趣,那么我们可以断言该法律有社会价值。因此在此意义上对于社会价值的研究是社会结构研究的一部分。

从这个观点来看,我早期所从事的研究可以称作仪式价值研究,也就是在仪式和神话中所表现的价值。宗教是把社会成员紧紧黏附在一起的黏着剂,这可能又是一个永恒的真理。但是为了科学上的理解,我们要知道宗教是如何做到这点的,而这是需要在不同形式的社会中进行长期的调查研究的一个课题。

在最后的例子中我要提及的是对巫术和魔法的研究,关于此项研究有广泛的人类学文献。埃文斯－普里查德博士的关于赞

investigated in terms of the part they play in the social relations of the members of a community.

From the point of view that I have attempted briefly to describe, social institutions, in the sense of standardised modes of behaviour, constitute the machinery by which a social structure, a network of social relations, maintains its existence and its continuity. I hesitate to use the term 'function', which in recent years has been so much used and misused in a multitude of meanings, many of them very vague. Instead of being used, as scientific terms ought to be, to assist in making distinctions, it is now used to confuse things that ought to be distinguished. For it is often employed in place of the more ordinary words 'use' 'purpose', and 'meaning'. It seems to me more convenient and sensible, as well as more scholarly, to speak of the use or uses of an axe or digging stick, the meaning of a word or symbol, the purpose of an act of legislation, rather than to use the word function for these various things. 'Function' has been a very useful technical term in physiology and by analogy with its use in that science it would be a very convenient means of expressing an important concept in social science. As I have been accustomed to use the word, following Durkheim and others, I would define the social function of a socially standardised mode of activity, or mode of thought, as its relation to the social structure to the existence and continuity of which it makes some contribution. Analogously, in a living organism, the physiological function of the beating of the heart, or the secretion of gastric juices, is its relation to the organic structure to the existence or continuity of which it makes its contribution. It is in this sense that I am interested in such things as the social function of the punishment of crime, or the social function of the totemic rites—of Australian tribes, or of the funeral rites of the Andaman Islanders. But this is not what either Professor Malinowski or Professor Lowie means by functional anthropology.

Besides these two divisions of the study of social structure, which I have called social morphology and social physiology, there is a third, the investigation of the processes by which social structures change, of how new forms of structures come into existence. Studies of social change in the non-literate societies have necessarily been almost entirely confined to one special kind of process of change, the modification of the social life under the influence or domination of European invaders or conquerors.

德人的著作就是个明显的例子，它通过系统调查巫术和魔法在社区成员的社会关系中所起的作用来说明我们应该做什么。

从我要简要描述的观点来看，在行为模式的标准化意义上，社会制度包含了一个机制，通过这个机制，社会结构即社会关系的一个网络实现了维持其存在和延续的目的。对与“功能”这一术语，我在使用时很迟疑，因为近几年中被频繁使用，它的多种词意也被滥用，大多用法含混不清。它没有起到科学术语应该起到的作用，即帮助人们分清事物，相反却使本应相互区别的事物相互混淆。它常被用来替代比较普通的词汇，例如“使用”、“目标”及“意义”。我认为，分别用斧子或挖土棍的用途、词或符号的意义，立法的目的比笼统地用“它们都有功能”更方便、明了、学术化。在生理学中，“功能”业已成为一个相当有用的科学术语，通过与它在科学中使用的类比，表明它能够在社会科学中方便地表述重要概念。与杜尔干和其他人一样，因为我已经习惯使用这个词，我将把行为模式社会标准化或思维模式定义成它和社会结构、它对社会存在及延续所起作用的关系。与此类似的是，在一活着的生命有机体中，生理机能如跳动的心脏或者胃液的分泌是与机体结构相关联的，并为其存在和持续发挥作用。正是基于此种意义，我对这样事物的社会功能产生兴趣，如犯罪惩戒、澳大利亚图腾部落、安达曼岛岛民葬礼仪式。但这与马林诺夫基和罗维教授所讲的功能人类学是不同的。

除了社会形态学和社会生理学这两个我已经提到的社会结构分支，还有第三个分支，即对社会结构的变化过程、新结构形式形成的研究。对前文字社会的变化研究必然会局限于一种变化的过程，即欧洲人侵者或征服者的统治影响了该社会的变化。

It has recently become the fashion amongst some anthropologists to treat changes of this kind in terms of what is called 'culture contact'. By that term we can understand the one-sided or two-sided effects of interaction between two societies, groups, classes or regions having different forms of social life, different institutions, usages and ideas. Thus in the eighteenth century there was an important exchange of ideas between France and Great Britain, and in the nineteenth century there was a marked influence of German thought on both France and England. Such interactions are, of course, a constant feature of social life, but they need not necessarily involve any marked change of social structure.

The changes that are taking place in the non-literate peoples of Africa are of a very different kind. Let us consider an African colony or possession of a European nation. There is a region that was formerly inhabited by Africans with their own social structure. Europeans, by peaceful or forceful means, establish control over the region, under what we call a 'colonial' régime. A new social structure comes into existence and then undergoes development. The population now includes a certain number of Europeans —government officials, missionaries, traders and in some instances settlers. The social life of the region is no longer simply a process depending on the relations and interactions of the native peoples. There grows up a new political and economic structure in which the Europeans, even though few in numbers, exercise dominating influence. Europeans and Africans constitute different classes within the new structure, with different languages, different customs and modes of life, and different sets of ideas and values. A convenient term for societies of this kind would be 'composite' societies; the term 'plural' societies has also been suggested. A complex example of a composite society is provided by the Union of South Africa with its single political and economic structure and a population including English-speaking and Afrikaans-speaking peoples of European descent, the so-called 'coloured people' of the Cape Province, progeny of Dutch and Hottentots, the remaining Hottentots, the 'Malays' of Cape Town, descendants of persons from the Malay Archipelago, Hindus and Mohammedans from India and their descendants, and a number of Bantu tribes who constitute the majority of the population of the Union taken as a whole.

The study of composite societies, the description and analysis of

近来,在一些人类学家中流行着一种做法,即把这种形式的变化称作“文化接触”。通过该术语,我们可以理解具有不同形式社会生活、制度、风俗和观念的两个社会、群体、阶级、宗教之间单方面或双方面的相互作用。因此,在18世纪英国和法国间有着重要的思想交流;在19世纪来自于德国的思想影响着法国和英国。当然,这样的相互作用是社会生活一个不变特征,但不一定会涉及显著的社会结构的变化。

在非洲前文字民族发生的变化有很大不同。现在我们再看一个非洲殖民地即欧洲国家领属地的例子。在这个地区以前居住着有自己社会结构的非洲人,但欧洲人通过温和或暴力的手段,统治了该地区,也就是我们常说的“殖民”统治。随之,一个新的社会结构诞生了并开始发展。这些人口中包含了一定数量的欧洲人,他们是政府官员、传教士、从商者和各种移民。因此,该地区的社会生活不再仅仅取决于当地人互相作用的关系。出现了新的政治经济结构,欧洲人尽管占人口少数却支配着影响力。在这个新的结构中,欧洲人和非洲人因有着不同的语言、不同的服饰、不同的生活模式、不同的思想观与价值观,所以组成了不同的阶级。可以用“复合”这个简便的术语来命名这种社会,但也有人建议用“多元”来称呼它。有着单一政治经济结构的南非联盟就是复合社会的复杂例子之一。南非联盟的人口中包括说英语和阿非利坎语的欧洲后裔;还有开普省的有色人种;荷兰与霍屯督后裔;开普敦马来人也就是马来群岛的马来人的后裔;还有印度人、穆斯林教徒的后裔;以及班图人,以上的这些民族和宗族构成了大多数南非联盟人口。

对于复合社会的研究,以及对它的变化过程的描述和分析是一项

the processes of change in them, is a complex and difficult task. The attempt to simplify it by considering the process as being one in which two or more 'cultures' interact, which is the method suggested by Malinowski in his Introduction to Memorandum XV of the International Institute of African Language and Culture on 'Methods of Study of Culture Contact in Africa' (1938), is simply a way of avoiding the reality. For what is happening in South Africa, for example, is not the interaction of British culture, Afrikander (or Boer) culture, Hottentot culture, various Bantu cultures and Indian culture, but the interaction of individuals and groups within an established social structure which is itself in process of change. What is happening in a Transkeian tribe, for example, can only be described by recognising that the tribe has been incorporated into a wide political and economic structural system.

For the scientific study of primitive societies in conditions in which they are free from the domination by more advanced societies which result in these composite societies, we have unfortunately an almost complete lack of authentic historical data. We cannot study, but can only speculate about, the processes of change that took place in the past of which we have no record. Anthropologists speculate about former changes in the societies of the Australian aborigines, or the inhabitants of Melanesia, but such speculations are not history and can be of no use in science. For the study of social change in societies other than the composite societies to which reference has been made we have to rely on the work of historians dealing with authentic records.

You are aware that in certain anthropological circles the term 'evolutionary anthropologist' is almost a term of abuse. It is applied, however, without much discrimination. Thus Lewis Morgan is called an evolutionist, although he rejected the theory of organic evolution and in relation to society believed, not in evolution, but in progress, which he conceived as the steady material and moral improvement of mankind from crude stone implements and sexual promiscuity to the steam engines and monogamous marriage of Rochester, N. Y. But even such antievolutionists as Boas believe in progress.

复杂而困难的工作。如果试图把两个或多个文化间的互相作用简单地认为是一个过程的话,正如马林诺夫斯基在他的著作《第15届非洲语言、文化国际机构备忘录·非洲文化接触研究方法·引言》中提出的一样,这仅仅是避开现实的做法。因为在南非,目前进行的是在一个本身就是一个变化过程,而且已经建立了的社会结构中个体间和群体间的相互作用,而不是英国文化、阿非利坎(或布尔)文化、霍屯督文化、各种班图文化及印度文化间的相互作用。也就是说,只有认识到特兰斯凯部落已经容入到一个宽泛的政治经济结构体系中这一现实时,我们才能描述那里发生的事件。

对于一个原始社会的科学研究要建立在不受比其先进社会的影响的条件下,然而不幸的是对于这种真实的历史数据我们几乎完全缺乏。我们没有史料可供研究,而只能臆测发生在过去的变化过程,而这种过程是没有任何记载的。人类学家推测以前发生在澳大利亚土著人社会、美拉尼西亚居民社会中的变化,但这种推测没有历史记载,在科学中是无用的。为了研究社会变化而不是研究已经有史可参考的复合社会,我们就不得不依赖于历史学家做出的真实记载。

你或许意识到了在一定的社会学领域中,“进化论人类学家”几乎是个被滥用的术语。这个术语没加区分就被应用。路易斯·莫根被称作进化论主义者,尽管他反对机体进化理论,并且在社会关系上他相信进步论而不是进化论。这种进步是人类持续的物质、道德的改进,即从野蛮的石器时代和性乱交到蒸汽机及纽约罗切斯特地区的稳定的一夫一妻制婚姻。但即使是像博厄斯一样的反进化论主义者也相信进步。

It is convenient, I think, to use the term ‘progress’ for the process by which human beings attain to greater control over the physical environment through the increase of knowledge and improvement of technique by inventions and discoveries. The way in which we are now able to destroy considerable portions of cities from the air is one of the latest striking results of progress. Progress is not the same thing as social evolution, but it is very closely connected with it.

Evolution, as I understand the term, refers specifically to a process of emergence of new forms of structure. Organic evolution has two important features: (1) in the course of it a small number of kinds of organisms have given rise to a very much larger number of kinds; (2) more complex forms of organic structure have come into existence by development out of simpler forms. While I am unable to attach any definite meaning to such phrases as the evolution of culture or the evolution of language, I think that social evolution is a reality which the social anthropologist should recognise and study. Like organic evolution, it can be defined by two features. There has been a process by which, from a small number of forms of social structure, many different forms have arisen in the course of history; that is, there has been a process of diversification. Secondly, throughout this process more complex forms of social structures have developed out of, or replaced, simpler forms.

Just how structural systems are to be classified with reference to their greater or less complexity is a problem requiring investigation. But there is evidence of a fairly close correlation between complexity and another feature of structural systems, namely, the extent of the field of social relations. In a structural system with a narrow total social field, an average or typical person is brought into direct and indirect social relations with only a small number of other persons. In systems of this type we may find that the linguistic community—the body of persons who speak one language—numbers from 250 to 500, while the political community is even smaller, and economic relations by the exchange of goods and services extend only over a very narrow range. Apart from the differentiation by sex and age, there is very little differentiation of social role between persons or classes. We can contrast with this the systems of social structure that we observe today

我认为使用“进步”一词是方便的，正是由于知识的增长及由发明和发现引发的技术改进使人类获得了更多的对自然界的控制。从空中就能把一些城市摧毁就是这种进步的最新的令人触目惊心的结果之一。尽管进步与社会进化是不一样的，但却和社会进化联系密切。

进化，从我的理解来看，特指的是一种新的结构形式的出现过程。有机体进化有以下两个重要特点：(1)在进化过程中，少量种类的有机体生成大量种类的有机体；(2)简单形式的有机体生成形式更加复杂的有机体结构。虽然我不能够对像文化进化或语言进化这样的短语下一个确切的定义，但我认为社会进化是社会学家应该认识到并展开研究的学科。和有机体进化一样，社会进化有两个特征：第一，它是一个社会历史过程即一个多样化的过程，在这样的一个过程中，大量不同的社会形式是由少量的社会结构形式衍生出来的。第二，在这个过程中，复杂的社会结构形式由简单的社会形式派生出来并取而代之。

如何根据社会结构体系的复杂与否来划分它们是个需要研究的问题。有根据表明，社会结构体系的复杂程度与社会体系的其他特征，也就是社会关系领域的广度有着密切的关系。在一个范围较小的社会结构体系中，一个普通人或典型人只是与其他的为数不多的人产生直接或间接的社会关系。在这种社会结构体系中，我们可以发现这样的一个语言社区，也就是说同一种语言的人群，他们人数为 250 人到 500 人，同时他们的政治社区更小，通过交换物品和服务而产生的经济关系只涉及到一个狭窄的范围。除了性别和年龄上的区分外，在人与人之间的社会角色或阶级上区别很小。我们可以把这种社会结构体系与我们今天看到

in England or the United States. Thus the process of human history to which I think the term social evolution may be appropriately applied might be defined as the process by which wide-range systems of social structure have grown out of, or replaced, narrow-range systems. Whether this view is acceptable or not, I suggest that the concept of social evolution is one which requires to be defined in terms of social structure.

There is no time on this occasion to discuss the relation of the study of social structure to the study of culture. For an interesting attempt to bring the two kinds of study together I would refer you to Mr. Gregory Bateson's book *Naven*. I have made no attempt to deal with social anthropology as a whole and with all its various branches and divisions. I have endeavoured only to give you a very general idea of the kind of study to which I have found it scientifically profitable to devote a considerable and steadily increasing proportion of my time and energy. The only reward that I have sought I think I have in some measure found—something of the kind of insight into the nature of the world of which we are part that only the patient pursuit of the method of natural science can afford.

的英国和美国的社会结构体系作一比较。因此，我认为用“社会进化”这个术语来说明人类历史是恰当的，这个人类历史过程可以被定义为一个过程，在这个过程中更宽泛的社会结构体系产生于狭小的社会结构体系或替代了狭小的社会结构体系。不管这种观点是否可以接受，我建议社会进化这个概念是一个需要在社会结构意义上进行定义的一个概念。

在此我没有太多时间探讨社会结构研究和文化研究的关系。我想向你们推荐格雷戈里·贝特森先生的《钠温》一书，它是把以上两种研究有意思地结合起来的一种尝试。我不想试图把社会人类学作为一个整体或把它作为不同的分支来探讨。我只是向你们展示了一个大概的关于此问题的研究，我觉得对此付出大量的时间和不间断的努力是有科学成效的。我认为我获得的唯一回报就是我找到了一种洞察世界本质的工具，我们是这个自然界的一部分，耐心地寻找，这种自然科学研究方法才会实现。

CHAPTER XI

Social Sanctions[①]

In any community there are certain modes of behaviour which are usual and which characterise that particular community. Such modes of behaviour may be called usages. All social usages have behind them the authority of the society, but among them some are sanctioned and others are not. A sanction is a reaction on the part of a society or of a considerable number of its members to a mode of behaviour which is thereby approved (positive sanctions) or disapproved (negative sanctions). Sanctions may further be distinguished according to whether they are diffuse or organised; the former are spontaneous expressions of approval or disapproval by members of the community acting as individuals, while the latter are social actions carried out according to some traditional and recognised procedure. It is a significant fact that in all human societies the negative sanctions are more definite than the positive. Social obligations may be defined as rules of behaviour the failure to observe which entails a negative sanction of some sort. These are thus distinguished from non-obligatory social usages, as, for example, customary technical procedures.

The sanctions existing in a community constitute motives in the individual for the regulation of his conduct in conformity with usage. They are effective, first, through the desire of the individual to obtain

---

① Reprinted from the *Encyclopædia of the Social Sciences*, Macmillan Co., New York, 1933, Vol. XIII, pp. 531-4.

第十一章　社会裁定[①]

在任何一个群体中，都存在一定的行为模式，这种行为模式被称为“习俗”。在所有的社会习俗的背后都存在着某种社会权威，但是，某些习俗得到允许，而另一些并没有得到允许。裁定是指社会的部分或相当大部分成员对某种行为模式的反应，这种反应可能是赞同（正面裁定），也可能是反对（负面裁定）。裁定又可以被划分为泛化裁定和组织裁定。泛化裁定是一种自发表达，源于作为单独行为个人的群体成员对于某种行为模式的赞同或反对；而组织裁定是一种社会活动，按照某种传统的、公认的程序进行。在所有的人类社会中，负面裁定比正面裁定更加明确，这一点具有非常重要的意义。社会义务可以被定义为行为规则，任何违反这种行为规则的人就要承担某种负面裁定。因而，它们不同于那种非义务性的社会习俗，如传统工艺程序等。

一个群体中裁定的力量促使人们遵守社会习俗，从而对自身行为进行调节。裁定的有效性首先源于人们渴望获得同伴的赞

---

① 重印自《社会科学百科全书》，麦克米兰公司 1933 年纽约版，第 13 卷，第 531 ~ 534 页。

the approbation and to avoid the disapprobation of his fellows, to win such rewards or to avoid such punishment as the community offers or threatens; and, second, through the fact that the individual learns to react to particular modes of behaviour with judgments of approval and disapproval in the same way as do his fellows, and therefore measures his own behaviour both in anticipation and in retrospect by standards which conform more or less closely to those prevalent in the community to which he belongs. What is called conscience is thus in the widest sense the reflex in the individual of the sanctions of the society.

It is convenient to begin a discussion of sanctions by a consideration of the diffuse negative sanctions, comprising reactions toward the particular or general behaviour of a member of the community which constitute judgments of disapproval. In such reactions there are not only differences of degree—for disapproval is felt and expressed with different degrees of intensity—but also differences of kind. Such differences are difficult to define and classify. In the English language, for example, there are a large number of words which express disapproval of individual behaviour; these vary from discourteous, unmannerly, unseemly and unworthy, through improper, discreditable, dishonourable and disreputable, to outrageous and infamous. Every society or culture has its own ways of judging behaviour, and these might conveniently be studied in the first instance through the vocabulary. But until comparative study of societies of different types has proceeded further no systematic classification of the kinds of diffuse negative sanction is possible. Provisionally the negative moral or ethical sanction may be defined as a reaction of reprobation by the community toward a person whose conduct is disapproved; moral obligations may thus be considered as rules of conduct which, if not observed, bring about a reaction of this kind. Another distinguishable sanction is that whereby the behaviour of an individual is met with ridicule on the part of his fellows; this has been called the satirical sanction. The varieties of diffuse positive sanctions, being less definite than negative sanctions, are therefore still more difficult to classify.

From the diffuse sanctions already described there should be distinguished what may be called (by a wide extension of the term) religious

同而并非责难,从而赢得群体给予的奖赏而并非惩罚的愿望。第二,每个人都与同伴一样,以赞同或反对的评判方式对某种行为模式做出反应,并根据群体中盛行的那些标准反复衡量自己的行为。因此,所谓的良心,从最广泛的意义上说,就是个体行为表现出的社会裁定的内容。

通过考察泛化负面裁定的方式来讨论社会裁定是很容易的。泛化负面裁定是指群体中某一成员对某一特殊或普遍行为所做的反映。这种反映构成了人们的反对评判。这类反应中,不但有程度的区别——由于人们感受到的和对这种反对表达的深度不同,而且反映的种类也有所区别。这类区别很难加以规定和划分。例如,在英语中,就存在很多对个体行为表示不赞同的词汇:不礼貌、粗鲁、不体面、可耻、邋遢、臭名昭著等词。每个社会、每种文化都存在自身评判行为的方式,在刚才的例子中通过所提及的词汇来研究这些行为是比较方便的。但是,在没有对不同类型的社会进行对比性分析以前,不可能对不同种类的泛化负面裁定进行系统分类。不过,负面道德或伦理裁定可以暂时定义为群体对行为受到谴责的人的一种责难反应。因而,道德义务就是一种行为规则,如果得不到遵守,就会导致这种反应。还可区分出另一种形式的裁定:即个人行为受到同伴的嘲笑,这种裁定被称为嘲讽裁定。因为泛化正面裁定没有负面裁定那么明确,所以仍旧很难对其划分。

“宗教裁定”(在引申意义上)是另一种含义的裁定,它与我们刚才描述的泛化裁定完全不同。这些宗教裁定曾被命名为超自然裁定和神秘裁定,但,这两个术语都没有能够让人满意的概念。在所有的群体中,宗教裁定都是以某些必须遵守的信仰存在为基

sanctions; these have also been named supernatural sanctions and mystic sanctions, but both these terms have unsatisfactory connotations. The religious sanctions are constituted in any community by the existence of certain beliefs which are themselves obligatory; it is therefore only within a religious community that these sanctions exist. They take the form that certain deeds by an individual produce a modification in his religious condition, in either a desirable (good) or an undesirable (evil) direction. Certain acts are regarded as pleasing to gods or spirits or as establishing desirable relations with them, while others displease them or destroy in some way the desirable harmonious relations. The religious condition of the individual is in these instances conceived to be determined by his relation to personal spiritual beings. The change in the religious condition may elsewhere be regarded as the immediate effect of the act itself, not mediated by its effects on some personal god or spirit, a view common not only in many of the simpler societies, but also found in a special form in Buddhism and in other advanced Indian religions. Sin may be defined as any mode of behaviour which falls under a negative religious sanction; there is no convenient term for the opposite of sin, that is an action which produces religious merit or a desirable ritual condition.

The religious sanctions involve the belief that most unsatisfactory ritual or religious conditions (pollution, uncleanness, sinfulness) can be removed or neutralised by socially prescribed or recognised procedures, such as lustration, sacrifice, penance, confession and repentance. These expiatory rites are also considered to act either immediately, or mediately through their effects on gods or spirits, depending upon whether the sin is regarded as acting in the one way or the other.

While in modern western civilisation a sin is usually regarded as necessarily a voluntary action or thought, in many simple societies an involuntary action may fall within the given definition of sin. Sickness—for example, leprosy among the Hebrews—is often regarded as similar to ritual or religious pollution and as therefore requiring expiation or ritual purification. A condition of ritual or religious impurity is normally considered as one of immediate or ultimate danger to the individual; it may be believed that he will fall sick and perhaps die unless he can be purified. In some religions the religious sanction takes the form of a belief that an individual who sins

础形成的。所以,宗教裁定只存在于宗教群体中。宗教裁定采取的形式是:个人采取的一定行为会导致其宗教状态发生变化,也许是令人不满的(不幸)状态。某些行为被看做是能够取悦上帝或神灵,或与神灵建立某种令人高兴的关系;而另一些行为则被看做是能够触怒神灵,或在某方面破坏了这种和谐关系。在这些情况下,此人与其个人神灵之间的关系是这个人宗教状态的决定因素。但在其他地区,人们认为,是行为本身而并非是由于这种行为和神灵之间的相互作用影响着宗教状态的变化。这种观点不但在较简单的社会中普遍存在,而且在佛教和其他形态较高的印度宗教中也可以找到它的特殊形式。罪恶可以被定义为任何一种受到负面宗教裁定的行为模式。但是,对于罪恶的对立面,即对产生一种宗教美德或令人满意的仪式状态的行为,我们还没有找到一个恰当的术语来指代它。

宗教包含这样一个信念:即最不令人满意的仪式或宗教状态(污染、不洁、罪过),可以通过社会规定了的或承认的方式如驱邪、祭祀、苦行、忏悔和悔悟,得以排除或化解。人们认为这种赎罪仪式能够通过直接或间接的方式对神灵加以影响,这取决于人们认为这种罪恶是以哪种方式得罪了神灵。

尽管在现代西方文明社会,罪恶通常被看做是自愿的行为或想法,然而,在一些原始的社会结构中,非自愿的行为或想法也会被划分到罪恶的范畴内。疾病——例如希伯来人的麻风病——被认为与仪式或宗教污染相似,因而,需要进行赎罪或仪式净化。仪式或宗教不洁的状态通常被看做是对个人的直接或最大的危害,人们会认为,如果此人不能够被净化,那么此人就会生病,也许会死亡。在一些宗教中,人们认为宗教裁定的行为方式是:如

in this life will suffer some form of retribution in an after-life. In many instances an individual who is ritually unclean is looked upon as a source of danger not only to himself but also to those with whom he comes in contact or to the whole community. He may therefore be more or less excluded for a time or even permanently from participation in the social life of the community. Frequently, if not always, an obligation therefore rests upon the sinner, or unclean person, to undertake the necessary process of purification.

Thus the religious sanctions differ from the other diffuse sanctions by reason of the beliefs and conceptions indicated above, which cannot be defined or described in any simple way. Somewhat similar beliefs underlie magical practices and procedure in relation to luck, but whereas religious observances and the beliefs associated with them are obligatory within a given religious community, the former are comparable with technical procedures, customary but not obligatory.

Organised sanctions are to be regarded as special developments of the diffuse sanctions, frequently under the influence of the beliefs belonging to religion. Organised positive sanctions, or premial sanctions, are rarely developed to any great extent. Honours, decorations, titles and other rewards for merit, including monetary rewards such as. special pensions, given to individuals by a community as a whole, are characteristic of modern societies. In preliterate societies a man who has slain an enemy may be given the right to distinguish himself by wearing some special decoration or in other ways.

Organised negative sanctions, important among which are the penal sanctions of criminal law, are definite recognised procedures directed against persons whose behaviour is subject to social disapproval. There are many varieties of such procedures, the most important and widespread being the following: subjection to open expression of reprobation or derision, as, for example, through forcible public exposure by confinement in stocks; partial exclusion, permanent or temporary, from full participation in social life and its privileges, including permanent or temporary loss of civil or religious rights; specific loss of social rank, or degradation, the exact contrary of the positive sanction of promotion; infliction of loss of property by imposition of a fine or by forcible seizure or destruction; infliction of bodily pain; mutilation or branding in which pain is incidental to permanent exposure

果某人在生前犯有罪恶,那么来世他会遭受到某种形式的报应。在很多地区,人们认为仪式不洁的人不但会给其本人带来危险,而且还会给那些与他有过接触的人,甚至是整个团体带来危险。因此,此人会被整个团体暂时驱除出去一段时间,甚至有可能永远地被禁止参与团体的社会生活。因此,有罪人或不洁的人即使不是一直,也经常会承担执行必要的净化过程的义务。

因而,由于以上所述的信念和概念的不同,宗教裁定区别于其他的泛化裁定,不能够对它们仅仅用简单的形式加以定义和描述。某些类似的信念构成了与幸运有关的巫术性活动和程序,但是,宗教仪式及其有关的一些信念在特定的宗教群体中是具有强制性的。而巫术性活动可以比做技术程序,具有习俗性,但却不具有强制性。

作为泛化裁定的某种特殊发展的组织裁定,通常受到类似于宗教信仰的影响。但有组织的正面裁定或鼓励裁定并没有多大发展。在现代社会中,由整个群体颁发给个人的荣誉、勋章、头衔或其他如特殊养老金等金钱上的奖励,体现了现代社会的特征。而在还没有产生文字的社会中,如果一个人杀死了仇人,他也会被授权佩带某种饰物或以其他的方式使自己引人注目。

有组织的负面裁定,其中最重要的是刑法裁定,是指对那些行为受到社会谴责的人施行的明确的得到公认的程序。这些程序多种多样,传播最广的是以下几种类型:公开的谴责和嘲笑受到责难的人,如强迫其带上枷锁示众;永久或暂时排除某人参与社会生活的部分权利或特权,包括永久或暂时地失去其公民或宗教的权利;社会地位的损坏或级别的降低,这恰恰是与正面裁定的升级相反;通过惩罚或强行没收或损坏的方式使人遭受财产的损失;使之遭受

to reprobation; permanent exclusion from the community, as by exile; imprisonment; and punishment by death. These sanctions are legal sanctions when they are imposed by a constituted authority, political, military or ecclesiastic.

In any given society the various primary sanctions form a more or less systematic whole which constitutes the machinery of social control. There is an intimate relation between the religious sanctions and the moral sanctions, which varies, however, in different societies, and cannot be stated in any brief formula. The primary legal sanctions of criminal law, in all societies except the highly secularised modern states, show a close connection with religious beliefs.

Besides these primary social sanctions and resting upon them there are certain sanctions which may be termed secondary; these are concerned with the actions of persons or groups in their effects upon other persons or groups. In modern civil law, for example, when an individual is ordered by a court to pay damages, the primary sanction behind the order is the power of the court to make forcible seizure of his property or to imprison or otherwise punish him for contempt of court if he fails to obey. Thus secondary sanctions consist of procedures carried out by a community, generally through its representatives, or by individuals with the approval of the community, when recognised rights have been infringed. They are based upon the general principle that any person who has suffered injury is entitled to satisfaction and that such satisfaction should be in some way proportioned to the extent of the injury.

One class of such procedures consists of acts of retaliation, by which is meant socially approved, controlled and limited acts of revenge. Thus in an Australian tribe when one man has committed an offence against another, the latter is permitted by public opinion, often definitely expressed by the older men, to throw a certain number of spears or boomerangs at the former or in some instances to spear him in the thigh. After he has been given such satisfaction he may no

身体上的疼痛;通过使其断肢或打烙印的方式使其受到永久的谴责;永久地被群体排除在外,如放逐;判处监禁;判处死刑。当这些裁定的执行依靠政治、军队或教会建立的权威得到保障时,它们就是合法裁定。

在所有的社会中,各种各样的基本裁定,或多或少都形成了一个可以构成社会控制机制的互相关联的整体。在不同的社会中,存在于宗教裁定和道德裁定之间的紧密联系的表现形式是有区别的,因此不能用简单的几句话加以陈述。除了高度世俗化的现代国家,在任何一个国家中,刑法的基本法律裁定都显示出它与宗教信仰的紧密关系。

除了这些基本的社会裁定之外,还存在某些以基本社会裁定为基础的所谓次生社会裁定。次生裁定是指人们或团体的行为对其他人或其他团体造成的影响。例如,在现代民法中,当某人被法庭判定要支付损害赔偿金时,那么,这个判决背后的基本裁定是:如果此人不服从法庭的判决,法庭就有权强行没收其财产或对他监禁,作为对他藐视法庭的惩罚。从而,当公认的权利遭到破坏时,次生裁定便会由团体(通常是团体的代表)或某个得到团体同意的人来执行某种程序。次生裁定基于这样一个总的原则:任何遭受到伤害的人都有权利要求得到补偿,并且这种补偿应当与受到伤害的程度比例相当。

其中的一种程序是由报复行为构成,但这种报复行为是经社会允许的,并得到控制和限制的。例如,在澳大利亚的一个部落中,当一位男子对另一个人有冒犯行为,那么,后者就可以在公众舆论(通常是由年长者给以明确表达)的允许下,向前者投掷飞镖,或在某些场合下,刺伤前者的大腿。在此人得到这种补偿后,

longer harbour ill feelings against the offender. In many preliterate societies the killing of an individual entitles the group to which he belongs to obtain satisfaction by killing the offender or some member of his group. In regulated vengeance the offending group must submit to this as an act of justice and must not attempt further retaliation. Those who have received such satisfaction are felt to have no further grounds for ill feeling.

Satisfaction for injury may be obtained also through the duel, a recognised and controlled combat between individuals, or through similar combats between two groups. Among Australian tribes duelling with spears, boomerangs, clubs and shields or stone knives, with the bystanders ready to interfere if they think things are going too far, is a frequently adopted alternative to one-sided retaliation. In these same tribes there are similar regulated combats between two groups, sometimes in the presence of other groups who see that there is fair play. It is often difficult to draw a dividing line between such group combats and warfare; in fact they may possibly be regarded as a special kind of warfare characteristic of primitive rather than of civilised societies. Frequently, therefore, war may be regarded as a secondary social sanction similar to the duel. A political group maintains recognition of its rights by the threat of war if those rights should be infringed. Even in the simplest societies it is recognised that certain acts are right in war and others are wrong and that a declaration of war may be just in certain circumstances and in others unjust, so that the conduct of warfare is to some extent controlled by diffuse sanctions. .

Indemnification is often found as an alternative to retaliation as a means of giving and receiving satisfaction. An indemnity is something of value given by a person or group to another person or group in order to remove or neutralise the effects of an infringement of rights. It may be distinguished from a propitiatory gift by the fact that it is obligatory (i. e. subject to a negative sanction, diffuse or organised) in the particular

他就不可以对那个人再存有任何恶意。在许多非文字社会中,如果某一群体中的一个成员被杀害,那么对这个群体的补偿方式就是它有权将杀人者杀死或把杀人者所属的团体中的一员杀死。在这种受到制约的报复行动中,冒犯方必须接受这种报复行为,并认为这是公平的,而不可以有任何继续进行报仇的企图。而那些获得补偿的人们也不许再存有任何恶意的情绪。

对伤害的补偿也可以通过一种得到承认的或受到控制的个人之间的打斗,即决斗来得到;也可以通过两个群体之间进行类似的争斗得到补偿。在澳大利亚的一些部落中,飞镖、"飞去来器"、棍棒、盾或石刀等,是他们在格斗时经常使用的武器。这种格斗通常是单方进行复仇采取的方法。在双方的格斗超出了某种界限时,旁观者便会对之进行干涉。同属一个部落的两个群体之间也会出现相似的受到一定约束的格斗,有时,格斗时还会有第三个群体出现,并观察格斗的公平性。通常来说,很难对两个群体之间发生的格斗和战争进行区分;事实上,这种格斗可以被看做是原始社会中特有的一种战争形式,而并不存在于文明社会中,因此,战争经常被称为是与格斗相似的次生社会裁定。当一个政治集团的权利受到侵害时,它可以通过发动战争的方式来维护其权利。即使在最原始的社会中,人们也会认为,在战斗中,他们的行为也有正误之分。宣战有时是合法的正义举动,而有时却被认为是非正义的。因此,从某种程度上说,战争的行为受到泛化裁定的制约。

赔偿也可以作为复仇的另一种选择,它是提供补偿或接受补偿的一种手段。赔偿金是指一个人或群体给予另一个人或另一群体的有价值的东西,目的是排除或消除对权利造成的侵害带来的

circumstances. A payment made in anticipation of an invasion of rights with the consent of the person or persons receiving it may be regarded as an indemnity. Thus in many societies taking a woman in marriage is regarded as an invasion of the rights of her family and kin, so that before they consent to part with her they must receive an indemnity or the promise of such. In these cases the process of indemnification bears some similarity to that of purchase, which is a transfer of rights of property for a consideration.

In many preliterate societies procedures of indemnification are carried out under the diffuse sanction of public opinion, which compels an individual to indemnify one whose rights he has infringed. In some societies there is a recognised right of an injured person to indemnify himself by forcible seizure of the property of the offender. When society becomes politically organised, procedures of retaliation and indemnification, backed by diffuse sanctions, give place to legal sanctions backed by the power of judicial authorities to inflict punishment. Thus arises civil law, by which a person who has suffered an infringement of rights may obtain reparation or restitution from the person responsible.

In a consideration of the functions of social sanctions it is not the effects of the sanction upon the person to whom they are applied that are most important but rather the general effects within the community applying the sanctions. For the application of any sanction is a direct affirmation of social sentiments by the community and thereby constitutes an important, possibly essential, mechanism for maintaining these sentiments. Organised negative sanctions in particular, and to a great extent the secondary sanctions, are expressions of a condition of social dysphoria brought about by some deed. The function of the sanction is to restore the social euphoria by giving definite collective expression to the sentiments which have been affected by the deed, as in the primary sanctions and to some extent in the secondary sanctions, or by removing a conflict within the community itself. The sanctions are thus of primary significance to sociology in that they are reactions on the part of a community to events affecting its integration.

影响。这与那种劝慰式的赠送礼物不同,因为,在某些情况下,它是具有强制性的(即受控于负面裁定,也许是泛化的,也许是有组织的)。在征得受款人的允许下,对某种可预期的权利侵犯事先进行支付,也被认为是一种补偿。例如,在许多社会中,由于婚姻关系,某女子会被带到另一个群体中,这种行为会被看做是对此女子的家庭和亲属权利的一种侵犯,因此,在此女子的家庭同意与她分别之前,他们必须得到一定的补偿金或类似的承诺。在这种情况下,补偿的过程与购买的过程有一定的相似性,都是对财产权的转让。

在产生文字以前的许多社会中,赔偿的程序是在公共舆论的泛化制裁下得以贯彻的。在这种裁定下,个人会被迫赔偿被他侵犯了权利的人。在一些社会中,存在一种普遍公认的权利:受到侵害的人可以通过没收冒犯者财产的方式弥补自己。当一个社会是一个政治组织化的社会时,被泛化裁定支持的复仇和赔偿程序,便由被法律权威所支持的法律裁定所代替。因而,民法就产生了。根据民法,权利受到损害的人可以从责任人那里获得补偿或赔偿。

考虑到社会裁定的功能,我认为,裁定对当事人的影响并不是最重要的,最重要的是裁定对整个群体所造成的普遍影响。由于任何一个裁定的应用都是对群体中社会情感的一种直接肯定,因而它构成了保持这些情感的重要的、也许是最基本的机制。次生裁定,尤其是有组织的负面裁定都是某种行为导致的社会焦虑的表达。因此,裁定的功能正如在基本裁定和某些情况的次生裁定一样,是通过对于某些行为引发的情感做出明确的集体表达,或通过消除社区内部的冲突来恢复社会安定。所以,裁定对社会学的重要意义在于:裁定是社区对那些影响到其团结的事件做出的反应。

CHAPTER XII

Primitive Law[1]

Many historical jurists in contrast with the analytical school have used the term law to include most if not all processes of social control. The term is, however, usually confined to 'social control through the systematic application of the force of politically organised society' (Pound). The limited application, more convenient for purposes of sociological analysis and classification, will be adopted in this article; the field of law will therefore be regarded as coterminous with that of organised legal sanctions. The obligations imposed on individuals in societies where there are no legal sanctions will be regarded as matters of custom and convention but not of law; in this sense some simple societies have no law, although all have customs which are supported by sanctions.

The confusion which has resulted in the attempt to apply to preliterate societies the modern distinction between criminal law and civil law can be avoided by making instead the distinction between the law of public delicts and the law of private delicts. In any society a deed is a public delict if its occurrence normally leads to an organised and regular procedure by the whole community or by the constituted representatives of social authority, which results in the fixing of responsibility upon some person within the community and the infliction by the community or by its representatives of some hurt or punishment upon the responsible person. This procedure, which may be called the penal

---

① Reprinted from the *Encyclop dia of the Social Sciences*, Macmillan Co., New York, 1933, Vol. IX, pp. 202-6.

第十二章　原始法[①]

许多历史法学家与分析学派的学者做法不同，他们都曾使用“法”这个术语涵盖绝大多数社会控制过程。然而，此术语通常被限定性的加以定义为“通过对政治组织的社会力量的系统运用而进行的社会控制”（庞德）。这种带有限制性的用法，便于做社会学分析和分类，因此本文会采用这种用法。因而，法在人们看来就与有组织的法律裁定具有相同的范围。在没有法律裁定的社会中，强制施加给个人的义务则被看做是习俗问题而不是法的问题，从这个意义上说，一些简单的社会就不存在法，尽管它们都拥有由裁定所支持的习俗。

如果试图把现代的刑法和民法应用于前文字社会中，势必会使我们感到迷惑，然而，如果用公法和私法来代替刑法和民法，那么这种迷惑就可以得到避免。一个社会中公认的不法行为是指，能使整个社区或既定的社会权威代表执行一个有确定组织和规则的程序的行为。执行这个程序的人会依照程序规定追究社区某成员的责任并对肇事者施以某种伤害或惩罚。这种程序也叫

---

① 重印自《社会科学百科全书》，麦克米兰公司 1933 年纽约版，第 9 卷，第 202～206 页。

sanction, is in its basic form a reaction by the community against an action of one of its own members which offends some strong and definite moral sentiment and thus produces a condition of social dysphoria. The immediate function of the reaction is to give expression to a collective feeling of moral indignation and so to restore the social euphoria. Its ultimate function is to maintain the moral sentiment in question at the requisite degree of strength in the individuals who constitute the community.

Comparatively little precise information is available concerning penal sanctions in preliterate societies. Among the actions which are known to be treated as public delicts in the simpler societies are incest, i. e. marriage or sexual congress with persons with whom such relations are forbidden; sorcery, or evil magic, by one person against another within the community; repeated breaches of tribal custom; and various forms of sacrilege. In many preliterate societies the penal sanction is applied principally if not solely to actions which infringe upon customs regarded by the community as sacred, so that the sanction itself may almost be regarded as a special form of ritual sanction. Ritual sanctions are derived from the belief that certain actions or events render an individual or a group ritually unclean, or polluted, so that some specific action is required to remove the pollution. In many examples of penal sanction it may plausibly be held that a deed such as incest produces a pollution of the whole community within which it occurs and that the punishment, which may mean the killing of the guilty persons, is a means of cleansing the community. Upon the establishment of a political or executive authority even of the simplest kind disobedience of that authority's commands may be subject to penal sanctions and treated as a public delict; moreover, direct offences against the constituted authority or against the persons in whom that authority rests may be subject to penal sanctions. Thus when the social authority rests in chiefs, an offence which would be a private delict if committed against a commoner may be treated as a public delict when committed against a chief.

In the procedure of a law of private delicts a person or a body of persons that has suffered some injury, loss or damage by infringement of recognised rights appeals to a constituted judicial authority, who declares

做惩罚制裁,其核心就是群体对因为内部成员侵犯了公认的群体道德观念而导致的社会动荡状态的反应。在这个反应中包含了集体道德愤怒的情感,从而起到使社会恢复安宁的作用。它的最终目的就是保持社区成员的最基本的道德情感。

在前文字社会中,关于惩罚制裁的准确资料相对来说很难找到。在那些简单社会中,被人们公认的不法行为包括:乱伦,即与那些禁止通婚或发生性关系的人结婚或发生性关系;巫术或是邪恶的巫术,由群体中的一位成员对其他成员恶意实施的巫术;不断的违反部落习俗;各种形式的渎圣行为。在许多前文字社会中,惩罚裁定除了这些方面可能还用于其他方面,但它的主要应用还是用于对付那些被群体认为是违背了神圣习俗的行为。因此,裁定本身也可以看做是仪式裁定的一种特殊方式。仪式裁定的信仰基础源于这样一种信念:某些行为或事件致使某个人或群体具有仪式不洁性,因此,人们就需要某种特定的行为消除这种污染。在许多有关社会裁定的例子中,人们都是这样认为的:如乱伦这样的一种行为会使发生这种行为的整个群体受到污染,那么,要想净化这个群体最常采用的办法就是将乱伦者处以死刑。对于建立了政治或行政权威的群体来说,即使是像不服从权威机构的命令这种最简单的行为,也要受到惩罚裁定并被看做是违犯公法行为;另外,如果直接冒犯了权威或有权威的人,也会受到惩罚裁定。因此,当这种社会权威交给酋长时,如果某人冒犯了一位普通人,那么此人就违犯了私法;但是,如果被冒犯者是酋长的话,那么此人就违犯了公法。

私法程序如下:当一个人或一组人的公认权利遭受到伤害、损失或损坏时,此人或此群体就可以向设立的司法机构上诉;司

some other person or body of persons within the community to be responsible and rules that the defendant shall give satisfaction to the plaintiff, such satisfaction frequently taking the form of the payment of an indemnity or damages. A private delict is thus an action which is subject to what may be called a restitutive sanction. The law of private delicts in preliterate societies corresponds to the civil law of modern times. There are, however, certain important differences. In general in modern law actions which fall simply under civil law are those which cause damage but are not subject to reprobation. Consequently, although the civil sanction expressed through the payment of damages causes loss to the defendant, it is not specifically punitive. Even in modern civil law, however, a magistrate may in special instances award ' punitive damages' , thereby expressing the view that the injury committed is of such a kind as to be properly subject to reprobation and therefore to punishment. In modern law when a deed is an offence against morality and at the same time inflicts injury it may become actionable under both criminal and civil law. The emphasis in the punishment for homicide or theft is on its aspect as an offence against the community rather than on the principle that restitution should be made to those who have suffered by the deed.

In preliterate societies private delicts are for the most part killing, wounding, theft, adultery and failure to pay debts; and while they are primarily regarded as constituting an injury to some member of the community they are subject also to moral reprobation as anti-social actions. The sanction is frequently both restitutive and repressive, giving satisfaction to the injured person and inflicting punishment upon the person responsible for the injury; for example, in some African tribes a thief is required to restore to the person whom he has robbed double the value of what he has taken. In its basic form the law of private delicts is a procedure for avoiding or relieving the social dysphoria which results from conflicts within a community. An offence committed against another member or group of the same community, by inflicting a sense of injury upon the victim, creates a disturbance of the social life which ceases only when satisfaction is rendered to the

法机构会宣称群体中的某人或某些人应对此负责,从而责令被告应对原告给予补偿,补偿方式通常是支付赔偿金或赔偿损失。在前文字社会中的私法可以看做与我们现代的民法基本相当,不过,它们之间还是存在着某些重要的区别。总的来说,在现代法律中,引起民法诉讼的行为只是那些引起损失的行为,而并非需要受到责难的行为。因此,尽管通过补偿损失而表现出的民事裁定会对被告造成损失,但是,这种方式并不具有惩罚性。然而,甚至是在现代民法中,地方法官在一些特殊的场合,也可以将一些案件判定为"惩罚性的损失",即认为被告人所造成的损失是属于应受到责难的类型,因而需要受到惩罚。在现代法律中,当一种行为是违反道德并同时又对他人造成了伤害,那么这种行为会同时涉及民法和刑法的诉讼。对于杀人或盗窃这类犯罪的惩罚强调以冒犯整个群体的原则进行,而不是以对受害人进行补偿的方式进行。

在前文字社会中,私法通常涉及的是以下行为:杀人、击伤、盗窃、通奸和欠债不还。尽管这些行为主要被认为是对群体中的某一个成员造成了伤害,但是,对于整个社会来说也是一种要受到道德谴责的违反社会的行为。因此,对它们的裁定通常就既具有赔偿性,又具有镇压性。这种裁定既需要违法者向受害者赔偿,同时,违法者还要遭受到惩罚。例如,在非洲的一些部落中,如果一个小偷盗走了另一个人的财产,那么他必须赔偿他所盗窃财产的两倍。对私法最基本的理解是:私法是一种程序,它避免或消除了由群体内部的冲突而引起的社会不安。群体内部某人通过对另一人或另一个群体造成的伤害,而使受害者感到一种受伤害的感觉,也为社会生活带来了骚乱。只有当受害者得到某种

injured person or persons. Thus in African native law a judge is not regarded as having properly settled a case until all parties concerned are satisfied with the settlement.

The distinction between public delicts and private delicts illustrates the fact that the law has no single origin. A deed committed by a member of the community which offends the moral sense of the community may be subject to three sanctions, the general or diffuse moral sanction, which makes the guilty person subject to the reprobation of his fellows; the ritual sanction, which produces in the guilty person a condition of ritual uncleanness that constitutes a danger to himself and to those with whom he is in contact—in such cases custom may require him to undergo ritual purification or expiation or it may be believed that as a result of his sin he will fall ill and die; the penal sanction, whereby the community through certain persons acting as its constituted judicial authorities inflicts punishment on the guilty person, which may be regarded either as a collective expression of the moral indignation aroused by the deed or as a means of removing the ritual pollution resulting from the deed by imposing an expiation upon the guilty person, or as both.

On the other hand, an action which constitutes an infringement of the rights of a person or group of persons may lead to retaliation on the part of the injured against the person or group responsible for the injury. When such acts of retaliation are recognised by custom as justifiable and are subject to a customary regulation of procedure, various forms of retaliatory sanctions may be said to prevail. In preliterate society generally warfare has such a sanction; the waging of war is in some communities, as among the Australian hordes, normally an act of retaliation carried out by one group against another that is held responsible for an injury suffered, and the procedure is regulated by a recognised body of customs which is equivalent to the international law of modern nations. The institution of organised and regulated vengeance is another example of a retaliatory sanction. The killing of a man, whether intentional or accidental, constitutes an injury to his clan, local community or kindred, for which satisfaction is required. The injured group is regarded as justified in seeking vengeance and

补偿后，这种骚乱才可以消失。例如，在非洲当地的法律中，只有当所有有关方都满足于对案件的审判，即获得赔偿之后，这个法官才被看做是公平地处理了案子。

公法和私法之间存在着区别的事实表明了法律的起源不只一个。某群体的一个成员所做的冒犯群体道德的行为会受到三种裁定：首先是一般的或广泛的道德裁定，这种裁定会使犯罪的人受到群体中其他成员的责难；其次是仪式裁定，这种裁定会使有罪的人处于仪式不洁的状态，处于这种状态的人以及与他有关的人都会面临一种危险。因此，习俗要求他进行仪式净化或进行补偿。否则，人们相信由于他的罪孽，他会生病甚至导致死亡；第三是惩罚裁定，即群体通过某些代表司法权威的人使犯罪者受到惩罚。这种方式是对那种罪恶行为的一种道德愤怒的集体表达，或是通过让犯罪者赎罪的方式来消除其仪式污染的一种手段，或者两方面都包含。

另一方面，受伤害方可能会因为这种对其个人或群体权利造成侵犯的行为而对侵害方发起报复行为。当习俗认可这些报复行为，并且对之规定了一定的习俗程序，那么各种各样的报复性制裁的形式就会出现。在前文字社会中，一般来说，战争就属于这类裁定中的一种。在一些像澳大利亚队群的群体中，发动战争通常是某一群体对另一个侵害方群体采取的报复行为。而且其程序受到公认的习俗制度的调节，这与我们现代的国际法大体相当。除战争之外，报复裁定的另一个例子是有组织的、受到一定规范的复仇习俗。无论是蓄意杀人还是过失杀人都会对受害人的氏族、地方群体或家族构成伤害，对于这种伤害，犯罪者需要给予补偿。受伤害的一方对此寻求报复行动被认为是合理的，通常来

there is frequently an obligation on the members of the group to avenge the death. The retaliatory action is regulated by custom; the *lex talionis* requires that the damage inflicted shall be equivalent to the damage suffered and the principle of collective solidarity permits the avengers to kill a person other than the actual murderer, for example his brother, or in some instances any member of his clan. When the institution is completely organised, custom requires the group responsible for the first death to accept the killing of one of their number as an act of justice and to make no further retaliation. Retaliatory sanctions may also appear in relation to injuries of one person by another; for example, the recognised right in certain circumstances of one person to challenge another to fight a duel. Among Australian tribes an individual who has suffered injury from another may by agreement of the elders be given the right to obtain satisfaction by throwing spears or boomerangs at him or by spearing him in a non-vital part of the body, such as the thigh. In all instances of retaliatory sanction there is a customary procedure for satisfying the injured person or group whereby resentment may be expressed, frequently by inflicting hurt upon the person or group responsible for the injury. Where it works effectively the result is to provide an expiation for the offence and to remove the feeling of injury or resentment in the injured person or persons. In many societies retaliation is replaced more or less by a system of indemnities; persons or groups having injured other persons or groups provide satisfaction to the latter by handing over certain valuables. The procedure of providing satisfaction by indemnity is widespread in preliterate societies which have not yet developed a legal system in the narrow sense.

Among the Yurok, who are food gatherers and hunters living in northern California in small villages with no political organisation, there is no regular procedure for dealing with offences against the community and therefore no law of public delicts. Injuries and

说,受伤害群体的成员有责任对其成员的死亡实施复仇行动。这种复仇行为是受到习俗调节的:复仇规则要求造成的损失要与遭受到的损失相等,并且集体团结的原则允许复仇者可以杀死真正的凶手以外的人,比如说凶手的哥哥,或在某种情况下,杀死凶手氏族内其他的成员作为代替。当一种习俗变得更加组织化和制度化,那么此习俗会要求对首先实施杀害行为负责的团体接受对方群体对其的报复,即杀害他的一个成员,并认为这种报复行为是公平的,而且不得进一步地反报复。复仇裁定也许会出现在一人对另一人造成伤害的关系中,例如,那种在某些情况下得到承认的决斗挑战权。在澳大利亚的部落中,如果一个人遭受到另一个人的伤害,那么根据长者之间的协定,受到侵害的人有权利通过向肇事者投掷飞镖或"飞去来器"的方式报复,或有权刺伤肇事者身体的非主要部分,如大腿。在所有复仇裁定例子中,都存在一种惯例性的程序补偿受害人或受害群体表达出的愤怒之情,这种补偿通常是使肇事者或肇事群体遭受到伤害。在这种程序有效发挥作用的地方,这种行为的结果是补偿了犯罪者的那种冒犯行为,并消除了受到伤害的人或人们的受伤害感和憎恶感。在许多社会中,这种复仇方式,多多少少被一种补偿金制度代替。对其他人或其他群体造成伤害的人们或群体,根据制度要求必须对受害者提供一些有价值的东西使其获得补偿。从严格意义上讲,提供补偿金进行补偿的方式在那些前文字社会中还没有形成法律体系,但这种方式的确广为流传。

生活在加利福尼亚北部的小村庄,以采集和狩猎为生的尤罗克人,由于没有任何政治组织,因而也就不存在处理那些冒犯群体行为的有规则的程序,即不存在公法。按照习俗规定,

offences of one person against another are subject to indemnities regulated by custom; every invasion of privilege or property must be exactly compensated; for the killing of an individual an indemnity or blood money must be paid to the nearkin. After a feud or war each side must pay for those who havebeen killed on the other side. Only the fact and amount of damage are considered; never the question of intent, malice, negligence or accident. Once an indemnity for an injury has been accepted it is improper for the injured person to harbour any further resentment. As the payment of indemnities is arranged by negotiation between the persons concerned and not by appeal to any judicial authority, the law of private delicts in the strict sense is not present. Among the Ifugao, who cultivate rice on terraced hillsides of northern Luzon in the Philippines and who have no political organisation and no system of clans, 'society does not punish injuries to itself except as the censure of public opinion is a punishment'; that is, there is no law of public delicts, no actual penal sanction. Nevertheless, a person who practises sorcery against one of his own kin is put to death by his kin; on the other hand, incest between brother and sister, parricide and fratricide are said to go unpunished. It is probable, however, that there are powerful and effective ritual sanctions against these acts. An offence committed by one person against another person or an infringement of the rights of one person by another is the occasion of a conflict between the kindred of the two parties, including relatives through btoh father and mother to the third or fourth degree. Retaliation by the killing of the offender or sometimes of one of his kin is the regular method of obtaining satisfaction in cases of murder, sorcery, adultery discovered *in flagrante*, refusal to pay an indemnity assessed for injury suffered, and persistent and wilful refusal to pay a debt when there is ability to pay. Satisfaction is provided in other cases by the payment of indemnities. There are no judicial authorities before whom disputes may be brought; the negotiations are carried out by a go-between who belongs to neither of the two opposed groups of kindred. Certain persons obtain renown for themselves as successful go-betweens, but such persons have no authority and are not

如果某人对另一个人有伤害性的冒犯行为，那么此人应该给予受害人以补偿。例如，对于某人的权利或财产的侵犯必须要如数给以补偿；对于杀人的行为，必须给受害者的近亲赔偿金或偿命金。对于群体的行为，例如在双方进行械斗和战争后，双方必须对死在自己方的对方成员给予一定的补偿金。这种赔偿只考虑事实和损失的数量，并不考虑意图是恶意的还是一种过失。一旦接受了伤害的补偿金，受伤害者仍旧对此事心存怨恨就是不适当的。由于赔偿金支付的数量是经过有关双方协调确定的，并不需要向司法权威诉讼，因此，从严格意义上讲，私法并不存在于这一地区。居住在菲律宾吕宋北部的山坡台地上的伊富高人，以种植水稻为生。他们这个群体也不存在任何政治组织，而且也没有氏族体系，“社会除了公共舆论谴责外，并不惩罚那些有损社会的行为”。也就是说，在这个地区中，并不存在公法，因而也没有事实上的惩罚裁定。然而，虽然家族会处死在本家族内部施行巫术陷害行为的家族成员，但在另一方面，据说却对兄弟姐妹之间的乱伦行为、弑亲和杀害兄弟姐妹的行为不加惩罚。也许对这些行为，他们还有其他的有力的或有效的仪式裁定。家族之间的冲突经常是由于其中一个家族的人对另一方成员做的冒犯行为，或是对其权利的侵犯，这种家族一般包括父母以及第三、四旁系亲属。对于谋杀、巫术、被当场发现的通奸、拒绝赔偿补偿金、有支付能力却拒绝支付欠款的这些行为，通常的补偿方式是用杀死冒犯者或冒犯者的一位亲属作为报复。在其他的情况下，也可以通过支付赔偿金施行赔偿。在这个地区中，不存在处理争端的司法权威，双方的协调是通过独立于双方之外的一个中间者执行的。一些中间人由于经常成功调解争端而获得了名望，但是，他们并

in any sense representatives of the community as a whole. During the controversy the two parties are in a condition of ritual enmity or opposition and when a settlement is reached they join in a peacemaking ceremony. A scale of settlement is recognised by custom and in certain circumstances the payments vary according to the class—wealthy, middle class or poor—to which the group receiving or making payment belongs. The Ifugao thus have an organised system of justice, which, however, does not constitute a system of law in the narrow sense of the term since there is no judicial authority.

An important step is taken towards the formation of a legal system where there are recognised arbitrators or judges who hear evidence, decide upon responsibility and assess damages; only the existence of some authority with power to enforce the judgments delivered by the judges is then lacking. It has been argued plausibly that in some societies a legal system for dealing with private delicts has grown up in this manner; disputes are brought before arbitrators who declare the custom and apply it to the case before them; such courts of arbitration become established as regular tribunals; and finally there is developed in the society some procedure for enforcing judgments.

A development similar to this is illustrated by the practices of the A-Kamba, A-Kikuyu and A-Theraka, Bantu peoples to the south and south-east of Mount Kenya in East Africa who live in scattered household communities, keep cattle, sheep and goats and grow grain in hand-tilled fields. They have no chiefs and are divided into well-defined age grades, one of which consists of elders who exercise both priestly and judicial functions. If there is a dispute in which one person believes his rights have been infringed by another, the disputants call together a number of elders of the district or districts in which they live and these constitute a court to hear the case. The court acts primarily as a court of arbitration and as a means of deciding upon the customary principles of justice by which the dispute should be settled; it usually takes no steps to enforce the judgment on the losing party

没有任何权力，并且，无论如何也不会成为整个群体的代表人。在争端中，双方处于一种仪式敌对或仪式对立的状态，但当他们之间的冲突得到解决后，他们就会参加一种和平典礼。由于解决争端的尺度会根据公认的习俗有所不同，所以有时候，支付会根据等级有所不同——即支付数量取决于接受和支付的群体是否富裕，是属于中产阶级还是穷人。所以，伊富高人存在有组织的维护正义的体系，但是，由于不存在司法当局，所以，从严格意义上讲，这个民族并不具有法律体系。

由得到承认的仲裁者或法官听证、追究责任和评估损失是构成法律体系的重要步骤。然而，只由某种享有权力的权威即法官执行审判是不够的。人们认为，在一些社会中，处理私法的法律体系一直在按这种方式发展：人们将某种争端带到仲裁者那里，仲裁者宣布习俗，并把这种习俗运用到案例中；这类仲裁的法庭已经被看做是一种有序的法庭；最终，这种法庭演变成社会中执行审判的某些程序。

与这一发展相似的现象可以从阿坎巴人、阿基库亚人、阿塔拉卡人的行为中得到解释。这三种人都属于班图人血统，分布在东非肯尼亚山东南部。他们生活在分散的家庭村社中，以饲养牛、绵羊、山羊和耕种为生。他们的部落并不存在酋长，整个部落按照明确的年龄等级划分，其中由长辈们构成的等级来执行祭祀和判决。如果某人认为权利遭受到另一个人的侵犯，那么争端双方就会召集许多居住在他们社区的长辈们，组成一个法庭听取证词。这个法庭主要担当起仲裁法庭的角色，并根据群体中约定俗成的公平原则，对争端进行审判。不过它通常不会对败诉方执行判决，而是把这个任务

but leaves this task to the claimant. In serious cases, however, when an offence affects the whole community or when the accused is regarded as an habitual and dangerous offender so that public indignation makes the affair one of public concern, the elders can exercise authority to enforce judgment. The usual procedure rests on the ritual powers of the elders; they can pronounce a curse, which is feared as inevitably bringing down supernatural punishment, on a person who refuses to obey a judgment. The killing of a member of one clan by a member of another, whether intentional or accidental, is treated by the court of elders as a private delict and is settled by the payment of an indemnity to the relatives of the victim by the killer and his relatives. The elders also possess limited powers of dealing with public delicts by a procedure known as kingolle, or mwinge. If a person is held guilty of witchcraft or is regarded as an habitual offender and thus as a public danger, the elders may inflict the punishment of death or may destroy the offender's homestead and expel him from the district. Before such action may be taken elders from remote regions must be called in for consultation and the consent of near relatives of the offender must be obtained.

The Ashanti afford a contrast to the system of the A-Kamba in that they have a well organised law of public delicts, which are designated by a native term which means 'things hateful to the gods'. These include murder, suicide, certain sexual offences including incestuous relations with certain relatives by descent and by marriage, certain forms of abuse, assault and stealing, the invocation of a curse upon a chief, treason, cowardice, witchcraft, the violation of recognised tribal tabus and the breaking of a command of the central authority issued and qualified with an oath. The Ashanti conception of the law is that all such actions are offences against the sacred or supernatural powers on which the wellbeing of the whole community depends and that unless these offences are expiated by the punishment of the guilty persons the whole tribe will suffer. The judicial functions belong to the king or chief (the occupant of a sacred stool), before whom the offender is tried. The punishment for the more serious offences

交给原告。然而,在某些严重的案子中,如果公众的愤怒使之成为公众关注的问题时;如某种冒犯影响了整个群体,或者被告被人们认为是惯犯或是危险性人物,这时长辈们通常会行使权威来执行判决。长辈的仪式权力是以上程序的基础,拒绝遵守判决的人会受到长辈们的诅咒。这种诅咒是任何人都感到恐惧的,因为他们认为这种诅咒会给他们带来超自然的惩罚。无论是蓄意的还是过失的,一个氏族成员如果杀害了另外的一个氏族的成员,由长辈们组成的法庭都会把它看做私法案件处理这件事,他们会判决让杀人犯本人或其亲属向受害方亲属支付赔偿金的方式来处理此案。根据"肯英戈尔"或"莫乌英"程序,长辈们对违犯公法的案例也拥有一定的权力。如果一个人犯有巫术的罪行,或者是个惯犯,那么此人就会被看做是个公众危险人物,长辈们也许会判处此人死刑或将其家园损坏后将其驱逐出境。这些行为必须在与远方地区的长辈们一起协商之后才能施行,而且还要得到犯罪者近亲的同意。

阿散蒂人的体系与阿坎巴人的体系恰恰相反,因为阿散蒂人拥有一套组织严密的公法。对公法的违犯在当地的术语中叫做"令神灵憎恶的事情"。这些事情包括谋杀、自杀、某些性侵犯(例如与有血亲或姻亲关系的亲属产生的乱伦关系)、某种形式的侮辱、袭击和偷盗、对酋长的诅咒,叛国、胆怯、巫术、违犯公认的部落禁忌或不服从权威的命令和擅改誓言等。阿散蒂人对法的概念是:所有这类行为都是对神圣的或超自然权威的一种侵犯,而这种权威是整个群体安宁的依靠。他们认为,除非这些冒犯行为通过对冒犯人施加惩罚的方式得到纠正,否则这些行为会给整个群体带来不幸。国王或者酋长(神圣坐凳的占据者)具有司

is decapitation, although in certain circumstances the condemned man and his relatives may 'buy his head'; that is, pay a redemption price by which his life may be saved. The courts of the chiefs do not concern themselves with private delicts, which are denoted 'household cases' and settled by the authority of heads of kinship groups or by negotiations. A dispute concerning a private delict may be brought before the chief indirectly if one of the parties involved swears an oath, which thus makes the dispute a public matter.

While the A-Kamba elders are concerned mainly with private delicts and the Ashanti chiefs with public delicts, there are tribes and nations in Africa and elsewhere in which the central authorities —the chiefs or the king and his representatives—administer both kinds of law, which may always be differentiated by reference to procedure. In the law of private delicts a dispute between persons or groups of persons is brought before the judicial tribunal for settlement; in the law of public delicts the central authority itself and on its own initiative takes action against an offender. Modern criminal law and civil law are directly derived respectively from the law of public delicts and the law of private delicts; but acts which are now regarded as characteristically public delicts, such as murder and theft, are in many preliterate societies treated as private delicts, while the acts which in such societies are most frequently regarded as public delicts are witchcraft, incest and sacrilege.

In its most elementary developments law is intimately bound up with magic and religion; legal sanctions are closely related to ritual sanctions. A full understanding of the beginnings of law in simpler societies can therefore be reached only by a comparative study of whole systems of social sanctions.

法权，犯罪者要在他们面前被审判。严重犯罪者有可能受到斩首的惩罚，尽管在某些时候，被判斩首的人及其亲属可以通过支付赎命金的方式“买回自己的脑袋”，从而保全性命。酋长法庭本身并不关注那些私法案件，因为这些案件被看做是“家庭案子”，是由氏族首领的权威或经过首领之间的协调解决的。如果争端双方中的一方可以发誓证明自己有理，那么这个争端就会成为一件公共事件，那么这种与私法有关的争端就会被间接地送到酋长那里审判。

尽管阿坎巴人的长辈主要处理私法案件，而阿散蒂人的酋长主要处理公法案件，但是，在一些非洲国家和世界其他地区，部落或国家的权威中心——酋长或国王及其代表——对于两种法律都进行管理，只是对这两种法律的执行程序有所区别。在私法中，人们之间或群体之间的争端也许会带到司法法庭上进行审判；在公法中，是由权威中心本身对违法者采取措施。由此我们知道，现代的刑法和民法分别是由公法和私法演变而来。但是，那些在现在被认为具有明显违犯公法的行为，如谋杀和盗窃，在许多前文字社会中却被看做是属于违犯私法的行为。在这类社会中，最常见的违犯公法的行为是巫术、乱伦和渎圣。

从法律的发展来看，最初它是与巫术和宗教紧密联系在一起的，司法裁定与仪式裁定紧密相关。只有对所有的社会制裁体系进行对比性研究，才能够透彻理解较简单的社会中法律起源的问题。

译者后记

本书著者 A. R. 拉德克利夫-布朗,1881 年生于英国伯明翰,卒于 1955 年,是英国社会人类学一代宗师,人类学功能学派带头人之一。在大学期间,他主攻精神和道德科学,于 1905 年以优异成绩获得剑桥大学荣誉学位,并在以后的研究中将一生中三分之一的时间献给了人类学的教学与研究。1922 年,他发表了个人的第一部专著《安达曼岛人》,其后的主要著作还有《社会的自然科学》等。《原始社会结构与功能》是布朗生前出版的最后一部著作,在这部著作中,作者反对用简单的因果关系来解释文化的起源,主张用较复杂的"函数"、"变量"或"功能关系"来解释社会文化现象。作者评论了各种构建于历史推测方法之上的论点,并与那些认为社会科学必须开始并终结于个人心理学的论点争辩。作者认为社会现象是一种独特的现象,都是与社会结构的存在相联系的产物。这本书集中体现了作者学术生涯最后 25 年间的思想发展历程,对人类学学科建设具有重大影响,既是他对自己一生学术思想的总结,同时也开启了后续学者研究的道路,是人类学的名著之一。

经过几个月辛苦的翻译,终于可以把这本书呈现在读者面前了。翻译工作虽然比较枯燥,可是沉浸其中又体会到另外的乐趣。每天坐在电脑前，体会着原著者的思想，在内心深处和他进行着交流。在翻译的过程中，通过对原著的仔细阅读，加上对原著者其他作品的研究，我深深感受到了作者作为一代人类学宗师的博大精深的思想，同时也为自己大胆接下这个翻译任务感到惶恐。自己的理论水平和思想深度难及大师之毫厘，要想充分表达大师的思想看似一个不可能完成的任务。我把每天的翻译都看做是和大师进行的一次心灵的对话，力求准确、完整、通顺地表达出原作者的思想。在每天翻译结束时，回想一天的工作，经常觉得受益匪浅，在睡觉前心中总是窃喜自己能得到这么好的机会。由于译者的水平有限，肯定有许多不足之处，恳请读者给予批评指正。

在本书的翻译过程中刘岩、刘美、朱彩云为本书进行了译校，张涛、于明清通读了最后的书稿，给予了十分中肯的意见，在此对他们一并表示感谢。

丁国勇

2006 年夏于花家地

《西方学术经典文库》(第一辑)

功利主义	[英]约翰·斯图亚特·穆勒
诗学·诗艺	[古希腊]亚里士多德 [古罗马]贺拉斯
经济发展理论	[美]约瑟夫·阿洛伊斯·熊彼特
经济学原理	[英]阿尔弗雷德·马歇尔
国民财富的性质与原理	[英]亚当·斯密
联邦党人文集	[美]亚历山大·汉密尔顿
就业、利息和货币通论	[英]约翰·梅纳德·凯恩斯
尼各马可伦理学	[古希腊]亚里士多德
道德情操论	[英]亚当·斯密
君主论	[意]尼科洛·马基雅弗利
新教伦理与资本主义精神	[德]马克斯·韦伯
古代法	[英]亨利·萨姆奈·梅因
第一哲学沉思集	[法]勒内·笛卡儿
查拉图斯特拉如是说	[德]弗里德里希·威廉·尼采
哲学研究	[英]路德维希·维特根斯坦
实践理性批判	[德]伊曼努尔·康德
社会契约论	[法]让·雅克·卢梭
理想国	[古希腊]柏拉图
心理学原理	[美]威廉·詹姆斯
精神现象学	[德]威廉·弗里德里希·黑格尔
神圣者的观念	[德]鲁道夫·奥托
小逻辑	[德]威廉·弗里德里希·黑格尔

论人类不平等的起源	[法]让·雅克·卢梭
道德形而上学基础	[德]伊曼努尔·康德
人性论	[英]戴维·休谟
政府论	[英]约翰·洛克
论法的精神	[法]查尔斯·路易斯·孟德斯鸠
代议制政府	[英]约翰·斯图亚特·穆勒
英国法与文艺复兴	[英]弗雷德里克·威廉·梅特兰
法律社会学基本原理	[奥]尤根·埃利希
论美国民主	[法]夏尔·阿列克西·德·托克维尔
原始社会结构与功能	[英]A. R. 拉德克利夫-布朗
政治学	[古希腊]亚里士多德
罗马帝国编年史	[古罗马]科尔涅里乌斯·塔西佗
普通语言学教程	[瑞士]费尔迪南·德·索绪尔
货币哲学	[德]格奥尔格·西梅尔
法理学讲演录	[英]约翰·奥斯丁
思想录	[法]布莱兹·帕斯卡
利维坦	[英]托马斯·霍布斯
意识形态与乌托邦	[德]卡尔·曼海姆
忏悔录	[古罗马]圣·奥古斯丁
西太平洋上的航海者	[英]布罗尼斯拉夫·马林诺夫斯基
历史学:理论和实际	[意]贝内德托·克罗齐
逻辑哲学论	[英]路得维希·维特根斯坦